School Business Management

School Business Management

Supporting Instructional Effectiveness

Thelbert L. Drake
Ball State University

William H. Roe
Professor Emeritus
University of Connecticut

Allyn and Bacon
Boston • London • Toronto • Sydney • Tokyo • Singapore

Series Editor: Ray Short
Editorial Assistant: Christine Shaw
Production Administrator: Susan McIntyre
Editorial-Production Service: Ruttle, Shaw & Wetherill, Inc.
Cover Administrator: Suzanne Harbison
Composition Buyer: Linda Cox
Manufacturing Buyer: Louise Richardson

Copyright © 1994 by Allyn and Bacon
A Division of Simon & Schuster, Inc.
160 Gould Street
Needham Heights, MA 02194

Library of Congress Cataloging-in-Publication Data

Drake, Thelbert L.
   School business management: Supporting instructional effectiveness /
     Thelbert L. Drake, William H. Roe.
     p. cm.
   Includes bibliographical references (p.   ) and index.
   ISBN 0-205-14699-6
   1. Public schools—United States—Business management. 2. School
management and organization—United States. 3. Education—United
States—Finance. 4. Educational planning—United States. I. Roe,
William Henry, 1917– . II. Title.
LB2823.5.D73 1993
379.1′1′0973—dc20   93-18857
                                                            CIP

Printed in the United States of America
10 9 8 7 6 5 4 3 2 1   98 97 96 95 94 93

This book is dedicated to Suzanne V. Drake and Viola R. Roe, our understanding spouses who gave up time with us, including summers and many weekends, because we often had stacks of paper in front of us. Sue and Vi noted that we were present but often not really there because we were working on some chapter of the book. For tolerating these long lapses and for understanding and supporting—thanks, Sue and Vi.

Contents

Preface

Schools exist so that students can learn and the central activity of schools is instruction. The popular terms "excellence" and "quality" have been linked to education conveying a message of importance and value to the purposes of schools. Urgent pressures have been placed upon the schools from all quarters of society to continuously improve instructional programs, but there is a concommitant demand to do so more efficiently—often with little or no increases in dollars or real purchasing power or other resources.

The efficiency and effective management of fiscal and physical resources can enhance instructional programs. The opposite is also true. If students have a series of poorly planned and prepared lunches, if the buses are continuously breaking down and running off schedule, or if rooms are too hot or too cold, parents become excited and move to have these deficiencies corrected. If a building is dirty and poorly maintained, if money is not carefully spent or accounted for, the public often loses confidence in the entire school, no matter how effective the teaching may be under the circumstances. In fact, inefficient management of support services often becomes apparent to the public more quickly than ineffective teaching.

If the management of resources makes a difference in the confidence of the public and if the maximizing of resources for increasing the effectiveness of instruction makes a difference in that effectiveness, then the school business manager makes educational decisions. As such he or she is in an educational leadership position and is an important part of the educational leadership team.

This text is written from that point of view. The principles, processes, practices, and questions raised are set in the context of enhancing instructional effectiveness. The book is addressed to professors, instructors, and students of school business management, and to superintendents or prospective superintendents and school business manager practitioners who will find the material useful in reviewing and possibly redefining their current practices.

The position of the school business manager should not dominate those positions associated primarily with instruction, nor should it be dominated by them. Rather, the position should, like the others, be focused on the purpose of the school—student learning. As such, the business manager works cooperatively with parallel position holders as well as with constituents at all levels in the school district. The interpersonal skills of the business manager are important districtwide.

More importantly, the school business manager's ability to articulate the vision of excellence held by the leadership of the district can make an important difference whether business management functions are merely mechanical services rendered or are part of the educational leadership effort toward excellence.

We believe that business management is a creative, planning/decision-making process rather than a series of routinized mechanical operations, and that it is best performed by a person who understands instructional practice and good leadership practice as well as business functions. The school business manager anticipates, initiates, organizes, staffs, coordinates, and guides activities and decision processes needed to facilitate learning, which is the school's "bottom line." He or she is part of an educational leadership team.

The days of the business manager being a person sitting at a desk wearing a green eye shade and hunched over a pile of ledgers or folder of purchase orders have long gone. A green cast in the office may come from a computer screen. The accountant's pointed pen is replaced by a keyboard and E-mail is flowing in and out at the speed of electricity. Just as antiquated an image of the school business manager is that of the person who controls for the sake of controlling, the one whose professional pleasure comes from "saving" a dollar for the sake of saving that dollar. The forward-looking business manager of today zeroes in on what the saving or the expenditure does to provide a positive slope on the learning curves for students. It is for this end that this book is written.

Acknowledgements

We wish to acknowledge the contributions of many people who provided information, responded to inquiries, filled out questionnaires, and spent time on the telephone explaining the way things were done in their districts. We wish also to thank the late Dr. Judy McConnell Jackson for her work on the personnel chapter and Dr. Ivan Wagner for his contributions to the budgeting chapter. Many thanks to Jerry Pulley, University of Texas, Pan-American, Philip Kearney, University of Michigan, and Robert Rossmiller, University of Wisconsin, Madison who critically read the first draft and made excellent suggestions for the final draft.

T.L.D. and W.H.R.

School Business Management

Chapter 1

The School Business Administrator

Managing the business of a school is a complex job requiring a great deal of knowledge and various skills. In colonial times and for decades thereafter, the tasks of collecting money, paying teachers, and maintaining buildings fell to laypersons serving on the committees or boards that were responsible for schools. It soon became too large a task for a part-time effort, particularly in the cities. In 1841, Cleveland, Ohio provided for an acting manager of schools to keep books, account for expenditures, purchase fuel, and keep the buildings in good repair. About the same time other cities were feeling the pressure of the tasks required to keep the city council or board of education current with the business management of the schools. As the cities grew, the work of the schools needed to be coordinated and by 1837 Buffalo, New York and Louisville, Kentucky had appointed superintendents of schools. The first superintendents were hired to perform a clerical function for the school board. As growth continued, in many cases the role of the superintendent moved toward that of a chief executive officer, responsible for both instruction and business management. In these instances the business management function became part of the overall school leadership team. In other cities the structure was divided into instructional and business functions in a dual-administrative arrangement in which the persons in charge of each area reported to the board independently.

Today in some places such as New Jersey, Iowa, Utah, Oregon, and Montana, variations of a dual system exist in which the board may have a secretary or clerk who reports directly to the board about fiscal and property matters. Some cities such as Milwaukee, Wisconsin and Omaha, Nebraska have a dual system. Such an arrangement is the exception rather than the rule. The great majority of school districts by virtue of their organizational structures consider the school business administrator as part of the educational administration leadership team. The school business manager reports through the superintendent to the board of education.

Jordan noted that "the philosophical question relative to school business administration as a profession or a specialty within the broader profession of school administration has not been resolved."[1] However, the authors view school business administration as an integral part of the larger field of educational administration.

It is clear that decisions and recommendations made by the school business administrator, whether he or she reports to the board through the superintendent or independently, affect the instructional program and thereby are educational decisions. For over a half-century the professional association for school business managers has viewed school business administration as one facet of educational administration. In its definition of school business administration, the Association of Public School Business Officials stated

School business administration is an evolving profession, coordinate with educational administration in its essentiality to the successful operation of the total school enterprise. It is subordinate in that its function is not a separate and distinct one originating within its own field, since all of its aims and objectives derive from, and many of its activities hinge upon, and are determined by the policies and programs established for the general administration of the school.[2]

Over four decades later, the Association of School Business Officials (ASBO) stated:

It is now recognized that decisions related to curriculum, school organization and personnel are interdependent upon decisions related to finance. . . . School business administrators must be trained and experienced in the field of education with emphasis on school business administration or trained and experienced in various phases of business with a knowledge of educational practices.[3]

In 1992, Ward noted, "School business administration can no longer stand aside as a staff function, separate and distinct from the other activities in the school. . . . The school business administrator will be part of a leadership team . . . flexible and open to participation in school district decision making from a wide variety of individuals."[4] The effective school business manager is one who sees the relationship of the school's business management functions to educational outcomes.

The main objective of the school is to educate children, and its central activity is instruction. Thus, all other activities are facilitating and service functions; they are means to an end rather than ends in themselves. Yet if they are not performed expertly and with precision the instructional program suffers, and the public's confidence in the total school enterprise is shaken. A breakdown in the business management side of the school's functioning becomes apparent to the public more quickly than a breakdown in the instructional side. The layperson feels on familiar ground where problems of business management are concerned, but he is inclined to leave instruction to professional teachers.

If bus service is bad or if school lunches are unappetizing, a mother is fairly sure of what she is talking about when she complains, and her criticism is justified. If taxes increase, but necessary supplies and equipment are not available and the school budget cannot be balanced, people will naturally wonder why and ask questions. A school administrator may have a master's and doctor's degree, he may be a person with outstanding leadership ability, have state or national recognition as an educational scholar, and yet if the business management details of the school are ineptly administered, the general public will consider him a poor administrator, and his opportunities for showing the splendid educational leadership of which he is capable are diminished.

Confidence or lack of confidence in the school administrator too often starts with confidence or lack of confidence in his managerial ability in the business and service areas of the school. Therefore, it would be easy for the school superintendent to succumb to the supposed realities of the situation and relegate his instructional leadership responsibilities to others in order to spend the major portion of his time in the business management of the school.

The importance of the business matters of the schools is not an issue. Rather the issue is what facets of the educational enterprise are serving which. It is easy to state that the school's main objective is to educate children. However, phrases such as "making tough decisions" or "the bottom line" come out of the great captains of industry images and belie the stated purpose. The hue and cry that education needs to link with business in order to shape up education can be found in book after book, articles, and conference speeches. Certainly there is little argument that partnerships with nearly all community agencies and businesses would be helpful. Until a major corporation executive can successfully teach for ten months a class of twenty-four sixth graders, five of whom are 15 years old; one who is a 13-year-old mother, four who are living on the street; and several who are active watchers and couriers for a drug ring officially associated with a national gang network, the executive's pronouncements about how to operate a school successfully should be tempered with appropriate disclaimers. The same holds true for the school business administrator whose knowledge of education extends little beyond having taken a survey course in American education and an introduction to school administration. She or he is at a serious disadvantage in making good decisions that directly affect the instructional program. All school business decisions must be made in the larger context of the mission of the school, that is, improving instruction and enhancing learning. Figure 1-1 illustrates some of the relationships influencing school business decisions.

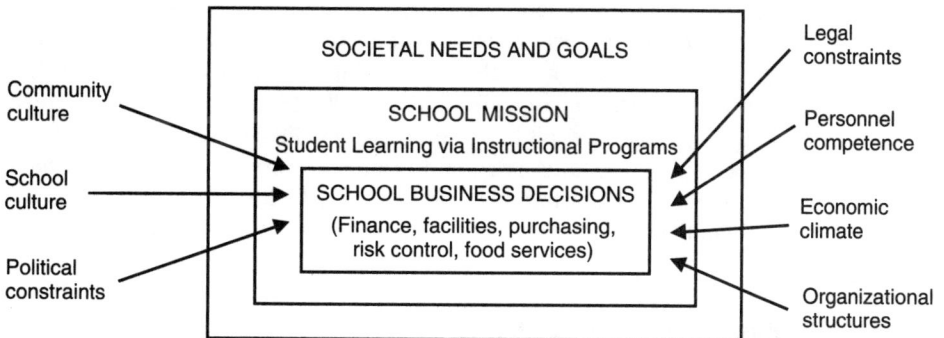

FIGURE 1-1   Contexts of and Influences on School Business Decisions.

Societal Needs and Wants

The 15,000 plus school districts in the United States must survive in an often unfriendly ocean of opinions, demands, needs, expectations, economic ups and downs, and personal and political gains, just to name a few of the currents affecting the sometimes battered school districts. The political changes of the early 1990s have shaken an increasingly interdependent world. Schools have to keep maps up-to-date on the computer or they will be outdated within days. Leaders of nations have always changed abruptly, but until recently those changes seldom affected businesses on "Main Street" the next day, or the school curriculum during the semester. The impact of new political alliances and the breakdown of others directly affect local industries, so that changes and competition oceans away can quickly erode the school district's tax base or allocations from the state.

In the context noted above, leaders from many quarters emerge to try to salvage the local, state, or national economy. There are new voices and new words in the din of new demands. Instead of dumping the perceived problem into the laps of the schools and saying "let the schools fix it," there are business and political voices saying that the schools have not coped with societal problems, but "we can fix the schools so they can." Traditional faith in the schools has eroded, rightly or wrongly. The school business manager is part of a leadership team of an institution in crisis. All this is happening in a time of rapid technological advances.

The rapid advances in technology provide opportunities for access to mountains of data and media; nearly instant information; and tools for a curriculum centered on problem solving and effective communication of ideas and solutions. The challenges facing various aspects of the school business office are many, but there are at the same time exciting opportunities for exerting wise leadership with results lasting into the twenty-first century. At the same time the business manager's enthusiasm must be tempered by the fact that whatever actions he takes, the results will be long range. His or her decisions and support information provided today in the areas of laser technology, interactive distance learning, or computer systems will affect the next school generation and may well affect other citizens who are dependent on the community's economic well-being and quality of services provided.

Those who view school business administration as a set of business-directed functions separate from the school's instructional functions may be encouraging goal displacement for the schools. When subserving means become the end an observer may find on the surface an efficient organization as evidenced by decisiveness, greater economic health, clean buildings and lovely grounds, low losses in relation to activities, and safe, well-operated buses. In its essential function, however, the school may be at a loss. The school business administrator should be charged with seeing that efficiency is achieved, but only in the context of the school's mission, as noted in Figure 1-1.

School Business Management Defined

School business management can be defined as that branch of educational administration which deals with the finances, facilities, and services that directly or indirectly support the instructional mission of the school. The Association of School Business Officials defines the school business administrator

> *as a member of the school staff who has been designated by the school board and/or the superintendent to accept general responsibility for the administration of the business affairs of a school district. . . . Unless otherwise specified by local law or custom, he shall report to the school board through the superintendent of schools.*[5]

The authors have avoided using the term "noneducational services" in the definition because many of the services are educational, planned or unplanned; provide opportunities for direct learning experiences; or if used improperly, may restrict the school's instructional programs in a harmful way.

Functions of the School Business Manager

The functions of a school business manager in one school district may be very different from those in another. Organizational structure, size, legal requirements, and many other factors have an influence on the manager's assigned functions. Hill et al. noted twenty-one typical functions in the school business management area[6]:

Financial planning and budgeting

Accounting

Debt service and capital fund management

Auditing

Purchasing and supply management

School plant planning and construction

Operation of plant

Maintenance of plant

Real estate management

Personnel management

Property records and custody of legal papers

Transportation of pupils

Food service operations

Insurance

Cost analysis

Reporting

Collective negotiations

Data processing

School board policies and administrative procedures as related to fiscal and noninstructional matters

Responsibilities for elections and bond referenda

Responsibilities for school assessment, levy, and tax collection procedures as may be set by law

Many other lists of functions are available and the reader must conduct his or her own cross walk between terms to see their similarities and differences. McGuffey reviewed several works and developed a list of ranked task clusters.[7] Among the task clusters was "general management." After a review of state and many local listings of functions the authors noted that the function identified as *general management* is overlooked or not specifically stated. Implied in the term are the concepts of coordination and leadership. The idea of the school business manager as part of the educational leadership team is appealing, for if emphasized in word and deed, the business decisions are indeed educational decisions. The school business manager can lead the office staff, regardless of size, in the direction of contributing to the main mission of the school—improving instruction and enhancing learning.

Communication with external public sectors whether directly or through the media is often an overlooked or underemphasized task facing many school business managers. The media relations role is sometimes difficult to ignore when confronted with media representatives seeking clarification or additional facts about the budget, or the cost implications of a decision or incident. The way the school business manager deals with the situation can be interpreted positively or negatively for the school system. A team approach may yield a united, consistent flow of communication to the internal hierarchy and external public sectors whether or not there is a crisis.

As examples of variations in the school business manager's functions noted from district to district, Figures 1-2 and 1-3 provide contrasts in organization and implied functions relative to school district size particularly in relationship to the school principal.[8] The first figure represents a relatively small school district of approximately 2,800 pupils, and the second a school district of approximately 21,000 pupils. Interviews with the superintendent or assistant superintendent of the districts yielded very different role expectations for the principals in each school. In the smaller district the principals were to be freed of any concern with "management duties" that would interfere with the school's instructional leadership role. In contrast, the larger school district expected the principal to be in charge of all facets including the maintenance of the building and personnel decisions regarding custodians and other noncertified personnel in the building. The jobs of principal and school business manager are essentially different, but in addition Figures 1-1 and 1-2 further point out that two similar lists of functions may be very different operationally. Chapter 2 provides additional organizational role implications.

Status of the School Business Manager

Few states have specific certification requirements for school business officials, and there is a great disparity between the actual and ideal educational qualifications of the school business manager. In the late 1950s a trend toward requiring graduate work beyond the bachelor's degree was noted. At that time the educational training of those who held prominent positions in school business management ranged from an eighth-grade diploma to a Ph.D. in educational administration.

The professionalization of the school business manager as a part of educational leadership continues primarily through the efforts of individual school districts and professional associations. It is difficult to see progress over the last several decades in state educational or licensure requirements for school business managers. Drake found that only fourteen states required a special license or certificate for the school business official and one additional state had a special certificate as an available option.[9] Thirty-five states indicated no minimum required educational background.

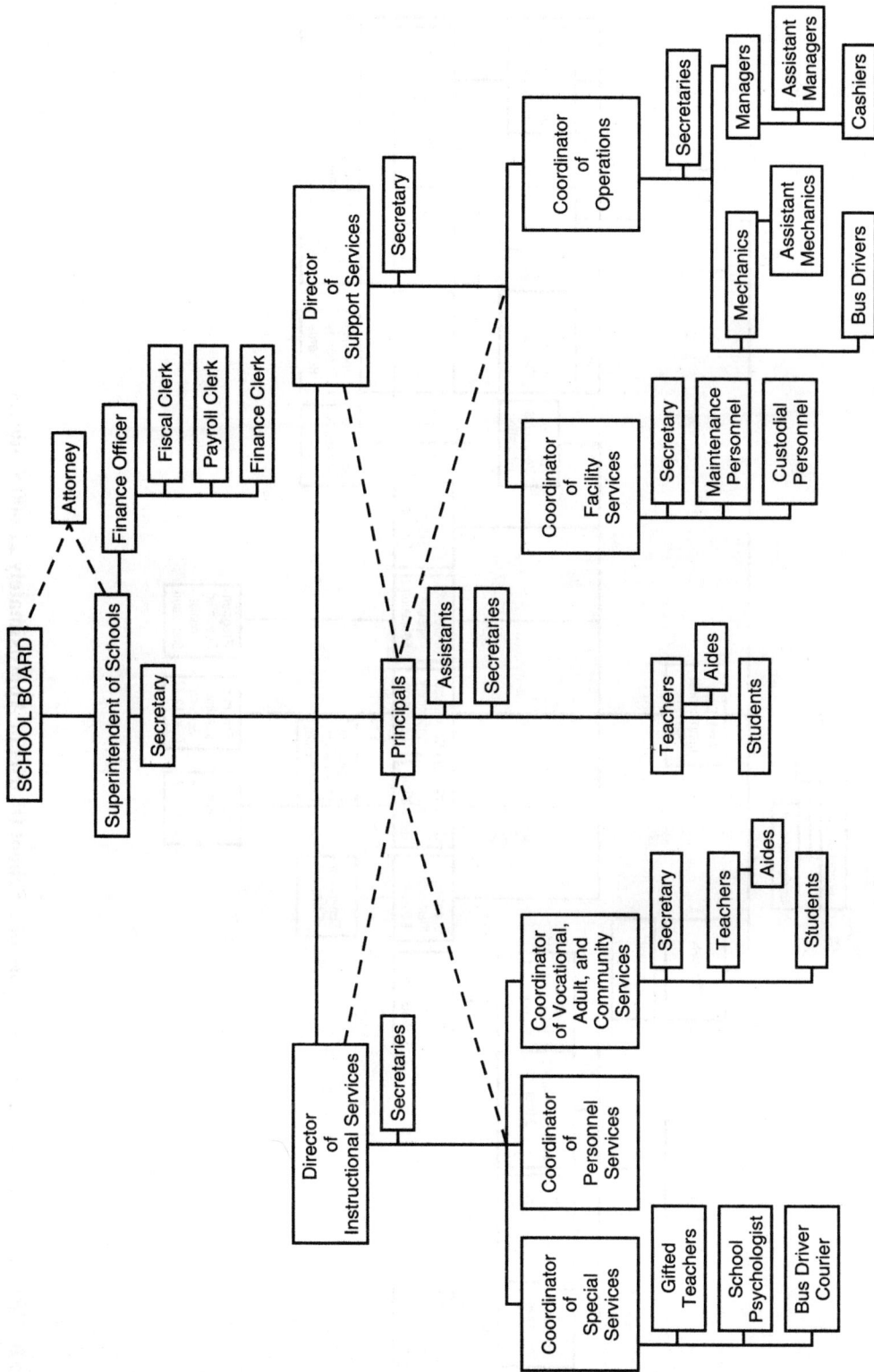

FIGURE 1-2 Organizational Structure of a Small School District of under 3,000 Enrollment.

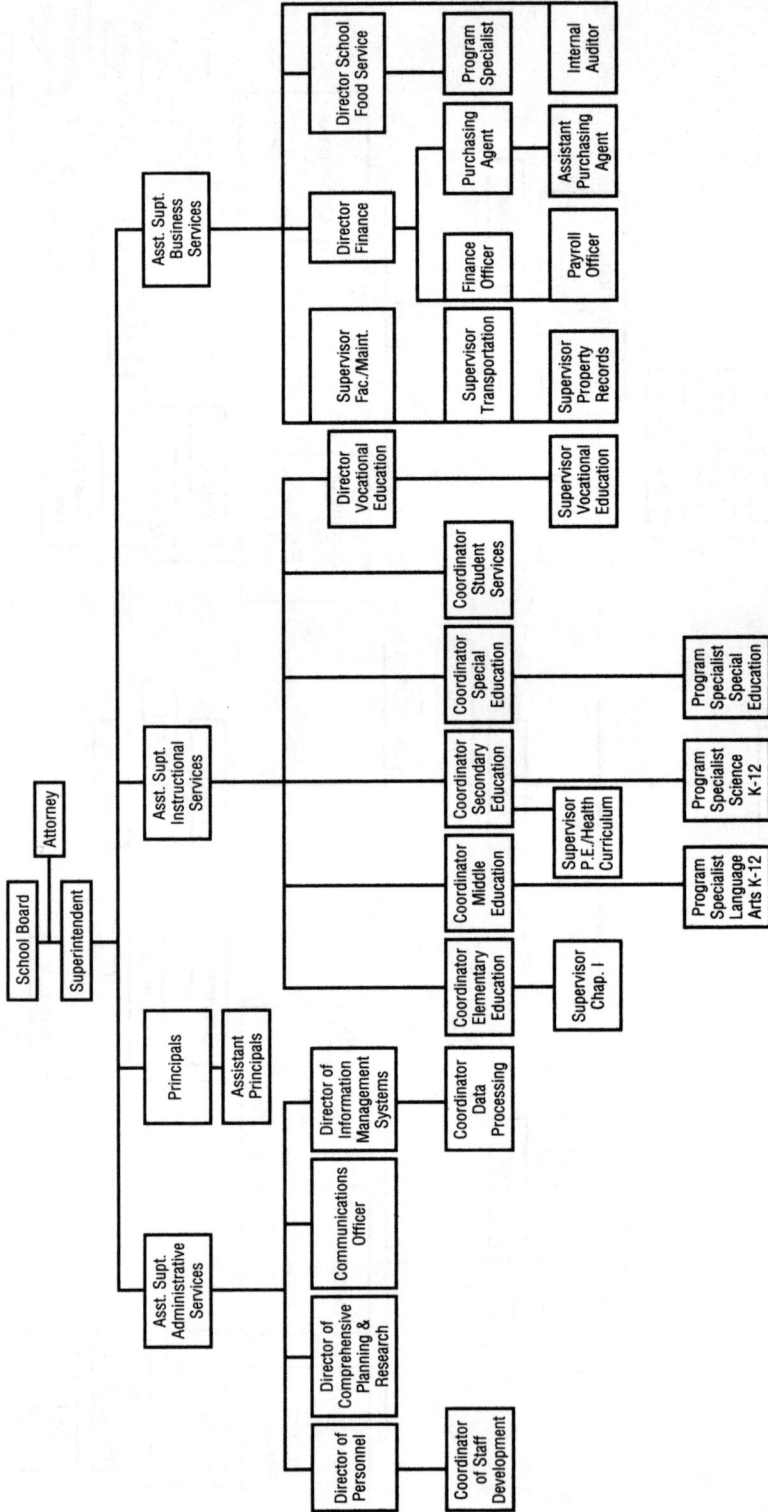

FIGURE 1-3 Organizational Structure of a School District of Approximately 21,000 Students.

TABLE 1-1   Frequency of Titles Used for School Business Managers

Title	Number of States	Percentage
Assistant Superintendent	9	18
Administrative Assistant	4	8
Business Manager/Administrator	24	48
Other titles mentioned first included: Director; Chief Business Official; District Clerk; Encumbrance Officer; Finance Officer	6	12

The picture is not as grim as first glance may indicate. The control point appears to be the local school district. Many school districts use the title of "assistant superintendent" for the person charged with managing school business functions. Such a title ordinarily requires an administrative certificate. The positive aspects of the assistant superintendent title is required graduate education and licensure/certification as an educator. Further, the title identifies the role as one of contributing educational leadership that assists in transforming dollars and services into applied educational values. When asked to list what titles were used most often in each state, state officials noted the title "assistant superintendent" as listed first in 18 percent of the states. Table 1-1 summarizes the results of a survey of the states regarding titles used for the school business administrator.

Standards of Conduct

Ethical problems have faced school officials since the early days of public education. The apple of unethical choice is often presented in subtle and innocent-appearing circumstances, but to take the bite offered may be a career-ending choice. To assist the school business manager, state and national professional associations have adopted codes of ethics and conduct for school administrators, and for school business officials in particular. The Association of School Business Officials adopted the following:

Standards of Conduct for the Association of School Business Officials

Now, especially, in this age of accountability, when the activities and conduct of school business officials are subject to greater scrutiny and more severe criticism than ever before, Standards of Conduct are in order. The association cannot fully discharge its obligation on leadership and service to its members short of establishing appropriate standards of behavior.

In Relationships Within the School District, It Is Expected That the School Business Official Will:
1. Support the goals and objectives of the employing school system.
2. Interpret the policies and practices of the district to subordinates and to the community fairly and objectively.

3. Implement, to the best of the official's ability, the policies and administrative regulations of the district.
4. Assist fellow administrators as appropriate in fulfilling their obligations.
5. Build the best possible image of the school district.
6. Refrain from publicly criticizing board members, administrators or other employees.
7. Help subordinates to achieve their maximum potential through fair and just treatment.

In the Conduct of Business and the Discharge of Responsibilities, the School Business Official Will:
1. Conduct business honestly, openly and with integrity.
2. Avoid conflict of interest situations by not conducting business with a company or firm in which the official or any member of the official's family has a vested interest.
3. Avoid preferential treatment of one outside interest group, company or individual over another.
4. Uphold the dignity and decorum of the office in every way.
5. Avoid using the position for personal gain.
6. Never accept or offer illegal payment for services rendered.
7. Refrain from accepting gifts, free services or anything of value for or because of any act performed or withheld.
8. Permit the use of school property only for official authorized activities.
9. Refrain from soliciting contributions from subordinates or outside sources for gifts or donations to a superior.

In Relationships with Colleagues in Other Districts and Associations, It Is Expected That the School Business Official Will:
1. Support the actions of a colleague whenever possible, never publicly criticizing or censuring the official.
2. Offer assistance and/or guidance to a colleague when such help is requested or when the need is obvious.
3. Actively support appropriate professional associations aimed at improving school business management and encourage colleagues to do likewise.
4. Accept leadership roles and responsibilities when appropriate, but refrain from "taking over" any association.
5. Refrain from using any organization or position of leadership in it for personal gain.

Source: Frank M. Pichel, "Professional Ethics for School Business Officials," *School Business Affairs 56,* No. 9 (September, 1990) p. 22.

The dollar amounts associated with school business management functions often make the school business decision maker a target for "deals." The K-12 sector spent over $215 billion in 1989–1990, and approximately one in four people in the United States are either students or employees of schools and colleges. A continued emphasis on the size of the operation may cause some perceptual problems. Although it is true that in most small communities the schools are the largest employer, feed more people per day and purchase more supplies than other organizations, while school bus drivers clock more miles than commercial transportation companies, schools are not "big business." They have functions that have big business dimensions. Drawing parallels with big business, however, does damage to the perceived mission of the schools. Turning out X number of graduates at the lowest cost to realize Y dollar amount of profit is not the mission of the schools. In fact, "turning out graduates" is not the essential mission of the schools. Such an achievement statement is too easily equated with turning out X number of machine parts without any qualitative criteria noted. The "bottom line" for schools is how much have the students learned. Perpetuating the big business myth may even give the board of education the idea that its main function is to hold tightly the purse strings rather than to represent the community in establishing a proper balance between the best education possible and what people need and want. The same myth may encourage the school business manager to become a watchdog of the treasury and warehouse instead of a servant to the instructional programs of the school.

Summary

The school business management branch of the larger field of educational administration continues to become more professionalized while at the same time growing more complex. The person performing some or all the functions noted in this chapter may be a specialist in accounting, facilities planning, or may be the superintendent of a small school district. The empowerment of building facility administrators to make curricular/instructional decisions, budget decisions, and often decentralized control of purchasing goods and services changes the role of the school business manager. The manager's quick response time in meeting compliance with numerous agency regulations emphasizes both his budgeting expertise and time management abilities. Although compliance with regulations, from disposing of underground fuel tanks, to eliminating asbestos, or to possibly guarding against electromagnetic fields in computer laboratories and offices may absorb a great deal of personal energy, the school business manager must keep the service dimension of his or her role in perspective. While business managerial efficiency is important, it is not the end, but merely a means to an end.

Much has been accomplished in professionalizing the school business manager's role. Much is left to be done. The Association of School Business Officials through its Registered School Business Administrator and Registered School Business Official (RSBA) programs is attempting to influence the profession positively. For example, one of the criteria for the RSBA is an earned master's degree in school business management or educational administration. As noted above, the school business administrator often carries the title of assistant superintendent, which ordinarily requires state licensure. States are continuing to look at testing or assessment as one step toward licensure or as part of the hiring process. Fifteen states now require some form of testing.[10] A growing number of states are using a test for administrators designed by National Evaluation

Systems. Some states require that prospective school business administrators go through
an assessment center process before licensure.

All these developments are encouraging, by attention being paid to selecting
competent people to serve as administrators in the schools. Although valid objections
can be raised regarding assessment or testing practices, and although "standards" are
sometimes adopted which demonstrate accountability without fundamental changes in
practice, some positive outcomes can be hoped for. As school business management
becomes recognized as an important part of educational administration, the future looks
even more promising.

Case Study

A Local Boy Makes Good

*Fred Fiver was a lifetime resident and nearly a living legend in the town of
Midcity. He won the state tennis title for Midcity High and went on to State
University to a great college tennis career. He majored in physical education and
minored in business education. After college he entered into a partnership in a
sports equipment business at the new country club and also served as the tennis
pro for the club. In a few years, the partners opened another sports equipment
store in the shopping mall. Times were good and Fred found himself on several
boards including that of one of the local banks, the YMCA, and Community
Health Group. His many business acquaintances often entertained Fred and
gave him privileges at their clubs or business/pleasure trips, and Fred recipro-
cated when the right occasions arose. He particularly enjoyed the Virgin Islands
fishing trip with the Alvin Gravel and Concrete Company. Two of his business
and sports friends were on the school board.*

*The auto industry crunch took its toll on Midcity and two major employers
closed their doors forever. Club membership dropped, and sports equipment was
not high on the "to buy" lists. Inventory and space rental costs at the club and
the mall still had to be met and there was talk about possible rent increases at
both locations.*

*The erosion of the tax base hurt the school district, caused some reduction
in the work force, and necessitated hiring some temporary, part-time people to
teach or coach in special areas. Fred welcomed the inquiry regarding his interest
in coaching tennis as a part-timer. The tennis team did well that year, and Fred
began a "farm club" operation at the middle school level. His summer tennis
program was well supported by parents whose children participated. The district
administrators asked Fred to teach a health course the next year. Given the
reduced business and need to keep the creditors satisfied, he agreed. That year,
Fred found he enjoyed the students in the health class as much as his tennis
charges. Again, the tennis team did very well and the newspapers in the area
were beginning to take note that Midcity was promising to become the region's
tennis power it was when Fred Fiver won the title.*

*However, another cloud was forming in that a major sporting goods chain
was pushing to get space in the mall. Fred and his partners decided to consoli-*

date back at the country club, reduce costs, and stop living on the edge of bankruptcy. At the same time, an opportunity opened for a full-time position for a health teacher and tennis and volleyball coach. Fred's friends on the board encouraged him to apply. Fred found himself employed full-time at his high school alma mater and enjoying an excellent year in volleyball and tennis. Two of his tennis players received full-ride scholarships at state colleges. Fred enrolled at State University in a master's program in school administration and completed it in two years. He became less involved in the sports equipment business at the club but maintained all his ties to business colleagues in the region. It was a good life.

During a late afternoon gathering at the 19th hole, a business acquaintance and school board member pulled Fred aside and told him that the Business Manager position would be open soon and that he would like Fred to apply. When the position became available Fred applied and was subsequently appointed to the position.

The next four years passed very quickly. Midcity had begun to recover from the economic blows and the club business was at least in the black. During that time Fred had done a creditable job and had convinced his central office colleagues that he had the good of the district at heart. The superintendent was supportive. A younger sports star at Midcity High School, Ted Tenner, had been appointed as the high school principal. Tenner had been a favorite of the superintendent since he starred in basketball while the superintendent was the high school principal.

Ted Tenner had a charismatic personality and was successfully moving the high school into site-based decision making and management. He was committed to the concept and had a clear idea where the school curriculum should be going. Ted was a "wheeler-dealer" and before long had developed a network of friends, including many of those Fred also counted as colleagues, including Fred's business partner.

The process toward planning the additions and renovation to the high school had been rocky. Ted had guided the high school management advisory board toward a firm commitment to an integrated media information system with total access from any part of the building. The upgrading and expansion of the sports facilities generated some heated responses from some parents and the community about keeping a balance between the academic mission of the school and sports. Fred was in the process of preparing for bids on the project.

Later, at a clubhouse gathering of long-time colleagues, the conversation turned to the school plans. During the course of the conversation, it became clear that Ted Tenner had been in personal contact with many of the local suppliers and contractors. Todd Alvin told Fred that he was looking forward to working with Fred on the project and hoped it wouldn't keep them all so busy that they couldn't get to the Virgin Islands for fishing. Fred's partner was exceptionally quiet.

For the first time in his tenure as business manager, Fred felt uncomfortable. He felt he was being pushed onto a train he didn't want to ride.

What are the issues involved? What basic problems might have contributed to the situation? What suggestions for action would you have for Fred Fiver? What might be the results of that course of action?

For Further Thought

1. If the school business manager is making educational decisions and is part of the educational leadership team, how do you define *leadership*?

2. Recall incidents in which means became the ends in an organization's life. What were the results of this displacement of goals?

3. If management of things should not be the primary goal of the school and yet excellent management of business resources provides the credibility to get on with the primary goal of the school—learning—how can the school business manager guard against business overshadowing learning?

4. Given the many functions of the school business manager noted in this chapter, how should he best be educated?

5. Compare job descriptions of school business managers from several school districts with the functions noted in the chapter. What discrepancies exist? Is there one area most often overlooked? Why do you think this is true?

6. Discuss the case "A Local Boy Makes Good." What implications are there not only for the school business manager, but also the superintendent and board of education?

Endnotes

1. K. Forbis Jordan, Mary P. McKeown, Richard G. Salmon, and L. Dean Webb, *School Business Administration* (Beverly Hills, Calif.: Sage Publications, 1985), p. 47.

2. Proceedings of the Thirtieth Annual Meeting of the American Association of Public School Business Officials (Kalamazoo, Mich.: The Association, 1941), p. 67.

3. Frederick W. Hill et al., *The School Business Administrator* (Reston, Va.: Association of School Business Officials International, 1982), pp. 4–5.

4. James G. Ward, "School Business Administration in an Information-Based Learning Society," *The Journal of School Business Management* 3, No. 4 (January 1992), p. 21.

5. Hill et al., *The School Business Administrator*, p. 8.

6. Hill et al., *The School Business Administrator*, pp. 28–32.

7. Carroll W. McGuffey, *A Handbook on Professional Certification of School Business Officials* (Reston, Va.: Association of School Business Officials, 1980).

8. The charts represent the 1990 organizational structures of two Florida county school districts.

9. Thelbert L. Drake, "State Requirements for School Business Officials," *School Business Affairs* 56, No. 3 (March 1990), p. 19.

10. Ulrich C. Reitzug, "Administrator Competency Testing: Status, Issues, and Policy Considerations," *Policy Bulletin*, Bloomington, Ind.: Consortium on Educational Policy Studies (May 1990), p. 2.

C h a p t e r 2

The School Business Manager as an Organizational Member

The school business manager is part of an organization and as a result is part of history, part of a culture, part of a political entity, part of sets of expectations and, as a result of the position, part of the leadership of the organization. Schools are more similar than different across the United States, although a greater range of differences are being encouraged from several sources such as parent groups, political figures, and coalitions of business leaders. The schools have developed in a unique fashion, serving unique needs. Although education is a state function and in nearly all instances the states have delegated the operation of schools to local communities, the 15,000 plus school districts, whether K-12, K-8, or overlapping high school districts, are very much alike in organizational appearances. They all have a chief executive, usually called superintendent; a legal entity composed of a policy making/administrative board; individual buildings have principals or head teachers, and nearly all are funded by a combination of local, state, and federal monies. Similarities are found in curricula, accreditation standards, daily schedules, and annual calendars. These similarities exist not only at a given point in time, but extend over a period of time. It has been noted that the organization of the high school of today has not changed significantly over the last 100 years. For the last century there has been little recognizable change in the overall structure of school districts. The most recent attempt to influence the shape of school organizational structure is the movement toward site-based decision making. Site-based decision making is an operational policy whereby the building administrator and staff, even a community advisory board, may make significant decisions affecting the school. These decisions frequently include curriculum, personnel, budget, and calendar. Each school operates within central district policies, but can meet student needs in its own way. Even this movement may be one of nomenclature and not substance.

In 1990 Drake conducted a number of telephone interviews with business administrators of school districts that had participated in a previous study of site-based schools.
The survey yielded no identifiable pattern of decision-making responsibilities at the
school level. In one district the impetus for site-based management came from an enterprising principal and grant money. The principal retired; the grant money ceased and so
did site-based management. Other conversations during the study began to underline the
idea that the definition of site-based decision making was local. Whether the decision was
made to comply with court orders or to join the "cutting edge," the practices were shaped
by local beliefs. One school system of approximately forty-five thousand students restricted building-level decisions to curricular matters and limited its purchasing of supplies and equipment. Such a pattern does not seem a departure from common practice over
many years, yet it may be a departure for that school system. The practice of hiring and
firing personnel at the building level varied greatly from selecting from a central office
list to complete freedom. What is it that makes school districts so much alike and yet so
different? Why do some districts that appear at least on the surface to be bureaucratic,
top-drawer organizations function well and others with very flat structures and participatory decision making function equally well? What is operating when change is imposed
by a federal court, economic trauma, or windfall and as soon as the external influence is
gone things return to the way they were prior to the external influence? What do people
mean when they say, "That's the way things are done around here"?

We contend that to be an effective leadership team member, over time, the school
business manager must be able to answer the above kinds of questions. He should be able
to go beyond the surface and interpret attitudes and behaviors as related to sets of norms
and expectations. In other words, the school business manager cannot remain content to
efficiently perform accounting and purchasing functions, but rather he or she must begin
to understand the educational needs of the whole organization and exert leadership as a
team member to meet those needs at an ever-increasing level of excellence.

Organizational Culture

People have observed that one can go onto a United States military establishment in
Oklahoma, California, or North Carolina and observe the same things, hear similar
sounds, and even smell the same odors. There are businesses that look exactly the same
physically, have the same "products," but in some way convey different atmospheres. In
some organizations employees work at their respective jobs, perform the tasks, and leave
without ever being part of the "big picture." The story is often told of the two bricklayers
who were asked what they were doing. One replied that he was laying brick. The other
replied that he was building a cathedral. Stories are told of the sense of mission and
belonging found among employees of a well-known cosmetics company. Contrasts are
noted in stories about certain airline flight attendants who do not identify with the
company that employs them. The stories provide the listener or reader insights into the
culture of an organization, and in some cases a subculture of an organization.

If school business managers are to understand the organization of which they are a
part and the suborganization which they lead, then a clear idea of the underlying, often
not stated, beliefs and values held in common is essential. Sergiovanni and Corbally stated

that "the battle for quality in loosely structured organizations . . . is won or lost on the basis of individual commitment—a cultural matter and not one of bureaucratic regulation or management technique."[1] Schools have been described as a loosely coupled organization; that is, schools are often viewed as having ambiguous goals. In a loosely coupled organization people attempt to reach their goals without tightly linked objectives and often without continuous communication. In the K-12 setting this is evidenced by the sparse communications among third-grade teachers, or between the high school and the elementary school, or between the school business office and the curriculum office. The activities of the loosely coupled organization may not appear to be directly linked with its stated goals. Is the solution to tighten the coupling with clearer goals and more specific procedures? Will a clearly drawn organizational chart bring the system together? At best, these are partial solutions.

What Is Organizational Culture?

Owens and Steinhoff offered the following definition of organizational culture: "Culture can be defined as the shared philosophies, ideologies, values, assumptions, beliefs, expectations, attitudes and norms that knit a community together."[2] Harman lists the following aspects of organizational culture: "Shared beliefs, myths, ideologies and other forms of expressive symbolism which serve as a normative guide for members' behavior."[3]

Expressions of these norms or shared values and beliefs are found in traditions, rituals, stories, often-cited heroes or symbols from the past. Buildings, art work, and language used to describe certain events or procedures, the sequence of events at commencement or athletic events, and countless other expressions seek to convey the culture. The problem for the school administrator is not so much identifying the expressions, but understanding the underlying values and beliefs on which they are based. One does not observe an organization long without finding conflicting, competing myths and symbols and their attendant underlying conflicts in values and beliefs. The leader, then, takes every opportunity to articulate his or her own values and beliefs and to underscore or create symbols or rituals that reinforce expected norms.

A clash of beliefs can be observed when a decision is made to go to site-based decision making. There are competing values regarding the worth of individual involvement in decision making as it relates to having an "efficient" and "accountable" organization. Tensions can develop, relationships can be strained, and role definitions can become less clear as the final points of approval for services, purchases, personnel hiring, and other ordinarily centralized functions shift away from the central office.

Bypassing Culture?

The perceived, clear-cut facts and figures associated with the management of the business aspects of educational institutions can provide a sense of a job well done, even a sense of comfort in not having to deal with the more difficult-to-measure educational goals of the school. The well-kept balance sheets, the clean, efficient buildings, and the orderly, on-time transportation system are essential. The school business manager properly may point with pride to them. Yet to stop at those facts and proclaim that the job has been done may stop short of true excellence. To do so may leave the school's business subunit with its own set of values whereby the *means* of good fiscal management become the only goal for the business management of the school district. To refer to the bricklayer story mentioned earlier, the end becomes X number of bricks laid into a straight, true wall in a given amount of time rather than making progress toward a magnificent cathedral.

Some questions become evident. Can a school business manager be fully functioning in a role that attempts to divorce the accomplishments of specific functions, no matter how well done, from the central values and beliefs of the total enterprise? Is it appropriate to bypass the culture of the school district by being content to simply lay bricks? If one were to ask the employees in the various roles in the business division what they did, would they respond with similar words that they were about the business of educating and helping the community's youth to become productive, contributing, caring people? Is that kind of response unrealistic? Is that a burden the school business manager should not have? Does expecting the business manager to relate to the underlying values of the school district imply too much of a heroic leadership role?

March noted that "much of what distinguishes a good bureaucracy from a bad one is how well it accomplishes the trivia of day-to-day relations with clients and day-to-day problems in maintaining and operating its technology."[4] Such a statement would seem to undermine the idea that emphasis on the broad goals and overriding mission of the schools is important or even appropriate. Individual tasks may be performed very well without reference to the development of contributing, caring citizens; therefore, the development of or change in a culture may be bypassed to the long-range detriment of the school system.

Other Views of Organization

An organization may be thought of as an entity, something that has a life of its own. This view conceives the organization as a system which receives inputs from and sends outputs into the environment. Processes occur within the organization to change the inputs. Berrien described a system as "a set of *components* interacting with each other and a *boundary* which possesses the property of filtering both the kind and rate of flow of *inputs* and *outputs* to and from the system."[5] Caplow noted that "an organization is a social system that has an unequivocal collective identity, an exact roster of members, a program of activity and procedures for replacing members."[6] Hall defined an organization as follows:

> *An organization is a collectivity with a relatively identifiable boundary, a nor-mative order, ranks of authority, communications systems, and membership co-ordination systems; this collectivity exists on a relatively continuous basis in an environment and engages in activities that are usually related to a set of goals; the activities have outcomes for organizational members, the organization itself, and for society.*[7]

The definitions imply interaction among the organization's components. The arrange-ments of and relationships between and among those components may help or hinder the system in achieving its goals. The intended hierarchical arrangements and relationships of an organization may be thought of as structure.

Designing Organizational Structure

Organizational structure establishes human and material relationships consistent with the objectives and resources of the organization and harmonizes activities through strategically placed administrative officers who can facilitate administrative details. The organizational structure should take into account the benefits of specialization, the limitations of authority, the problems of communications, and the need for stimulation and leadership; it should also provide a balance so that positive personal relations are encouraged.

A pattern of organization describes the bounds of action of a particular individual; it outlines the way he or she is expected to work and provides a framework within which to work. We must emphasize, however, that organizational structure is a pencil-and-paper affair and the way it operates is a matter of human relationships. An organization may be thought of as a set of social/personal relationships within the boundaries of the organization. When dealing with people, we must have principles that provide for flexibility. This is most important in a school system. Any school organization which institutionalizes its working relationships, stratifies its personnel, and develops a solid hierarchical form of control without utilizing the reservoir of staff abilities will fail to reach its full potential.

In designing an organizational structure, one logically starts with the objectives of the enterprise. These must be planned and with minor modifications accepted as constants. How should people and responsibilities be grouped in order to function best? What organization and structure will best utilize the expertise of personnel? It is not possible to prescribe a precise formula appropriate for all school districts. Many conditions within a state or local community affect the character of the school's organizational structure. These include (1) custom, tradition, and local cultural patterns; (2) constitutional provisions; (3) the degree to which statutes define the authority and responsibility of school districts; (4) school board policy; (5) the way courts have interpreted the state constitution and statutes; (6) the number, competency, and ability of personnel; (7) finances available for operation; (8) educational needs in the state and community; and (9) the importance of education to the people of the community.

Some of these conditions may be altered, but American education, because of its closeness to the people, demands an organization flexible and adaptable enough to fit local conditions. Therefore, although structures and patterns of organization and the way they operate vary locally, basic principles to guide their adoption should be followed.

Principles of Organization

The following principles are suggested as guides to the development of proper organizational structure for schools.

1. The value of all the organization's structures, agents, agencies, and practices should be based on and evaluated according to their contributions to the achievement and objectives of education.

2. The plan of organization should help obtain and hold the most able leadership as well as stimulate leadership activities on the part of all persons in the structure.

3. The organization should provide for the division of the total work into related parts which will ensure the most effective utilization of the skills and services of available personnel.

4. The organization should attract and retain the most competent men and women in the service by providing, insofar as possible, conditions under which they can do their best work.

5. The organizational structure should emphasize unity. It should facilitate effective coordination of the efforts of all educational agencies toward fulfillment of the objectives of education.

6. The organizational structure should be as simple as possible, consistent with the need to coordinate the work of the school, and be flexible to meet new demands and opportunities.

7. Each unit in the structure should have a clear definition of its functions and of the authority and responsibilities of the individuals comprising the unit. Everyone should participate in the exercise of authority, commensurate with job responsibilities, and without confusion or duplication.

8. An individual should be responsible to only one administrator in the performance of a particular function. This does not preclude an individual being accountable to more than one person for different functions; however, final authority should be clearly vested in one place. Whenever authority is vested in a group, the group should have a single executive officer who is responsible for the execution of group decisions.

9. The number of persons directly responsible to an individual should not be greater than he or she can supervise effectively. Activities should be grouped into the smallest feasible number of units without creating an inflexible administrative hierarchy.

10. The organization of the school should reflect the complete service offering in education. The organization should be such that it is possible to identify the various activities both individually and in relation to broader areas.

11. All personnel within the school should feel that they belong to an identifiable group and have a definite home base. Therefore, administrative units within the school should have similar and compatible groupings so that the units and subgroups within the units have real group identity.

An organization chart with its attendant job descriptions is sterile and without life. To be effective it must meet the test of reality: it must function in day-to-day operations. The principles of operation are discussed in the next section.

Principles of Operation

The following operational principles are as important to success as is the organizational structure itself.

1. A school district cannot exceed the restrictions placed on it by the popular understanding of its function. On the other hand, it cannot ignore the expectations placed on it. Expectations must be addressed. A low degree of public confidence and understanding limits the effectiveness of the school.

2. The importance of education demands that the school organization be aware of the vagaries of partisan politics; how they affect the schools; and how to protect itself while at the same time not succumb to closed system behavior and ignore external influences.

3. The educational function is so complex that it can only be carried out through a number of institutions, agencies, and activities. Encouraging the cooperation and coordination of educational and social agencies are essential activities of any school. The structure should reflect the interaction with the external environment.

4. An effective organization emphasizes and constantly utilizes in proper balance the four constituent elements of administrative activities: (a) planning, (b) execution, (c) appraisal, and (d) interpretation.

5. Persons affected by policies, both within and outside the organizational structure, should have a part in shaping those policies. The level of democratic action at any time depends on the competence and conscience of the individuals involved.

6. The aim of administration is to facilitate the instructional process. Administrative personnel should provide leadership in improving instruction and should see that the members of the staff have the necessary time, sufficient materials, and proper working conditions for the performance of their functions.

7. The effectiveness of a school is measured at least in part by the kind of job it does and by the achievements of all its personnel including students as they work individually and cooperatively. To achieve excellence, staff members must be allowed to avail themselves of opportunities to make significant contributions locally, nationally, and internationally.

8. A school organization should have enough flexibility and adaptability to handle newly developing needs. Its structure, policies, and programs should be subject to continuous evaluation. However, there should be sufficient continuity of organization and program to provide the necessary feeling of security for both the staff and the public at large.

9. Barriers to communication should be minimized both in structure and practice.

10. A process for reviewing the organizational structure should be part of the long-range planning process.

Traditional Organizational Structures

The organization of a school system is actually a translation of its purposes, principles, and activities into a structural, functional plan. A realistic approach is to review and clarify if necessary the purposes of the school; list all the tasks that are to be accomplished; relate them to the goals; then group them into related areas. Traditionally there are three major areas: instruction, fiscal functions, and support services. The prevailing pattern is a unit district with the superintendent as the chief executive officer to whom all major subunit heads report and they may report to the board only through the superintendent. Figure 2-1

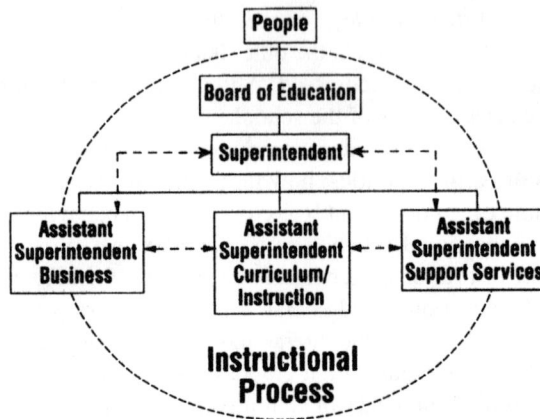

FIGURE 2-1   Traditional Unit Organization.

illustrates the traditional organizational pattern. The broken lines indicate that the subdivisions of the organization must be in continuous interaction to keep the organization effective.

There are almost as many variations of structure as there are districts, particularly as size of enrollments increases. School districts that experienced very rapid growth sometimes found their organizational structures growing like the New England farmhouse, a room here, a room there made from different materials and little relationship to the rest of the house except proximity. Others have found themselves bound by traditions of decades and simply patch and caulk to keep the house intact. The many influences on school districts have resulted in a variety of structural accommodations. No one way to structure a school district is best; however, any structure that inhibits effective instruction, or finds itself replacing the learning of students with other "more pressing" goals is a poor structure.

With the above in mind, the reader may find examining the following organizational charts to be of interest. Figure 2-2 shows the organization of a school district of about ten thousand students. There are at least two interesting features in the organizational structure: transportation services is separate from the business management functions and the director of special education is separate from instruction. A detailed chart of the business functions can be found in Figure 15-2 on page 256. The prominent positioning of the coordinator for communications may provide consistent information reporting to the public. On the other hand, it may imply a form of "gag rule" resulting from some previous negative experiences. Such possibilities simply underscore the fact that the organizational structure expressed on paper does not convey either the way the school organization operates or the principles, assumptions, beliefs, and values that form the foundation for the operation.

Figure 2-3 on page 24 shows the structure of a school district of forty-five thousand students. The chart provides a good example of a traditional division of functions. A possible exception is the separation of classified personnel functions from the business division. The district is divided into three geographical areas with an assistant superinten-

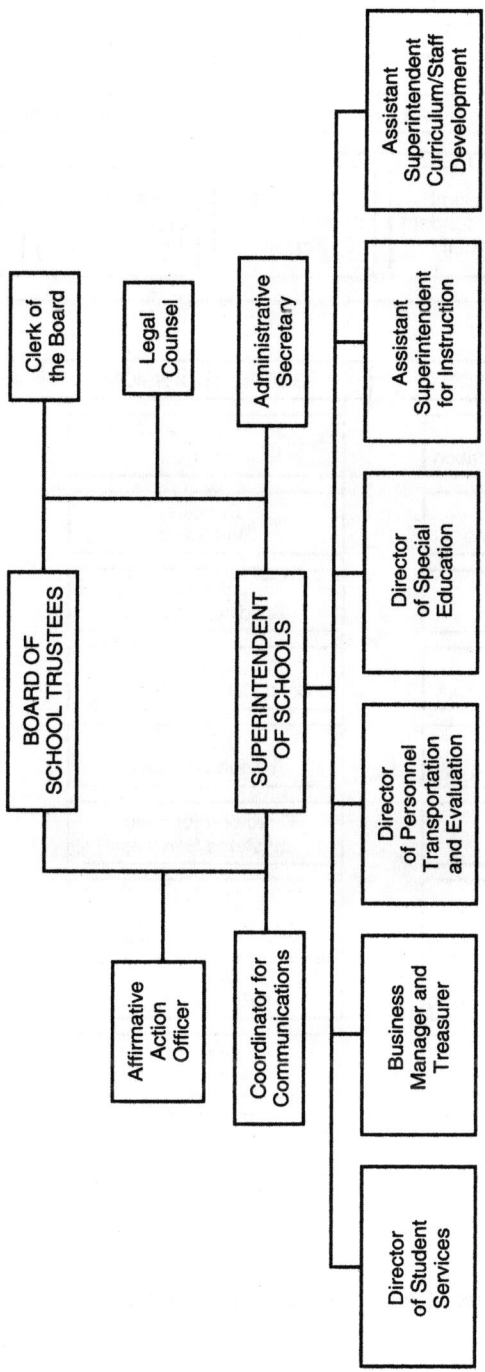

FIGURE 2-2 Administrative Organization of a School District of 10,000 Enrollment.

BOARD OF SCHOOL TRUSTEES

Clerk of the Board

Legal Counsel

Affirmative Action Officer

SUPERINTENDENT OF SCHOOLS

Administrative Secretary

Coordinator for Communications

Director of Student Services

Business Manager and Treasurer

Director of Personnel Transportation and Evaluation

Director of Special Education

Assistant Superintendent for Instruction

Assistant Superintendent Curriculum/Staff Development

MANAGEMENT TEAM

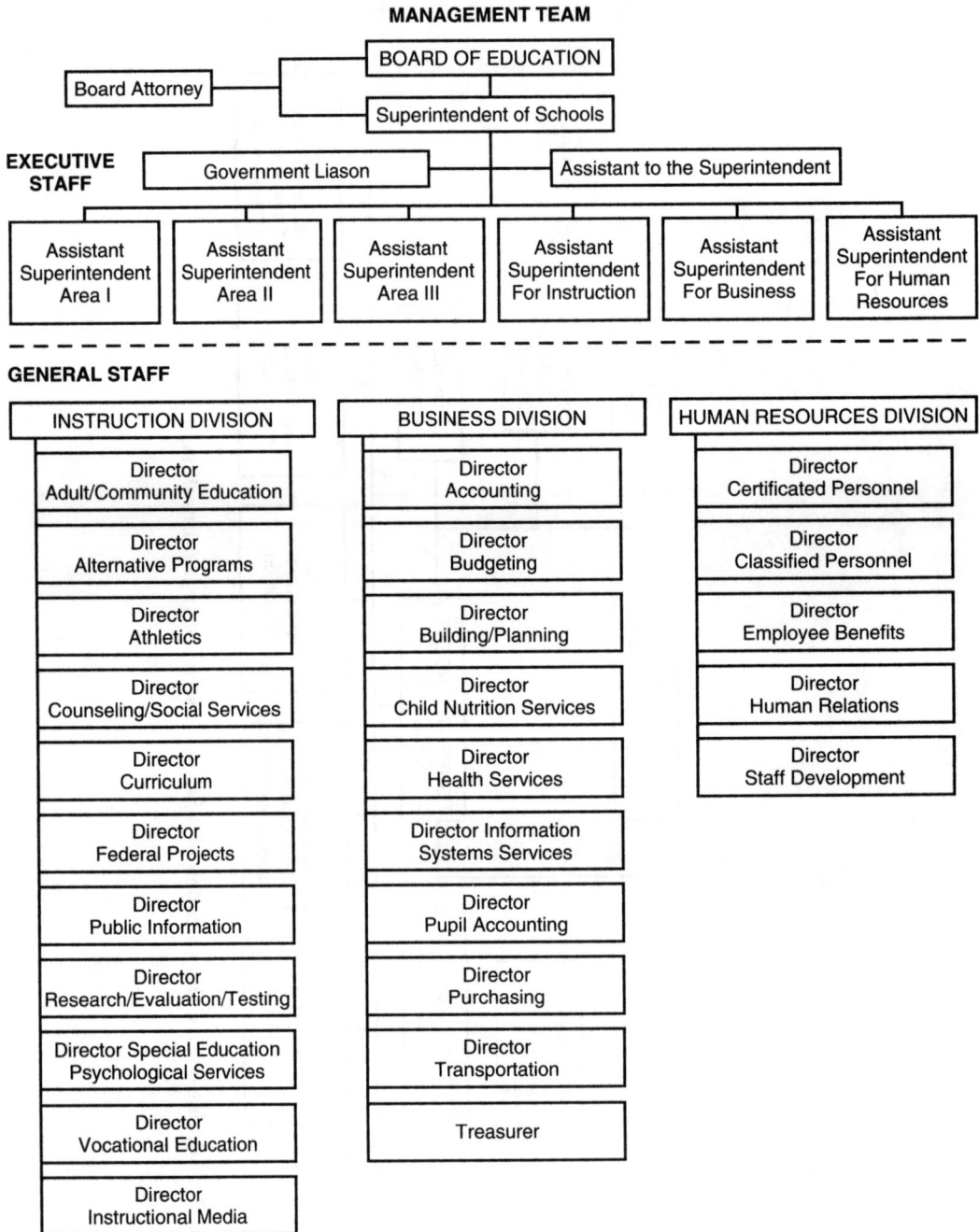

FIGURE 2-3   **Structure of a School District of 45,000 Enrollment.**

dent over each area. The assistant superintendent for instruction is primarily responsible for specialized areas. The communications requirements are important in this organizational structure, but to even further complicate the requirements, the district has a form of site-based management.

The two organizations described are unit type of districts in which all functions report through the superintendent. The chart shown in Figure 2-4 is a dual-executive type of district in which the treasurer reports directly to the board of education. Figure 2-5 details the divisions of the treasurer's functions.

As noted in chapter 1, there still exist some districts that by city charter or state law have a dual-executive type of organizational structure. Because business management is the phase of education with which the layperson is most familiar and because its activities are perceived to be easily separated from the instructional program, a few school organizational structures show a dual or multiple form of administration.

Under dual-administrative control, the administration of a school system is vested in two or more coordinate executive officers, each responsible directly to the board of education. The system is an outgrowth of the belief that the educator does not know enough about business affairs, that the educator should be entrusted only with the instructional phases of school operation, and that practical management problems should be assigned to an experienced businessman who is hired as a major executive of the school and is responsible directly to the board of education. This executive officer may be given the title of business manager, business executive, business agent, treasurer, or secretary to the board of education. The business officer and the superintendent independently report directly to the board of education. When most school districts were small the responsibility for performing the necessary business functions was, as one might expect, assigned to members of the board, committees of the board, or the board secretary. As the school system became larger the secretary was called on to give an increasing proportion of time to schoolwork. Thus, in the larger school systems the secretary of the board of education very often became the business manager or controller, a full-time executive officer on a par with the superintendent of schools. Too often the person holding this position had neither educational nor business training, but local politics frequently made him a more powerful executive than the superintendent.

Another look at Figures 2-4 and 2-5 show potential duplications of effort or at best the right hand not knowing that the left hand is generating and analyzing the same data. To reinforce by way of organizational structure the idea that the business functions are not part of the educational team effort to improve student learning could prove to be counterproductive. It is easy enough to lose sight of the original purpose of any organization given the press of deadlines and problems, but to create or maintain a structure that facilitates goal displacement is not wise. The elected or even appointed school board members may find the separate finance officer or controller an ally in their bids to maintain office. Friction can develop between the finance/business officer who reports to the board of education and the separate business manager who reports to the superintendent. Such an arrangement erodes the idea of cultivating shared values and vision within the leadership team. If the board of education feels it cannot trust the superintendent to operate a complex system efficiently and honestly, then the board should find another superintendent rather than maintain a structure which serves as a breeding ground for

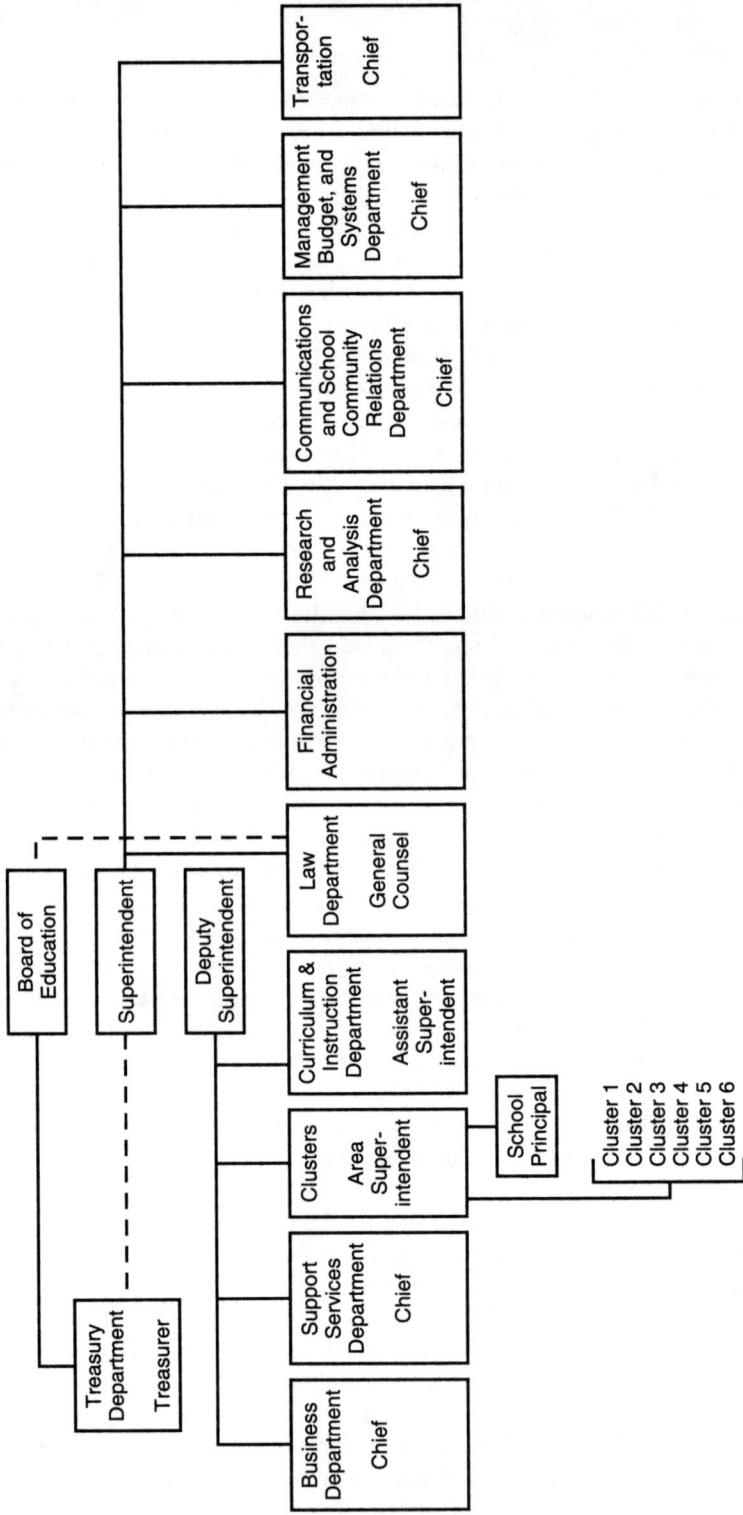

FIGURE 2-4 Organization of a Dual-Reporting School District of Approximately 13,000 Enrollment.

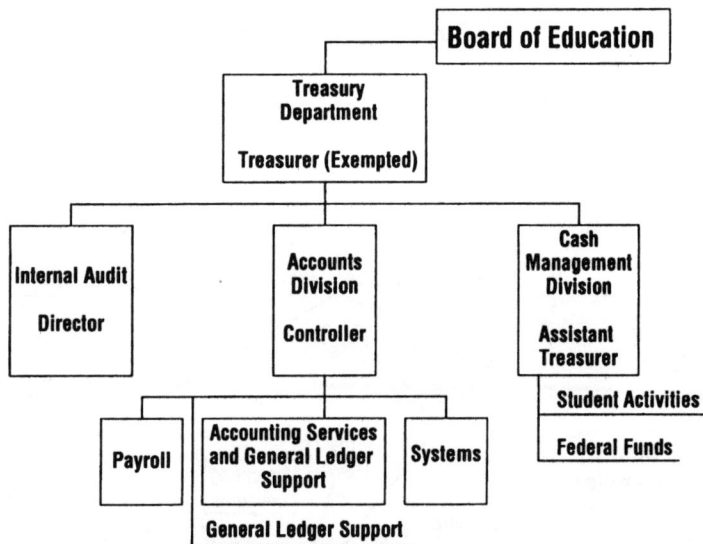

FIGURE 2-5 Detail of One Department Reporting Directly to the Board of Education and Not through the Superintendent.

these potential problems. Again, the authors acknowledge state laws and charters that require a dual-executive arrangement. A united effort to change those situations may be in order.

Nontraditional Organizational Structure

The reader has seen several examples of line/staff organizational charts depicting the structures of school districts such as presented earlier in this chapter. These were presentations of the traditional form of organization. There is an assumption about most of the representations of structure—this is the way it is until we have to change. A second form of structure looks a great deal like the first in that the squares and rectangles and the lines that join them are static on a page of paper. One cannot show movement except by video techniques. The second form of structure is the nontraditional type and has the assumptions that (1) the current functions may become obsolete because the tasks were accomplished, internal or external changes occurred, or newer, more important functions supplanted the existing functions; and (2) the changes necessitate new configurations continuously.

Often in the second type of structure functional groups are called centers or clusters rather than departments or divisions. The semantics seems to imply fluidity and change and the real possibility that a center could easily expand or cease to exist as new

Board of Directors

President			NC (Region 3)
Secretary	President Elect	NW (Region 1)	NE (Region 2)
Past President	Officers	WC (Region 6)	Regional Coordinators
Executive Secy/Treas		SW (Region 8)	EC (Region 4)

Officers — Regional Coordinators

Trustees
317
219
317
812   812

Standing Committees
Organizations & By Laws
Program Planning
Membership
Information & Publications

Ad Hoc Committees
Critical Issues
Parenting Concerns
Awards and Recognition
Elections
Nominations
Resolutions
Research
Diverse Cultures, Ethnic & Racial Concerns
Conference Committee
Professional Preparation & Certification

Board Members At Large
ICPT
DOE
IAEMSP
ISCA
ISSA

SW (Region 8)   Cen (Region 5)   SE (Region 7)

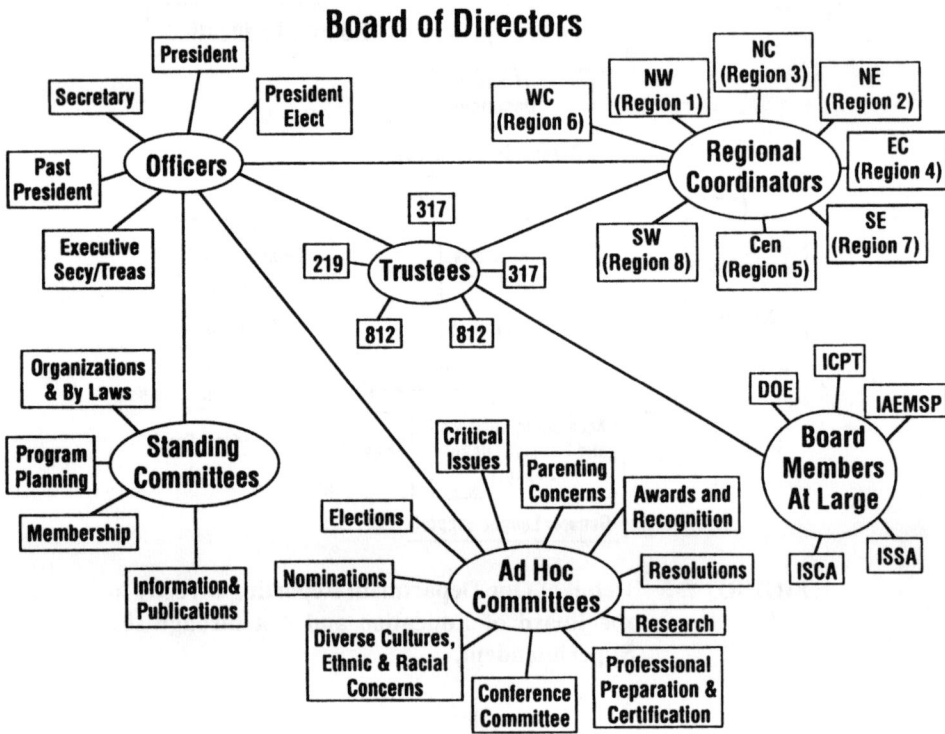

FIGURE 2-6   Nontraditional Organization Chart.

challenges arise. Turf gives way to task. Reaching goals becomes more important than defending departmental boundaries.

The nontraditional structure may be represented as a series of labeled circles surrounded by other circles, with each cluster of circles connected to each of the other clusters (Figure 2-6). Regardless of the way it is presented on paper, the underlying assumptions are the important differences. So it is with all attempts to organize people to accomplish a task. The idea is to shape the structure to get the right things done the right way in an ever-expanding environment of excellence.

Communications in Organizations

Electronic mail, fax machines, and video telephones do not make communications. All of these help make communications easier, but the keys to communication include willingness, clarity, timeliness and, of course, knowledge.

The school district business offices are the recipients and generators of massive amounts of communications. There are many times when both received and sent communications may seem to be less important than absolutely necessary. Too often there are people in the organization who rely almost completely on information coming from the district's central offices. Hodgkin found that when effecting mandated changes, secondary principals rely most on communications from the superintendent's office and occasionally from the state department of education.[8] The use of other sources dropped off quickly. The implication is clear for the communications efforts of the school business administrator. People responsible for the operation of units within the school district look to the central offices for information and direction.

As organizations become flatter and more decentralized, communications demands can increase, but from a somewhat different point of view. In the top-down organization, the central office instructions and directives might have been accepted as "This is the way they want it" or any number of variations on one waiting for directions from on high. As accountable responsibility becomes decentralized, as more functions move to remote sites and decisions at one site differ from those at another site, expectations regarding communications change. The central office may be viewed as a service agency to the remote sites. Communications may be viewed as a service to the site so the school mission can be accomplished.

As noted in chapter 7, Purchasing, the business office needs to anticipate the reactions of teachers and other staff to the information made or not made available at the building level. The business office personnel ordinarily communicate with the teachers through the principal; however, the way the communications are filtered to the users and how they interpret them are important considerations. It might be useful to provide the principals with written explanations of or the rationale of changes that have occurred, even though teachers may have been part of the decision to make the changes. Internal communications between peers at the building level may not be as extensive or as accurate as central office personnel may expect. A newsletter aimed at the building level telling what has happened, what is being worked on, anticipated events, and who is involved in making input may be very useful to the school business office in getting out the message as well as generating positive input.

Not only does the internal community look for reliable input, the external public sectors do also. The district needs consciously to develop an internal communications network for everyday operations as well as for emergencies. What office is to provide what kinds of information to what units? Are there "clearinghouses" for information going to the organization as well as to the external public sectors? How are responses handled during rapid change?

As noted in chapter 1, the school business manager may find it necessary to respond to media inquiries or to initiate communications for the media. Nearly always, the business manager is in a support role for the superintendent, but the same rule of thumb applies: honesty is the best policy. On occasion the media does not receive a detailed statement because of the potential harm to individuals or to the schools, but the reason should be clarified for media personnel. Over a period of time, this kind of honesty will be respected. Another rule for those dealing with the press is to have realistic expectations. Errors of fact and interpretation inevitably creep into deadline-pressure stories. A calm presentation or correction of facts may be the best approach rather than cutting off any further communications or storming the media ramparts with accusations of poor work or irresponsible reporting.

In a 1990 study, Drake interviewed a number of school business officials in school districts identified with site-based decision making. Most of the business officials noted an increase in the reporting function because separate reports had to be generated for each site. Given different grade levels and programs among the buildings, the increase in the paper flow seemed exponential. The importance of another form of communication emerged—the in-service education of the users of the paper flow. One school business manager cited electronic mail as a means of keeping meanings of communications clear. Another said he spent much more time communicating by telephone than in the past. His in-servicing was done on an individual basis rather than in groups, partly because of the geographical distances between schools and the central office. These were typical responses from school business officials who were in site-based school districts and they serve to underscore the need for better communications into and from the school business manager's office. There did seem to be a substantive change from communiqués, memos, and directives toward that of enhancing communication through one-on-one interactions, working with small groups, or teaming with the purpose of understanding and working toward a common goal. Such a change seems to imply a qualitative shift rather than just quantitative.

Organizational Leadership

If the reader accepts the ideas that the school business manager is part of the educational leadership team and does make educational decisions, then it is appropriate to expect the school business manager to exert leadership in a broader context than the business office alone. This is not to say that the demands of the business office do not consume much time, energy and continuous learning, but rather that the responses to those demands must be determined in light of effects on student learning. In addition, the business manager must be able to influence the educational decisions of others to achieve fiscal responsibility. As a case in point, a brilliant fiscal decision that harms opportunities for learning is a bad decision. On the other hand, an equally brilliant educational decision that puts the district at financial risk is equally bad. The business manager then is required to be a team leader continuously considering both the instructional and fiscal responsibilities of the schools.

Leaders and leadership have been observed, analyzed, and theorized about for millenia. When groups were small in families or clans, leadership fell to the patriarch. As groups become larger and more complex, so did the accrual of leadership authority and power. As needs increased, specialized groups developed to meet those needs. Soldiers, priests, builders, and herdsmen were needed to keep the organization going. The early Christian church found that they needed deacons to use resources to care for the poor. Organizations that made products required designated leaders to oversee the workers. The industrial revolution spawned many needs, not the least of which was how to lead large numbers of people to accomplish the work to produce the products. The image of the great captains of industry seemed to reinforce images of kings and national leaders. The idea emerged that successful leaders must have some common traits. So for many years the traits of leaders were studied to determine why Charlemagne, Churchill, Hitler, or Hammurabi were acknowledged leaders. The studies have yielded little of value to identify sets of inherent traits that make a leader. One would only have to look at the differences among Churchill, Gandhi, De Gaulle, or J. F. Kennedy to suspect that traits may not be useful predictors.

Max Weber[9] looked at an organization's potential to become efficient. The main ideas he proposed regarding bureaucracies are: (1) there is a clear hierarchy of authority positions, (2) written rules and regulations govern behavior, (3) specialization occurs, (4) rational behavior is espoused, and (5) there is internal control of resources.

Encounters with bureaucracies as an insider quickly cause one to question the assumption that those who do the work do so in a rational way to maximize the organization's goals. In somewhat the same way it is easy to question the proliferation of rules that seem to be spawned when a negative situation occurs. The bureaucracy tends to try to operate as a closed system, one which makes every attempt to control its inputs and to limit interactions with its environment. For instance, the school business office can adopt the attitude that there is only the business office way of doing things—their timing for reports, their formats, their list of materials and vendors, etc. With such a limitation on inputs, the operation is perceived from within to run more smoothly and efficiently. Chances for the unanticipated are reduced and routines can be refined. The vision of the business area with the above orientation might be summed up in "Let them run the schools; we'll run the business area." Such a view limits everyone to a prescribed set of functions, expectations, and procedures, with any variance from those prescribed perceived as a problem, if not intrusions on territory. The ideas of mutual goals and cooperative efforts can be displaced with a compartmentalized view of functions. The fragmentation of efforts can erode the accomplishment of an overall mission even though each unit may be doing well what it has carved out for itself to do, or has been told to do.

During the same period as Weber's work, Frederick Taylor and Henri Fayol were investigating the complexities of organizations. Taylor[10] suggested through his time-motion studies that there was one best way to perform a task. Leadership consisted of finding the best way and inspecting to see that the task was done that way. The *scientific management* era had begun. The contributions of scientific management research have been helpful and continue to be helpful; however, additional considerations such as human relations, human resources, and behavioral and cultural considerations have filled in the leadership picture so that it is more complete, although not finished. The scientific management movement tends to put the role of the supervisor into that of inspector, that is, the supervisor merely had to inspect to see that the work was being done in the one best way that had been determined by someone other than the person doing the work.

For the administrator to simply inspect to see that the work is being done in the exact way a person other than the worker determined puts both the administrator and the person performing the tasks into an infancy mode of behavior. The administrator is not leading but inspecting and in a sense may be performing no higher order function than a laser scanner recognizing bar codes. Such a level of "scientific" management tends to reinforce both the manager and the producer at the level of being told what and how to do something. The inadequacy of such an approach is obvious. It denies that the worker is capable of being a thinking contributor and limits behaviors to prescribed routines and compliance. The potentials of the office secretary, purchasing clerk, or bus driver likely will never be tapped under inspectorial supervision.

On the other hand, the school business manager may limit his own potential contribution by defining the role narrowly and confining his contributions to routine duties, along with those of his staff encompassing several areas of the business division. Such an approach limits solutions to school district challenges, and at the same time denies the business manager the rewards of continuously growing and contributing to a larger picture.

Fayol articulated his principles of management in *Administration industrielle et generale* (1916)[11]. He also dealt with the issue of centralization versus decentralization as related to the importance of subordinates' roles. Today the reader has encountered many articles and speeches using such terms as "participatory management" or "empowerment" as related to optimizing roles and therefore the productivity of the subordinates in an organization. Dewey stated:

> *Absence of participation tends to produce lack of interest and concern on the part of those shut out. The result is a corresponding lack of effective responsibility.*[12]

School business office personnel are no exception to the above as far as their commitment to the organization. It may be important for the business manager to reflect on his behavior as it relates to the involvement of others in making decisions about the operations in the business area. This is not to prescribe a routine set of behaviors as the reader will see later in the chapter.

In the 1920s studies of human reactions to workplace changes were the beginning points of the *human relations* movement. The Western Electric studies confirmed that psychological factors did affect the output of workers. There was a frenzy of writing to support the idea that "democratic" administration would produce the best work results. On occasion these exhortations were mistranslated into "happy workers equal productive workers." As the song from the musical *Showboat* states, "T'aint necessarily so."

Researchers continued to look at the human relationships dimension of leadership behaviors. Many terms have been used to describe the dimensions of human relations versus those of task or goal orientation. The relationship of leader behavior is often expressed as a point or a line on a two-dimensional grid. The terms listed on each axis of the dimensions illustrated in Figure 2-7 have been taken from a number of research studies of effective leadership. The studies performed at Ohio State University identified "initiating structure" and "consideration" as major factors relating to leadership behavior. Others have studied the relationships between various forms of productivity (e.g., items produced, achievement, sales) and the people/task behaviors of leaders. Generally, the studies show a direct relationship between subordinate satisfaction and a leader's high rating on a "people" dimension score. Halpin,[13] Blake and Mouton,[14] and other researchers in the private sector and in public schools support the idea that leaders must give attention to both people and task dimensions of leadership behavior.

A simplistic approach to leadership behavior would call for the leader to exercise a high level of people consideration and a high level of organizational task behaviors and

HUMAN	
Consideration	
Concern for people	
Idiographic	
Human relationships	

ORGANIZATIONAL

Initializing structure	Task	Production	Goal-Oriented	Nomothetic

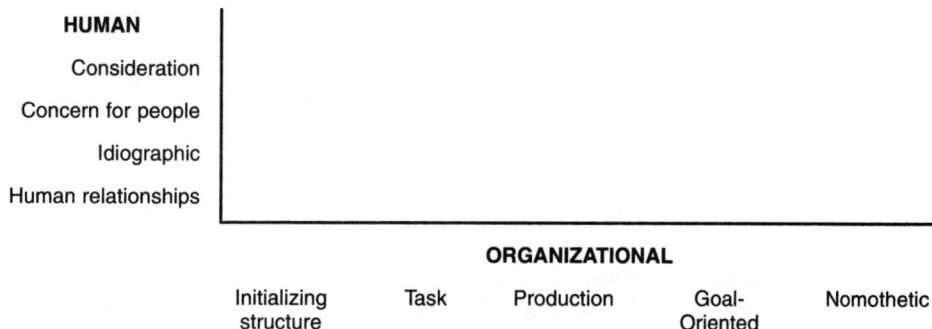

FIGURE 2-7   Terms Used to Identify Human and Organizational Leadership Behaviors.

Adapted from: T. L. Drake and W. H. Roe, *The Principalship* (New York: Macmillan, 1986), p. 110.

the results would be positive. The reader can think of instances when the results did not turn out quite that way. A study of achievement in city schools indicated that achievement was higher in those schools whose principal was task oriented.[15] Staff were more satisfied in schools in which the principal was human-relations oriented, but higher achievement was not reflected in teachers' satisfaction. It should be pointed out that the schools were not noted for their high achievement or motivation; therefore, the application of Hersey and Blanchard's "telling" mode of leader behavior is reinforced by the findings.

Fiedler studied leadership behaviors and classified them as either task oriented or human-relations oriented.[16] His work popularized the *situational approach* to leadership style. He concluded that task-motivated leaders were most effective in either low control or high control situations and that human-relations–motivated leaders were most effective in situations of moderate control. Hersey and Blanchard capitalized on the research and theories developed and noted that as the maturity, strengths, and willingness of the followers change, so should the leader's behavior.[17] They use terms describing a leader's behavior as "telling, selling, delegating" to relate to various levels of followers' maturity. Their contention, along with others, is that the leader should change his or her behavior depending on the situation.

The discussion of organizational culture earlier in the chapter and the brief presentation of leadership behavior raise the question of how the leader is to behave so that he can be effective in a variety of settings. It appears clear that one formula does not work in all situations the leader may encounter. If the leader is to be effective it does appear that he needs to (1) understand the prevailing values held in the organization; (2) interpret occurrences to colleagues (internal changes, external pressures, etc.) in light of the values and goals of the organization; and (3) articulate the purposes and goals of the organization. Vaill suggests that in a high-performance group, what the leader stands for and communicates is very important.[18] The leader needs to reflect on what he "stands for," that is, what message is being conveyed by his behaviors and words to the work group. Is the message consistent? Is it clear? How does it relate to the belief system in the organization?

Does it convey the idea that if no one is complaining, then everything must be okay? Does that kind of message encourage an ever-expanding vision of excellence?

There are many smoothly operating, efficient school business offices. The business manager may only need to keep his staff informed of events and new techniques and provide the best materials and equipment to keep the level of efficiency high. Underlying this is the assumption that the tasks needed are the tasks that have always been done. Yet the environment not only changes around any operation, the ways to successfully meet the challenges may be different as well. Not only will the tasks performed by the school business office personnel change, so will the manager's tasks change. Kanter noted that "managerial work is undergoing such enormous and rapid change that many managers are re-inventing their profession as they go; . . . they watch traditional sources of power erode and the old motivational tools lose their magic."[19] The management function in some organizations is becoming less hierarchical and more interactive with peers, a communications-based cooperative venture focused on problem solving. School systems have adopted the semantics and may have changed the job descriptions, but the way of thinking may not be too different from the traditional, bureaucratic model of top-down management. As experience grows, the empowerment of others may be seen as an opportunity for growth rather than a potential loss of power. Everyone in the office becomes a source for improvement. Through a continuous improvement approach new standards for excellence are established as each improvement is tried, tested, and adopted. One need not wait until the new academic year or the next budget to move the standards up a notch. Total quality management (TQM) being implemented in some governmental agencies as well as in competitive private businesses encourages everyone to be a problem solver but primarily through anticipating problems and avoiding their occurrences whenever possible. Wilson and Schmoker[20] noted the focus on statistical data which elicits the expression, "Give me the data" in problem-solving discussions in a Toyota plant in Kentucky. The approach makes every employee concerned about and expert in quality control. Incremental improvements are made as needed to improve quality. The school business manager is in an excellent position to foster statistical controls given the massive amount of data available in his or her offices, but to make it relevant to the school's mission a cooperative effort among all team members of the school's leadership is needed. Within the business office domains, statistical controls used by everyone could affect the system in a very positive way. Siu-Runyan and Heart[21] in discussing Deming's fourteen points for effective management noted Deming's preference for an atmosphere of receptivity and recognition over measuring performance by the numbers of items completed. Statistical controls then are not quotas, but rather supporting quantifications of problems to be solved or solutions reached. It is continuous and pervasive quality control and improvement. The emphasis on statistical controls is not to avoid valuing, but rather to provide a common set of data and information for those involved to make judgments.

The TQM approach to management leadership may be distinguished by at least the following commitments:

- *Recognizing quality as value rather than the absence of defects.* Quality can be viewed both internally (within the school business office operations) and externally.

Quality may be viewed as the product of a task and the contribution of that task to the overall mission of the school organization. While the absence of error may be a part of quality (e.g., the maintenance of buses so there are zero breakdowns), the concept of quality goes beyond zero errors to the contribution of zero breakdowns to the larger picture of providing all students with access to learning opportunities.

- *All employees seek continuous improvement.* Instilling the desire to do one's tasks even better requires ownership in the overall mission, in one's own area of responsibility, and a degree of freedom to make changes within a collegial structure.
- *An orientation for cross-functional teamwork.* The ability of people within a particular area to work across departmental or division lines to accomplish their work better is important to the TQM approach. To disallow this kind of teamwork can limit seriously the quality emphasis noted above.
- *Reduction of costs while improving technical performance.* It is easy to say that one can do better if more resources are available, and in some instances it is true. The challenge of doing better with the same or with fewer resources in one area in order to provide resources in another area may appeal to the entrepreneurship and creativity of those charged with the responsibility of producing excellence.
- *Preventing error rather than just fixing errors.* Of course errors should be found and fixed, but the emphasis is on anticipating what could go wrong and preventing it from happening. This includes people error possibilities and well as mechanical error. For instance, a new requirement comes in from the state. It would be easy to send a copy of the requirement to building administrators or treasurers with the directive to make certain changes in reporting or accounting. What other parts of the system might be affected? What misunderstanding could occur? Is the software able to handle it? Does it require new training? Are there needed pieces of information not now being generated? Are there additional time requirements and if so what might be dropped or put off so that the new procedure can be implemented?

In a sense, adopting or adapting TQM may well be changing the existing organizational culture. Changing shared beliefs in how things ought to be done is a challenge to the bravest, but may be an effective way to make lasting change.

Leadership is complex and effective leadership appears to be affected by the situation and by the would-be leader's behaviors. What then is leadership? The authors support the following:

Leadership is a planned process *that results in the following:*[22]

1. *The challenging of people to work toward an ever-expanding vision of excellence in the achievement of organizational goals and objectives.*
2. *The creation of a threat-free environment for growth so that the creative talents and skills of each person are used to best advantage.*
3. *The encouragement and building of working relationships that are individually and organizationally satisfying, unifying, and strengthening in the realization of mutually determined goals and objectives.*
4. *The optimization of available material and human resources.*

Summary

Schools and school systems are organizations that have their own sets of acceptable behaviors (ways of doing things around here) and sets of values—in short, their own cultures. The school system behaves much like any other organization toward its environment in that it decides how it will relate to that environment. The school may choose to recognize itself as an open system and ready itself for changes and in turn to influence its environment, or it may choose to behave as much like a closed system as it can. The school business manager is part of the leadership group responsible for accomplishing the school's goals; therefore, it is incumbent on the manager to proactively help shape the organization toward a shared vision of excellence by communicating, by nurturing an open organization, and by dealing with the business management areas in a way that exemplifies linkages between on-the-job behaviors and the stated goals of the school.

For Further Thought

1. Cite an example of an organization that could best be described as nontraditional (see Figure 2-6 for the organizational chart). What characteristics caused you to select the organization?

2. What provisions for planned interaction with the school's environment can you identify in your school district's business management functions? What messages might be conveyed to persons outside the school in the way they are carried out?

3. What communication barriers exist between the school business office and other units of the schools? What might be done about lowering those barriers?

4. Since inadequate supervision is ordinarily identified as a source of dissatisfaction by workers, what provisions can be made to ensure that the various areas of activity associated with the school business management function have adequate technical supervision?

5. Collect several school organizational charts. Identify all the school business management functions. Are they under one administrator? Are there potential conflicts built into the organization?

Endnotes

1. Thomas J. Sergiovanni and John E. Corbally, eds., *Leadership and Organizational Culture* (Urbana: University of Illinois Press, 1984), p. ix.

2. Robert G. Owens and Carl R. Steinhoff, "Towards a Theory of Organizational Culture," *Journal of Educational Administration* 27, No. 3 (1989), p. 11.

3. Kay Harman, "Culture and Conflict in Academic Organizations: Symbolic Aspects of University Worlds," *Journal of Educational Administration* 27, No. 3 (1989), p. 34.

4. James G. March, "How We Talk and How We Act: Administrative Theory and Administrative Life," in Sergiovanni and Corbally, eds., *Leadership and Organizational Culture*, p. 23.

5. F. K. Berrien, *General and Social Systems* (New Brunswick, N.J.: Rutgers University Press, 1968), pp. 14–15.

6. Theodore Caplow, *Principles of Organization* (New York: Harcourt Brace Jovanovich, Inc., 1964), p. 1.

7. Richard H. Hall, *Organizations: Structures, Processes, & Outcomes,* 5th ed. (Englewood Cliffs, N.J.: Prentice-Hall, 1991), p. 32.

8. Russell E. Hodgkin, "Information Sources Utilized by Secondary School Principals," Ph.D. dissertation, Ball State University, 1990, p. 71.

9. Max Weber, *The Theory of Social and Economic Organizations,* trans. Talcott Parsons, New York: The Free Press, 1974.

10. Frederick Taylor, *The Principles of Scientific Management,* New York: Harper and Row, 1911.

11. Henri Fayol, *General and Industrial Management,* trans. by Constance Storrs, London: Sir Isaac Pitman & Sons, 1949.

12. Morris Mendelson et al., "Social Power and Commitment: A Theoretical Statement," in Morris Mendelson (ed.) *Interdisciplinary Foundations of Supervision* (Newton, Mass.: Allyn and Bacon, Inc., 1970), p. 219.

13. A. W. Halpin, "How Leaders Behave," *Theory and Research in Administration* (New York: Macmillan, 1966), pp. 81–130.

14. Robert Blake and Jane Mouton, *The Managerial Grid* (Houston: Gulf Publishing Co., 1964).

15. Dixie W. Garner, *A Comparative Study of the Leadership Styles of Elementary Principals from Chapter I Schools with Principals from Non-Chapter I Schools to Determine if Leadership Style Is Related to the Achievement of Third Grade Students,* Unpublished doctoral dissertation, Ball State University, 1989.

16. Fred E. Fiedler and M. M. Chemers, *Leadership and Effective Management* (Glenview, Ill.: Scott Foresman and Company, 1974).

17. Paul Hersey and Kenneth Blanchard, *Management of Organizational Behavior,* 5th ed. (Englewood Cliffs, N.J.: Prentice-Hall, 1988).

18. Peter B. Vaill, "The Purposing of High-Performing Systems," in Sergiovanni and Corbally, eds., *Leadership and Organizational Culture,* p. 9.

19. Rosabeth Moss Kanter, "The New Managerial Work," in Amy Cohen Paul (ed.), *Managing for Tomorrow* (Washington, D.C.: International City Management Association, 1990), p. 95.

20. Richard B. Wilson and Mike Schmoker, "Quest for Quality," *The Executive Educator* (January 1992), pp. 18–22.

21. Yvonne Siu-Runyan and Sally J. Heart, "Management Manifesto," *Executive Educator* 14, No. 1, January, 1992, pp. 23–26.

22. Drake and Roe, *The Principalship,* p. 115.

Appraisal of School Business Management Functions

Without evaluation of the effectiveness of the various school business management functions, the school business manager would be adrift as far as setting a course for improvement. To rely on the idea that "if everything is working don't fix it" will at best keep operations going at the current level of productivity, but seldom improves the quality of performance. Given continuous changes in the organization's environment, the "don't fix it" approach usually results in a reduction in effectiveness. A *planned* evaluation process is essential to the business management functions just as it is important to instructional processes. The purpose of this chapter is to establish a workable evaluation process.

Focus on Performance

Most people find satisfaction in their work to the point that they identify themselves as managers, accountants, drivers, and so on. To the extent that a person identifies himself with the job, he associates his self-worth with that job. The leader of an enterprise must exercise care in appraising job performance so that the focus of the appraisal is on the results of job performance, and not on the person's feelings of self-worth. Although this is a difficult task, it is worth the effort to separate effective task performance from the idea of the evaluator's regard for the value of the person as a human being.

Case Study

Glenda Eishayd had been serving as the Director of Accounting for seven years in the Westside School District. She had a reputation for arriving early, leaving late and generally being a positive, helpful person. Glenda looked forward to working with the new business manager because she was confident in her abilities and had a sincere desire to please. A good portion of her own time was spent reading journals and newsletters in her field and attending conferences. At meetings she would often introduce herself as Director of Accounting and not mention her name at first.

The new business manager met with the department directors and announced that she wanted to get an idea of the levels of performance within the business areas. To this end, the business manager planned to conduct a series of job performance evaluations beginning at the director's level. She outlined the evaluation as including the accomplishment of established goals; directors' personal goals; evaluation techniques used by each director to ensure continuous growth on the job; records of those evaluations; usefulness of the reports generated by the departments as perceived by the users of the reports; retention of employees; problems referred to the business manager over the last two years; innovations within the last two years; savings or efficiencies generated by those innovations; and supervisory processes used to upgrade the technical skills of employees. The new business manager made it clear that she "enjoyed working with good people—people who moved their departments toward excellence in service to the mission of the schools."

Ms. Eishayd had always been proud of her track record in accuracy and perceived that the four persons in her department respected her knowledge and dedication. She always responded to any questions her four employees had about their tasks, and she had divided the relatively repetitive tasks into nearly equal workloads so that if a new employee came on board, it was only a short time before there were very few questions. Over the years the turnover in the department was one per year, but last year there were two and already this year one had left the office. Glenda was very proud that it took very little time to orient a new person to the job. She had noticed recently that the applicants did not seem to be as well-prepared or committed to the school district.

On the way home after the new business manager had outlined the evaluations she planned, Ms. Eishayd could not get her phrase, "good people" out of her own mind. She began to wonder if she fit into that category, and if not, where did she fit?

Glenda's situation and her reactions to it are not unique, or even rare. Most people equate their individual worth with their jobs. When the rules change or are interpreted differently by a new person, time and thoughtful communications may help each employee to focus on opportunities for growth and his contribution to the organization.

The above does not imply that regardless of poor performance an individual's feelings should outweigh a decision for dismissal or to change work assignments. Focusing on task performance as opposed to the worth of an individual does not mean mediocrity should be tolerated. The focus simply should be articulated so that the evaluator and those persons whose work is being evaluated view the process from the same perspective. Notice the semantic difference between the phrases "the persons being evaluated" and "the results of the person's work being evaluated." To evaluate a person as a human being is different from evaluating his work and the results of that work.

Appraisal of programs or functions has the same emphasis: the results of the program are evaluated, not the human worth of the persons associated with the program. Most evaluators would agree with this statement, but there is a need to convey the concept to those persons associated with the function being evaluated. Overlooking this aspect of appraisal can cause a morale problem, with workers covering up their deficiencies, and lead to reduced productivity because employees view the appraisal as an assessment of themselves rather than of the function or program. On the instructional side, too, teachers often view the appraisal of a student teacher's performance or evaluation of the student teaching program as a threat to their own value. As a result they write inflated evaluations or avoid negative aspects. It is the same with maintenance personnel, bus drivers, and the accounting office. All must develop the perspective that the purpose of evaluating is to improve the program and not to judge the worth of individuals. The follow-up on an evaluation should result in decisions made to move to the next higher level of perform- ance. In the case study presented, it was not apparent to Glenda that program improvement was the intent. To her it was a process to determine if she were a good person.

A Beginning Point of Evaluation

At the outset, the evaluator should realize there is no such thing as a purely objective evaluation. The term itself emphasizes "value" or "valuing" which results from subjective judgment. One can try to make the evaluation of an investment program objective by limiting it to criteria such as "the return on money invested shall be at 5% or higher" and "the investment program caused no cash flow problems." It is clear that subjective judgment entered into setting the return of investment percentage and defining "cash flow problem." The same situation exists in evaluating the performance of a task. The setting of performance standards is a valuing activity and may be even a political activity. One may reflect on the performance of a coach or a physician to understand the complexity and subjectivity of the evaluation process. An act completely unrelated to wins and losses may result in a coach's removal. The physician's diagnostic and surgical skills may be superb, but the client's evaluation may be based on the physician's communication skills.

The Purposes of Evaluation

Ordinarily, evaluation of task performance or program effectiveness is thought to be limited to (1) improving the performance or (2) determining the continuation of the person in the role under evaluation, or continuation of the program. The words used to describe evaluative processes associated with the purposes are "formative" (improvement) and "summative" (decisions to continue). To try to separate formative evaluation from sum- mative evaluation may result in neither process being effective, or at best confusion regarding how they are related. If one makes the assumption that all evaluation is intended

Purposes of performance → Gathering data/ information pertinent to performance → Applying value judgment by establishing criteria → Decisions regarding continuation or steps toward improvement

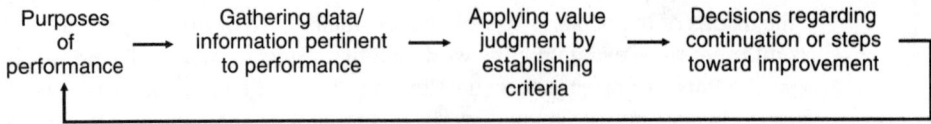

FIGURE 3-1   A Generic Evaluation Model.

to improve the situation, then if no improvement occurs is the evaluation faulty? Or if no improvement occurs, does the evaluation become summative? The lines are not drawn clearly. It may be best to regard evaluation as a process of gathering data and information about task or program performance so that a judgment may be made regarding the effectiveness of the performance. After the judgment has been made, decisions need to focus on what might be done to improve performance or whether to hire or retain an individual or to continue the program. Figure 3-1 depicts a typical evaluation model. The model may be applied to task or program performance and may involve a number of techniques involving the persons whose performances are being evaluated. The management by objectives process, clinical supervision, or a simple solo act on the part of the evaluator may be employed. The last choice may be the best choice in the long run.

Clarifying Purposes

Every job and every function or program has a purpose. The purposes are generally stated in the job description or in documents approving programs. The school board's minutes may be a source of program or function purposes for such functions as cash flow and investments, personnel, food services, and so on. Both job descriptions and program purposes should be reviewed on a planned schedule so they can be updated. The job description written on paper yellowed with age is highly suspect. The same is true of a function which has a purpose that only would fit well in the nineteenth century, or a function whose connection with the unit's mission or the school's mission is difficult to determine.

There are at least two perspectives from which to review statements of purpose: (1) Do the stated purposes provide enough specificity to seek evidence about performance and (2) Have stated purposes been overlooked which are implied, however, in the evolved tasks of the job or program being evaluated. Another view of the latter perspective is to determine whether the tasks are incumbent-specific and should be there at all. The reader can probably cite many instances in which a person has incorporated a number of tasks into the job which were not in the job description. Should the evaluation be limited to just those things written in the job description, or seek to identify and describe the other tasks being performed as well.

As noted in other chapters in the text, evaluation of good purposes is sometimes avoided because no one wishes to take the responsibility or cannot imagine a way to determine their effectiveness, for example, the educational dimension of a food services program. Documenting such purposes is avoided occasionally because the evaluator does not perceive a way to quantify data so that the evaluation remains as objective as possible.

Holistic evaluation is gaining another look from the evaluation profession as a legitimate way to arrive at judgments about performance. One cannot imagine judging a work by Michelangelo only by measuring the percentage of this color or that color, or weighing the amount of paint he used per square inch compared with that used by Claude Monet. Even if one were to do so, it is clear to the reader that the effect of Michelangelo's works would be lost. Holistic or global evaluation may also avoid the problem of looking at only one or a few parts of the performance, although a one-step global evaluation in some instances may yield good results. Scriven noted the following:

> *The analytical approach naturally takes several times as long as the holistic one, and costs in proportion. Of course, it looks more scientific; but research suggests the holistic ratings may be more accurate. Hence, the common presupposition that analytical evaluations are preferable must be treated very cautiously. They are certainly more expensive and slower to get, and at least sometimes less accurate.*[1]

Neither evaluating separate components nor using a holistic approach should be used exclusively. Whether using analytical or global evaluation, purposes must be clear and inclusive.

Gathering Data

Data are valueless, but the selection of such data is not. An evaluator can skew the results simply by excluding some data; limiting or extending the time period the data represents; selecting a known-to-be-biased outside evaluator; using little or no comparative data from the past or similar current jobs or programs, and many other ways. Decisions regarding the data to be gathered or judged are very important. To evaluate a grounds maintenance program on weed control and dollars spent on equipment use/maintenance in an exceptionally hot, dry year could lead to poor decisions about the program. Gathering data separate from a larger context can be misleading.

One set of data or data from only one source can provide the evaluator with a false impression. The number of pupil bus riders may not give an accurate picture of the job a bus driver is doing. Nor will just the records regarding their on-time performance along with average fuel consumed per mile. When put into a larger context of number and level of students being transported, terrain, length of route, and fuel consumption the data become more meaningful.

The timing of data gathering should also be considered. In the bus driver performance evaluation above, would there be differences in students' reactions on the second week of school as contrasted with the last week? Would a clearer picture of performance emerge if performance evaluations were made quarterly?

In all evaluations, cost should be considered. Not only are there costs in the time it takes to conduct the recording of data, but costs in developing the instruments, producing them, and organizing and analyzing the results. The school business manager must determine if the expenditure is achieving the results needed: the generating of evaluable data useful for decision making.

The Rating Form

A common means of evaluating job performance is using a rating form. The rating form does not make the evaluation objective nor even approach that goal unless a great deal of preparatory work is done on the part of evaluators and those whose work is being evaluated. As an example, the performance levels on the form shown in Figure 3-2 range from "Satisfactory" to "Unsatisfactory." The best rating a person's performance can receive is "Satisfactory." There should be some understanding that satisfactory regular attendance means not absent more than a specified number of times within a certain time period. Note that there is no recognition for the person who never misses work unless "Satisfactory" means zero absences and any absence would result in "Needs Improvement." Care must be taken to avoid misunderstandings about the terms used.

Another potential problem is the tendency for the evaluator to give top ratings. A term used in a military branch was "firewalling"; that is, the pressure on the evaluator to not hurt the chances of an officer to be promoted resulted in top ratings unless there was a serious deficiency. We all hope that practice is not the case when we get on an aircraft. Yet, the practice is widespread. We have reviewed many employee rating forms on which there were negligible differences in the ratings, with nearly every employee getting top ratings. In fact, it often was so indiscriminate that an area marked "Good" instead of "Outstanding" was cause for concern. Less than honest ratings over time cause a great deal of difficulty when a serious problem occurs and dismissal proceedings are considered.

Common definitions shared among evaluators are important. When more than one person is evaluating performances or programs, differences result when the raters have different meanings for the terms used.

A problem inherent in many rating forms is that seldom are the relative values of the terms or descriptors considered. For example, in Figure 3-2 is performance in the area of "Punctuality" of equal value with "Quality of Work?" In Figure 3-3 on page 46, are the areas of "Time on Task" and "Ability to Work With the Public" equivalent in importance? If not, how are the results to be treated. Obviously, the evaluator does not wish to create a total score or an average unless weightings for the areas are established and understood.

Recording an MBO Process

Figure 3-3 shows an example of a two-part form used to record a management-by-objectives (MBO) process. The Spring Evaluation rating form raises a question that most forms do: "What is the standard?" Who was involved in setting the standard? The process implied by the two-part form in Figure 3-3 involves the employee at the outset. A process that goes beyond stating words, such as, "exemplary quality of work," will be helpful to all. The employee will be able to make specific adjustments as needed. The supervisor will have sharper perceptions of quality performance. The schools should profit by having a job performed better.

CLASSIFIED STAFF EVALUATION

NAME _____   DATE _____

ASSIGNMENT _____   BUILDING
ASSIGNMENT _____

I. WORK HABITS	SATISFACTORY	NEEDS IMPROVEMENT	UNSATISFACTORY
Regular Attendance	_____	_____	_____
Punctuality	_____	_____	_____
Responsibility	_____	_____	_____
Ability To Complete Assigned Tasks	_____	_____	_____
Ability To Follow Directions	_____	_____	_____
Adherence To Job Description	_____	_____	_____
Quality of Work	_____	_____	_____
Initiative	_____	_____	_____
Concern/Care For School Property	_____	_____	_____

II. ABILITY TO WORK WITH OTHERS

Students	_____	_____	_____
Co-Workers	_____	_____	_____
Public	_____	_____	_____
Teachers	_____	_____	_____
Administrators	_____	_____	_____

III. PERSONAL QUALITIES

Appearance	_____	_____	_____
Receptive To Suggestions	_____	_____	_____
Receptive To Constructive Criticism	_____	_____	_____
Positive Attitude Toward Work Situation	_____	_____	_____
Appropriate Attire For Assignment	_____	_____	_____

COMMENTS: _____

_____

_____

_____

_____   _____
Signature of Employee   Administrator's Signature
(Does not necessarily indicate agreement)

FIGURE 3-2   An Example of a Rating Form.

NAME _____

SCHOOL _____

POSITION _____

CLASSIFIED PERSONNEL PERFORMANCE APPRAISAL

INSTRUCTIONS

FALL EVALUATION (October 15)

1. Employee establishes specific objectives for the year.
2. Supervisor discusses objectives, documents positive performance, and specifically outlines any areas needing improvement.
3. If step advancement is in jeopardy, it will be necessary to conduct another evaluation by December 15. If deficiency is not resolved by that time, employee may be placed on probation or considered for termination.
4. Evaluation is signed by employee and supervisor.
5. Employee receives one copy, one copy is sent to Director of Classified Personnel, and original is retained at building to be used for Spring Evaluation.

SPRING EVALUATION (April 30)

1. Supervisor completes checklist regarding employee's performance for the year.
2. Supervisor and employee discuss and document:
   a. Success in meeting objectives established in the Fall.
   b. Positive performance and any areas needing improvement.
   *Additional comments can be attached to this form.
3. If step advancement is in jeopardy, it will be necessary to conduct another evaluation by May 30.
4. Evaluation is signed by both parties. One copy is given to the employee and original is sent to the Director of Classified Personnel for review and placement in employee's file.

FALL EVALUATION: October 15

OBJECTIVES FOR SCHOOL YEAR

_____

_____

_____

_____

POSITIVE COMMENTS/AREAS NEEDING IMPROVEMENT

_____

_____

_____

_____

Is employee's overall performance satisfactory?

Yes _____   No _____

Is step advancement in jeopardy?

Yes _____   No _____

Employee _____   Date _____

Evaluator _____   Date _____

FIGURE 3-3   Example of a Two-Part Management-by-Objectives Evaluation Form.

SPRING EVALUATION: April 30

	Exemplary Performance	Meets Standard	Needs Improvement	Unacceptable
Quantity of Work				
Quality of Work				
Ability to Organize and/or Prioritize				
Cooperation				
Initiative				
Judgment and Common Sense				
Attendance and Punctuality				
Time on Task				
Confidentiality				

EVALUATION OF SUCCESS IN MEETING OBJECTIVES

_____
_____
_____

POSITIVE COMMENTS/AREAS NEEDING IMPROVEMENT

_____
_____
_____
_____

Is employee's overall performance satisfactory?

    Yes _____   No _____

Is step advancement in jeopardy?

    Yes _____   No _____

Employee _____ Date_____

Evaluator _____ Date _____

FIGURE 3-3 *Continued*

The next step in an MBO process is assessing whether or not the objectives have been met. The supervisor can do this alone, or both the supervisor and the employee can make assessments of the job performance independently. Shortly thereafter, the assessments may be exchanged and a conference is scheduled to discuss the results. If there are discrepancies between the assessments, the conference will clarify the "standards" and point toward the next cycle.

The evaluator is faced with another decision in the MBO process. How shall he or she value improvement in a job area by one employee over his previous performance even though a second employee's performance in the same area is consistently better? Both need recognition provided for a job well done. If Joan has an excellent record of attendance, punctuality, and time spent on the task, but George has quite a bit less than excellence in all those areas, it may be easy to make a differentiation at the conference or even in some more tangible way. If, however, George makes tremendous strides and matches Joan's record in the next evaluation period, how shall his turnaround in performance be recognized as opposed to Joan who is consistently excellent? How can the evaluator recognize George without alienating Joan? Obviously some tools must be available to the evaluator to recognize both employees. In areas in which promotion possibilities are remote and/or the union contract disallows pay differentials, other rewards such as more involvement in decisions, greater flexibility in time, and public recognition may serve well for the consistently high performer.

The Staff Development Linkage

If the evaluation process is individualized enough to identify specific and sometimes unique areas needing improvement, then it points directly to individualized staff development needs. There should be a direct linkage between the evaluation process and staff development. General staff development sessions are needed for many situations, for example new transportation regulations or changes in software/hardware, but they are only part of an effective program. It would be unusual on the completion of a set of evaluations to find that all of the business staff needed improvement in business arithmetic or that all custodians needed to learn floor stripping techniques. To maximize the benefits of an evaluation program, individualized staff development as part of an overall staff development program may yield positive outcomes that benefit the school.

Analyzing Data

Data should be viewed in relation to a larger context. A program is not successful when it produces good short-term gains but perpetuates or creates long-term problems. The menus of a food service program might be changed to use less expensive foods or preparation shortcuts resulting in the elimination of a deficit or even gleaning a small profit. If over time the participation falls off, then the program faces the same problems. Looking at the "bottom line" for the short-term gain would result in a false evaluation.

There is another question to be raised: How important is the profit line relative to participation, or relative to nutritional concerns?

No one can collect all the data needed to evaluate a program or job performance completely. It is important to establish essential outcomes, those which are most important to a successful program or job performance. Limiting the analysis of data to a single outcome (e.g., safety record of transportation; losses of supplies; number of staff development meetings held) and basing decisions on the relative effectiveness of that outcome is questionable and may be irresponsible.

Results of data analyses may be used in many ways. They may be compared to a previously set "standard"; compared to results from similar programs in similar districts; compared to historical data from the same program or job performance; compared to opinions of experts regarding appropriate outcomes; or used in all of these ways. Again, using a single comparison may not yield the complete picture needed to make good judgments.

It is important to analyze data having a set of criteria that were established at the outset. It is also important to look for the unexpected. Some positive or negative results may emerge that were not part of the original evaluation criteria. The evaluator should always be ready to look at the data from a different perspective, or to pursue the question about why something occurred. Limiting one's decisions to just the established criteria may result in decisions that ignore important considerations.

Valuing

The real evaluation decision takes place when the evaluator (whether singly, several, or as a group) decides if the results are desirable or not desirable. Valuing has taken place at the very beginning of the process when decisions were made regarding criteria, standards, data to be collected and type of analyses to be used. Valuing again occurs when the data are gathered and analyzed. An important, though sometimes overlooked, facet of evaluation is the underlying set of beliefs and values held by the evaluator. Recognition of these values are important so that one approaches the situation from a realistic point of view. For instance, does the evaluator really believe that persons who are qualified (by license, training, experience) and have been on the job for a long period of time do not need to be evaluated except to document that the jobs are still being done in a satisfactory manner? Would such a belief lead to rather perfunctory evaluations even though the same format and cycle were being used for new employees? Would such a belief help the experienced employee to grow on the job, to assume ownership in achieving excellence? Would the evaluator grow as the process and criteria were refined? While no one knows what has shaped our views of reality, each of us might profit by examining what influences our views and the effects those views have on a valuing program or job performance outcomes. If one has the view that each program or job is part of a very complex set of relationships designed to enhance the achievement of students, our valuing will be different from someone else who views business jobs and programs as discrete and separate from the "learning enterprise."

Starting Points

The superintendent or school business official has several sources available to begin evaluating various aspects of the school business management program. Many state affiliates of the Association of School Business Officials (ASBO) have manuals which provide starting points. Often these contain state and federal mandates and guidelines as well as "yes/no" checklists for various functions, such as transportation, maintenance, etc. The checklists serve merely as starting points, since they merely document the presence or absence of a particular facet. An example of such a checklist for the transportation function is provided in Figure 3-4.

Decisions must be made about each of the items under no. 4 in Figure 3-3 since the form merely asks for a "yes" or "no." The fact that the district has documentation of the frequency with which trips are completed on schedule tells little about the merit of job

	YES	NO	NI*	NA**
1. Is the school identifying problems in transportation and seeking their solutions?	( )	( )	( )	( )
2. Are the State policies being followed?	( )	( )	( )	( )
3. Are the local policies being followed?	( )	( )	( )	( )
4. Does the corporation have documentation of the following?	( )	( )	( )	( )
(a) Injuries to passengers, the driver, and others	( )	( )	( )	( )
(b) Property damage accidents involving buses	( )	( )	( )	( )
(c) Moving traffic violations of drivers	( )	( )	( )	( )
(d) The frequency with which trips are completed on schedule	( )	( )	( )	( )
(e) The nature and frequency of road failures	( )	( )	( )	( )
(f) The frequency and nature of complaints received from drivers concerning bus operations	( )	( )	( )	( )
(g) The number of vehicles used when viewed against the geographical size and number of students transported	( )	( )	( )	( )
(h) The amount of nonpassenger miles	( )	( )	( )	( )
(i) Number of stops	( )	( )	( )	( )
(j) The amount of time students spend on the bus	( )	( )	( )	( )
(k) The number of vehicles used when viewed against the geographical size and pupil population density	( )	( )	( )	( )

FIGURE 3-4   An Example of a General Evaluation of Transportation Service.

*NI = No Information
**NA = Not Applicable

performance and provides no clue of the cause if the frequency of completed-on-schedule trips is too low.

Herman suggested that an evaluation cycle be established prior to the beginning of the new fiscal year.[2] Whether the cycle begins in July or at the beginning of the school year, it would include an orientation conference, quarterly formative evaluations, and a summative evaluation to determine job status and, in some instances, salary. Since the data/information generated for the formative evaluations are used also for the summative evaluation, distinctions are not always clear.

Action Planning

Each evaluation should result in decisions. Decisions imply action, which in turn requires planning. Evaluation is not a stand-alone function but rather a part of the continuing planning process, which is described in Chapter 4. Once the forms have been filled out and filed, the real job is just beginning. What will be done in regard to what has been found? The cycle repeats itself, as illustrated in Figure 3-1.

Summary

Evaluation is at best imperfect, and at worst it can be destructive. It is necessary to keep the organization and the people in the organization focused on doing the job well and continuously improving. The following principles may be helpful as the manager refines the evaluations of school business functions.

1. *The data to be generated and the analyses of the data should be planned at the outset of the program or if an ongoing program is being evaluated such as (food services, transportation), lead time should be sufficient so that an overall view of the program can be formed.*

2. *The persons involved in the activity should participate in planning the evaluation.* There will be instances in which full or representational participation cannot occur, however, the process can be strengthened by a cooperatively developed design. Participation can become a springboard to meaningful in-service education and training.

3. *Multiple sources of data and data generated over time provides a more defensible base for decision making than single-source, one-shot data.*

4. *All evaluations should be done taking the context into consideration.* External influences always play a part in task or program performance. An ugly divorce situation can affect a person's job performance whether it be that of the school business manager or a bus driver. A war in the Middle East or a coup attempt in a superpower can depress markets and may cause serious changes in what had been a well-planned investment program. To evaluate without considering the context in which the performance takes place is to make decisions on incomplete data.

5. *Feedback regarding performance should be as carefully planned as any other part of the evaluation.* Whenever possible, the evaluation process should be developed cooperatively. One part that often remains unplanned is the feedback phase to individual workers or those associated with an evaluated program. Terms should be mutually understood. Rating intervals, if used, should be clear, as well as computations used to arrive at totals, weighted scores, and other quantitative data.

6. *Evaluations should result in planned actions to improve personal or program performance.*

7. *There is no best way to evaluate.* The reader is justified in asking why then all the words and energy spent on writing or reading this chapter. The answer: Because there are some very bad ways to evaluate, and we are learning more each day about evaluation. A few years ago quantitative data and inferential statistics constituted the "best" way, while currently qualitative analyses are gaining in acceptance. The reader is encouraged to remain current regarding developments in the field and not to become locked into the "we've always done it that way" mind-set.

For Further Thought

1. What relationships should exist between the evaluation program and the staff development program?

2. How can internally evaluated programs avoid the problem of being "doomed to succeed?"

3. Is building self-esteem and ownership compatible with high performance expectations? Explain.

4. How would you determine if an evaluation process is too costly?

5. Who should provide data input for the evaluation of the

   School business official
   Bus driver
   Insurance manager

6. Should self-evaluation be part of a job performance evaluation? Explain.

7. How can the practice of giving only top ratings in job performance areas be avoided?

Endnotes

1. Michael Scriven, "Beyond Formative and Summative Evaluation," in Milbrey W. McLaughlin, and D. C. Phillips (eds.) *Evaluation and Education: At Quarter Century* (Chicago: The National Society for the Study of Education, 1991), p. 30.

2. Jerry J. Herman, "Evaluating the Performance of School Business Officials," *School Business Affairs* (February 1990): 11–14.

Chapter *4*

Planning

The School Organizational Setting: A Review

If the leaders of a school district are going to plan successfully, they must be able to see the district within a larger context and how it will deal with changes in that context. Schools do not exist in splendid isolation regardless of how much some persons within the schools would like to have them be autonomous entities separate from the "evils" of politics and economic realities. Schools are affected by almost every major change in their environments and by many smaller changes. As examples, one need look no further than population shifts, economic upturns or recession, or party changes in the governor's office and in control of the state legislature. Too often, school personnel may see these changes as something to survive, another storm to get through so that when the waters calm the schools can continue to sail along on the same course in the same way. A critical question to ask is whether the change is one which provides an opportunity for growth or a situation which requires internal changes to be made in order to maintain or improve the school's position in the larger context.

Given the fact that change is the only constant that one can be sure of, the school's leadership needs to anticipate changes and predict their outcomes on the school's role, procedure, and technology. The following is a partial list of potential influences on schools:

Governmental	Legislation, regulations, reporting requirements
	Political issues, e.g., funding, accountability, certification
	School board elections/appointments
	Power shifts from one party to another which may influence the labor environment, funding sources, special programs, social priorities
Demographics	Population shifts, in/out migration, ethnic and racial changes
	Land utilization
	Birth rates

Economic	Health of local, state, national, and global economics
	Consumer preferences and trends
	Weather downturns in agricultural and/or tourist-dependent regions
	Energy-related costs, availability of alternative energy sources
	Shifting sources of revenue from/to local or state sources
Technological	Job requirements, changing communication needs and patterns
	Effects of health care breakthroughs
	Home-school linkages via technology
	Developing breakthroughs in technology and means to access information
	Pressures to acquire new technology for instruction
	Changes in work environment
	Available personnel services
National/World	Increased interdependence
	National interdependence
	National agendas
	War/peace and societal value fallouts
	Ecological trends
Sociocultural	Values regarding family, responsibility, acceptable "losses" of youth, elderly, and social deviants
	Meanings attached to events
	Cultural aberrations engendered by the media becoming accepted values

The school is part of a larger, complex societal picture. School leaders can choose to comply with laws and regulations, file accurate reports on time, and get the most return on the resources available. This is obviously a reactive posture and one which works in relatively stable environments. Such environments are becoming more rare and therefore the school leader must assess continuously the meanings of changes or trends relative to the school's mission and its organizational success.

Realistically, we all live in ever-changing environments in all the areas noted above, plus many others. The school leader's task is the awesome one of predicting future events and their implications for the schools and planning appropriate changes to deal with that future, not just for survival, but for successfully meeting goals. Schools exist to make learning possible. Not only are there new concepts, facts, and skills to be learned, the learners (students) and teachers themselves are changing continuously.

We have just discussed external influences on the school organization. Internal influences shape the future of the organization as well; therefore, planning cannot ignore the internal influences pressuring the organization to react in particular ways. Again, the partial list presented below may stimulate school planners to consider the scope of the internal influences playing a part in the life of the organization.

Personnel	Ages by service/instructional area
	Levels of expertise, licensure, density of expertise
	Turnover factors by area
	Potential for reallocation of human services
Organizational culture	Values, traditions (reviewed in chapter 2)
Perceptions of school's mission	Teachers, parents, students, administrators, staff
Physical plant	Utilization
	Useful life left, change potentials
Interaction with community	School board relationships
	Utilization of agency expertise
	Utilization of human resources
	Extremist views
Available technological resources	Useful life, utilization, upgrading potential
Available equipment/materials resources	Useful life, applicability to future programs

Local influences added to the above list will yield a planning process tailored to the specific organization. For example, the suburban school district in a wealthy tax base area experiencing rapid enrollment growth will have a different set of personnel considerations from those of the older center-city school district experiencing enrollment decline and an eroding tax base. Even a partial list of internal influences underlines the complexity of designing and participating in an effective planning process. Although it is not the intent of this chapter to teach expertise in planning functions, an overview of the definition and types of planning as well as the steps involved in effective planning may help the reader to see the role of the school business manager in the planning process.

Role of the School Business Manager

The school business manager is important to the planning process not only because he or she can supply abundant data and information to others in leadership/planning groups, but because of his or her potential to influence the outcomes of the planning process. The school business manager faces the dilemma of influencing the planning process on two levels: meeting the business office definitions of excellent practice and carrying out the role of an educational statesman on the district planning level. The potential for conflict between these two positions is high. Totally centralized processes with centrally dictated forms and time frames usually mean better control and efficiency in a school business office. Reduced time ordinarily means reduced costs. Yet there are pressures to go toward decentralization and then more people become involved, more complex and time-consuming reports are needed, and turnaround times may be lengthened. What position should school business managers take?

The manager could take the position that after all, he or she is there to handle business functions and educational functions are best left to the superintendent. If the business manager's proposals are overridden, then so be it. It is the authors' contention that such a position falls short of carrying out the role of the fully functioning school business manager. He or she must assume the educational dimension of the role, particularly in the critical task of planning. The manager must go beyond the roles of provider of data and advocate for the business areas. He or she must make accommodations and proposals that relate to the main purpose of the schools—student learning.

What Is Planning?

Planning has been described as a means to reduce uncertainty; as a process of anticipating unwritten history; and as a way of converting pressures and problems into opportunities and new goals. Frank Eikenberry provided the following list of "shoulds" and "should-nots" for the school planner's consideration[1]:

Planning Is (or Should Be):

A way of thinking, an attitude
An effective direction-setting tool
An ongoing process
A framework for examining alternatives and making decisions
A way of identifying problems
Hard work over long periods
An endeavor in statesmanship; facilitates consensus
Concerned with the whole
Almost totally occupied with the "futurity of present decisions"
Participative; bottom up and top down
A special type of communication activity
A basic management task
A way to organize and formalize old practices
A thinking and doing activity, in that order
Only as good as the planners

Planning Is Not (or Should Not Be):

A projection or forecast
An on-and-off process
A substitute for good judgment
A problem solver
A quick-fix gimmick
A political process

Immune to risk and uncertainty
New at every session
A way to deal with future decisions

Muther included the following as one definition of planning:

To condition one's mind with future opportunities, obstacles, possibilities and alternative courses of procedure so the mind will be open and quicker to respond to new circumstances or more creative solutions in subsequent, more-definitive planning.[2]

Planning then is not a one-time exercise or even a process that evolves into a tradition practiced year after year. It cannot avoid the trauma of extreme changes that the schools are experiencing, but it may assist in coping with changes. One positive outcome may be the sensitizing of the administrators and staff to the larger, somewhat interdependent communities influencing the schools and thereby enhancing the adaptability of the school district to its environment.

The results of planning, that is, the action plan implemented, cannot be set in stone to run for the chosen planning period of one, five, or ten years. The process is ongoing. An often overlooked aspect of planning is building adaptability and responsiveness into the plan. Without such provision most plans run into trouble as the sands shift to change the terrain.

The school planner is left with the task of defining what the planning process will yield for the school. Will it primarily focus on internal awareness and incremental program adjustments? Will it primarily yield a document for external consumption (really a public relations device)? Will it address issues that may lead to fundamental change? Since the school business office is at the center of much information gathering that is pertinent to the planning process, the school business manager should be a key player in formulating the planning policy as well as participating in the complete and ongoing process of school planning.

Pre-Planning Decisions

Planning itself needs to be planned. School organizational leaders must determine which person performs which function when and for what period of time. Immediately school planners face the question of what is meant by long-range or short-range planning: One year? Five years? Ten years?

Another set of questions centers around who, or what units, shall be the initiators of ideas. Shall the ideas bubble up from the staff or come from the top? If they come from the top, will the results include apathy on the part of those lower in the administrative hierarchy? If the initiators are the departments or schools or teacher groups, will the unit plans fit with the school district's goals and mission? Will the planning process become a political battle for budget?

It is clear that a school district board or administration cannot jump into the planning process without carefully thinking out and answering these questions and many others. The structure of the planning process must be resolved first.

Where Should Planning Start?

There seem to be as many planning "models" as there are organizations planning or consultants helping them plan. Many of the models follow the *rational approach* to planning. Its other names include the *formal-rational* or *rational-technical approach*. The organization of the planning process in the rational approach and many of its assumptions parallel those of the classic concept of a bureaucracy. In particular, the rational planning approach assumes that individuals behave rationally relative to accomplishing the organization's goals. Another assumption is that the officeholders in the hierarchy are those with the expertise to carry out the planning. The beginning point in this model is clarifying and articulating the mission and goals of the organization and the process flows from that point. Richard Muther noted that "the logical sequence of getting things done is: goals, plans, actions and results."[3] He saw planning in four phases: (1) *orientation* (seeing the problem/project in its surroundings); (2) *overall* (the long-term solution); (3) *detail* (short-term plans); and (4) *do/act* (the plan implemented). Figure 4-1 delineates a rational planning model gleaned from reviewing school district models and higher education models. On the surface the components appear to be clear, logical, and not impossible to implement. In fact, the apparent simplicity may be one of the weaknesses of the rational model, since too often the results of the planning process become the written plan itself and not the desired program changes. The written plan may serve as a political document and not be implemented beyond that. In other words, the planning process remains static. When this occurs, the planning process may be rational, but is not implemented and thereby is an ineffective process. The planning process needs to go beyond making political statements and providing a forum for posturing, with results seen in real work, real changes, and real assessment.

Understanding external/internal environments
and probable changes
↓
Mission of the schools
as related to the environments
↓
Programs/Specific objectives
↓
Translation into budget
↓
Evaluation

**FIGURE 4-1   Model of the Rational
Planning Process.**

Cautions and disadvantages of the rational approach to planning include the following:

1. The school's processes, governance, and mechanisms may not be as rational as the model presumes.
2. Fiscal and human resources required are usually high.
3. Programs may not have the same time periods as the planning cycles and therefore become lost to the planning process.
4. There is a tendency to develop a planning staff isolated from the school's real worlds.
5. Tends to foster incremental changes as opposed to basic changes.
6. May not be able to be responsive to opportunities or instant pressures.

The above list is not intended to discourage rational planning, but to raise awareness of potentially shaky assumptions that could lead the school district into misplaced faith, especially in one-shot applications of the rational model. That is, a single effort at developing a five or ten year plan and assuming it will be useful for that period of time without change can lead to disastrous results.

Who Should Be Involved?

One city school district organized a planning structure as depicted in Figure 4-2 on page 60. The purpose of the planning process is stated as providing a means to identify educational and related concerns and to translate the concerns into recommendations to be used in establishing the school district's priorities for a three-year period. The limitations of time frame and responsibilities are clearly stated. The process was perceived to have yielded a good base of data in a variety of areas noted by the subcommittee titles; it generated community confidence in the schools, and led to certain decisions, particularly those dealing with facility utilization. The "interlocking directorate" of central office personnel assured that communications were not lost to them as they developed the district's priorities for the next three years. Community leaders and citizen's representatives were informed of the school district's situation and proposals. Information sessions were held throughout the community to provide the opportunity to reach all citizens.

Figure 4-3 on page 61 demonstrates an intended idea-exchange format using the rational planning model. This format may be adaptable to school districts that have a relatively mature site-based management program. The statement of the mission came to the planning team from the school board by way of its chief administrative officer. The institution was divided into planning units and each planning unit was further divided into subunits. Subunit ideas and requests were to go through their respective units to the planning table. An interesting feature of the structure was the ad hoc, or wild card, group which if recognized by the Planning Council could constitute a stand-alone unit with the authority to submit a plan to the council. Several plans from ad hoc groups were recognized.

Units could vary in the way they planned with their subunits. In units in which planning was conducted in an open, democratic manner, unit and subunit teams appeared

```
                          ┌─────────────────────┐
                          │  Board of Education  │
                          └──────────┬──────────┘
                                     │
                          ┌─────────────────────┐
                          │   Superintendent     │
                          └──────────┬──────────┘
                                     │
┌──────────────────────────────┐    │
│ Advisory Committee            │    │
│ Board Members (3)             │    │    ┌──────────────────────────────┐
│ Superintendent                │    │    │ Planning Committee           │
│ Associate Superintendent      │    │    │ Superintendent               │
│ Assistant to Superintendent   ├────┼────┤ Associate Superintendent     │
│ High School, Junior           │    │    │ Assistant to Superintendent  │
│ High School, Elementary       │    │    │ Central Office Division Heads│
│ Principals (3)                │    │    └──────────────────────────────┘
│ Teachers (3)                  │    │
│ Citizens Advisory Council (7) │    │
└──────────────────────────────┘    │
```

Operational Subcommittees					
Pupil Population	Educational Programs	Supporting Programs	Personnel	Facilities and Equipment	Finances

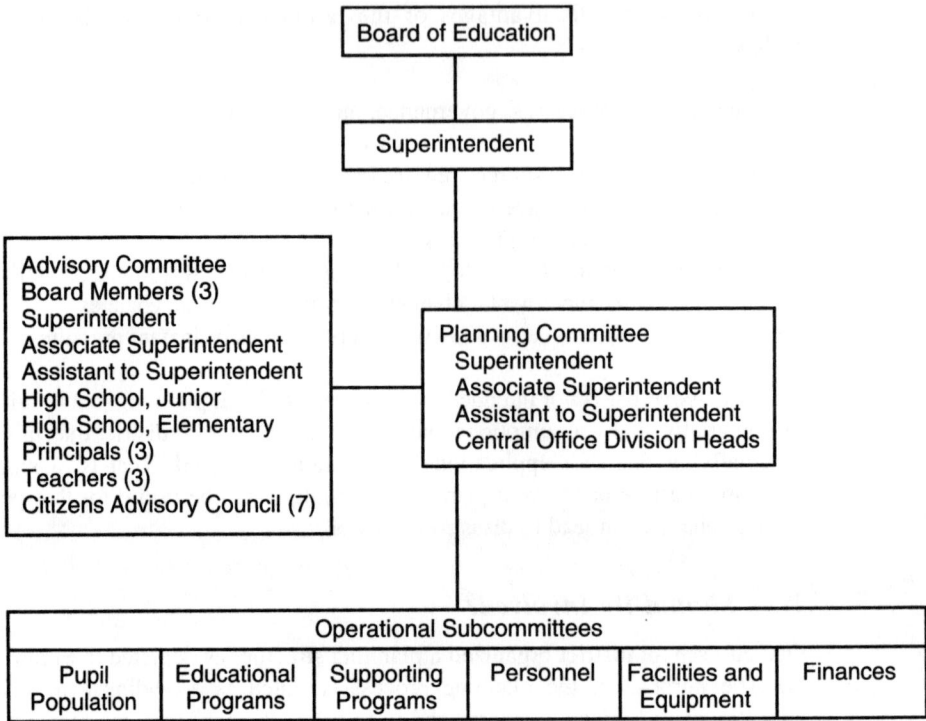

FIGURE 4-2   Structure of the Planning Task Force in a Three-Year School District Plan.

to be committed to the process. In other units in which the unit head behaved like royalty listening to the pleas of the serfs, interest dropped off quickly.

The purpose of the planning process is stated as being a guide to the development of the internal operating budget. A zero-sum concept was introduced and articulated as "If you want to add something, tell us what you are going to drop." Before long, the planning process was perceived to be political and many comments were heard like, "I've never received anything out of this, so why participate?" The end result was to limit in deed, if not in word, the number of persons actually involved in the planning effort. In a short time it was perceived to be a top-down process with the units serving as a supporting cast. Initiative was perceived as being by invitation only.

The two structures discussed (see Figures 4-2 and 4-3) are workable and the intentions appeared clear, yet the first went according to expectations and the other developed negative side-effects causing changes in procedures. Planning the plan requires clear, honest thinking and communication. Initiating such a process nearly always raises expectations on the part of subgroups. The scope, the way decisions will be made, and the limitations placed on the planning process (e.g., budget, legal requirements) need to be articulated early in the process to all the participants.

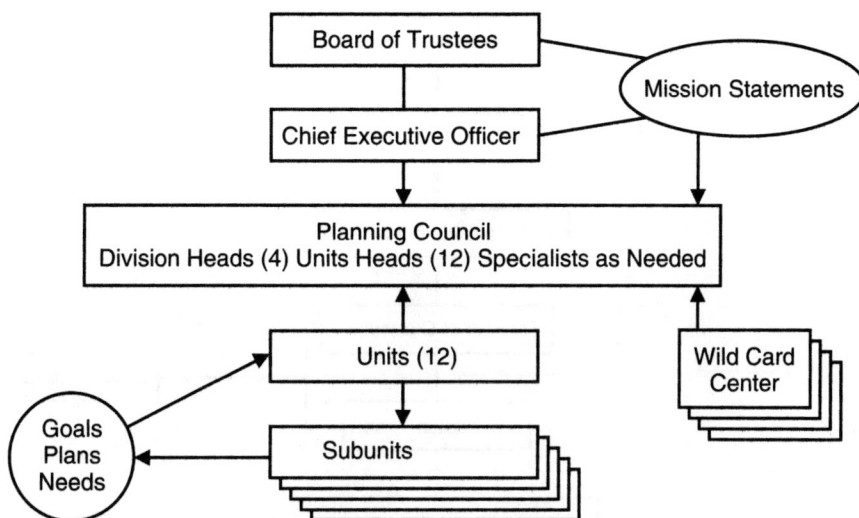

FIGURE 4-3   A Planning Structure Showing Interactive Flow of Ideas.

Scope of the Plan

A plan can attempt to include every phase of the school or institution, or it may be limited to a single emphasis, e.g., mathematics K-12, or elementary school music. Often the planning process is limited to curriculum. Figure 4-4 illustrates the planning structure for a small school district that limited its planning to curriculum. The broad-based committee consisted of representatives from each building, administration, parents, school board, the community at large, and students. The facilitation team consisted of seven people representing building administrators, parents, school board, and teachers. The purpose of this group is to cross-link state/national organizations, networks, and information bases to the broad-based committee.

Some institutions have set the scope of the planning process to include everything but athletics. Others have found subgroups reporting to the central administration to be useful. The latter does tend to result in somewhat incremental budget building rather than addressing larger issues facing the school.

Another question that must be answered is the time frame which is to be used. Does the resulting plan cover one, three, or five years? If it is a five-year plan, are there checkpoints along the way for adjusting the plan other than annual budgets? Is adaptation built into it? Adaptation is a necessity in a humanistic institution like the school in which its leaders must be able to adjust to the continuously changing clientele and outside environments.

Assessing the Environment

As noted earlier, the school district is part of a very complex, changing environment. Keeping abreast of the changes that have occurred is an impressive task, but anticipating

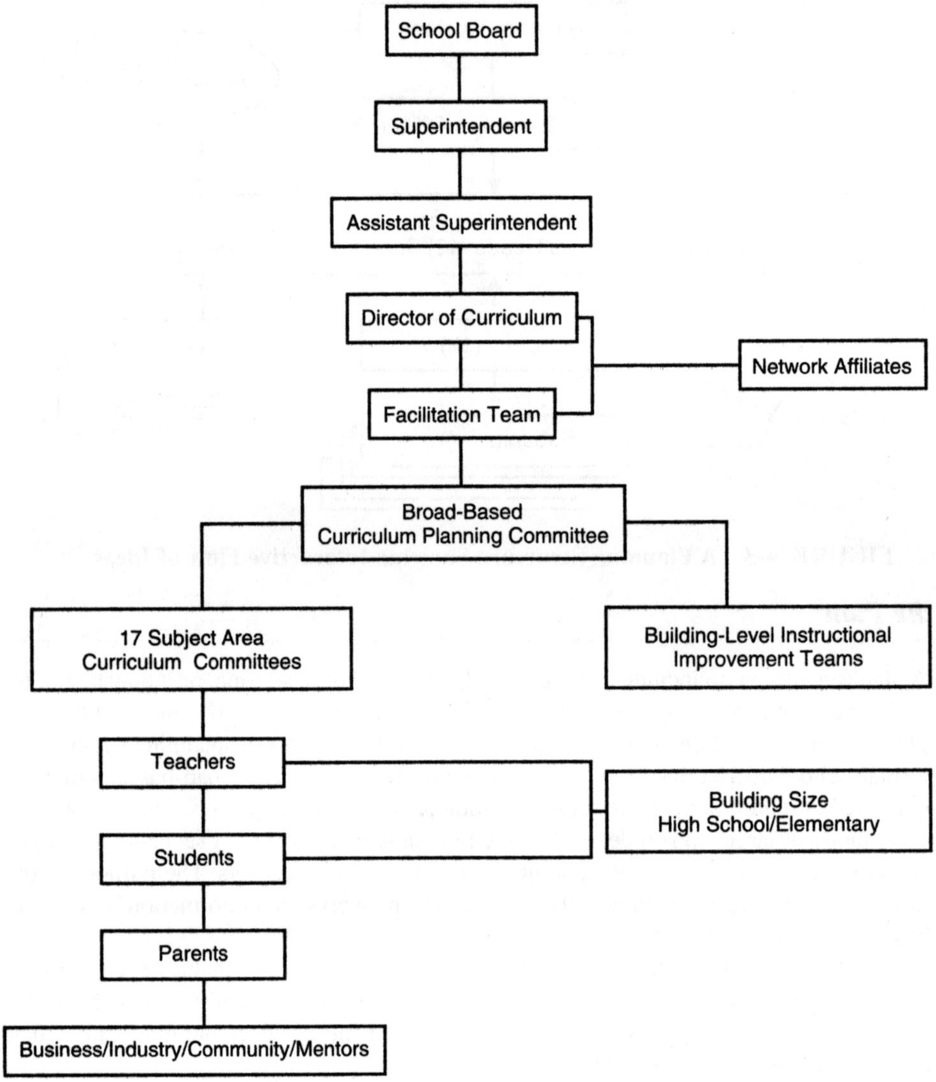

FIGURE 4-4   Planning Stucture for Curriculum Planning.

what changes may occur in the future challenges the bravest soul. Large corporations, school districts, and institutions of higher education continuously scan the environment for shifts in political policies, changes in the economy, or demographic trends that may affect the organization. These forecasters may be part of a planning group or may be individuals selected across the organization. Upcoming legislation, news items, forecasts, and polls become grist for the forecaster's mill in raising questions about the future direction or reactions of the organization.

More formal techniques are sometimes employed to forecast trends. These techniques include the "Delphi process" of seeking opinions, choices, and forecasts about the future. As wide a group of participants is involved as is practical in terms of time and expense. Wide participation lends validity to the process by incorporating views that range from reactionary to futuristic.

Keeping abreast of current literature is essential. A person may be assigned the task of identifying appropriate reports, analyses, books, documents, or periodicals that keep planners informed of new issues and trends in the external environment. A committee of persons may be established not only to widen the possibilities for input, but to interpret the implications of environmental changes on the school system. The school business manager or his representative is essential to such a process. Financial information, bond markets, investment trends, and real property use and trends are important to the planning team. The business manager ordinarily has access to several print and/or electronic media sources to glean useful information. Beyond the financial data he usually gathers, his close contacts with the business community at large brings concerns, perspectives on problems, and opportunities and interpretations from the community that complement input gained by the superintendent or provided by community members of the planning team.

Morrison et al. noted three types of scanning the environment: passive, active, and directed.[4] *Passive scanning* of the external environment is almost by chance or results from someone having a particular interest at a given time. *Active scanning* is limited to a selected field of resources and focuses more on issues that will have an influence on the educational enterprise in the relatively near future—one or two decades. Narrowing the fields of interest and the issues further from a selected range of resources puts the scanning team into a *directed scanning* mode.

From a wide range of input, the administrative team scanning the environment may develop a list of areas of concern that appear to be important to the school system over the next ten to twenty years. The lists noted at the beginning of the chapter may provide a starting point. Sources can then be identified to keep the team informed. Persons may be designated selected areas to scan. The issues may become more complex as time passes or may point toward newer issues with greater impact potential. The team needs to be ready to respond as new issues and data emerge.

A Word of Caution

Honing fishhooks to surgically sharp points and keeping line free from tangles and checking for weak spots are commendable activities for the fisherman. The fisherman must bait the fishhook and cast his line to put fish into the skillet. In the same way, scanning, analyzing, and generating planning data are important for the school that wishes to provide excellent education, but stopping short of deciding what to do and doing it leaves would-be planners nothing more than articulate about potential issues. Nothing will be given to students to prepare them for the future. If many companies in the very near future will operate with 200 employees or fewer, and if participative and consultative management models will be the rule rather than exception, what instructional goals and format changes will be required of the schools? How do these changes relate to legislatively imposed testing of students for rote memory or repetitive processes? Are schools addressing the potential intergenerational conflicts as the aged population comprises a larger and larger percentage of the population? Probably the ultimate evaluation of the planning process is what actually happens as a result.

Communicating the Plan

A sure way to generate rumor, distrust, and misinformation among members of the school organization is to keep a plan under wraps. It is necessary to communicate what the issues are, what the plans are to address them, and what effects the participants can anticipate. Dill in reviewing John W. Gardner's book, *On Leadership* notes that the function of planning is communication.[5] The limited circulation of another dust-gatherer may result in wasted activity. A planning document, or report, does not have to be a thick volume; in fact, it may be much more effective if its size and scope are limited. If the intent of planning is to communicate a working vision of the school organization's future, then a few goals and the direction to be taken in the future based on clear values stated in straightforward language may be more effective to most readers than too many charts and graphs in an overflow of wordiness.

Priorities must be established and the school system needs to focus on its top priorities. Dissipation of resources and energy can result when a school system attempts to deal with too many goals and issues at once.

Planners need to determine their audiences and tailor the communications about the plan to those audiences. The goals and direction are the same, but communicating the basic plan and how it is to be implemented will be different in impact and action for parents, teachers, maintenance crews, and many other groups.

Discussions about the plan need to occur. These discussions not only provide an opportunity to explain the plan, but afford a chance to resolve misunderstandings and further clarify issues as perceived by the various audiences. Well-run discussions refine the plan and the planning process. They can provide starting points and offer fresh perspectives for the continuing planning process. Carefully recording and analyzing the input from participants in the discussions provides an important component for evaluating the planning process. It is important that the discussion be perceived as a two-way interaction, not a one-way discussion of the planners merely to inform an audience.

Evaluating the Process

As with any good evaluation process, the evaluation of the plan began at the beginning rather than at the end of the planning process (see chapter 3). One of the first questions to ask is, What do we expect this planning process to do for us? The second question is, How will we know if those things happened? A set of questions following the first two should deal with what levels will be considered successful.

Concurrent with these questions and their answers should be a sensitivity to and conscious awareness of the circumstances surrounding each stage of the planning process. What was happening in the community or nation that might change the results or cause different reactions from community groups? A recession? A natural disaster? An outbreak of violence? Although these situations may be easily identified as having an impact on planning, much more subtle influences may need to be accounted for, such as the reactions of a local group of workers to a Supreme Court decision or a congressional decision not to limit the interstate transportation of waste materials. In short, the whole context within which the planning process takes place should be recognized as part of the evaluation. Evaluating the planning process is complex but essential to keep the process vital and ongoing, not merely an annual or biannual exercise with little meaning to anyone but those producing the planning documents.

The State as an Influence

Part of the context of the school district's planning includes long-range and current objectives of the state government. Many states have a long-range plan of their own in place and a process whereby updates to implementing their plan are communicated to school districts. Just as individuals do not live in contextual vacuums, neither do school districts. The current trends toward city-county or metro service regions is an example. What effects have the creation of metro service areas had on school districts within the region? Mergers? Access to more service agencies?

Education is recognized as both a state function and a local responsibility. This means that the state, through constitutional provisions, legislative enactments, and state department of education directives, sets a pattern for school operation, and then the local communities operate their schools within that pattern. This has worked very well for normal school operations. However, in the area of long-range statewide planning for education there is a noticeable weakness. It is well-known that what happens in one school district affects another. A child educated in the poorest school district in the state may later live and work in the richest district. A school district with overcrowded, poorly staffed buildings creates a community emergency, but it also creates a state emergency. Poorly organized districts, inadequately trained teachers, and overcrowded and outdated buildings are actually statewide problems. The state, then, through its opportunity to examine the overall picture should rise above local and provincial interests and stimulate a broad and intelligent consideration for the needs of all its citizens.

Statewide planning in which lay citizens participate improves public understanding of the problems faced by the schools and stimulates the desire to solve them. This does not mean that the state should merely help local groups plan within their own school districts; rather, it means that the state should define the problem as a statewide issue. The problems should be studied on a broad base so that if school districts need to merge to provide a better and more economical educational program, the avenues for their merger are already set up. No matter how strenuously local people work, unless they understand and consider regional, state, and national educational problems, their planning will be ineffectual and in many cases worse than no planning at all. There can be no question that the changes in our society demand greater understanding and integration among individuals, school districts, regional areas, and states. The broad understanding which is necessary cannot be created by adhering to a narrow local provincialism. It must be created by having people from various communities work together so that they come to understand that some problems can be solved only by joint effort and cooperation.

The Private Sector as an Influence

Given the well-funded groups from the private sector attempting to restructure education in their own images, and given the private foundations attempting to effect change by funding special projects, the private sector cannot be ignored. Influences exerted by private foundations have affected grade structure, types of learning activities, and school organization. The middle school movement is an example of the effects of private sector influence. Public awareness and attitudes have been changed regarding such issues as middle school education or corporal punishment through the efforts and influence of private funding agencies.

Summary

Much has been said in previous chapters about the new leadership responsibilities which are developing in the school business management field. Certainly it is logical that the job of gathering much of the financial and physical plant data which make up part of the information base for planning and of keeping such data up-to-date should be assigned to the assistant superintendent for business because of the job responsibilities and the technical know-how of the staff. A major task in line with this job is to set up a reporting and record system for each area of work which ties in with planning to bring the plan up to date at each reporting period. The school business manager, along with the school superintendent, should take the lead in encouraging the school district to develop a planning board and, as a member of this board, contribute as fully as possible of his or her technical know-how and previous experience in planning.

For Further Thought

1. Review the planning documents of several school districts. What changes would you make regarding involvement, focus, or style of reporting?

2. Identify the sources of information in your community for the following: birth rates over time; land use; population changes; economic indicators.

3. Present pro and con arguments regarding the idea that a small school district does not need to engage in formal planning since nearly everyone knows everyone in the community.

4. What advantages or disadvantages are there to joining other agencies in their planning efforts, as well as their joining in the school district planning?

5. Review techniques of forecasting public school enrollments.

6. Identify data bases needed to analyze the internal influences affecting the school organizations noted at the beginning of the chapter.

Endnotes

1. Frank Eikenberry is director of the Office of Analytical Studies and Planning at Ball State University.

2. Richard Muther, *High Performance Planning,* 2nd ed. (Kansas City, Mo: Management and Industrial Research Publications, 1988), p. 1-1.

3. Muther, *High Performance Planning,* pp. 2-2 through 4-1.

4. James L. Morrison, William L. Renfro, and Wayne I. Boucher, *Futures Research and the Strategic Planning Process.* Association for the Study of Higher Education, Report No. 9. (Washington, D.C.: The Association, 1984), pp. 19–21.

5. David Dill, "Qualities That Make an Academic Leader," *Planning for Higher Education,* Society for College and University Planning, Vol. 19, No. 1, (Fall 1990): 42.

Chapter 5

Budgeting*

Education has been experiencing a fiscal ride somewhat like a roller coaster. In recent years there have been varying periods of rapid growth, decline, population shifts and economic development and doldrums. Added to these are voter apathy, taxpayer revolts, and state caps on tax increases contrasted with increased pressure to provide more services for more segments of the population and unfunded mandates from the state and federal levels. These volatile situations too often seem to whipsaw the schools into frustration. Finances have always been a governing factor in running the organization and they shape the effectiveness of schools. Regardless of the amount of dollars available, whether perceived to be more than adequate or dismal, the decisions about how to spend those dollars is crucial to the relative welfare of the students entrusted to the school board and professional staff.

Money, or the lack of money, will govern the way an organization is managed and the way it succeeds. An educational activity may be encouraged by increasing its revenue, or it may be discouraged or enfeebled by denying it financial support. Thus, finance can become an instrument of control. The important linkage between school policy and planning and school finance is easily seen. Left uncontrolled, finance can lead the way to a poorly functioning school out of touch with its mission. Properly controlled and used as a tool for education, money can serve as the lifeblood for a quality school. For this reason, neither the citizen, the board of education, nor the school administrator can afford to leave to chance the distribution or management of money. The stakes are too great. Thus "budgeting" as the device for translating the educational plan into a financial plan has become a more important administrative process each year.

*The authors wish to acknowledge the assistance provided by Dr. Ivan D. Wagner, Professor Emeritus, Ball State University, for his contributions to this chapter.

Definition

The budget has been defined in a variety of ways. Bartizal defined it as follows: "A budget is a forecast, in detail, of the results of an officially recognized program of operation based on the highest reasonable expectation of operating efficiency."[1] Buck, speaking of governmental budgeting, declared: "The budget in the strict sense of the term is a complete financial plan for a definite period, which is based upon careful estimates both of the expenditure needs and the probable income of government."[2] Koontz and O'Donnell conceive budgeting as "essentially the formulation of plans for a given period in the future in specific numerical terms. As such, budgets are statements of anticipated results."[3] Candoli et al. defined the school budget as " . . . basically an instrument of educational planning and, incidentally, an instrument of control."[4] Hartman called the budget "a document which specifies the planned expenditures and anticipated revenues of a school district in a given fiscal year, along with other data and information relating the fiscal elements to the educational philosophy, programs and needs of the district." Others somewhat facetiously have called budgeting "a method of worrying before you spend, instead of afterwards."[5]

The authors would define the yearly *educational budget* as the *translation of prioritized educational needs into a financial plan which is interpreted to the public in such a way that when formally adopted it expresses the kind of educational program the community is willing to support, financially and morally, for a one-year period.*

It is clear from the definitions selected from a span of many years that an element common to all, or implied, is a "plan." The budget is an expression of planning, a window through which all may view the educational values of the school board and administration. If an effective planning process is in operation, it may be difficult to distinguish when planning ends and budgeting begins.

The budget is an extremely important item in all government activities. Government activities and services cost money and taxation is a method of securing money to pay for them. Americans can well afford better educational services but they are not going to give school authorities carte blanche to decide what services are needed and to provide them. This is a matter for the public to decide. Thus with expanding social demands for services and governmental mandates, the dynamic give-and-take forces of democracy are operating with increasing tempo. National and state government budgets have been in the spotlight in recent years, but with the pressures on property taxation and litigation relative to school financing, it can be expected that citizens will continue to carefully scrutinize both their local community budget and the school budget.

So much of our thinking as citizens is tied up with budgeting that we are inclined to assume that our government's budget system has existed ever since the establishment of the United States. This is not true. Not until 1921 did Congress pass a law requiring the federal government to have a budget.

Emphasis on public school budgeting as an administrative process is also of recent origin. In 1922 Twente made a study of the budgetary procedures of schools in 363 cities.[6] He found that budgetary processes in public schools were relatively undeveloped. Because of the various procedures followed and the lack of standardization, it was difficult to find any overall agreement about how a school budget should function. Arthur B.

Moehlman's *Public School Finance,* published in 1925, was the first book to present a functional approach to the scientific management of school money.[7] It is not surprising nor inappropriate that many volumes have been written since then about funding schools. By 1985 Jones noted that elementary and secondary schools in the United States spend more than $100 billion each year, a sum greater than the total budget of most nations in the world, yet less than the sales of some corporations and far less than is spent for U.S. defense.[8]

Nationally, the dollar amounts spent for education appear to show a strong, positive value for education, yet the United States spends a smaller percent of its gross national product on education than most other developed countries. The attention given to student achievement and economic competitiveness over the years has given rise to even more scrutiny of dollars spent on education.

Views of Budgeting

Traditionally, business and industry have viewed budgets as an instrument of control. This is a restricted view of the budget, for a budget should be an instrument resulting from planning and only an instrument of control within a specific period of time. The budget reflects the organizational pattern and the programs offered by translating the elements in a total plan into its various components, thereby allowing costs to be more easily estimated and analyses to be made. It then forces a coordination of these elements by reassembling costs in a whole so that a comparison may be made with total revenues. This very process requires a kind of orderly planning that otherwise might never take place. Budgeting, then, forces the administrator and staff to plan together on what needs to be done, how it will be done, and by whom.

The benefits of budgeting may be listed as follows:

1. Establishes a plan of action for the coming year
2. Requires an appraisal of past activities in relation to planned activities
3. Necessitates the establishment of work plans
4. Provides security for the administration by assuring the financing and approval of a year's course of action
5. Necessitates foreseeing expenditures and estimating revenues
6. Requires orderly planning and coordination throughout the organization
7. Establishes a system of management controls
8. Provides an orderly process of review and planning for both personnel and facilities needs
9. May serve as a public information device

Varying Philosophies of Budgeting

The school budget has become a conventional administrative tool, and several philosophies have developed regarding the way it is conceived and thus the way it is used. These philosophies have not been formalized into universally accepted systems. In practice, they are interwoven in varying degrees; but they may be documented as follows: (1) mechanical budget or functional budget, (2) yearly budget or continuous budget, (3) administrator-dominated budget or participatory budget, (4) centralized budget or decentralized budget.

Mechanical Budget or Functional Budget

Simply stated, the mechanical type of budget shows two sheets of paper, one presenting the estimated yearly receipts of an institution and the other showing how the money can be divided in order to run the school. Under this philosophy, budgeting is strictly a revenue-and-expenditure operation—a bookkeeping chore, required by law, which is feverishly pored over near the end of the fiscal year and, once established, is forgotten until the next year rolls around. This method tailors the suit to fit the cloth. Any planning that takes place is rather a negative operation performed by calculating what can be eliminated or what can be padded so that the budget will come out right according to revenues in sight. The eternal hope is, "If we have money left over after we figured out how much it will cost to do the same things we did last year, maybe we can cut taxes." Or Joe, the typical high school student's father, says, "The people are getting tired of paying these exorbitant school taxes, so let's cut out that stuff about interactive TV or buying all those computers."

On the other side of the coin is the functional view of budget building, in which school budget planners attempt to determine the educational objectives of the community, state, nation, and even the world, and develop an educational plan suited to these objectives. Then they explain the plan and its costs to the community. The result is usually a compromise between what the people are willing to pay for and what educational leaders think is needed. Thus, the adopted budget represents the best education the people of the community will buy at a particular time.

Given a functional view, the budget planners consider the educational plan before they consider money. The qualitative and quantitative aspects of the educational program are translated into expenditures and show the people what the educational needs are so that they will provide the money.

Yearly Budget or Continuous Budget

Those who view the budget as a yearly or periodic task may see the budget as a chore that must be accomplished once each year during a three- to four-week period before the budget is presented to the board of education or approving body. During that period the administrative staff works at high speed to gather figures and supporting data. Thoughtful consideration of programs and personnel is brushed aside in the face of the time crunch. Well-intentioned plans to study and appraise community and school needs are now discarded and finally another deadline is met with a grateful murmur, "Thank heaven we won't have to go through this again until next year!"

When the continuous-budget approach is followed, on the other hand, budgeting is seen as a planning process which is an integral part of daily operation. The day the budget is formally approved by the board of education, work immediately starts on the budget for the next year. Strengths and weaknesses in the operation of the previous year's plans are appraised, and proposed budget corrections are made. Hastily conceived educational programs, quick faculty changes, and faulty facility changes are eliminated or greatly reduced by long-range planning which includes proposed financing *with planning*. Thus with year-round budgeting, school programs can be better coordinated, and the board of education can be given time to consider an addition or deletion on the basis of educational merit as well as cost. The continual consideration of the budget is not an automatic operation; certain administrative devices must be used to set it into motion. In order to be sure that budgeting is a continuous process, the administration may schedule a number of information/discussion meetings involving citizens and teachers throughout the year regarding program needs and costs, and proposed plans for improving the facilities of the school district. Valuable feedback is thus obtained. By involving a number of audiences, school administrators are presenting value choices for community members to think about throughout the year.

In a continuous budget a calendar of events is established. The calendar assists all who are involved in the budgeting process to gather pertinent information and consider alternatives throughout the year rather than in a hectic last few days or weeks at the end of the fiscal year. Priorities can be established in a more considered manner than with a yearly budget. Even given the last-minute or even past-the-last-minute special sessions of the legislature to act on education funding, the view of budgeting as a continuous process holds promise.

An additional device to help encourage a continuous-process view of budgeting is to require reports at specific time intervals which force proper consideration of items and programs that must be included or excluded from the budget. Facility/equipment maintenance, renovation, and replacement are examples of areas which can be evaluated earlier than other items. The relationship of the continuous development approach to the planning process discussed in chapter 4 is obvious. It is hard to separate one from the other particularly since financial planning is involved at each step of an effective planning process.

Administration-Dominated or Participatory Budgeting

The administrator or board member who views her or his role autocratically, that is, as the one who makes all decisions, the one who dispenses favors or punishments, or the one who by virtue of office *deserves* to be in charge likely will view the budget as a personal tool.

When it comes time to develop a budget that is administration-dominated, no help is asked and no help is desired in making up the budget. The teachers, staff, and principals take what they get as far as the budget is concerned. The central office creates the impression that the budgeting process is beyond the understanding of ordinary human beings and that, in obtaining funds, it is grappling with some mystic elusive "they" which cannot be approached by anyone else. Budget reporting is done only as required by law and then in an ambiguous manner so that parents, citizens, and professional staff will not ask too many questions. When the administration-dominated budget is controlled by the board of education it can be used as a club over the head of the administrator or the teacher's union, and it becomes a strait jacket rather than a dynamic plan.

Those who view citizens, faculty, and staff as being contributors of ideas and persons who wish to take responsibility tend to view budgeting as a participatory process. In a participatory budget the principle is recognized that schools as tax supported institutions need to work with the community not only to gain support but to enrich the ideas for programming to meet the needs of the children in the community. Furthermore, the principle is recognized that both professional and support staff as well as students are important stakeholders in the educational enterprise and should be involved in the budget process.

Public education is the largest governmental budgetary unit controlled and administered at the local-community level. In the long run it does not matter whether the school board has fiscal independence or not. In either case, community members must be convinced of the desirability of a particular educational program before they will support it. By the same token, teachers must believe in and understand the school's educational plan before they will support it properly as school representatives.

The site-based approach to budgeting, whereby building administrators are given a wide range of responsibility over the school's financial resources, can be viewed as an example of the participatory view of budgeting. On the other hand, the site-based approach may only serve as a veneer over a truly administrator-dominated process, that is, it is participatory on the surface, but not in philosophy. The administrator may in various ways simply send the proposed budget items back "until they get it right"—meaning until it is congruent with the administrator's already determined parameters.

The long-range effect of psuedo-participation is easily predicted. As noted in the examples in the previous chapter on planning, the "participants" quickly find other ways to spend their creativity and just walk through the budgeting process in a perfunctory way. The administrators must be committed to the participative view in belief as well as form or the process will simply deteriorate into added work in an administrator-dominated budgeting approach. Participatory budgeting does not mean that the administrator should abdicate responsibility for making decisions about the overall budget. Rather it suggests there is another way, possibly even a stronger way, to arrive at a continuously improving use of available resources.

Centralized or Decentralized Budgeting

Whether centralized or decentralized, the budgeting process can be either administrator-dominated or truly participatory. The advantages of centralized or of decentralized is affected greatly by the underlying view of the administrator regarding control or power: if the administrator is making up "my budget," then the chances for a participatory budget probably do not exist, even in a decentralized setting.

The centralized organization of the budgeting process is ordinarily a top-down approach that is administrator-dominated. Carefully conceived centralized budgeting, using all techniques possible, can obtain teacher, staff, and citizen participation in planning, and will reap practically all the benefits of decentralized budgeting without running the danger of over compartmentalizing the educational process.

Site-based decision making has put some budget decision making at the building level. A survey of school business managers in districts claiming to have site-based management showed no common definition of site-based management among the budget practices.[9] In this survey, budget practices as described by school business officials ranged from decisions about a very narrow range of functions, e.g., materials, to deciding at the building level how to allocate a block of money across all functions.

Hartman suggested five elements appropriate to the individual school site-budgeting process[10]:

1. The establishment of an overall school district budget target
2. The establishment of basic (non-school-site) costs
3. The assignment of all remaining funds to individual schools on a per capita basis
4. The development of individual school expenditure plans
5. The assembly of individual school expenditure plans into a comprehensive district budget in accordance with Item 1.

Whether the school principal or a policy group with wide representation is involved, budget decisions can be made at the site level. One key to successfully decentralizing the budgeting process is clear communications from the central offices and board of education regarding decisions to be made. The early problems which surfaced with site-based decision making in Chicago serve as a caution to planners. It was quickly evident that the local decision-making boards did not understand the nature, limits, or implications of their power. Inappropriate decisions led to fiscal hardships for the schools as well as loss of credibility for key individuals in the schools. So it could be if the limitations of budget decision making were misunderstood by the principal or by other local decision-making groups.

Decentralized budgeting by its very nature forces wider participation in budget making. It envisions the principal, teachers, and community working together, planning together, creating a custom-made program. It stresses the individuality and culture of each particular building and staff. It breaks down the highly populated school district into units which are small enough to permit face-to-face planning and follow-through. School districts using this plan encourage variety in programs, experimentation, group unity, and spontaneous creativity within school board guidelines regarding how best to meet educational goals.

One of the major disadvantages of decentralized budget planning is that it may compartmentalize education in the community. Each school may become a small kingdom in itself. Rivalry and competition could take the place of cooperation throughout the school district. Furthermore, people in a community could become confused over the variety in methodology, the apparent differences of philosophy, and the lack of overall unity.

There are additional dangers: the principal and teachers may become so tied up with the mechanical aspects of budgeting and operation that they do not have time for personnel and program improvement. Pressure groups may become overaggressive in attempts to gain some particular advantage for their building. Internal politics with the central office and the board of education may get out of hand, and the board of education and the central administration may find it difficult to handle public reaction to differences among schools in the system.

While the above are possible pitfalls, the other side of the picture which emphasizes the expenditure of efforts to achieve excellence, not in a competitive way, but rather in an atmosphere of exciting possibilities and responsibilities may offset the negative potential. Careful planning and clear communications are essential to the success of a decentralized budgeting process.

Budget Techniques

Several techniques or methods of developing budgets have evolved over the years. The reader should note that most of them can be placed into more than one category of philosophies or approaches to budgeting, as described above. For example, the zero-base technique may be used in an administrator-dominated, yearly, mechanical budget, or it may be used in a continuous budget with wide participation in making up the budget. Although it is not the intent of this chapter to make the reader an expert in each budgetary technique, especially since volumes are available on each, brief descriptions of each are in order.

Incremental Budgeting

The starting point for incremental budgeting is this year's budget. Each line item is examined along with overall expected revenues. Decisions are made for each existing line item, either to add or subtract dollars. Certain "fixed" costs such as utilities may be easily adjusted assuming stable rates, no new construction coming on line, and stable weather conditions. Salaries may be forecast, particularly when employees are on a multiple-year contract and/or a formula-based salaries agreement. If anticipated revenues permit, then additional amounts may be added to the remaining lines by across-the-board increases, or by differing dollar amounts.

A common practice is to gather requests from individual buildings and for individual programs. Each building administrator prepares a request for each appropriation/expenditure area for which that building is responsible. In school systems where site-based management is translated into a full spectrum of costs such as utilities, transportation, etc., this process can become quite a chore. More often, the building-level budget planners deal with items excluding fixed costs. Appendix I is an example of a form that can be used by an elementary school principal to detail his budget requests. As noted on the form, supplemental information is required for detailing equipment, and library books and periodicals. Special requests such as building repair or renovation are made separately, often in concert with the director of buildings and grounds or, in smaller school districts, with the school business manager.

After the requests have been received from the buildings and for the programs, a total request budget can be put together. Some school districts use a form similar to that shown in Appendix II. Amounts are categorized into various funds and whatever additional breakdowns are required by the state and preferred by the school district. In Appendix II, for example, instructional and support salaries and supplies are broken down by individual cost unit.

When the totals are done for all expenditure areas, preliminary decisions can be made regarding proposed appropriations for the following year. Appendix III shows a sample sheet which provides figures for each expenditure area from the "last year" (which is actually the current year) and the request totals and tentative decisions regarding proposed appropriations for the following year. This spreadsheet application also gives the management team the percentages of increases or decreases, as the case may be.

At this point a number of options are available regarding how to arrive at the increases or decreases to existing lines in the budget. Program performance, popularity, or perceived promise may tip the budget maker's pencil up or down. Decisions may be made by group process or by one individual. These decisions may be made at the central office level or the building level. Given the nature of incremental, line-item budgeting, the likelihood of dramatic change is slim. In fact, this is one of the major criticisms of the technique, namely that it does not encourage innovation and seeking new ways to meet needs. Rather it assumes that what exists is working and and so there is no provision for new needs. A new program idea tends to be viewed as needing new money, hence, it may be a threat to the well-entrenched programs that have been counting on their fair share of increases each year. Part of the problem may be that seldom can the real costs of a specific program (e.g., elementary language arts, counseling, mathematics) be determined on a line-item, incrementally developed budget.

Zero-Base Budgeting (ZBB)

A technique introduced or at least popularized in the 1970s at the federal level, zero-base budgeting addresses some of the criticisms of incremental budgeting noted above. The organization is divided into cost or budget units. The fact that a program was budgeted for this year does not mean it will be funded next year. All programs begin the budget building project with zero dollars. The head of each unit is required to justify the continuation of the programs or activities in the unit each year. Justifications are made relative to the goals, goal achievement, and cost of alternatives available to achieve the goals. Budgets or budget packages are developed to reflect a level of basic survival of the unit's activities, a budget reflecting current operating levels, and an improvement level(s). As in the incremental technique, a number of options are available for determining priorities among the various units' proposals and the levels proposed by each unit.

One advantage of zero-based budgeting is that the school district must continuously examine and set priorities and, theoretically, the highest priorities get funded. Another advantage is the increased knowledge of program or unit costs. An obvious disadvantage is the increased time needed to prepare budget requests and to analyze and prioritize requests to form the budget.

Planning, Programming Budgeting System (PPBS)

A variation of PPBS is the planning, programming, budgeting, and evaluation system (PPBES). The insertion of the term "evaluation" emphasizes the evaluation of goals, effectiveness, and alternate routes to goal achievement over a period of time both past and future. Many of the elements in zero-base budgeting are present in PPBS. The technique integrates planning with the allocation of resources to achieve goals over time. Although annual budget documents are produced, a long-range plan to fund programs is the basis for annual allocations.

The PPBS technique requires the generation and analysis of data about specific program costs, projections of need (e.g., pupil enrollments, technological developments) goals realization, alternative possibilities, and associated personnel and facilities costs. The continuing development of site-based decision making will impact on this technique and will require greater financial analysis on the part of the school business manager. Fortunately the computer is available to assist, but a person with expert judgment finally decides what data are collected at what time and applied in what way. An example is pupil enrollment data collected at a specific time and the single-time data applied to allocation decisions. In one school system the usual pattern was a drop in enrollment during second semester for all units except one. That unit had stable or increasing enrollments during the second semester, but the fall counts adjusted for a second-semester drop was uniformly applied to all units. The result was a punitive situation for the unit not experiencing enrollment drops. Providing for the exceptions should be the rule.

No Pure Form

As expected, one cannot find a common application of any of the above techniques or approaches noted earlier. Variations and mergers of processes occur from district to district. This is as it should be given the different needs, traditions and goals. Faced with an ever more complex set of demands and constraints, schools need to be positioned to be flexible, yet not drifting at the whim of this or that current. A budgetary process based on good data, with the input of important stakeholders, and integrated into a long-range planning process may place the schools in that needed position.

The Budget Document

The budget document itself is the written presentation by the school administrator which translates the educational program proposed for the school district in coming year into costs and indicates by sources the revenues expected and needed. The following might be a sample table of contents for a comprehensive type of budget embodying a full working policy for education within the school district, along with costs and supporting data. The formal budget document ordinarily includes these elements:

> Title Page
> Table of Contents or Index
> Letter of Transmittal (from the district board of education to the public)
> Budget Message (from the superintendent to the district board of education)
> Budget Philosophy
> School District Profile—Staff

The Educational Plan
   Mission Statement
   School System Goals/Priorities
   Educational Plan including Proposed Changes

Estimated Expenditures
   Summary of Expenditures
   Detailed Estimate for each Budget Classification
   Data Supporting Detailed Estimates

Estimated Revenues
   Summary of estimates
   Analysis of Revenue Sources
      Federal
      State
      County
      Local (Taxation Structure)

Comparative Data
   Comparison of Revenues and Expenditures for previous years

The budget document, as seen from the format for a formal budget, ordinarily includes three major divisions: the educational plan, the expenditure plan, and the revenue plan. The educational plan provides an overview of programs and services provided by the school district. The expenditure plan should translate programs and services into dollar amounts so that constituents can see the appropriated amount for the next budget year. The revenue plan identifies sources of income the school district expects to access in order to operate all school sites, centralized services, and the delivery of programs and services to students.

The Educational Plan

The educational plan is the heart of the budget. It is the center around which everything else is built and the determining factor for both expenditures and revenue requests. In any educational plan which has been developing over the years through a long-range planning process, many matters are taken for granted and have received public acceptance. The intimate details of the educational plan do not need reiteration in each budget document. However, to achieve a greater understanding of the purposes of an educational plan, let us assume that we are developing a comprehensive budget document for a community that has sprung up overnight. All future budgets will be built around this educational plan; therefore it will require thorough treatment. What then are the first steps in developing the educational plan?

A plan must have a pervading philosophy and specific objectives developed and accepted by the community and professional staff. These should be simply written and understandable so that they can guide decisions on educational problems which may arise in the future. Professional jargon should be avoided in order that the document can serve as an understandable way to communicate with all the school's public sectors.

The way the school is organized to accomplish educational objectives is the next logical step to consider in the development of an educational plan. This includes the organization of the administration as well as that of the grades or classes. For example, shall it be a graded school with preschool, kindergarten and grades 1 through 4? Shall it be kindergarten through grade 12? Shall it be kindergarten-6-3-3? Kindergarten-8-4? Kindergarten-6-6? Shall there be ungraded classes in the elementary school and graded classes in junior high and high school, for example, kindergarten-ungraded-7-12? Should there be rooms set aside to accommodate those who are not ready for the next grade level?

How broad a curricular program is needed to fit the stated philosophy and objectives? Will it require an approach to teaching which is different from the traditional approach? Should the middle levels be partially self-contained and partly departmentalized?

How large an administrative staff is required? How many supervisors? Special teachers? Consultants? What kind of teachers do we want? How many years of preparation and experience shall we require? What should be the average class size and teaching load?

What educational services shall we provide in guidance, counseling, medical checkup, psychiatry, visiting teachers? What mandated services for the disabled will be required? What is the incidence of various disabilities in the district?

What kinds of hardware and software are needed to prepare students for dealing with today's and tomorrow's demands for information and analyses? What implications for the next ten years at the high school levels derive from the present successes of kindergarten and primary level children using computer word processing? Will hardware be furnished by the schools to handicapped students at home who cannot afford it? All the preceding considerations will have an effect on the type of school buildings and facilities needed, and, of course, on costs.

In any school system which has been in existence for some time it is presupposed that the board of education has developed policies covering the multitude of questions regarding such educational plans. These should be formally adopted and documented, although there is no need to republish them each year. However, the educational plan section in the yearly budget document should serve to inform people of changes in policy, of innovations, or of particular points that need to be reemphasized.

In developing the educational plan, we must remember that state minimum requirements must be an integral part of it. As states move toward performance-based accreditation, the relationship between educational planning and budget development becomes stronger. If schools choose to meet requirements for regional accreditation, additional budget implications are added.

The Expenditure Plan

The expenditure plan is the main focus of the school budget. Although it is important to include goals and priorities in the formal budget document, local and state agencies responsible for reviewing and approving the budget are mainly interested in the expenditure plan. The expenditure plan is a composite of appropriations, the intent to spend, and the translation of the educational plan into anticipated costs. In 1957, the U.S. Office of Education developed Handbook II providing basic guidance to school districts in classifying expenditures. Most states adopted Handbook II, *Accounting For Local and State School System*, to use as a financial format for reporting school expenditures to state education agencies. Handbook II was revised in 1973 and continues to serve as a point of reference for state and local school districts. To ensure proper accounting of expenditures, budget classifications are, in general, uniform from state to state. Classifications still represent major categories, but in addition, some states have developed a program format for purposes of classifying and reporting expenditures. Local school districts are required to prepare the budget and account for expenditures according to state statutes. However, a local school district may choose to provide more detailed information in the expenditure plan. For example, state reporting procedures may require a major category of, *Instruction*, be used to classify all expenditures having to do with the delivery of instructional services. The local school district may wish to further delineate this budget category accordingly i.e., Instruction, Secondary, Foreign Language, and French, and even by level (elementary...) in each of the subdivisions. Below are function divisions used by most districts to report the expenditure plan.

Master Chart of Accounts: Function Accounts

Expenditures
1000	*Instruction*
1100	Regular Program
1110	Elementary
1120	Junior High
1130	High School
1200	Special Program
1300	Adult Program
2000	*Supporting Services*
2100	Pupils
2200	Instructional Staff
2300	General Administration
2400	School Administration
2500	Business
2600	Central
3000	*Community Services*
4000	*Nonprogrammed Charges*
5000	*Debt Service*

The Association of School Business Officials International has been instrumental in assisting the U.S. Department of Education in developing a uniform system for classifying expenditures. Historically, ASBO has been called on to choose from the membership a task force to recommend desired changes in the classification system. The school business manager selects from the state expenditure classifications systems those accounts to be used in preparing the local expenditure plan. Data is gathered and organized to help determine the cost of each classified item. The budget becomes a "before the fact" estimate of the intent to spend, but it is based on facts. It is, therefore, essential that data is gathered from multiple sources to assist in justifying budget figures.

A primary source of data is always student enrollment. Larger school districts, in general, have a child accounting office which monitors student mobility. Child accounting is generally organized and reported according to grade level, school sites, and special program areas, i.e., vocational, special education, and so on. Data gathering for budget preparation begins with an accurate accounting of students with an estimate of future enrollments. Data gathering also includes cost accounting "after the fact" expenditures utilizing last year's budget. Fixed costs such as social security, retirement payments, insurance, bond payments, and others are factored into the expenditure equation.

Miller and McClure suggested the following steps to help the budget forecast to be reliable as possible:[11]

To Get Started

- Clarify the purpose of the forecast.
- Match the time frame with the purpose of the forecast.
- Be sure the basic data are correct.
- Specify the assumptions.
- Be consistent in calculations.
- Examine data critically.
- Recognize that forecasting requires insight and intuition.

To Survive the Forecast Process

- Compare apples with apples.
- Identify the competitors for school district revenues.
- Obtain accurate enrollment data and track population.
- Discern trends in the regional economy and local business climate.
- Clarify data on assessed values and market values.
- Understand current trends in the housing market.
- Monitor the tax collection structure to uncover obsolete practices.

Basic to budget development is the *objects of expenditure*. Almost all programs or support service areas include the following objects of expenditure as a foundation for estimating expenditures.

Salaries
Employee Benefits
Contracted Services
Supplies and Materials
Capital Outlay
Debt Service

Larger school districts rely on the accounting department to provide a historical review of budget data and budget estimates. They will also provide important data on anticipated expenditures on fixed costs, which represents those costs the school district cannot control, i.e., utilities, insurance, employee benefits. Smaller school districts must generate a similar data base for budget preparations, but are likely to do so through the superintendent and the secretary/bookkeeper.

Preliminary budget estimates are often needed to assist local school boards in strategic planning. For this purpose, baseline data from the previous year's budget should be readily available, which includes the following informational categories:

Number of Teachers/Administrators
   Elementary Staff
   Secondary Staff
   Special Needs Staff
Number of students
   Elementary Schools
   Secondary Schools
   Special Needs Programs
Average Teacher Salary
Cost Per Pupil
Fixed Charges
Employee Retirement/Replacements
Assessed Valuation

Supporting data providing comparative data from previous years and other school districts would also be of assistance to decision makers in determining the expenditure plan. State statutes ordinarily require school budgets to be advertised. This provides an opportunity for public review of (a) the intent to expend funds, (b) source of revenues, (c) employee classifications, (d) salary and wages, (e) student enrollment data, (f) assessed valuation, and (g) certified tax rates. Thus, the budget becomes a *public relations* document as it is legally presented to the media to inform the public of the financial condition of the school district.

Figure 5-1 is an example of a required legal notice showing the expenditures and receipts of a school district.

Some budget documents in their original form present more than one estimate. One might be listed as minimum and another as desirable. In the final adoption of the budget the board of education can make a choice based on its knowledge of the school district and the supporting data presented to aid in its decision. Supporting data might include such documents as comparison with expenditure of previous years, percentage distribution of costs between various budget items, cost analyses, a brief description of the advantages of various services, studies and research on specific budget items, comparisons with other school districts, the state or national averages, and cost-of-living indexes.

Revenue Plan

The revenue plan is a carefully prepared estimate of receipts which can be used to finance the educational plan. Revenue may be classified as follows:

Local sources	Sale of bonds
Taxes and appropriations	Loans
Intermediate sources	Sale of property
State sources	Transfer tuition
Federal sources	Special revenues

In a fiscal/political climate which finds everything from political redistricting to social or health welfare issues tied to legislative decision making about educational funding, it is little wonder that school district revenue forecasters find themselves frustrated. At one time arguments about whether the revenues should drive the program or

---

ANNUAL REPORT

County Number 1
School Corporation Number 1
Nonawantee Community School Corporation
Any questions regarding this report should be directed to:
Dr. Jane Doe, Treasurer, 396-012-6437

EXPENDITURES COMPARISONS
Calendar Year 1990

Expenditure Accounts	1990 Approved Budget Expenditures	1990 Actual Expenditures	1991 Approved Budget Expenditures
GENERAL FUND			
11,000 Instruction/Regular Programs	$5,503,145.61	$5,503,134.72	$5,888,353.20
12,000 Instruction/Special Programs	81,227.85	81,226.22	86,913.95
14,000 Instruction/Summer School	85,111.00	85,109.39	91,006.63
21,000 Support Services/Pupils	149,149.00	149,140.12	159,588.46
22,000 Support Services/Instructional Staff	195,622.62	195,699.94	209,301.30
23,000 Support Services/General Administration	299,780.11	299,777.47	320,764.19
24,000 Support Services/School Administration	343,710.10	343,709.75	367,769.75
25,000 Support Services/Business	1,300,824.82	1,300,820.09	1,391,882.17
26,000 Support Services/Central	733,392.00	733,390.64	792,063.42
30,000 Community Services	53,993.00	53,990.50	57,772.77
40,000 Nonprogrammed Charges	489,920.00	489,918.29	524,215.36
50,000 Debt Services	212.00	224.00	236.00
TOTAL	$9,236,083.11	$9,236,051.13	$9,889,922.00

FIGURE 5-1   Example of a Required Public Report of Expenditures.

vice versa were interesting and consumed a great deal of ink. Today school revenues may be affected by strong programmatic arguments, but the realities of tax ceilings and economic belt-tightening in all sectors of public service dampen the idea of program-driven revenues.

The school business manager needs to have current information about state and federal funding trends. The state education department along with state professional associations ordinarily provide current information in this regard. Data on local and internal funding sources need to be kept current so that periodic checks of the data can be made to refine the revenue forecast.

The Budgeting Process

The budget process is a cyclic, never-ending process consisting of planning, coordinating, interpreting, presenting, approving, administering, and evaluating. Each of these seven steps are continuous, although at any given point in the school year one or the other may be intensified by special deadlines and/or evolving state requirements. Coley noted that "... the budget process ... is probably the most important routine activity undertaken by the school administration and the board."[12] Since dollars are essential to operating educational programs, it is easy to see why budgeting is important, but its importance goes beyond that. The budget is a statement to the community and staff about the priorities and values of the school board. It is a public relations document. It can be the culmination of the best thinking of the best people in the school and community.

Figure 5-2 depicts the sequence of the budgeting process, but the reader is reminded that parts of each of the steps may be occurring simultaneously. Planning for the budget two years away can be taking place while the next year's budget is up for formal approval.

Planning

The approaches to planning have been discussed in chapter 4. The authors believe that whatever budgeting approach is used, the planning phase of the budgeting process should involve a wide range of participants, especially those affected by the outcomes. Budgeting is political whether one wishes it to be or not. The school administrator who best utilizes the "brain power" of the staff and community is the one who will lead the schools in addressing the critical questions necessary to creating or maintaining their excellence in the community.

Answering difficult questions in the planning phase can avoid embarrassing silences when those questions come up during the interpreting or presenting phases of the budgeting process. The school business manager is in an excellent position to anticipate many of the questions and to provide data helpful in answering them. It may seem to the informed professional that some of the questions should not be asked given the amount of information available, but rest assured, they will be asked. The perpetual question regarding why the school budget is increasing faster than inflation when enrollments are holding constant or declining is asked. Questions regarding the expenditures for special

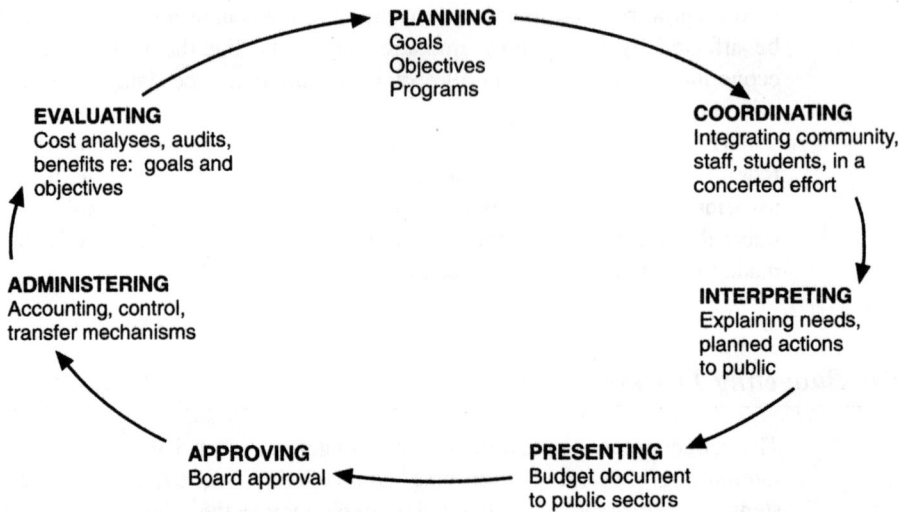

FIGURE 5-2   The Budgeting Process Cycle.

education or sports or fine arts may be anticipated. An important question to anticipate deals with the relationship between increased expenditures and the learning results being obtained. In a 1990 survey of school business managers, a question was asked regarding the relationship between academic achievement and site-based budgeting practices. In far too many cases, the business managers did not know about the "academic end of it" and seemed to wish not to respond to the question. This is inexcusable on their part and on the part of the superintendents. No matter what facet of the school business manager's role is being considered, he or she should conduct the role as a part of the instructional leadership team rather than as a somewhat detached observer of the team.

Coordinating

Coordinating a process that is not totally sequential, in as much as each phase is continuous, is a challenge to any administrator. The efforts of many people need to be focused on the task of budgeting and a key to its success is maintaining long-term efforts in a never-ending process without it degenerating into routines that have lost their meaning. Good communications among the participants help maintain the focus on the larger task of providing excellent education to the community's youth.

Interpreting

Public support requires public understanding. Therefore, schools must continually interpret their plans and actions to the public. Only a shortsighted administrator will wait until the budget needs to be adopted before explaining its ramifications to the public. Interpretation is an integral and continuing part of the budgetary process.

Presenting

The budget may be presented to the public sectors in many ways. Formal presentation involves publication of the final budget document; however, presentation in its broadest form consists of hearings, committee reports, research findings, accounting reports, and so on. Many schools develop a simplified version of the formal budget document; it contains pictures, diagrams, graphs, and an interesting but limited narrative, which will educate the average taxpayer.

Approving

Approval occurs when the board of education formally adopts the budget. Approval as a part of the cyclic budgetary process, however, goes on throughout the year when the school board deliberates on various projects proposed for the school. The enterprising administrator brings to almost every board meeting studies, research projects, experimental programs, and proposals that require the careful consideration and deliberation of the board of education before their final approval. Adoption of the budget is the formal acceptance of many projects that have been carefully studied, considered, and approved throughout the year.

Administering

The budget serves as a guide for action throughout the year. Once adopted it is an established part of the accounting records, which themselves are a part of budgetary control. Although the budget shows the essential activities that should take place, the administration attempts to get the most return for the money spent. Administration calls for sound purchasing of goods, along with proper distribution, care, use, and control. It requires the employment of superior personnel, their proper assignment, and the establishment of work loads, standards of performance, and supervision. Administration means the sound management of all the classifications that go to make up the budget.

Evaluating

Appraisal too is a continuous process. It is the means by which the board of education and the administrators know whether the budget is really functioning. There are many ways of appraising the budget system. Just daily observation and supervision provide one way. More formal devices include cost accounting records and reports; inside and outside surveys; audits; and comparisons with established criteria, checklists, standardized procedures, and staff studies. As noted in chapter 3, evaluation requires accurate data that are collected in a way planned prior to initiating the evaluation. The analyses of large amounts of data are possible by use of computer programs. Dembowski has provided basic information on computer applications that may be useful to the school business manager in planning for gathering and analyzing data.[13] Baldwin provided a stimulating discussion of the potentials of quantitative decision making that is now possible thanks to the computer.[14] The school business manager now can respond to questions from a much firmer base than in the past, which in turn should yield more accuracy in decisions based on the evaluation phase of the budgeting process.

The Budget as Public Relations Device

The interpreting and presenting phases of the budgeting process provide the school administrators an excellent opportunity to educate the public. Through their knowledge and understanding of the community, school administrators may see that it is unreasonable and impractical to ask for money to finance certain programs at a particular time, yet in the long-range educational plan the time may be appropriate for stimulating people's thinking and getting them to consider the need.

The layperson can never know what an outstanding educational program is unless the professional educator points the way. There is nothing better than a proposed budget to stimulate discussion about a superior program. Even though a budget for an enriched curriculum is not adopted one year, the discussion that takes place may lead to the success of the program the next year or the year after that. Certainly if a superior program is never presented, it can never be adopted. Community members can learn much about the educational plan through the central theme of the annual budget.

Encouraging the State Department of Education

The school business manager may be in a position to encourage the state department of education personnel to go several steps beyond the mundane roles of regulation, inspection, and auditing. It seems that many state departments of education are overlooking the springboard to dynamic educational leadership that a finance office can become. The need is apparent; it has been expressed by constant requests for help. Although most requests from the school business office have been for help in overcoming mechanical and technical difficulties, administrators who have a firm belief that financing is a true reflection of the educational plan can do much to raise the educational level of the state. If this challenge is to be met, finance departments must revise their concept of their function. They must be staffed by educators who have had training and experience in public school work supplemented by special training in accounting and educational finance. Above all, the staff of the finance office should understand the place of finance in education and accept the fundamental principle that their leadership can extend far beyond the traditional supervisory and inspectional functions. After legal commitments are satisfied, the greatest improvement can often be accomplished in areas beyond the requirement of law. School business managers can continue to encourage state department personnel to provide leadership beyond regulation.

Responsibility of Local, State, and National Citizens

Local school budgeting may seem far afield from citizenship responsibilities of local people. Yet there is a connection. Consider revenue as a prime example. Every school budget lists three prime sources of revenue—local, state, and federal. When local revenue needs to be increased, citizens are exhorted to vote additional millage for the good of their children and the nation. However, when state and federal revenues need to be increased, the local citizen is forgotten and the typical educator begins lobbying personally or through state and national educational agencies that work on the legislative scene. Often forgotten by school administrators is the fact that the local citizen is a citizen of both state and nation. Additional state and federal aid is provided through legislation at the state capitals and in Washington D.C., but the legislators who pass the laws to provide that aid are elected by local people and often they will listen to their constituency people more closely than they will to lobbyists and professionals. One of the most effective ways for schools to increase revenues from state and federal sources is to start a grassroots movement to demand more revenue. This means that in each community the schools are responsible for educating the populace to the overall need and then reminding them of their duties as state and national citizens. There is no better place than the budget document itself to present some of the shortcomings of our present method of financing schools.

Summary

In the educational budget, educational needs are translated into a financial plan which is interpreted to the public in such a way that when it is formally adopted it represents the kind of program the community is willing to support, both morally and financially, for a year's period. The document itself should not be a mechanical financial statement. It should be a dynamic, enlightened plan; when translated into costs and supported by revenues, it can serve as a leadership device and guidepost for future years.

The budgetary process is not a step-by-step operation; rather, it is a continuing, cyclic process, consisting in planning, coordinating, interpreting, presenting, approving, administering, and appraising.

For Further Thought

1. Would you advise public budget hearings if they were not required by law? What are some of the dangers? Advantages?

2. Select several budgets and compare their contents. Make a list of the strengths and weaknesses of each.

3. What are the laws of your state regarding budget form? Approval? Review?

4. List ten "tough" questions you would anticipate community members would ask at interpretive or budget presentation meetings. What sources of data would you use to respond to those questions?

5. What is the relationship of budgeting to the democratic process?

6. Interview several school superintendents and categorize their dominant philosophy of budgeting, using the philosophies described in this chapter. What techniques do they use to arrive at the budget?

7. What is the main purpose of an educational plan in a school budget?

8. Discuss the theoretical and the practical aspects of relating revenue to the educational plan.

9. What kinds of assumptions can you identify in the budgeting process selected by school district administrators? In the type of budget presented?

10. If you were a new school superintendent where would you go to get help on budgeting?

Endnotes

1. J. R. Bartizal, *Budget Principles and Procedures* (Englewood Cliffs, N.J.: Prentice-Hall, 1942), p. 1.

2. Arthur E. Buck, *Budget Making* (New York: Appleton-Century-Crofts, 1921), p. 2.

3. Harold Koontz and Cyril O'Donnell, *Principles of Management*, (New York: McGraw-Hill Book Company, 1955), p. 435.

4. Carl Candoli, Walter G. Hack, John R. Ray, and Dewey H. Stollar, *School Business Administration: A Planning Approach*, 2nd ed. (Boston: Allyn and Bacon, 1978), p. 146.

5. William T. Hartman, *School District Budgeting* (Englewood Cliffs, N.J.: Prentice-Hall, 1988), p. 2.

6. John W. Twente, *Budgetary Procedure for a Local School System* (Montpelier, Vt.: Capital City Press, 1922).

7. Arthur B. Moehlman, *Public School Finance* (Chicago: Rand McNally & Company, 1925), p. 474.

8. Thomas H. Jones, *Introduction to School Finance Techniques and Social Policy*, (New York: Macmillan Publishing Company, 1985), p. 1.

9. T. L. Drake, Funded research, Ball State University, 1990.

10. Hartman, *School District Budgeting,* p. 39.

11. Linda D. Miller and Maureen W. McClure, "Reliable School Budget Forecasts: Seven Tools that Work," *School Business Affairs* 54, No. 11 (November 1988): 18.

12. Joe D. Coley, "Beating the Budget Blues," *The School Administrator* 54, No. 5 (May 1988): 9.

13. Frederick L. Dembowski, *Administrative Uses for Microcomputers,* 3 vols. (Reston, Va.: The Association of School Business Officials International, 1983 and 1984).

14. Grover H. Baldwin, "Quantitative Decision Making," in *Principles of School Business Management* (Reston, Va.: The Association of School Business Officials International, 1986), pp. 175–206.

C h a p t e r **6**

Accounting and Reporting

Successful administration of a public school system depends on keeping accurate records of the many financial transactions required in its operation. Inasmuch as educational systems are financed primarily through various forms of taxation and inasmuch as schools belong to the people, it is appropriate that agencies of government, as well as private individuals and organizations, have available to them financial information from school administrators. Therefore, a complete accounting of all financial transactions is required at each administrative level, whether district, city, county, state, or federal.

Financial transactions of a school district range from the collection of a $1 student fee for club dues to the financing of multimillion-dollar buildings. Public school revenues come largely from state and local tax sources, some come from federal funds, and some are locally generated funds from rents, sales, and interest.

Accounting consists of recording, accumulating, presenting, summarizing, and interpreting financial data for a school district. It is one of the most important aspects of school business management, for it is the base from which decisions may be made on a wide variety of administrative questions. It is not an end in itself but a service function, responsible for supplying accurate informative data to management in the form of reports that describe the school's financial position and measure its operating results. Accounting is an important part of the language of school business administration.

Many people incorrectly use the term "accounting" and "bookkeeping" interchangeably. One of the major functions of a good accounting system is to furnish a continuing and easily, if not immediately, accessible instrument of budgetary control. Bookkeeping is that aspect of accounting which is concerned generally with the recording of financial data on forms or electronic formats selected by, and in compliance with procedures established by, the accountant in accordance with state or federally mandated forms or guidelines. The broader aspects of accounting, however, involve evaluation and measurement, presentation, and interpretation.

Neither the school business manager nor the superintendent can be expected to do the detailed work required in accumulating business documents, analyzing and recording the transactions, or summarizing all financial transactions for the school system's accounting period. However, they must be able to administer accounting and internal auditing functions and oversee a staff of technically trained people working in these areas. Under the supervision of the school business manager, the accounting department prepares summaries, analytical reports, and financial statements which serve as a basis for decisions by administrative officers and the board of education. In this task the school business manager must understand the theory and practice of both accounting and education and relate one to the other in proper perspective. He or she must then be able to adapt the results so that they can be easily used and understood by the rest of the administrative staff and the board of education. This places a huge responsibility on the school business manager because administration means not only observing the techniques of good accounting in all instances, but also the proper interpretation of financial and statistical data, which leads to better schools and improved school programs and results in greater student achievement.

Accounting Serves the Central District Administration

One of the main purposes of accounting is effective control and management of school monies. The following list illustrates some principal ways accounting serves the central school administration in this activity:

1. It provides data for use in controlling costs.
2. It provides information needed to control the assets, liabilities, revenues, and expenditures.
3. It provides information needed by the board of education and school patrons in judging the efficiency of operation.
4. It provides information required by law for local, state, and national governments. For instance, information about social security, federal income tax, sources of revenue, and purposes of expenditures is provided.
5. It provides information needed for comparing school systems of communities and states.
6. It provides information that will facilitate and improve reliable reporting to the public sectors on the condition and progress of education.
7. It provides data that are necessary in long-range studies and research for the school system.
8. It provides information required by prospective investors in bonds issued by a school district or other governmental agency for the construction of school buildings.
9. It provides the necessary information for budget development, construction, and execution.
10. It provides information needed in dealing with teachers' organizations and labor unions when establishing salary schedules and negotiating wages.
11. It provides data for citizens' committees, survey teams, legislative hearings, and similar study groups concerned with education locally and statewide.

Although this list is not exhaustive, it is comprehensive enough to dispel the notion that the accounting process is strictly a bookkeeping operation that can be cast off with a shrug of ignorance by the administrator and delegated to a clerk who practices a mysterious craft on a number-crunching CPU. The accountant should normally be in a position to understand, analyze, and interpret financial data, but cannot and should not make final policy decisions. The accountant must present data clearly, however, so that all executives of the school system can analyze the facts and make their own interpretations as far as policy and administration are concerned.

Johnson and Kaplan reminded the business world that the accounting function can cease to

> *become a means to make managerial decisions to reduce costs and increase productivity, but rather to become an end in itself, serving its own cycles, aggregations and refinements. Accounting can become its own world in education as well, serving the district well in accurately creating required reporting forms and accounting procedures mandated by the state. On the other hand, the administrators may need different kinds of reports so they may not only exercise fiscal responsibility, but make sound educational decisions. The business manager carries a large measure of responsibility to see that the accountant's office shares in the responsibility to communicate, to suggest assistance in providing information in such a way that the school's "bottom line," student achievement, is improving.*[1]

Womble suggested that the monthly budget report listing revenues and expenses is insufficient for controlling for budget overruns. He suggests a form of *projected* financial reports that integrate information from enrollment projections, utilities histories, interest, and salaries until all the revenue and expenditures are included. For example, Womble suggests locating the June overruns in September *prior* to the end of the year rather than after the overrun has occurred.[2]

Administration and Supervision of the Accounting Function

While it is not expected that the steps for supervising accounting can be outlined in a few statements, the following are basic to proper supervision:

1. Each of the prescribed steps of accounting is completed in the recommended pattern and, where applicable, according to government mandates.
2. Various functions are assigned to workers or employees by means of a job description.
3. A record is kept of each separate operation.
4. Necessary comparisons and provings of independent records are undertaken at proper intervals.
5. All financial records are adequately protected against loss and damage.

6. The work of one employee serves as a check on the work of another.

7. All employees who handle any significant amount of cash are covered by a surety bond.

8. Cash receipts are so handled that each can be traced directly into a bank.

9. Special safety practices are used to insure secure check writing and recording.

10. Signed, serially numbered receipts are required when money passes from one person to another.

11. Two or more individuals must share the responsibility of disbursing money.

12. A good system of financial publicity is maintained.

Characteristics of Good School Accounting and Reporting

In a nonprofit institution such as a school system, good accounting practice must also include adherence to the school's educational mission.

1. All records must be preserved in a manner adequate for the purposes of the organization, and reports prepared therefrom must fit effectively into the framework locally, and at state and national levels.

2. Accuracy, consistency, simplicity, and completeness must be faithfully pursued.

3. Accounting processes must be adaptable to changes in a dynamic school system.

4. Explanations and interpretations must be clearly set forth to avoid misinterpretation of data.

5. Accounting and reporting are means to an end, not ends in themselves. There can be no justification for either unless it improves and enriches the educational system.

6. Schools are not operated for profit, nor are they operated to save money for the sake of savings itself. The accounting function has a basically different purpose for schools than it has for businesses and industry.

7. School district accounting must follow the dictates of state directives and statutes, with local adaptations being built on the minimal requirements established by the state.

8. School districts operating on a system of appropriations and authorizations from public funds must conscientiously keep the reporting process simple so that the use of funds may be easily interpreted to the public.

9. For the purpose of presenting an adequate and accurate state and national educational picture, a uniform core of terminology, classification, and reporting is necessary. Local adaptations should be built around this national core.

10. School district records should be audited periodically by competent and disinterested auditors and the results made available to the public.

11. Accounting processes should be consistent. Methods should be changed only when the advantages to be gained will be greater than the disadvantages which may arise if a new method causes loss of comparability between different chronological periods.

12. The form in which accounts are to be kept and the classifications to be used should be formally adopted by the board of education and included in its minutes.

13. An accounting system must be designed so that permanent records may be easily kept over a period of years and so that they will be available for research purposes.

14. The accounting function should be centralized as much as is possible.

Public School Fund Accounting

Public school fund accounting is concerned with the property of the school system and rights related to that property. Its objective is to provide all interested parties with reliable information concerning public school property and property rights and to indicate the effect of financial transactions on that property right. This objective is accomplished by combining the two components of a complete and effective accounting system, which are: (1) documenting, analyzing, recording, and summarizing budgeted and actual financial transactions of the public school district; and (2) providing adequate safeguards to preserve and conserve the property rights of the public school district through the use of both internal and external auditing procedures and standards.

Documenting, Analyzing, Recording, and Summarizing

Public school fund accounting should provide all desired and necessary fiscal information for the management of the school and for the public sectors. Every financial transaction affects property or rights to it. Therefore, every transaction must be considered in view of a consistent and systematic process. The systematic process requires that each financial transaction be properly (1) documented, (2) analyzed, (3) recorded, and (4) summarized.

Documenting

All financial transactions are initiated by documents that indicate the authority by which the transaction is entered. If these transactions are to be analyzed and recorded, complete information about each transaction must flow to the accounting department by written documentation to provide evidence that the transaction occurred and was properly authorized. It is to be emphasized that the accounting department does not initiate the document or entry. The power to initiate the basic document rests with the superintendent, principal, or other properly authorized administrative officer. Along with the authority to initiate a transaction goes the responsibility of incurring debt within the limits of the allotment or appropriation. Because the accounting department is charged with the responsibility of maintaining all financial records of a school district, it must be closely associated with those departments which collect revenue, incur debt, or preserve property.

Systematic process requires that each transaction be identified with a particular unit for both administrative and accounting purposes. The unit is referred to as a "fund." Customarily several funds exist in each school system, and each fund has certain property set aside for its restricted and limited use. For example, in the state of Indiana four funds are designated: general, debt service, capital projects, and transportation.

Analyzing

In addition to gathering basic documents evidencing completed public school fund transactions, the accounting department analyzes and classifies each transaction in terms of debits and credits to the accounts affected by the transaction in the fund. Debits and credits record increases or decreases in individual account balances.[3] Each fund may have accounts for assets, liabilities, fund balance, reserves, estimated and actual revenues, appropriations and appropriation expenditures, and encumbrances. The use of budgetary accounts within a fund makes it possible to restrict the purpose and the amount that may be expended. Budgetary accounts also reflect the department's adherence to legal provisions applicable to resources and expenditures of public funds, a most important matter to the school business manager, the board of education, and the community.

Recording and Summarizing

Summarizing is presenting the mass of financial data in a useful and meaningful manner. It is not the recording of the single financial transaction but the sum of all the transactions of a fund for a day, a week, a month, or a year that is significant in the operation of a school system. When the school business manager knows what changes take place within each of the public school funds and is able to make certain comparisons and analyses, he can exercise intelligent administrative control over the school funds as required by law.

Generally speaking, the need for a summary report of accounting data grows with the size and complexity of a school's business affairs. As business activities grow more varied and numerous, accounting descriptions and measurements also tend to increase, and managers, administrators, boards of education, and the community at large rely more on accounting data in making sound decisions.

A study of figures collected over a period of years can be particularly useful to the school administration if they are broken down into various categories of operational activity and then graphed, charted, or placed in some visual form which shows trends, so they may be easily used and understood by those not skilled in accounting. Comparable long-term finance figures when used in conjunction with services, enrollments, and number of persons employed will clarify financial forecasting and increase accuracy in estimating needs. The power of the computer to generate graphics directly from data have enhanced the financial reporter's capabilities to communicate effectively.

Costs when compared to function and services performed or benefits gained may show up waste and excessive expenditure. Although it is not the function of schools to make a profit or to save money for money's sake, it is the function of school administration to make possible economic and efficient school operation by getting 100 cents worth of service out of every dollar spent.

Another important need for summarizing and reporting is asserting itself. In a period when education is under the surveillance of the public because of rising costs, increasing pressures on tax rates, the knowledge explosion and rapidly changing societal patterns, the matter of summarizing information and reporting to the public is extremely important. Further complicating the accounting and reporting function is the increasing numbers of schools operating on some form of site-based decision making. Boards of education and school administrators are becoming increasingly aware of their obligation to keep their communities adequately informed. Thus, proper accountability is not only an imperative of good management but it is also necessary to keep and maintain proper public support for educational goals.

Providing Adequate Safeguards for Public School Property

Safeguards of public school property operate in the following areas:

1. By use of various funds, each existing as an independent accounting entity
2. By use of budgetary accounts which record estimated revenues and appropriations
3. By use of the encumbrance system to avoid the possibility of overexpenditure of an appropriation
4. By use of internal auditing procedures within the school district
5. By use of special examinations made by the state department of audit or finance
6. By use of external financial examinations by certified public accountants

Accounting for public school monies requires the use of various kinds of funds. By the creation of a fund, it is possible to break income and expenditures into simplified, understandable units and to restrict the purpose for which money may be spent and the amount that may be spent. This is, of course, important to the taxpayer. The use of funds also makes possible adherence to legal provisions applicable to specific resources and expenditures of public money. Each fund may have a number of possible sources of cash. In order to know how much cash is available or how much will be available for disbursement, how much tax remains receivable, etc., a separate account is used for each individual asset of a fund. It is necessary that each fund's financial position be shown, and that the results of its operation be reflected. This may be done in a variety of ways such as showing the balances of funds for the current year and comparing them with one or more past years. School administrators may wish to know the current status of funds and probable income and expenditures to date. Figure 6-1 (pp. 98–105) shows some entries in a sample appropriations report generated on a desktop computer in a superintendent's office. At a glance the superintendent can see the current status of a fund and percentage of the fund that has been spent or encumbered to date.

Use of Budgetary Accounts

In addition to recording actual transactions as they occur within a fund's assets, liabilities, reserves, fund balance, revenues, or expenditure accounts, the accounting system also maintains other accounts that reflect the budget. The budget concerns itself with estimated revenues and appropriations. Therefore, the budgetary account structure for both estimated revenues and appropriations must be consistent with the account structure for actual revenues and appropriation expenditures. These accounts serve as the most effective administrative tool available to school business administrators because they reflect

(text continues on page 106)

EXEMPLAR SCHOOL DISTRICT #1

Appropriations Report

FND	PROGRAM	OBJECT	CC	TITLE	NET APPROP	MTD EXPENDED	YTD EXPENDED	UNEXPENDED BAL	OUSTAND ENCUM	UNENCUM BAL	PERCENT ENCUMB
010	.00	.00	000	BANK MASTER FILE							
010	11100.00	110.01	000	ELEM SALARIES (CERTIFIED)	5,435,565.00	862,409.42	2,895,629.71	2,539,872.29		2,539,872.29	53.27
010	11100.00	110.02	000	ELEM SALARIES (CERTIFIED) SUBS	90,878.31	2,560.00	43,252.37	47,625.94		47,625.94	47.59
010	11100.00	120.00	000	ELEM SAL — PRIME TIME ASSIST	212,580.00	25,190.29	65,370.55	147,209.45		147,209.45	30.75
010	11100.00	120.01	000	ELEM SALARIES TEACH ASSIST N/C	173,327.00	21,635.75	103,395.42	69,931.50		69,931.58	59.65
010	11100.00	311.00	003	ELEM INSTRUCTION SERVICES CG	2,392.00			2,392.00		2,392.00	
010	11100.00	311.00	006	ELEM INSTRUCTION SERVICES WG	2,559.00			2,559.00		2,559.00	
010	11100.00	311.00	007	ELEM INSTRUCTION SERVICES — PG	2,600.00			2,600.00	2,600.00		100.00
010	11100.00	323.00	003	ELEM REPAIRS & MAINT CG	11,171.00	1,508.42	2,215.48	8,955.52		8,955.52	19.83
010	11100.00	323.00	004	ELEM REPAIRS & MAINT MG	3,120.00	1,159.51	1,310.51	1,809.49		1,809.49	42.00
010	11100.00	323.00	005	ELEM REPAIRS & MAINT NG	2,841.00	1,349.31	1,970.68	870.32		870.32	69.37

Fund	Account	Object	Sub	Description	Budget	Month	YTD Expended	Balance	Encumbrance	Available	%
010	11100.00	323.00	006	ELEM REPAIRS & MAINT WG	6,676.00	34.33	4,075.10	2,600.90	300.00	2,300.90	65.53
010	11100.00	323.00	007	ELEM REPAIRS & MAINT PG	17,600.00	5,378.58	7,360.06	10,299.94		10,299.94	41.68
010	11100.00	325.00	003	ELEMENTARY RENTALS — CG	11,232.00	1,145.00	7,843.50	3,388.50		3,388.50	69.83
010	11100.00	325.00	004	ELEMENTARY RENTALS — MG	10,400.00	1,230.37	7,767.30	2,632.70		2,632.70	74.69
010	11100.00	325.00	005	ELEMENTARY RENTALS — NG	10,345.00	1,238.73	8,064.69	2,280.31		2,280.31	77.96
010	11100.00	325.00	006	ELEMENTARY RENTALS — WG	6,510.00		2,879.98	3,630.02		3,630.02	44.24
010	11100.00	332.00	003	ELEM TRAVEL CG	613.00	106.37	660.34	47.34—		47.34—	107.72
010	11100.00	332.00	004	ELEM TRAVEL MG	728.00		921.44	193.94—		193.44—	126.57
010	11100.00	332.00	005	ELEM TRAVEL NG	624.00	22.00	143.92	480.08	180.00	300.08	51.91
010	11100.00	332.00	006	ELEM TRAVEL WG	800.00		125.47	674.53		674.53	15.68
010	11100.00	332.00	007	ELEM TRAVEL PG	572.00	103.59	586.29	14.29—		14.29—	102.50
010	11100.00	342.00	003	ELEM POSTAGE CG	700.00		580.00	120.00		120.00	82.86
010	11100.00	342.00	004	ELEM POSTAGE MG	728.00	290.00	290.00	438.00		438.00	39.84

Continued

FIGURE 6-1 A Partial Sample Appropriations Report.

EXEMPLAR SCHOOL DISTRICT #1

Appropriations Report

6/30/92
9 : 19 : 45

FND	PROGRAM	OBJECT	CC	TITLE	NET APPROP	MTD EXPENDED	YTD EXPENDED	UNEXPENDED BAL	OUSTAND ENCUM	UNENCUM BAL	PERCENT ENCUMB
010	11100.00	342.00	005	ELEM POSTAGE MG	728.00		578.00	150.00		150.00	79.40
010	11100.00	342.00	006	ELEM POSTAGE WG	676.00		290.00	386.00		386.00	42.90
010	11100.00	342.00	007	ELEM POSTAGE PG	832.00	290.00	580.00	252.00		252.00	69.71
010	11100.00	360.00	003	ELEM PRINTING & BINDING CG	416.00	201.60	234.17	181.83		181.83	56.29
010	11100.00	360.00	004	ELEM PRINTING & BINDING MG	624.00	201.60	234.17	389.83		389.83	37.53
010	11100.00	360.00	005	ELEM PRINTING & BINDING NG	1,040.00	201.60	312.17	727.83	1,463.50	735.67–	170.74
010	11100.00	360.00	006	ELEM PRINTING & BINDING WG	364.00	201.60	234.17	129.83		129.83	64.33
010	11100.00	360.00	007	ELEM PRINTING & BINDING PG	624.00	201.60	234.17	389.83	422.50	32.67–	105.24
010	11100.00	411.00	003	ELEM SUPPLIES CG	7,320.19		5,032.04	2,288.15	450.00	1,838.15	74.89
010	11100.00	411.00	004	ELEM SUPPLIES MG	11,646.50		4,348.44	7,298.06	2,317.59	4,980.47	57.24
010	11100.00	411.00	005	ELEM SUPPLIES NG							

010	11100.00	411.00	006 ELEM SUPPLIES WG 7,635.00	2,558.27	5,076.73	3,541.26	1,535.47	79.89
010	11100.00	411.00	007 ELEM SUPPLIES PG 9,712.86 762.18	3,500.29	6,212.57	3,782.63	2,429.94	74.98
010	11100.00	411.00	009 CENTRAL STORES SUPPLIES — CG 4,206.41	4,206.41	4,206.41			
010	11100.00	411.00	010 CENTRAL STORES SUPPLIES — MG 3,632.77	3,632.77	3,632.77			
010	11100.00	411.00	011 CENTRAL STORES — NG 3,993.51	3,993.51	3,933.51			
010	11100.00	411.00	012 CENTRAL STORES — WG 3,387.58	3,387.58	3,387.58			
010	11100.00	411.00	013 CENTRAL STORES — PG 2,413.68	2,413.68	2,413.68			
010	11100.00	540.00	003 ELEM CAP OUTLAY EQUIP CG 359,497.34 183,030.00 250,972.92	108,524.42	105,445.60	3,078.82	99.14	
010	11100.00	540.00	004 ELEM CAP OUTLAY EQUIP MG 31,715.10 912.00 3,189.70	28,525.42	59,467.10	30,941.70—	197.56	
010	11100.00	540.00	005 ELEM CAP OUTLAY EQUIP NG 127,425.15 2,340.13 124,643.61	2,781.54	3,370.00	588.46—	100.46	
010	11100.00	540.00	006 ELEM CAP OUTLAY EQUIP NG 94,634.50 1,220.00 50,707.54	43,926.96	122,547.75	78,620.79—	183.08	
010	11100.00	540.00	007 ELEM CAP OUTLAY EQUIP PG 142,273.45 6,791.95	135,481.50	137,315.00	1,833.50—	101.29	
010	11100.00	540.01	004 PROJECT 4R'S 1992 — MG					

FIGURE 6-1 *Continued*

Continued

EXEMPLAR SCHOOL DISTRICT #1

Appropriations Report

6/30/92
9 : 19 : 45

FND	PROGRAM	OBJECT	CC	TITLE / NET APPROP	MTD EXPENDED	YTD EXPENDED	UNEXPENDED BAL	OUSTAND ENCUM	UNENCUM BAL	PERCENT ENCUMB
010	11200.00	110.00	000	MS SALARIES (CERTIFIED) 1,734,634.00	258,887.06	904,987.58	829,646.42		829,646.42	52.17
010	11200.00	110.01	000	MS SALARIES (CERTIFIED) SUBS 30,900.00	2,124.24	26,675.67	4,224.33		4,224.33	86.33
010	11200.00	120.00	002	MIDDLE SCH SAL — N/C TEACH ASS 32,935.00	2,124.24	14,412.08	18,522.92		18,522.92	43.76
010	11200.00	314.00	002	NORTH CENTRAL — MS 4,000.00	200.00	225.00	3,775.00	300.00	3,475.00	13.13
010	11200.00	323.00	002	MIDDLE SCHOOL REPAIRS						
010	11200.00	325.00	002	MIDDLE SCHOOL RENTALS 10,076.00	818.75	4,168.75	5,907.25		5,907.25	41.37
010	11200.00	332.00	002	MIDDLE SCHOOL TRAVEL 2,982.50		1,825.32	1,157.18		1,157.18	61.20
010	11200.00	342.00	002	MIDDLE SCHOOL POSTAGE 2,371.00	145.00	1,640.00	731.00		731.00	69.17
010	11200.00	360.00	002	MS PRINTING & BINDING 3,342.08		254.65	3,087.43	675.00	2,412.43	27.82
010	11200.00	411.00	002	MIDDLE SCHOOL SUPPLIES 15,493.66	2,307.97	21,444.81	5,951.15–	2,979.59	8,930.74–	157.64
010	11200.00	411.00	015	CENTRAL STORE SUPPLIES — MS 3,787.67			3,787.67		3,787.67	

010	11200.00	540.00	002 MIDDLE SCHOOL CAP OUTLAY EQUIP	97,683.05	3,113.61	57,910.05	39,773.00	16,872.55	22,900.45	76.56
010	11300.00	110.00	000 HS SALARIES (CERTIFIED)	3,543,236.00	563,616.75	1,862,855.72	1,680,380.28		1,680,380.28	52.57
010	11300.00	110.01	000 HS SALARIES (CERTIFIED) SUBS	56,100.00	2,588.61	23,301.90	32,798.10		32,798.10	41.54
010	11300.00	120.00	001 HIGH SCH SAL N/C TEACHER ASSIS	55,263.00	3,523.31	23,338.17	31,924.83		31,924.83	42.23
010	11300.00	314.00	001 NORTH CENTRAL — HS	4,000.00			4,000.00		4,000.00	
010	11300.00	317.00	001 HIGH SCHOOL STATISTICAL SERVIC	2,600.00			2,600.00		2,600.00	
010	11300.00	323.00	001 HIGH SCHOOL REPAIRS & MAINT	33,524.90	1,612.68	13,712.12	19,812.78	847.43	18,965.35	43.43
010	11300.00	325.00	001 HIGH SCHOOL RENTALS	23,300.00		6,828.00	16,472.00	2,276.00	14,196.00	39.07
010	11300.00	332.00	001 HIGH SCHOOL TRAVEL	5,564.00	155.28	5,580.94	16.94–		16.94–	100.30
010	11300.00	342.00	001 HIGH SCHOOL POSTAGE	3,560.00	1,145.00	2,290.00	1,270.00		1,270.00	64.33
010	11300.00	360.00	001 HS PRINTING & BINDING	8,320.00		1,096.86	7,223.14	6,857.41	365.73	95.60
010	11300.00	411.00	001 HIGH SCHOOL SUPPLIES							
010	11300.00	411.00	014 CENTRAL STORES SUPPLIES — HS	14,497.80			14,497.80		14,497.80	

Continued

FIGURE 6-1 *Continued*

Appropriations Report

6/30/92
9 : 19 : 45

FND	PROGRAM	OBJECT	CC	TITLE	NET APPROP	MTD EXPENDED	YTD EXPENDED	UNEXPENDED BAL	OUSTAND ENCUM	UNENCUM BAL	PERCENT ENCUMB
010	11300.00	540.00	001	HIGH SCHOOL CAP OUTLAY EQUIP	192,787.32	30,687.38	54,837.59	137,949.73	95,336.46	42,613.27	77.90
010	11450.00	110.00	001	VOC ED HOME EC SALARIES (CERT)	86,294.00	13,244.83	45,772.60	40,521.40		40,521.40	53.04
010	11450.00	411.00	001	VOC ED HOME EC SUPPLIES	3,004.00	790.82	2,207.87	796.13		796.13	73.50
010	11450.00	540.00	001	VOC ED HOME EC CAP OUTLAY EQUI	2,381.39		1,643.05	738.34		738.34	69.00
010	11510.00	110.00	001	ICE SALARIES — CERT	25,504.00	5,848.50	15,039.00	10,465.00		10,465.00	58.97
010	11510.00	332.00	001	ICE TRAVEL	222.00	42.00	42.00	180.00		180.00	18.92
010	11590.00	411.00	000	APPLIED BIO/CHEM 92/93 SUPPLY					1,731.40	1,731.40–	
010	11590.00	540.00	00	APPLIED BIO/CHEM 92/93 — EQUIP		481.28	4,943.19	4,943.19–	10,123.13	15,066.32–	
010	11900.00	110.00	000	COMP TEST REMEDIATION-SAL-CERT	16,640.00			16,640.00		16,640.00	
010	12100.00	110.00	000	GIFTED & TALENTED SALARIES-CER	125,157.00	29,814.66	76,452.32	48,704.68		48,704.68	61.90

010	11200.00	332.00	000	GIFTED & TALENTED TRAVEL					
				1,016.00	28.80	623.02	392.98	392.98	61.32
010	12100.00	411.00	000	G & T SUPPLIES					
				676.00	100.00	576.00	576.00		14.79
010	12350.00	110.00	000	HOMEBOUND SALARIES (CERTIFIED)					
				5,650.00	1,393.00	5,356.12	293.88	293.88	94.80
010	12350.00	332.00	000	HOMEBOUND TRAVEL					
				200.00	53.89	53.89	146.11	146.11	26.95
010	14100.00	110.00	000	ELEM SUM SCH SALARIES (CERT)					
				92,328.00	28,689.36	29,126.36	63,201.64	63,201.64	31.55
010	14100.00	120.00	000	ELEM SUM SCH SALARIES N/C					
				1,300.00	988.85	988.85	311.15	311.15	76.07
010	14100.00	411.00	000	SUM SCH ELEM SUPPLIES					

FIGURE 6-1 *Continued*

adherence to legal and administrative provisions prescribed by law, the tax levy, an ordinance at the city level of administration, an appropriation at the state level, or by minutes of meetings of the board of education.

Budgetary accounts permit comparison of estimated revenues with actual revenues. On the revenue side, then, administrative steps can be taken to do all that is within the power of the board of education or superintendent to bring actual revenues up to estimated revenues. Appropriation expenditure accounts are compared with the appropriations authorized by the legislative body or the board of education. Constant reference to these accounts which compare budgeted amounts with actual amounts reveals variances between actual and budgeted revenues and expenditures. If a variance is unfavorable but controllable, and if attention is brought to the variance by administrative officers in sufficient time to allow appropriate action, losses which occur as a result of a controllable unfavorable variance can be minimized, thereby safeguarding public school funds.

Use of the Encumbrance System

Financial accounting normally involves the receipt of a given sum of money, the recording of approved expenditures on accounting forms, and the clearance of checks through banks. Many school districts, however, extend their accounting process back to an earlier point, for long before cash is actually disbursed, obligations may be incurred within a fund. In other words, a portion of a fund may be promised or encumbered without actually disbursing it at that specific time. Encumbrances are those obligations in the form of purchase orders, contracts, or salary commitments which are chargeable to an appropriation and for which a part of the appropriation is reserved. An encumbrance is recorded when preliminary negotiations are initiated to incur a debt. When a debt is actually created, the encumbrancing entry is revised and the actual liability is recorded or the debt paid. Therefore, as good fiscal policy, prior to the final issuance of a document creating a liability on the part of a public school fund, the document is processed through the accounting department or budget officer's office to determine from the accounts whether unobligated funds are available for the purpose stated on the document.

By comparison of appropriations with expenditures plus encumbrances, uncommitted balances of appropriations are determined. The unobligated balance of an appropriation is the amount most important to the school superintendent or other administrative officer and serves as a basis for a decision to incur or to refrain from incurring additional obligations on the part of the school district. Comparison of proposed expenditures with unobligated appropriations prior to incurring a debt will avoid overexpenditure of appropriations, an act which if committed is often beyond the authority granted by the board of education, or even illegal if it puts the school district into a deficit situation at the end of the fiscal year.

Cautions should be taken to safeguard fund balances especially when individual schools make their own fiscal decisions and when obligations are made by telephone and electronic communications. A failsafe system needs to be installed to reduce or eliminate encumbrance problems.

Accounting Department in Relation to Other Departments

Although the accounting department is called on to assist in preparing basic documents necessary to substantiate financial transactions, to put the budget into final form, and to indicate the availability of unobligated appropriations, it must be remembered that the accounting department does not and should not have the power to initiate documents that incur debt. That power is vested in the school board or superintendent or other administrative officer specifically authorized to do a particular part of the school district's job. Even though the final budget is summarized and prepared in the accounting department, this department does not have power to direct the educational program. That power is vested in professional educators and educational administrators. However, in order that financial transactions may be recorded, all documents which evidence financial transactions must be processed in the accounting department.

The use of various funds which constitute separate legal, administrative, and accounting operations is highly technical. Each fund has its own group of accounts which are self-balancing as a result of the application of appropriate accounting principles. Thus, each fund has its own set of financial statements to reflect its position and the results of its operation. When financial statements are prepared for each fund, they are then combined to give a full and complete financial report on the overall operation of the school district.

Administration of the accounting and auditing function of a public school system requires an understanding of the background and the foundation on which each fund's financial statements came into existence. Adherence to generally accepted business methods and procedures creates public confidence in school business management. Through a knowledge of what the employees of the accounting department are doing and why, and through a knowledge of how financial statements come into existence, school administrators may take efficient and effective action when faced with the practical problems involved in carrying out the policies established by the board of education.

There is a basic communications requirement on the part of all, especially given the "satellite" purchasing and accounting occurring in the individual schools. The school business manager in the site-based management environment finds a much greater demand for frequent communications and report generation than ever before.[4] Communications technology helps, but identifying and even anticipating needs in order to provide clear direction as well as the desire to respond to the communications received are as important as the "E" mail or other mechanics of quick communications.

Maintaining an adequate accounting system for each fund and keeping records available for public inspection through orderly and well-organized periodic examinations provide the best evidence that the board of education, superintendent, and school business manager have complied with the various federal, state, and local laws that govern the handling of money and that these public officials are fulfilling the school system's objectives.

Public School Funds

Traditionally a budget, indicating the purposes and objects for which money is needed, is prepared prior to the actual appropriation of the money. When the amount necessary for the operation of the school district is known, it is compared with estimated revenues. Estimated revenues must equal or exceed estimated expenditures; otherwise a deficit will occur. The appropriation act by the board of education or by the governmental unit appropriating money to a school district gives authority to the administrative officers of the school district to expend money within the limits of the appropriations for specified purposes. Since money available through taxation is limited in amount, and in order best to serve the school system, its use is restricted. Restrictions are placed by the appropriation act, and the budget's execution is reflected in financial statements prepared from the accounts of each separate fund of the school system. As a result, the fund system of accounting has been developed for use in the operation of public enterprises, such as schools, colleges, universities, hospitals, and libraries, and of city, county, state, and federal governments.

Tidwell cited the Association of School Business Officials (ASBO) definition of a fund:

> [A fund is] an independent fiscal and accounting entity with a self-balancing set of accounts. These accounts record all assets and financial resources together with all related liabilities, encumbrances (or commitments), reserves, and equities which are segregated for the purpose of carrying on specific activities or attaining certain objectives in accordance with special regulations, restrictions, or limitations.[5]

Money is not the only property or resource that a fund may have. Therefore, it is necessary to account for a fund's other property as well as for its money. Property other than cash is as important to the operation of a school system as cash itself, and this property must be preserved, conserved, and safeguarded. To accomplish this, each fund is a separate and independent accounting administrative entity and has sufficient accounts to reflect the amount and nature of each of its assets, liabilities, reserves, fund balances, estimated and actual revenues, appropriations, and appropriation expenditures. Only those accounts necessary for the specific fund are used.

Classification of the Various Kinds of Funds

Each fund is a separate entity and the nature of each fund may vary according to state, county, city, federal, or school district rule, regulation, or law. However, the accounting principles and procedures which apply to the various accounts of each fund are uniform and it is on this concept that uniformity is possible in accounting for public school funds.

All public school funds may be classified under one of the following heads: ownership, expendable or nonexpendable, purpose, source of revenue.

Classification by Ownership

Public school funds may be either public funds or trust funds. *Public funds* include those resources which are available for expenditure for general school system purposes and objectives. *Trust funds* include those resources which arise from public or private sources, the benefits of which are for specified individuals or groups or are held subject to certain restrictions. Examples of trust funds are pension funds, withholding taxes, and income from endowments.

Classification by Expendability

Funds may be classified by expendability when their entire resources or assets may be used in carrying out the purposes for which the fund was created. The most common type of expendable fund in the field of public school administration is the *general fund.* However, expendable funds also include *bond funds,* frequently referred to as capital projects or building funds, or funds arising from grants, gifts, and bequests, when the assets may be consumed. Nonexpendable funds are those whose resources when originally transferred to it are represented by a permanent fund balance, principal, or capital account. This account, whatever the title, must be maintained intact and cannot be reduced or otherwise depleted. In order to retain its nonexpendable nature, such a fund has to be reimbursed for services rendered. Examples of nonexpendable funds are working-capital funds, such as central warehouse, central printing plant, and central building and grounds department. Endowment funds are often created; the principal amount of these is nonexpendable but income from them may be expendable.

Classification by Purpose

Public school funds may be classified as revenue funds, working capital funds, trust and agency funds, bond funds, sinking funds, general fixed assets group of accounts, or general bonded debt and interest group of accounts. This classification implies that each kind of fund has a specific purpose; therefore, each is discussed separately.

Revenue Funds.   Revenue funds include those arising from revenue and are related to the current operation and activities of the public school district. Generally, revenue funds are governed by a budget. The most common type of revenue fund in use is the *general fund.* The general fund may be referred to by many different titles; however, each school district has a fund which may be so classified. This is the fund from which the regular day-to-day operations of a school district are conducted. As the scope and methods of its operation are understood, the relationship and functioning of the other funds which may be needed in a school district's operations become clear. This fund receives all cash, whether from a revenue source or a nonrevenue source, which is not required by law or contractual agreement to be placed in a special fund. This, then, is the most important of public school funds, for it is the central one, and its purpose is to carry on the current operation of the school district.

Special revenue funds are those created for specific purposes such as transportation or for purposes other than general operation of the school district. Examples of special revenue funds are those which may receive revenue from such sources as class plays, athletic events, cafeterias, and sale of school newspapers. To be a special revenue fund, however, the purposes for which revenues may be expended must be specifically designated, otherwise revenues would go into the general fund for regular school operating purposes. Therefore, when revenues from these special sources are restricted as to use, such funds are referred to as special revenue funds. To illustrate, the proceeds from athletic events may be restricted to paying the costs of operating the event, with the remainder, if any, to be used for purchase of additional athletic equipment, property improvement, and additional cafeteria facilities. In the state of Indiana, funds generated by sales to students must be spent toward student activities or welfare. In these cases, the money should not be used for general operation of the school system.

Activity Fund Accounting.   This fund deserves special consideration because it is so often neglected and poorly managed. We are speaking in particular of monies derived from extra class fees, athletic contests, plays, concerts, sales, and special programs of all kinds. From these sources even in a small school many thousands of dollars may be handled each year, and in the large school system the money easily reaches six digits and beyond.

The weight of legal opinion is that monies collected as a part of school activities must be considered public money and therefore, as decided in the German Township case, "the proceeds of these activities belong to the board of school directors and must be accounted for in the same manner that other funds of the school district are accounted for."[6] As far as the courts are concerned, the fund is public in nature if it is produced through public facilities, by public employees as a part of public services for which they are employed.[7] In essence, boards of education in all school districts are required to identify and control the funds of any school-approved and school-administered student organization or school service agency.

While these funds are without question under the jurisdiction of the board of education they may be handled in a manner slightly different from that in which ordinary school funds are handled. An effort should be made to keep these funds as close as possible to the students, providing learning situations for them and imparting to them a personal concern and feeling of responsibility for the proper control of money.

The centralized fund accounting system in which a specific person, often known as the activity fund manager, does the accounting of activity funds for all schools of the district has proved to be a success. The centralization process assures uniformity of procedure and security, and at the same time facilitates reporting, aids in postauditing, and provides uniform data for planning and administrative purposes. The activity fund manager is responsible only for financial control and serves as the representative or arm of the business office and therefore the board of education. The management of the various activities rests with the student officers and faculty advisors.

The school business manager through appropriate authorization from the superintendent and by policies adopted by the school board should fix the responsibilities for the administration of activity funds. The ASBO suggested the following as responsibilities of the principal and sponsors[8]:

> Principal—*The principal or other authorized administrator shall be responsible for the approval of requisitions for the expenditure of funds, and any other duties as assigned by the superintendent of the school district.*
>
> Advisors/Sponsors—*The duties and responsibilities of the advisor/sponsor should consist of the following:*
> (a) *Preparing annual budgets and purpose clauses of the activity group;*
> (b) *Supervising the activities of the activity group, including preparation of fund-raising potentials and proofs of cash and*
> (c) *Any other duties as assigned by the proper administrative authority.*

Working Capital Funds. These funds are created to provide a specific type of service for various departments within the school district, and each working capital fund, regardless of title, is self-supporting because it is reimbursed for the cost of services performed. Examples of working capital funds found useful in the operation of public school districts are the central purchasing and warehousing fund, the central building and grounds fund, and the school's bookstore. Capital with which such a fund operates is transferred to the working capital fund by special appropriation and the amount of the capital must be retained intact. The working capital fund is not to operate at an amount of revenue in excess of expenditures, but adequate records are required in order to compute costs of services rendered and to permit reimbursement for these services.

Trust and Agency Funds. Trust and agency funds are created to account for cash or other resources held by a school system as a trustee or as an agent. These funds may be either expendable or nonexpendable. For example, endowments generally are handled as trust funds, the principal amount of which, according to the terms of the trust agreement, must be retained intact. However, income earned from investments or endowment funds may, under the terms of agreement, be placed in an expendable trust fund to be used for the purposes specified. If the resources of a fund can be depleted, it is said to be an expendable fund.

Bond Funds. Bond funds are created to account for all transactions related to authorizing the issue of bonds and accounting for the proceeds from the sale of bonds. Generally, bonds are issued by a school district for major capital outlays such as facilities construction and equipment. Therefore, bond funds are frequently referred to as "building funds." The liability of the school district is accounted for through a group of accounts referred to as the "general bonded debt and interest group of accounts." A separate bond fund is required for each bond issue. This is necessary because a bond issue is authorized for specific purposes and its proceeds are restricted. Bond funds can be created when bonds are issued for purposes other than facility construction, such as for absorbing operating deficits, refunding maturing bond issues, or establishing capital for a working capital fund where permitted by the state.

The continuing use of a term building fund may imply a combination of sources for cash which may be expended for facility construction. Such a fund may receive money from the sale of bonds issued for that purpose plus money from a capital projects fund using state monies. Under these circumstances, it is best to establish a separate fund which will account for the use of the money from these two sources. If capital outlays are to be made for construction from current revenues alone, however, no separate fund is necessary, since the general fund can handle such transactions adequately through its expenditure accounts under the classification of "capital outlay," or in a separate fund of capital projects if required to be kept separate from the general fund.

Property acquired by the use of money provided through a bond fund or a building fund continues to be accounted for in a group of accounts known as the "general fixed assets group of accounts." This group of accounts is discussed later in the chapter.

Bond Sinking Funds. Bond sinking funds are useful to school business managers, superintendents, and boards of education because they reflect required, as well as actual, progress made toward accumulating sufficient money with which maturing bond issues can be properly retired. This type of fund is particularly useful when money is being raised through taxation and other sources over a period of years. Annual contributions are computed as a part of the budget, and annual earnings required from investment of resources of the fund are computed. Comparison of required contributions and required earnings with actual contributions and actual earnings permits close administrative supervision of bond sinking funds and assures adequate time during which accumulations of money may be made in order to retire outstanding issues. Separate bond sinking funds have the advantage of a separate and distinct accounting; they also help to avoid oversight of bond retirement provisions in the budget. One school system reported a large deficit because of its failure to consider bond interest as a required expenditure from current revenues in its budget.

General Fixed Assets Group of Accounts. Proper safeguards require permanent records of each fixed asset owned by the school district. This group of accounts, kept on a cost basis, shows the kind of assets owned, the amounts and sources of investment in those assets, and the location and age of each asset; it also provides proper control over proceeds from the sale of or exchange of each and every asset. Therefore, this group of accounts can serve as a most effective tool of administration, particularly in planning adequate annual expenditures in the budget for maintenance, repairs, upkeep, replacements, retirement of assets, etc.

Without the use of a set of accounts for general fixed assets, a public school district may lose complete control, possession, and accountability of its assets. Equally important to taxpayers is appropriate control over cash or other assets acquired when a fixed asset is sold or exchanged. Maintenance of perpetual fixed assets accounts does incur additional operating expense, but the interests of the taxpayer and the board of education are best safeguarded when adequate accounting controls for these accounts are maintained.

General Long-Term Debt and Interest Group Accounts. A separate group of accounts is recommended in order to provide adequate administrative controls for the total general bonded debt and interest obligations of the public school district. Generally, bonds are retired from amounts accumulated in sinking funds established for that purpose. Current interest is paid from the general fund. However, the general fund carries no accounts nor do sinking funds or bond funds carry accounts which show the school district's indebtedness due to outstanding bonds and indebtedness now and in the future due to interest on bonds outstanding. This part of the accounting job is accomplished by the general bonded debt and interest group of accounts. These accounts show each year's amount to be provided for payment of principal and interest. In addition, these accounts show the amount already provided in sinking funds to offset that liability for which funds for retirement have been provided. This group of accounts best gives administrative control over the present status of all bond programs and can serve as a basis for forecasting future construction and bonding programs under existing or contemplated bonded debt limitations.

Determining the Number of Funds to Be Used

Consistent terminology for the funds selected may be found by consulting the ASBO resources and the various state departments of education. The terminology should be in congruence with other governmental agencies given that the Governmental Accounting Standards Board (GASB) sets the requirements for accounting in the public sector.

The number of funds to be used by a school district may be prescribed by state statute, rule, or regulation or by policy established by the board of education. Accounting for compensated absences is an example of recent changes in accounting requirements. The GASB standards note the types of absences and which funds should be used to account for the obligations incurred for employees.[9] Generally accepted accounting principles have been established which account for each fund under the major classifications required by the GASB.[10] Only those funds called for either by legal provisions or by sound business judgment should be used. An example of making sound business judgments may be related to the idea of depreciation accounting. Although it will generate costs, depreciation accounting may be "the first step in a move towards developing a system that will show a truer economic measurement of the use of physical plant assets."[11] The use of depreciation accounting so that comparisons can be made over time to reduce costs may provide better educational facilities and wiser use of taxpayers' dollars for student generations to come.

Because of local circumstances, funds of various kinds must be adapted to the needs of the particular school district. When these funds are in operation, a type of financial administrative procedure and control is developed that is quite different from that used in commercial accounting. School accounting and reporting must be geared to one end—the continuous improvement of the total educational program so that student achievement is maximized for all students.

Cash Management

Unlike the monthly paycheck and the rent, the income and payments due dates for a school district do not come at the end or beginning of each month. Payments from the state, whether received annually or quarterly, sometimes are delayed during recessions when the revenues are not forthcoming as anticipated. Expenditures in salaries are easy to anticipate. A drastic jump in oil prices may quickly affect utilities, transportation, food costs, travel budgets, and a number of other budget lines. The peaks of income do not match the peaks of expenditures. The cash manager will need to plot income and expenditure patterns to determine how much cash will be on hand for what periods of time. Once this is done, one must decide how to safely maximize returns on the available cash. Emphasis is on the word "safely" because no one wants to lose the taxpayers' money by a bad investment. On the other hand, neither do we wish to get poor returns on the investments made.

Flynn[12] suggested certificates of deposit for most small school districts with relatively small amounts to invest for short periods of time. He also suggested the following possibilities given time and sufficient amounts available:

Repurchase agreements
State investment pools
Brokerage money market funds
Banker acceptances and commercial paper

The cash manager can find a number of opportunities and given good advice and the ability to act on it can turn those opportunities into educational dividends. A number of formulas may be developed to assist in the decisions regarding how to optimize investment opportunities.[13]

Auditing Procedures

Internal Auditing

The term "audit" when applied to public school funds refers to that accounting procedure used to determine whether legal and administrative provisions applicable to the fund are being followed and whether public school property and funds are being properly safeguarded through the use of an effective and efficient system of internal control. Three types of audits related to public school funds are in general use today. The first kind of audit may be conducted by technically trained and experienced persons who are regular employees of the school district. Because this kind of audit is conducted by the school district's own employees, it is referred to as an "internal audit." Internal auditing is a part of an effective system of internal control and has as one of its objectives the prevention of improper administration of funds caused by intentional or unintentional error at the time transactions occur or as they are being recorded. This type of audit, however, does not guarantee elimination of fraud, because collusion can exist between employees and losses can continue to occur.

Internal auditing, of necessity, concerns itself with basic documents which give evidence of the business transaction. Therefore, a primary function of the internal auditing procedure is to secure adequate documentary evidence for each transaction. The objectives of internal auditing may be summarized as follows:

1. To determine that all financial transactions for each fund of the public school district have been recorded.

2. To determine that the recording of documents is verified to the greatest practical extent by a person other than the one recording it. This is done by requiring approval by someone besides the person recording the transaction.

3. To verify prices, quantities, and receipt of goods or services, and to verify mathematical accuracy in the case of extensions, footings, and discounts.

4. To provide safeguards against theft of physical property and to assure that property taken off the premises of the school district is removed by proper authority and under sufficient control to safeguard its return.

5. To determine that all transactions recorded are entered in the proper accounts of the appropriate public school fund.

6. To determine that balances of each fund's accounts are correctly computed.

7. To provide proper clerical control over journals, registers, summaries, ledgers, statements, and reports.

While 70 percent of school districts in 1988 did not utilize internal auditing,[14] the decision may be a function of size and complexity rather than not recognizing the need for the activity. Districts using internal audits averaged over 18,000 students and over $100 million in general fund budgets. Although the internal audit is a desirable practice, the external audit may be a more practical option for the small school district.

Examinations by the State Department of Audit, Finance, or Accounts

The second type of audit frequently used in cases concerning public school funds is examination of accounts by the state department of audit or finance. The objective, generally, is to determine that the appropriations made by the state to the public school district are being handled under the provisions prescribed by state laws. However, an examination of expenditures of state money only would be insufficient and at times impossible because of the mingling of local and state money; therefore, in a proper state audit all the school district's funds must be examined thoroughly and in accordance with generally accepted auditing standards, including enterprise funds and their expenditures.

Because of the vast number of other agencies which are subject to periodic examination by the state, states find it increasingly necessary to restrict the scope of examination or the frequency of the examinations. If the inspections do not bring to school business administrators the kind of assistance that will help them do a better job with the accounting function, school administrators may need to seek additional assistance. Although it is important to be in compliance with mandated procedures, leaders need more from the accounting-reporting process than affirmation that the school district is in compliance with state procedures.

Independent Audits

The third type of audit is an examination of the financial statements and supporting records of the school district by outside, independent certified public accountants. Certified public accountants are technically trained and licensed by the individual state to practice accountancy as a profession under its laws. Reports of examination, frequently referred to as "audit reports," contain professional opinions and comments resulting from analysis of the accounting system of the school district and about the way it is managed and implemented. An independent audit has many advantages over that made by employees of the school district or by the state department of audit or finance, for the professional opinion is free of the employer-employee relationship, which can destroy the independent judgment of the examiner. If the accountant finds irregularities, they are brought to the attention of the school administrative officers, and recommendations can be made to correct them. Such services can be provided at the time requested by the board of education, and the scope of the examination can be extended to satisfy the needs of the individual case. This type of examination best serves the board of education and the community because of its timeliness and adaptability to each particular school district.

A brief word of caution might be inserted at this juncture. School and institutional accounting differs from accounting in a profit-making organization. It must not be expected that any auditing firm will be able to give the most helpful professional service. As much care must be used in selecting an auditing firm as in selecting an architect.[15] There have been occurrences when an auditor unfamiliar with school accounting and its basic purpose have thrown the school administration into a turmoil because his final report was based on the profit-and-loss concept found in business and industry.

Summary

Presentation of financial position and results of operation of one of the funds of the public school district will not reflect the entire picture of the school system. Each fund's financial statements have to be presented and combined with the financial statements of each of the other funds maintained if complete financial control is to be obtained in the school district. A system of accounting which failed to report the financial position or the results of operation of any one of these public school accounting funds would be inadequate for the present needs of school administrators, business managers, superintendents, boards of education, and taxpayers. Wise management decisions are as important in the effective and efficient operation of our educational system as in the operation of our industrial system in America. Accounting for public school funds provides the foundation on which wise management decisions and policies can be made.

This chapter on the administration of the accounting and auditing functions and kinds of public school funds has not attempted to explain accounting procedures in detail, nor has it been possible to present completely the basis of accounting for public school funds. However, it has attempted to present in a concise way the area of technical understanding necessary if a school business administrator is to be in a position to successfully supervise the accounting and auditing functions of present-day public school business offices.

For Further Thought

1. What is the difference between accounting and bookkeeping?

2. Review various accounting references and then set up a list of criteria which could be used in rating or evaluating a school system's accounting process.

3. What is the difference between an encumbrance and an expenditure?

4. Study the accounting manual for your state and compare its list of funds, account numbers, and titles with the manual published by the Governmental Accounting Standards Board.

5. Are the student activity funds adequately controlled in your state? Are all funds generated by students required to be expended for students?

6. How does accounting for a business enterprise differ from accounting for public school system? What is a school's profit line?

7. Investigate several school districts to determine the accounting hardware and software in use. Determine the strengths and weaknesses of each. If possible, determine costs connected with the initial startup of the program and its operation.

8. What steps might be taken to help the staff in the accounting office feel part of the educational team effort of the schools?

Endnotes

1. H. Thomas Johnson and Robert S. Kaplan, *Relevance Lost: The Rise and Fall of Management Accounting* (Boston: Harvard Business School Press, 1987).

2. A. G. Womble, Jr., "Predict Expenses, and Nip Budget Overruns in the Bud," *The Executive Educator* (October 1987): 30–31.

3. The reader is encouraged to read an explanation of debits and credits in Sam B. Tidwell, *Financial and Managerial Accounting for Elementary and Secondary Schools* (Reston, Va.: Research Corporation, Association of School Business Officials, 1985), pp. 47–56.

4. Thelbert L. Drake and Ronald M. Hall, "Business Managers Must Adapt to Site-Based Management," ASBO Accents, 11, No.8, (August, 1991): 1.

5. Tidwell, Financial and Managerial Accounting, p. 18.

6. In re German Township School Directors, 46 S. and C. 562 (1942).

7. *Petition of Auditors of Hatfield Township School District,* 161 Pa. Sup. Ct. 388, 54 A.2d 833 (1947).

8. Association of School Business Officials, *Guidelines to Student Activity Fund Accounting* (Reston, Va.: ASBO, 1986), p. 8.

9. For further details see Rita H. Cheng and Robert B. Yahr, "The Basics of School District Accounting: How They'll Change in the 1990's," *School Business Affairs* 56, No. 10 (October 1990): 11–23.

10. In June 1991 the Governmental Accounting Standards Board (GASB) approved and issued "Statement 14," which will affect reporting for 1993 or FY 1993–94. The reader is encouraged to study this statement regarding financial reporting by governmental agencies.

11. Louis R. Morrell, "Depreciation Accounting: Friend or Foe?," *NACUBO Business Officer* (October 1988): 42.

12. Jeffrey B. Flynn, "Cash Management and the Small School District," *School Business Affairs* (January 1990): 43–44

13. For a discussion of formulas applicable to investment decision making the reader may wish to read Guilbert C. Hentschke's models for cash management in *School Business Administration* (Berkeley,

Calif.: McCutchan Publishing Corporation, 1986), pp. 240–244.

14. Charles E. Cuzzetto and Daniel D. Moran, "School's Still Out in Internal Auditing," *School Business Affairs* 54, No. 10 (October 1988): 38.

15. See Richard Seidell, "Selecting an Independent Auditor," *School Business Affairs* 54, No. 10 (October 1988): 43–45.

Chapter 7

Purchasing

A listing of the supplies, equipment, and facilities needed to operate a school district looks like the items needed for operating a city or town. Pencils to playground equipment, buses, buildings, paper clips, brooms, computers, and tons of paper add up to large purchases and spending, approximating 20 to 25 percent of the budget. Nationally, school purchases represent billions of dollars and opportunities to lose or to save millions of dollars each year depending on the purchase practices employed. As discussed in more detail later in the chapter, the school business manager has an opportunity to exert leadership in the purchasing function. To obtain an excellent price for a quality item is poor practice if the item is not used. It is a false economy to acquire materials that do not work well with other components of the operation. Often the "people factor" is the key to wise purchasing practices. The purchasing agent's knowledge of the operation, whether instructional practice or transportation is concerned, will affect the decisions regarding the purchasing process.

Legal Bases for the Purchasing Function

Purchasing is regulated by state law, court decisions, and local school board policy. All states have deemed it necessary to pass legislation controlling certain aspects of purchasing. The most common are (1) laws that make it mandatory that purchases above a certain amount be submitted for bids and (2) laws that prohibit board members and executives of the school from selling goods to the school district in which they are employed or from receiving personal rebates on goods purchased for the district.

All states have laws that regulate purchasing to some extent. The regulations may limit the amount of the purchases allowable without going through formal bidding processes. Many school business officials have viewed formal bidding regulations as distasteful because it exacts time from an already heavy load. They also realize it is a safeguard that must be lived with.

Only under certain contingency circumstances specified by law can the purchasing agency negotiate terms and prices. The major source of protection and flexibility comes under the proviso that no contract will be awarded on bids "contrary to public interest." The law may be worded that advertising for bids shall be made in "sufficient time," that specifications and invitations to bid shall permit "full and free competition," and that all bids shall be publicly opened at a specified time and place.

In a sense these state and federal laws put purchasing on a higher professional plane. Instead of resisting the laws and trying to get around them, school business officials would be wise to develop model legislation which would correct weaknesses and strengthen certain aspects of purchasing in which technical professional judgment is necessary. Many of the disadvantages of bidding legislation could thereby be eliminated and the good features could be maintained. Bidding restrictions should not fence in a purchasing agent. They should be flexible enough so that the school business manager can exercise professional judgment and expertise.

While bidding is at its best when there is a surplus of goods and at its worst when there is a scarcity of goods, laws can be devised which are flexible enough to allow for these economic fluctuations so that the advantages of bidding are maximized and the disadvantages are minimized. For example, a clause might be inserted which states that "in the event the submitted bids on items are higher than the prevailing market price the local board of education may declare all bids void and purchase on a negotiation basis." The federal government's "saving" clause mentioned above also provides flexibility; it states that "no contract will be awarded on bids contrary to public interest."

The Courts and Purchasing

Because of its very nature, purchasing has attracted far more than its share of litigation. Although few cases have gone up to the higher courts, they have been frequent enough at the local and regional levels to serve as a warning to all schools that this is an area of operation scrutinized carefully in all its stages by private business and industry. The question, "What are the limitations on purchasing that are placed on a board of education?" has been answered in this way: "Supplies and equipment *essential* to effect operation of the schools may be purchased by local boards. Other items may not be purchased in the absence of statutes so permitting. The line between these two categories, however, cannot be drawn clearly, and frequently the courts must resolve controversies."[1]

Courts have consistently ruled, even in the absence of prohibiting statutes, that contracts negotiated for the school district in which school administrators and board members have a personal financial interest are illegal. In most questionable situations and when public monies might be subject to misuse for private gain, the courts scrutinize the case with the greatest intensity. A quotation from a court decision in Pennsylvania as far back as 1865 exemplifies the philosophy of the courts in this regard:

> *The older we grow as a people the more systematized and difficult of detection do the schemes become for plundering the public; and among them all, none are more prominent or successful than those which concern contracts and jobs. The very elections of the people are sometimes guided and controlled by the unseen*

hands of rapacity. Fraudulent claims, fraudulent prices, fraudulent receipts, and fraudulent practices, are often winked at or shared in by officials in disregard of honor, honesty, and oaths.[2]

Numerous cases in our federal government from the Teapot Dome scandals right up to recent savings and loan cases have created national controversy. Out of these has come a definition of the public attitude: "There must be no hint of personal monetary gain as a result of a public official's acts while performing his job, or the integrity and honor of this official may be questioned."

In accepting and deciding on bids on certain items to be purchased or constructed, boards of education can expect occasional litigation from unsuccessful bidders, especially when statutes are flexible and allow some judgment and discretion by the school board. Roe cited Dean R. R. Hamilton, College of Law, University of Wyoming, who had reviewed a large number of cases involving litigation over bidding procedures and arrived at some general conclusions which might be useful to boards of education and administrators[3]:

1. *Statutory "lowest responsible bidder" requirements are not construed strictly by the courts. Boards have wide discretion under them.*
2. *Boards are not required to specify the grounds upon which their decision of lack of responsibility of bidders is based.*
3. *Proposed cash discounts may not legally be taken into account in determining the lowest bidder.*
4. *If there is reason to suspect a mistake in a bid, and such a mistake exists, it may not legally be accepted by the board.*
5. *Goods or services furnished to districts* without *compliance with competitive bid statutes may not be legally paid for by the district. Of course, if the goods can be* returned *the district must return them.*

To summarize briefly the philosophy of the courts in considering the numerous cases coming before them, we may say that their major concern is the protection of the public. They show little sympathy in situations where collusion is evident, personal gain suspected, or intent of the law evaded. On the other hand, unless proven guilty of collusion, a public official must be assumed to be acting in good faith and according to his best judgment in making any public decision.

A New York court may be quoted in this regard: "It is the well settled law of this state that in the absence of fraud, corruption, or abuse of discretion, the judgment or discretion of the proper officials will not be disturbed by the courts."[4]

School Board Policy

The state laws, the court decisions, and the administrative rulings of the state department of education provide the general overall framework for purchasing procedures.

Boards of education must perform the purchasing procedures in a manner prescribed by law. There is no alternative. Permissive legislation does, however, give school boards wide discretion in the way they may operate within the law. Local school boards must then write policies and procedures which provide for the most intelligent application of these laws and rulings according to local needs and circumstances.

Clearly stated, carefully considered policies show the public that there is nothing to hide in one of the most sensitive areas of operation in the public schools. Policy statements should present the best judgment and thinking of the school board about problems which might become critical issues and result in emotional conflicts. They should seek to eliminate petty politics, "favor doing," and patronage. They should be clear-cut guides which translate laws into action.

School board policy in regard to purchasing should include the following:

1. An interpretation or summary of state statutes affecting purchasing.
2. An interpretation or summary of state court cases having implications for local purchasing.
3. A summary of administrative rulings on purchasing by state boards of education or state departments of education.
4. A statement on authority and responsibility in purchasing for the school district.
5. A designation of the purchasing agent for the school district.
6. An outline of steps for approval and disapproval of purchases, designating different situations according to amount and type of purchase.
7. A clarification of local purchasing practices.
8. A statement clarifying how those who use materials and equipment shall work with the purchasing agent in selecting supplies and equipment.

Guidelines for School Policies on Purchasing

The following guidelines will help school district administrators purchase wisely, with the educational plan and the best interests of each child in mind.

1. The educational welfare of the child should be a foremost consideration when making any purchase.
2. Purchasing should be a centralized function of the school. Even when provisions are made for site initiatives, the central office should be involved either by electronic reporting or actually processing the paperwork.
3. Those who use materials should have a decision in the selection of materials. Variations on degrees of freedom can occur especially in school districts using site-based management.
4. Supplies and equipment must be so handled that there are checks and balances at each step of supply administration starting from their selection to the time they are used up or become obsolete.
5. Purchasing should be so organized that the user will have the right quantity and quality of equipment at the appropriate time.

6. There should be sufficient flexibility in the purchasing program to allow for experimental programs, unusual expansions, changes in curricula, and emergencies.

7. Means should be provided to assure the proper use, care, storage, and control of equipment and supplies.

8. New and untried materials should be purchased in quantity only after a period of experimental use.

9. Scientific selection and testing of materials should be undertaken to the limits appropriate to the size and capacity of the school district.

10. The public should expect the greatest possible return for every dollar spent.

11. All records of the purchasing office should be open to public scrutiny. Absolutely no activities should take place which would throw a cloud of suspicion on the integrity of the school.

12. Making and controlling the budget for equipment and supplies and the purchasing function are highly related and should be centralized. Expenditures on supplies and equipment, like all expenditures, should be subject to budgetary control.

The Purchasing Agent

The person doing the purchasing for a school performs a service function and has two major responsibilities: (1) to furnish supplies, materials, and equipment of the right quality and quantity when needed, and (2) to purchase supplies and equipment at the lowest possible cost. Often these obligations may seem at odds with each other and the necessity of effecting a compromise that will satisfy both is a heavy responsibility.

The purchasing function is considered one of the most touchy jobs in public service. When it is performed fairly, judiciously, and with good management techniques, few people outside the purchasing department concern themselves with it. Let any questionable practices come to light, however, and the public spotlight focuses with ruthless intensity on the total organization. Mismanagement in purchasing can throw an entire organization into turmoil and disrepute. Thus, the purchasing agent is placed high on the staff level, and must be a person of impeccable reputation, a person who operates on principle, who will not allow anyone—either fawning, backslapping salespeople with an offer of gifts or entertainment, or the important citizen with an interest to serve—to sway him or her from the honest and unbiased performance of duty. In addition, the purchasing office must have the technical skills and the ability to handle the intricate process of purchasing.

The board of education, by policy and regulation, should appoint a purchasing agent. In the small school district, the superintendent may act as the purchasing agent; in the medium-sized school the administrative assistant or school business manager is the logical person to do the purchasing; and in the large city school, a full time purchasing agent who reports directly through the assistant superintendent for business is warranted. In no case should the school board or individuals on the board act as a purchasing agent.

There are various patterns in schools throughout the nation as evidenced by the organization charts shown in other chapters. The centralized purchasing office is most common and most practical in terms of efficiency and accountability. Good practice has made the purchasing agent the only point of initial contact for vendors. Even in a site-based school district, it may be wise practice to have all initial contacts with the centralized purchasing agent. When the purchasing agent is someone other than the school business manager, it can become a re-education process to direct vendors to the purchasing agent rather than the school business manager.

The continuing development of site-based decision making increases the pressure to decentralize the purchasing function. Various responses to the decentralization of the purchasing function have ranged from "no way" to *carte blanche* within certain dollar guidelines or allocated budget totals. Self-pay purchase orders as discussed later in the chapter have been employed to help both centralized office responsibility and responsiveness of administrators at the school-site level.

The school business manager and the purchasing agent need to shoulder the responsibilities of sound, districtwide procurement practices and at the same time to maintain school objectives in guiding their procedures. Accountability can be enforced, but at cost of discouraging initiative and even fostering hostility at the user's level. A message of "It's your job to teach and it's my job to do the purchasing" can result in very negative reactions according to the context of the message. The mature, thinking purchasing agent will use her/his role as an educational leader and a "builder of a cathedral" and will work with the constituencies accordingly.

The Purchasing Cycle

The mechanics of purchasing ordinarily include every step, beginning with consideration of the item to be purchased to the final approval of the invoice for payment. The steps may vary from one school to another, depending on the size and general characteristics of the school, but the essential features of the purchasing cycle are universal. A system of supply management must be adapted to the local situation. Steps may be eliminated, expanded, or combined, according to the local needs. Final evaluation depends on getting the right kind and amount of equipment and supplies at the right place at the right time with the most economical expenditure of money. A hypothetical case follows.

Case Study

Mary Tary, a high school English teacher, attended several lectures where a computer and overhead projector coupled with an LCD panel or electronic chalkboard were used very effectively in the presentation. She saw the possibilities of using this aid in her own classes. Her inquiries took her to fellow teachers, the English supervisor, the media consultant, and the principal. It was soon discovered that the school district did not have any computer projection equipment (an LCD panel or electronic chalkboard). The principal suggested that if Miss Tary would initiate a formal requisition, stating exactly what she wanted, he would put it through necessary channels. Miss Tary again visited the media consultant, and they drew up a formal requisition, which the principal approved and sent to the central administration office.

In the meantime ten teachers in other schools throughout the system had seen LCD panels coupled with overhead projectors and heard of their classroom possibilities, and they too had made formal requisitions. Since the ten requisitions were not for routine supplies or equipment, they were referred to the assistant superintendent for instruction. He in turn discussed the requisitions with the media director, and they agreed that an LCD panel could be a valuable teaching aid. They thereupon ordered a limited number for the media center. These would be made available to the teachers who requested them and would be tried on an experimental basis for three months. The teachers were informed of this staff decision, and they expressed a willingness to help with the experimental evaluation.

The requisitions were sent to the school business manager and purchasing agent with the notation that the LCD projection panels should be delivered to and credited to the media department of each school and, for accounting purposes, classified as equipment rather than supplies.

The first thing noted by the purchasing agent was that eight of the ten requisitions specified different types and brands, and only three requested an overhead projector. The purchasing agent immediately began an investigation. He looked through supply catalogs; he called a nearby school district to find what its experience with the LCD panels had been; and he sent a letter to the media center of the state university to obtain advice on what to use. He also discussed his problem with the two school supply houses and two computer vendors in the city.

Since the teachers had requested various types of LCD panel to be used with different computers, and had seemed to have little knowledge of their quality and structure, the purchasing agent decided to meet with the media director and the teachers concerned to see if requests could be standardized and some general specifications developed. He presented the results of his investigations and demonstrated sample LCD panels which he had obtained from vendors. He proposed specifications that standardized the LCD panels for purposes of comparison. This was agreeable to all the teachers.

Quotations were then requested on the ten LCD–overhead projection panels. The Omni-All Supply Company gave the best price, and an order was signed by the purchasing official for purchase of the goods. The order was entered into the computer and a copy was generated and sent to the vendor. Notices were also sent by electronic mail to the unpaid bills file and to the warehouse where the LCD panels were to be delivered. In a few days the purchasing agent received an invoice from the vendor which he compared with the quotations and contract figures. On receipt at the warehouse, the LCD panels were counted and checked and the warehouse entered a "received and OK" message onto their records file and sent the information to the purchasing agent. The purchasing agent then placed a copy of the vendor's bill with a second copy of the purchase order, marked the bill ready for payment, and sent it to the accounting office where prompt payment was made to take advantage of the time discount.

The media director was notified by electronic mail that the LCD panels had arrived, and one was sent to the media department of each of the schools involved. Previously the purchasing agent had met with the research consultant and the assistant superintendent for instruction to devise an evaluation sheet for use in assessing the LCD panels under various conditions. The media director notified each teacher by memo that the LCD panels could be checked out from the media department. With each memo he enclosed an evaluation sheet, along with instructions for using it.

The temporary purchasing cycle was complete. Mary Tary had her teaching tool, but she also had the responsibility of testing it to help determine future purchases. The complete purchasing cycle for this item, however, would go on for a long time. Like many items, the projection device would probably never have such perfect specifications that they would never again need to be changed, particularly in a rapidly changing technological environment.

A Flow Chart Showing Steps or Mechanics of Purchasing

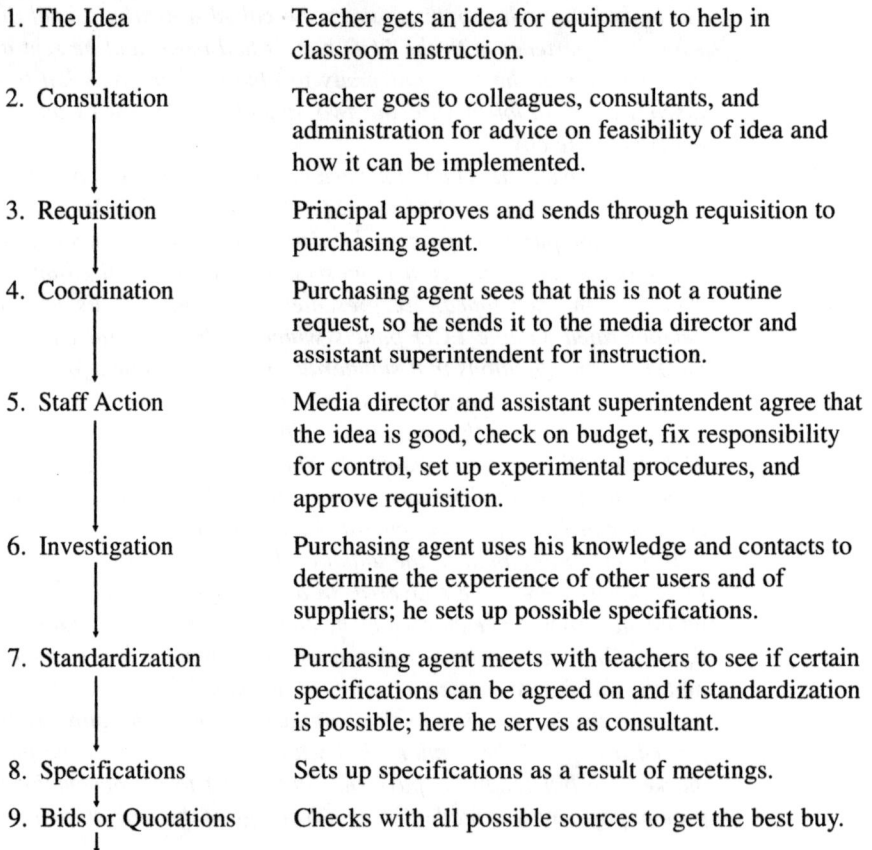

1. The Idea — Teacher gets an idea for equipment to help in classroom instruction.

2. Consultation — Teacher goes to colleagues, consultants, and administration for advice on feasibility of idea and how it can be implemented.

3. Requisition — Principal approves and sends through requisition to purchasing agent.

4. Coordination — Purchasing agent sees that this is not a routine request, so he sends it to the media director and assistant superintendent for instruction.

5. Staff Action — Media director and assistant superintendent agree that the idea is good, check on budget, fix responsibility for control, set up experimental procedures, and approve requisition.

6. Investigation — Purchasing agent uses his knowledge and contacts to determine the experience of other users and of suppliers; he sets up possible specifications.

7. Standardization — Purchasing agent meets with teachers to see if certain specifications can be agreed on and if standardization is possible; here he serves as consultant.

8. Specifications — Sets up specifications as a result of meetings.

9. Bids or Quotations — Checks with all possible sources to get the best buy.

10. Purchase Order	Purchasing officer and designated cosigners sign purchase order in quadruplicate. One copy each goes to vendor, warehouse, purchasing agent, and accounting office.
11. Follow-up	Purchasing agent makes a follow-up if equipment is not received when due.
12. Receipt of Goods	Warehouse personnel receive goods, check them according to specifications, and return purchase order with their OK.
13. Payment	Purchasing agent and board of education approve purchase for payment, and accounting office pays.
14. Accountability	Goods are sent to the department which is held accountable for the equipment.
15. User Receives	Teacher picks up equipment at designated place.
16. Quality Control	Equipment is used experimentally and tested under different conditions.

Electronic Purchasing

Given the technologies available and the move toward site-based management, the purchasing process may be enhanced by substituting the computer keyboard and screen for paper. Inquiries, vendor searches, requisitions, and receiving reports may all be done by computer, reducing time spent, forms used, and the endless filling out of data for files.

Figures 7-1 through 7-6 show examples of the screens that can be made available to the requisitioner at remote sites. Figure 7-1 shows the purchasing menus. The requisitioner selects the menu needed and can initiate, check on the status of a purchase order, or check the balance in a supplies/equipment budget before initiating a request.

Figure 7-2 shows a screen listing potential vendors in a particular area of the curriculum. Vendor numbers are available to be put on the proper forms such as the one shown in Figure 7-3, a sample requisition screen or on the inquiry screen (Figure 7-4) to determine the status of a requisition. Once the requisition has been made, the requester can check on the status of the purchase order by looking at the purchase order inquiry screen (Figure 7-5). When the item has been received at a remote site, a receiving report may be filed (Figure 7-6).

In addition to selecting the software and supporting hardware that does what the purchasing officer wishes, a very important key to initiating and operating a computer-based purchasing system is the early and continuous training of all who use the system. Confusion can reign if the process is not thoroughly understood; lags in timing occur or errors creep into the system to destroy its credibility. Training sessions for remote-site teams (building secretary or treasurer and an administrator) with central purchasing personnel will make the transition to and the operation of the system more effective.

(text continues on page 131)

```
    Ref No.:
    Qty Recd:                        Qty Inv:                  Amt Inv:

 201   Purchasing Menu                                         FPR Version 1.10
                                                               Fiscal Year: 92
 Screen: _____  Vend:   P0000279960   PO: 243824   Inv: _____   Line: 001

                          20M   Vendor Maintenance Menu
                          22M   Purchase Order Processing Menu
                          23M   Receiving Menu
                          24M   Invoicing Menu
                          25M   Requisition Processing Menu
                          26M   Master Order Processing Menu
                          27M   Future Order Processing Menu
                          2QM   Purchasing Inquiry Menu
                          2TM   Purchasing Table Maintenance Menu

                          41M   Bid Processing Menu
                          45M   Commodity Maintenance Menu

                          FIN   Financial Systems Menu
```

FIGURE 7-1   Sample Purchasing Menu Screen.

```
 202   Vendor Name Search

 Screen: _____  Vend: BUSINESS   PO: 243824   Inv: _____   Line: 001

 LN   VENDOR NAME/ADDRESS              CITY/STATE        VENDOR NO.   DROP   ALIAS

 1    BUSINESS & HEALTH                                  P0000101240    0      N
      SUBSCRIBER SERVICES DEPT         MARION, OH
 2    BUSINESS & HEALTH                                  P0000101241    0      N
      CIRCULATION DEPT                 ORADELL, NJ
 3    BUSINESS & LEGAL REPORTS                           P0000075260    0      N
      64 WALL ST                       MADISON, CT
 4    BUSINESS BOOK THE                                  P0000138000    0      N
      MILES KIMBALL COMPANY            OSHKOSH, WI
 5    BUSINESS CLASS INC                                 P0000285790    0      N
      PROFESSIONAL CASSETTE CTR        PASADENA, CA
 6    BUSINESS COMMITTEE FOR THE                         P0000145710    0      N
      ARTS INC                         NEW YORK, NY
 7    BUSINESS COMMUNICATIONS GROUP                      P0000203700    0      A
      7755 E 89TH ST                   INDIANAPOLIS, IN

 Line Number: _____     Previous Screen: 248     Search Key: BUSINESS
```

FIGURE 7-2   Sample Vendor Information Screen.

```
250   Requisition Header Maintenance

Screen: _____   Vend: _____   PR: 082794   Inv: _____   Line: 001

Req Date: _____   Req Type: _____
Ref No.: _____   Buyer/Phone: _____

Delivery Date: _____

Status: _____   Print Req: _____
Suggested Vendor: _____

Account No.          Pct.          Amount          Account No.        Pct        Amount
_____   _____   _____   _____   _____   _____
_____   _____   _____   _____   _____   _____

Division: _____         School: _____         Dept: _____
Sub Dept: _____          Exec Lvl: _____          Fd. Grp: _____
Purpose: _____           Campus: _____            Security: _____

Delete:            Freeze:            In Proc:            Tfr/Appr:            Req. Total:
```

FIGURE 7-3   Sample Requisition Screen.

```
258   Requisition Line Item Inquiry

Screen: _____   Vend: _____   PR: _____   Line: 001

Line     Quantity     Commodity     UOM     Unit Price   Trd Disc     Extended Price   UPO

         Account No.:
         Inventory No.:
         Reference No.:

         Account No.:
         Inventory No.:
         Reference No.:

         Account No.:
         Inventory No.:
         Reference No.:
```

FIGURE 7-4   Sample Inquiry Screen.

```
*W-Z0137 — SECURITY — YOU MAY NOT UPDATE ON THIS SCREEN
 228   Purchase Order Line Item Inquiry

Screen: _____   Vend: _____   PO: _____   Inv: _____   Line: 001

                                                         Trd    Disc    Extended
Line    Quantity    Commodity    UOM    Unit Price        Disc   Type     Price     UPO

        Acct No.:                   Desc:
        Ref No.:
        Qty. Recd:                  Qty Inv:                     Amt Inv:

        Acct No.:                   Desc:
        Ref No.:
        Qty. Recd:                  Qty Inv:                     Amt Inv:

        Acct No.:                   Desc:
```

FIGURE 7-5   Sample Purchase Order Inquiry Screen.

*Note: Central Purchasing controls certain functions using security measures.

```
 239   PO Receiving Report Line Deletion

Screen: _____   Vend: _____   PO: 238500  Inv: _____   Line: _____

Purchase Order:
Line    Commodity        Qty Ord   Qty Recd   UOM    Dt Recd   UPO
                                                                          Enter "D"
        Desc:                                                             to delete

Receiving Report:                                                Del
Seq     Loc ID Carr Bol          Qty Recd   UOM    Dt Recd   Stat  Qly  Flg      Del Dt
                                                                          __ _____
        Rejected:
        Comments: _____
                                                                          __ _____
        Rejected:
        Comments:_____
                                                                          __ _____
        Rejected:
        Comments:_____
```

FIGURE 7-6   Sample Receiving Report Screen.

A clearly understood phase-in process should be in place before the first requisition is keyboarded. A decision has to be made whether or not dual paper and electronic processes will be part of the phase-in. The dual system may perpetuate the paper system longer than expected by providing those resistant to change a way to avoid the new complete system.

Opportunities for Leadership

At a professional meeting some time ago, a seasoned purchasing veteran had this to say when the leadership function of the purchasing agent was addressed. "You know, this is an innocuous subject for us to discuss and I presume my good friend the professor proposed it. How many of us here are really leaders when it comes to purchasing? It's our job to squelch, not lead!"

"Squelched" aptly describes a teacher's or custodian's feeling when he is not allowed materials which would help him in his work. The exact correlation between squelching and morale is probably unknown, but it certainly would be a high negative one. Supplies and equipment have to be purchased, and the difference in cost between what the purchaser buys and the user really wants is generally negligible.

In the case of Mary Tary and the electronic chalkboards, the purchasing agent served as a valuable consultant. He used technical knowledge, contacts, and know-how to gather information. He met with the teachers and gave them ideas and possible varieties to choose from. In the end the product was standardized, but it also was approved and accepted by the users. The chances are that this was a more economical purchase for the school district because it was used and appreciated. The morale of the teachers was not damaged because they understood the purchasing process and appreciated being asked to help.

Leadership can be exerted by a purchasing agent in many ways. He or she can obtain supplies for demonstration, evaluate supplies by a check sheet or an interview, and meet with teachers to discuss their problems. The purchasing agent can send studies and reports on equipment and supplies to teaching and nonteaching personnel, brief them on the process of obtaining supplies, and ask their help on some of the difficulties encountered in purchasing. Purchasing begins and ends with the user. The purchasing officer must get the most out of the dollar spent, but it is actually a waste of money if supplies are purchased and then not used because they are not satisfactory.

There are many cases in which supposed good management of supplies and equipment is really poor management. There was the case of the bragging superintendent who asserted that his school used only one-third the amount of chalk that another school of the same size used. Investigation revealed that the chalk was so hard that the teachers simply did not use the chalk. He saved dollars on chalk and the custodian did not have to wash so many chalk boards, but the children must have been shortchanged because the teachers could not work to capacity.

In another case, the costs for media repair and upkeep on equipment was negligible at School A compared with nearby School B. Reports showed that equipment was used eight times more often in School B than in School A! School A issued its equipment from the business office supply room. It was so difficult to check out equipment that teachers just did not bother to use it.

There are many cases in which accounting shows that the cost of supplies in some schools is much lower proportionately than in other schools. The purchasing agent proudly pats himself on the back. At the same time, teaching and nonteaching personnel are grumbling because they cannot get supplies and equipment to do their jobs as they should be done. Invariably a school will spend more money in the long run in wasted learning opportunities if adequate supplies are not available to do an efficient job.

Standardization and Specification

There has been a great deal of writing and discussion about standardization and specification of supplies and equipment. In many cases the subjects have become so involved and technical that they command more of the purchasing agent's time than is necessary or desirable. Yet they are important. Industrial progress in the United States has been made possible through both these important processes. Standardization of the gauge of railroad tracks throughout the nation put us ahead of other nations in transportation. Interchangeability of parts of machines and all types of equipment and exactness in standards and specifications have been a boon to industrial development. Professor Henry Linn of Columbia University in a speech entitled "Standardization and Relations to Specifications" delivered at the New Orleans Convention of Business Officials on October 22, 1954, had this to say about standardization:

> *It is interesting to note what simplification has meant to industry; for example, when the United States Department of Commerce first established a division of simplified practice, the number of varieties of paving brick dropped from 64 to 4, the number of varieties of wheelbarrows from 168 to 22, the number of varieties of control abrasive products from 8,000 to 1,976. In later years the simplication program sponsored by the National Bureau of Standards reduced the number of different sizes of steel drums and barrels from 66 to 26, the variety and sizes of slate blackboards from 120 to 6; and the variety and sizes of steel horizontal firebox heating boilers from 2,328 to 38. These are only a few illustrations of the results of simplified practice recommendations.*

Standardization within a school can be relatively simple because it requires merely an agreement by the users on size, weight, general ingredients, and what the item is to do under certain circumstances. In most cases, users are not so particular about these specifications as one might think. Although construction of custom-made items, particularly in buildings and facilities, requires exact and unique specifications, few items in the line of equipment and supplies need to be custom-made. Most are mass-produced, most have been standardized, and most have been tested and found acceptable under varying conditions. Experience has proved that often the cost of developing "homemade" specifications is more than the savings that might be realized.

When determining a set of specifications, the purchaser must convey to the seller a precise description of what should be delivered, how much of it is needed, and where it should be delivered. The last four items are quickly decided. The first item becomes highly technical. Few schools can profitably analyze ingredients and construct specifications; therefore, persons in charge of purchasing must locate sources where they can get this technical help.

Opportunities for Savings

The business manager can find opportunities for savings in addition to those already noted. Several states have lists of state-approved items and vendors from which state agencies, including schools, can select. The state's listing of prices needs to be checked carefully because it may not always be the lowest possible price, given other savings opportunities such as cooperative purchasing. The patterns for utilizing state purchasing assistance vary from ordering through a central agency to making contact with approved vendors to work out the details of satisfying purchasing needs.

Cooperative Purchasing

Increased buying power usually means lower prices. The school system of 1,200 students will not be able to obtain price breaks on expendable materials that a school system of 100,000 students will easily obtain unless the small school system joins with others to equal the buying power of the larger system. In some instances school districts form a cooperative purchasing group. On occasion a school district and a city and/or county will cooperatively purchase selected items.

This arrangement might take the form of a school district buying commonly used office supplies and paper which is in turn purchased by the city or county. The city or county may purchase fuel and transportation commodities and the school district could purchase these from the city or county. In some states regional educational service areas may provide a cooperative purchasing service for school districts within the region.

Cooperative purchasing may not be as positive as it sounds, although if it is carried out wisely the positive aspects tend to outweigh the negative. From a survey of Association of School Business Official (ASBO) members, Sanders and Knapp list the advantages and disadvantages of cooperative purchasing. The primary benefits were[5]:

Better prices
Better quality—improved testing and selection
Savings in administrator's time
Carry-over of cooperation into other areas
Improved public relations
Benefit of counsel of fellow business managers
Standardization of specifications
Keeps competition honest
Reduction in visits from vendor salesmen

Development of a central file on specifications, product testing and evaluation by various cooperative members on supplies and equipment

The disadvantages most often mentioned by the survey respondents were:

Delivery, warehousing and distribution problems
Difficulty in agreeing to product specifications
Red tape—increased paper work
Loss of individual attention by vendors
Coordinating dual purchasing functions—local and cooperative
Coordination of cooperative purchasing with various local agencies' budget
  preparation

The following points need to be considered when thinking about cooperative purchasing arrangements:

- The cooperative must be established under proper authority as a legal entity.
- A clear structure needs to be established to operate the cooperative purchasing process. The following questions need to be answered:

—Who shall communicate with vendors?
—Who shall sit on the decision-making board?
—How shall the leadership of the board be determined?

- Policies of each board of education should be established in relation to the purchasing cooperative.
- The cooperative should have its own policies and procedures clearly stated in writing.
- A school district should not be permitted to opt in and out at will.
- Storage and distribution policies need to be established.
- A schedule of events needs to be adopted by all participants.
- An annual review of items agreed on should occur.
- Care should be given to minimize added paperwork to cooperating districts/agencies.
- Dispersed deliveries should be required whenever possible.

School districts have realized significant savings over time by increasing their purchasing power through cooperatives, some realizing over 38 percent on total purchases.[6] The school business manager will find it useful to contact successfully operating school purchasing cooperatives to gain insights regarding the process.

Reducing Need for Warehousing

Agreements may be made with vendors to deliver immediately on demand certain supplies that are used frequently and in relatively large quantities. The vendor absorbs the costs of warehousing and any losses connected therewith. The schools save warehousing costs, delivery costs, and often paperwork costs. The "stockless purchasing" ordinarily carries higher prices or service fees; however, if the savings realized are greater than the higher prices or fees, the arrangements may prove useful over time.

Self-Pay Purchase Orders

Wills provided an excellent overview of the development and current practice of self-pay purchase orders.[7] The self-pay purchase order is a purchase order with a check that is attached to or is part of the purchase order form. The amount is limited and the items for which the order can be issued are limited. The self-pay purchase order can serve individual buildings very well and at the same time realize some savings of time and labor in the central purchasing office. The self-pay orders should represent a very small percentage of the total purchase dollars spent by the school district but may represent a much larger percentage of the total transactions made. Clearly stated procedures will guide the initiators to assure proper accounting and control at the central office.

Automation

Automation of purchasing functions using networked computers and software can save time and energy in a variety of ways. Paper handling is reduced, time delays reduced, bid solicitation can be streamlined, and historical data and analyses can be generated to assist in decision making. Bonner reminded readers that automation of purchase orders, encumbrances and accounts payable do not constitute an automated procurement system.[8] As noted earlier in the chapter, the crucial part of the purchasing process precedes ordering.

Specifications, selection of vendor(s), bidding when required, insuring the proper input into the process, evaluating the item, and tracking it for storage/inventory purposes should be considered if an "automated" system is being planned. The same considerations of installation and training time must be taken into account when contemplating a new system.

Networking automation can be a help to systems using site-based decision making. Budget encumbrances, storage and/or distribution, and central accountability and planning can benefit. Although not a panacea, automation has a contribution to make.

Purchasing Locally

Good purchasing principles require that the purchaser buy the quality needed at the best price. The requirement overlooks the pressures exerted on schools to purchase locally. Yet this is a problem facing almost every school. State laws which require schools to advertise for bids and to accept the lowest quotations take the school off the "hook" to some extent in this regard. Even then, for purchases below a certain figure in which bidding is unnecessary the problem still arises. There is some justification for patronizing local vendors as far as public relations are concerned, but there is no justification for subsidizing a local merchant at the expense of the taxpayers of the school district. Purchasing problems created by pressure to buy locally can only be relieved by a sound, well-conceived, and thoroughly understood policy established by the board of education.

Intelligent businessmen soon recognize that sound business procedures require careful buying. In most cases, local concerns can successfully compete with outside sources because of their proximity to the school system if they can provide thorough and reliable service. These factors should be considered in the bidding, and conceivably they could be the determinant for bid acceptance. They are justifiable items. However, school board policy should be firmly stated so that local merchants will realize that good purchasing principles will prevail over local favoritism when the school buys supplies and equipment. Unless a policy is so stated, so understood, and so administered the local purchasing officer will find himself in an untenable position and unable to do his job as he should.

Personal Integrity in Purchasing

The new school business official or purchasing agent will be immersed into opportunities for compromise. Some will be blatant; others much more subtle. The dividing line between a gift and a bribe may be hard to discern once one develops a rationale to accept a gift. The ego-building attention of a very personable salesperson may ignite a glow of importance and power in the new administrator. There is always the possibility of the rationale that, after all, there is very little difference in the products; therefore no harm is being done to go with the one represented by someone who offers advantages to the buyer. The fawning, super generous salesperson should serve as a flashing danger signal for the purchaser.

The Potential Conflict of Interest Problem

A school district with one purchasing agent and a very limited input from others regarding the purchasing decision can easily prepare for and monitor compliance with a conflict of interest policy. There are many school districts in which there are several people involved in the purchasing decisions. In fact, the authors have encouraged a wide involvement of people to assure the best decisions regarding use of the items. Site-based decision making further complicates the situation. Cuzzetto and Race provided the following guidelines to identify a potential conflict of interest[9]:

> *A conflict of interest may exist when an employee has direct or indirect financial interest in, or receives any compensation from, any individual or business firm:*
>
> - *From which the district purchases supplies, materials, or property*
> - *Which renders any service to the district*
> - *To which the district sells or leases any of its materials, services, facilities, or properties*
> - *Which has any other contractual relations or business dealings with the district.*

School board policy should state that employees must avoid conflict of interest or even the appearance thereof. The school board may wish to direct that a "right to audit" statement be used in all purchase orders and contracts. Cuzzetto and Race suggested that a review by the local chamber of commerce may generate support for reviewing vendors' records.[10] The school should aggressively pursue the nonconflict of interest in all its dealings.

For Further Thought

1. What centralized state assistance for purchasing supplies and equipment is provided schools or other government agencies in your state?

2. What cooperative purchasing arrangements are operating in your geographical area? How are decisions made regarding qualities of items? How are materials stored and distributed?

3. Compare automated purchasing systems in use in your area. What pro's and con's are noted by the administrators who use them?

4. What different behaviors and attitudes would you anticipate might result from a purchasing philosophy expressed as "We're here to hold things down" as contrasted with one expressed by "We want to help schools get the best we can in a responsible way." How would you as superintendent try to ensure one or the other?

5. What limitations on bidding, non-bid ceiling, and local purchasing requirements exist in your state?

Endnotes

1. Robert R. Hamilton and E. Edmond Reutter, Jr., *Legal Aspects of School Board Operation,* (New York: Bureau of Publications, Teachers College, Columbia University, 1958), p. 88

2. *Hague v. City of Philadelphia,* 48 Pa. 527.

3. As quoted in W. H. Roe, *School Business Management* (New York: McGraw-Hill Book Company, 1961), p. 129.

4. *Pioneer Coal Company v. Board of Education of City of Rochester,* Monroe County Sup. Ct., Wheeler, J., Sept. 10, 1949.

5. Frank Sanders and Herbert Knapp, *Cooperative Purchasing Guidelines* (Park Ridge, Ill: Association of School Business Officials, 1979), p. 4.

6. Sanders and Knapp, *Cooperative Purchasing Guidelines,* p. 14.

7. Chuck Wills, "Self-Pay Purchase Orders," *School Business Affairs* (April 1989): 12–17.

8. Larry Bonner, "Myths, Misconceptions, and Realities About Public Procurement Automation," *School Business Affairs,* 55, No. 4 (May 1989).

9. Charles E. Cuzzetto and Susan L. Race, "Conflicts of Interest in Purchasing: An Aggressive Plan for Prevention and Detection," *School Business Affairs* 56, No. 4 (April 1990): 17.

10. Cuzzetto and Race, *"Conflicts of Interest in Purchasing,"* p. 19.

C h a p t e r *8*

Supplies Control and Distribution

Supply management involves the purchasing, receiving, storing, distributing, and accounting of supplies and equipment used in the operation and maintenance of a school. Operationally each element of the process hinges on the others. How much is purchased for the school depends on how much is needed. How much is needed depends on how much was used in the past under varying circumstances. Knowledge of past use must include an appraisal of quality, quantity, availability, economy, utility, and other use factors. Efforts to separate these essentials of supply management either when writing about them or when administering them become most frustrating, because one element is so closely tied to another that the implications and effects of executing one phase affect others.

Discussion in chapter 7 dealt mainly with purchasing and receiving. As noted in that chapter, irregularities in purchasing will cause the public to lose faith in the integrity of the entire school. By the same token the way supplies are handled and used will create an impression of extravagance or thrift, for public attention most often is focused on the physical, the material, and the tangible. Mismanagement and waste will weaken public confidence and thereby handicap the total operation of a school.

Several questions arise regarding the management of supplies. Among those questions are:

1. Shall supplies be ordered on an "as needed" basis, on an annual basis, or some variation in between? Not only is the purchasing process affected by the answer, but additional questions arise.

2. How much central storage is available? In the individual schools?

3. If there is adequate storage, what distribution system should be used?

4. What track records have the vendors established regarding on-time deliveries?

5. What technology is in place to assist the supply management process?

6. What changes will site-based decision making have on the answers to the above?

7. What supplies and/or equipment deteriorate as a result of storage? What rotation system is in place to avoid losses due to missing shelf-life limits?

8. What should be done with building or centrally stored obsolete material or equipment? How will obsolete or nonfunctional equipment be identified on a timely basis?

9. What additional equipment and operating costs will be needed to handle and distribute supplies if centrally delivered and/or stored?

10. What is the proper view of how people will use supplies if they know the amount available, that is, should users know the inventory?

The above questions and others are discussed in this chapter. Although answers to some of the questions may seem painfully obvious to the reader, it might be noted that strong opposing arguments and feelings exist about most of the questions.

Storage

An adequate supply of materials with which to carry out an assigned task is a must in any organization. If equipment and materials essential to the job are missing or are insufficient, employees will not be able to work at maximum efficiency. Therefore a much greater loss is incurred than the cost of the materials alone, because the cost of less effective personnel must also be taken into account.

On the other hand, an oversupply can be troublesome and expensive. The business manager will need to compute the added costs of keeping supplies over a long period of time. The added costs include such factors as obsolescence, deterioration, costs in handling, storage space, insurance, and loss in use of money. Schools, unlike businesses and industries, ordinarily cannot have a yearly inventory or warehouse sale to get rid of excess equipment, so unless special emphasis is placed on using up old stock no longer being purchased, the accumulation becomes larger, more out of date, and less usable each year.

Elements of the Storage Function

The elements of the storage function include identification and coding of the complete item and related parts, internal organization of the warehouse by nomenclature and number, proper protection, scientific development of space requirements, packaging, shipping sequence, inventorying, and similar details. These aspects of storage and issue are in the province of personnel specially trained in warehouse techniques. Schools in the process of constructing warehouses and improving their warehouse system can save money by bringing in a specialist to help with the organization of the system and the training of the personnel.

Principles
While proper organization of the system and proper training of personnel are becoming increasingly technical, there are principles of storage and issue that are basic and easily implemented.

1. Storage space should be free of excessive heat, cold, and moisture, and damage by insects and rodents.

2. Storage space should provide flexibility for storing different types of materials that might deteriorate under different conditions or which through odor or leakage might damage other equipment.

3. Storage space must be centralized and easily located through an orderly storage system or through coding.

4. Stock should be inspected and rotated so that old stock will be used up first.

5. Continuing records should be kept of all materials received and disbursed; inventories should be "on line" for immediate updates or analyses. A backup of these records should be kept in a place separate from the storage facility.

6. Responsibility for the storage operation should be specifically assigned and understood by all.

7. Stock should be handled with a minimum outlay of time for unpacking, shelving, and if part of a central storage system, repacking for distribution.

8. The number of distributions should be kept to a minimum.

9. Stocks should be released only on written requisition.

10. Refusal to honor a requisition should be made only by a member of the administrative staff or by a supply officer on written memo from a member of the administrative staff.

11. Periodic analyses should be prepared which can indicate current supply levels, use patterns, potential surplus items, delivery information, and other information useful to the business manager in making purchasing-related decisions.

12. Prevention of loss by employee misuse can be a concern; therefore, some type of internal security should be planned.

13. Precautions against losses by fire or theft should be instituted including proper insurance if the school district is not self-insured.

Centralized versus Decentralized Warehouses

Centralized storage requires a central storeroom or warehouse(s) where all goods for the school system are delivered, stored, and maintained. These goods are then distributed to individual school buildings only on approval of a requisition.

Decentralized storage also requires some kind of storage facilities, but it also requires the delivery, storage, and maintenance of all materials needed by an individual school usually in that particular school building. Supplies and equipment are then disbursed to the users by the building principal or his or her designated representative.

Given the economics inherent in centralized purchasing, it may appear at first glance that centralized storage is best. The growth of site-based decision making may affect both centralized purchasing and supply management. Many factors enter into answering centralized versus decentralized storage. Among those factors are the adequacy of storage areas both central and in individual buildings; distances between buildings; staff availability; administrative expectations of the building principal and staff; and track records of vendors relative to timeliness of deliveries.

Advantages of Centralized Storage

There are many advantages to centralized storage:

1. Centralized storage makes it economical to employ and train specialized supply persons.
2. Principals, office personnel, and teachers can be relieved of much clerical work.
3. Supplies and equipment are more easily controlled by perpetual inventory and records of receipts and disbursements.
4. There is little chance of mistakes or duplicate ordering when one person controls the supply storage for the entire school district.
5. Materials are kept in good condition because of better storage facilities and closer administration.
6. There can be close coordination within the purchasing office, the storing office, and the accounting office.
7. Obsolete and unused materials may be easily detected and disposed of.
8. Flexibility of purchasing is maintained so that large orders may be placed at any time of the year without disrupting an individual school or worrying about where to store it.
9. A wide range of supplies may be provided for each school.
10. Clerical, packaging, and shipping expenses may be eliminated for the supplier when he or she can send supplies in large lots to one location.
11. Safety considerations are ordinarily more easily accommodated.
12. The need to add personnel to help with supplies in each building may be reduced.

Advantages of Decentralized Storage

However, decentralized storage offers its own advantages:

1. Supplies and equipment are stored in the user's building and are available when needed.
2. Each school building is a self-sufficient administrative unit.
3. The need for a large central supply staff is avoided.
4. Internal operational costs are cut down through elimination of deliveries, cost of warehouses, and specialized warehouse equipment.
5. All employees are close to the supply situation; they understand it and feel that little red tape is required to obtain supplies.
6. Employees are inclined to be more careful and economical in their use and consumption of supplies when they are aware of the supplies available to them.
7. Variations in materials can be accommodated according to curricular differences resulting from local decision making.

In the small school district, with as few as six or seven school buildings, the economic advantages of maintaining centralized warehousing are questionable. The district is too small to provide a full-time person to handle the operation, centralized warehouse space may be too expensive to provide, and time and money are often poorly spent in transportation and running errands for supplies and equipment.

Centrally Administered, Decentralized Storage

The answer to the supply problem for the smaller school district may be the centrally administered, decentralized storage method. This plan provides for centralized purchasing, centralized receiving (except on some major items of furniture and equipment), dispersed storage, minimum distribution, and centralized control and accountability.

The centralized receiving goes along with the centralized purchasing, so that the purchaser may follow through the purchasing cycle until the goods are received and inspected. The completion of this purchasing cycle by one or two responsible people eliminates many of the loose ends in purchasing. No one wonders, Did we receive it? Was it in good shape? Has it been entered on the proper accounting records? Did the right person get it? Was it assembled correctly? These questions are all automatically answered because the function is centralized in one office.

Dispersed storage locates supplies and equipment as close to the place they are used as possible. Materials are normally stored in three locations:

1. *In facilities immediately available to the user.* Approximately a month's supply of materials in regular use is kept by teachers in classroom storage closets and by custodians in the custodial closets and the central custodial room. Teachers and custodians perform their own continuing inventories and records and requisition from the central office of the school by large order.

2. *In school building stockroom.* This provides a close source for replenishing exhausted supplies. A more or less standardized supply of common materials is stored here, including central office supplies and emergency materials used daily by teachers and custodians plus materials used less often but with some regularity throughout the year. Two or three months' supply is stored here, depending on the storage facilities available.

3. *In central school district warehouse or stockroom.* This provides a central source of supply for the entire district. It houses a limited amount of standard supplies and is a place where materials bought more in quantity can be stored, in addition to materials used infrequently and for emergencies. Supplies for central administration are stored here. Under this system the central warehouse does not need to be a complicated, highly organized storage operation requiring many permanent personnel, intricate equipment, and specialized space. This warehousing operation provides opportunities for combining with other service functions, such as a central maintenance shop, bus repair shop, and garage.

The warehouse serves as a weekly or monthly source for replenishing supplies rather than a daily and hourly requisition center. However, it is the nerve center for supply, so to speak, where records are initiated and where the coordinating process for supplies takes place. The distribution process is minimized by dispersed storage. Deliveries may be made once a week or perhaps less often instead of several times a day or week. Fewer trucks and drivers are needed and less operational money is expended.

The key to this entire process is centralized control and accounting. The main trouble with decentralized storage is that too often the administration in individual school buildings is not careful in stock management practices. Supplies and equipment once issued to a unit are presumed to be the exclusive property of that unit. Often too little attention is given to rates of consumption and to the actual use of the equipment and materials. Sometimes inventory records are not maintained, and each year, stock which could have been used in other buildings accumulates and goes out of date.

Centralized control and accounting correct this. Because of their special training and because of their involvement in accounting and control processes, personnel cultivate a positive attitude toward the welfare of the entire school district. The central warehouse keeps a continuing inventory of all supplies and equipment along with a record of where they are located. Everyone understands that the material in a sense belongs to and is reclaimable by the central warehouse. Periodic inspections are made of supplies and equipment in individual buildings. Each summer a total inventory is taken. Supplies are replenished, and excess and damaged supplies are reclaimed. The old account is then closed and a new one begun.

Continuous inventories of supplies can be maintained via networked computers. All requisitions are in quantity, therefore, an undue burden is not placed on the record keeping function.

Furniture can be handled in much the same way as far as accountability and control are concerned. After being coded and marked, each piece is assigned to a room by the central warehouse. Yearly inventories by the central office and occasional reviews of room needs by the principal and business manager provide flexibility for necessary changes and removal of obsolete pieces. Teachers themselves may request additional furniture through the normal requisition process or the yearly budget requisition summary.

Equipment may be controlled by assigning it to a person, department, or building principal. A use chart affixed to the equipment or maintained by the department determines the value of this equipment to the total organization.

Most of the above inventory control activities can be aided by computer applications readily available. Some schools and colleges have found a "home grown" vision of inventory control and analysis by using Hyper card or Super card applications. The computer can provide a floor plan of any building and the supplies or equipment items that are supposed to be there. In the event a request for a particular item comes to the central administration for supplies, the computer can pinpoint its location quickly.

Professional Responsibility of Users

Is it wise to provide supply information to users, or if they know what is available will they abuse the use of supplies? Is limited knowledge a safeguard against waste? Are the teachers and principals responsible professionals who will use wisely the supply resources available to them? These authors contend that the principals and teachers (the users) can and most often do act responsibly, especially if given the information necessary to so behave. The Pygmalion effect may apply in supply management in that if one treats the users as irresponsible and unable to deal with complete information, they will behave that way. On the other hand, if pertinent information, a history of use, and a projected supply schedule are provided, users can plan well and use supplies judiciously rather than "Let's use this up so we can get more."

Successes and failures can be shared with users. The time it takes to provide information and in-service training up front may save time and money as well as generate ideas for better supply management.

Standard List of Supplies

The need of adequate supplies does not call for extravagance in furnishing them. Although every imaginable kind of item cannot be kept in stock, a standard list of those supplies needed under normal teaching conditions should be developed by teachers in cooperation with the administration. A minimum allotment can then be set up by grade, and this can serve as a guide for use and for reorder. After several years of study and implementation, a responsible and effective standard list of supplies will emerge. The school business manager may find a good start in neighboring school districts.

Those who fear that teachers will go wild when allowed to establish standard lists and budget their own supplies will learn from experience that they have little to worry about. With proper in-service education, there will be less hoarding, waste, and misuse of supplies because the teacher will come to feel a part of the system. Morale also improves when the teacher understands that he or she is operating in a professional atmosphere with the tools and supplies necessary to carry on the job.

Control and Accountability

Through proper control and accountability of supplies and equipment, the administration can follow and account for the supplies within the school system from the time they are planned and purchased until they are expended or are declared obsolete. This can be accomplished by placing definite responsibility on specific persons at each step in the supply process and by establishing a system of records to evaluate each of these steps.

Accountability and control are just as important in handling supplies and equipment as in handling money. Supplies and equipment are assets of the school, just as money is. Control and accounting are illustrated by the steps shown in Table 8-1.

Property management, as may be seen in Table 8-1, does not begin with purchasing but with the supply planning which necessarily precedes procurement. An administrative agency needs systematic information about requirements for equipment and supplies; it needs to know how supplies have actually been used in the past, the consumption rate, breakage, loss, their utility, and the inventory turnover. Only when management has this information can it appraise and reorder. Any system of management which does not have these controls is based on guesswork.

Risks of Overmanagement

The authors recall a visit with a school principal who was enamored with the traffic flow inside and outside the building. He happily shared a number of charts showing the

TABLE 8-1 The Supply Process and Its Control

Process of Purchasing and Control	Staff Member of Department Involved in Process
1. Develop standard list of supplies and equipment	1. By users in cooperation with business manager
2. Stock catalogs refined from standard list; includes all possible supplies normally handled with necessary ordering data	2. Business office
3. Annual supply and equipment request (detailed statement of requirements for year)	3. Entire staff, including teachers and custodians
4. Budget document (listing in general supplies and equipment authorized and money available)	4. Supply and equipment budget developed by business office, approved by superintendent and board of education
5. Requisition and approval	5. Initiated by individual approved by designated administrative officer
6. Purchase order	6. Designated purchasing office
7. Note of receipt in good order on invoice or original purchase order	7. Receiving clerk
8. Spot checks made on weight and quality and quantity; notations made	8. Business office
9. Material placed in supply or equipment accounting ledger	9. Supply clerk
10. Bill paid by accounting office	10. Sent to accounting office by purchasing officer
11. Distribution records material sent to accountable individual buildings periodically, based on annual requests and periodic requisitions	11. Principal of school held
12. Building distribution records each teacher who gets basic supplies at beginning of year and periodically as requested	12. Principal administers. May be coordinated with central office computer
13. User accountability: user signs for supplies	13. Users (teacher, custodians, etc.) and equipment in room at beginning of year; list provided by supply
14. User "use" chart: materials checked off as used; form provided by supply, appraisal may be computerized	14. User (teacher, custodian, etc.)
15. Spot checks and inspections	15. Business office and principal
16. Yearly inventory of all areas of supply storage	16. Business office (supply)
17. Use charts, reports, summaries	17. Business office (supply)

school's current conditions and planned changes. Signs had been ordered and plans had been made to assign monitors for following traffic flow. In visiting with him it soon became apparent his obsession for orderly movement was out of control. A similar danger lurks in supply management. Very sophisticated systems exist for purchasing, receiving, accounting, storing, and distributing materials. The systems can become an end rather than a means.

School business managers can establish systematic processes for operating and controlling supplies, but in the end the human being is the one who will be using both the materials and the controls. Thus the human element must be a major consideration when developing procedures. There is grave danger that overstructured requisitioning, recording, and reporting systems will create so much frustration and disgust among employees that they will actually confuse and misuse the process. The art of management, then, must predominate over the science of management.

In addition to lowering morale, complicated procedures can cost more in time and personnel services needed to accomplish them than they are worth. This is true in both supply administration and accounting. Experiences have taught that a school district can overcompensate for losses of supplies. Buildings have been built, vans purchased, people hired, and indeed losses were reduced. The problem that remained was that the expenditures to reduce the losses were far greater than the original losses.

Sometimes it is cheaper to consider certain supplies expendable than to worry about controlling them and accounting for them individually. The military discovered that it was spending two to three times the cost of certain supplies and equipment trying to control them. Often it is better to teach employees how to use supplies properly than to try to control each individual item. For example, supplies like paper, pencils, and paper clips must be controlled in some way, so that management can know approximately how much is being used and where, but rigid and complicated control procedures cost more—in morale as well as in money—than they are worth.

Instead of worrying about where each paper clip has gone, management can more profitably build up an appreciation of the proper use of school supplies and equipment. The cultivation of this desired attitude in all school personnel is a real challenge to management.

Summary

Supply management deals with the purchasing, receiving, storing, distribution, and accountability of supplies used in the operation and maintenance of schools. The way this management process is carried out is important; it can create among the public an impression of waste and dishonesty, or one of thrift and integrity.

Many improved methods, and technologies have been developed in the area of supply management over the past few years. Large city schools are almost compelled by the immensity of their task to maintain a comprehensive central warehouse that operates daily. Smaller schools look with favor on the centrally administered, decentralized storage method. This plan combines the advantages of both the centralized and decentralized methods of storage. At the same time, it provides adequate control by placing definite responsibility on specific people and by establishing a system of records that follow the flow of supplies from the planning and purchasing stage to the expendable stage.

In the end it must be understood that systems are carried out by people. Thus when developing procedures, school administrators must give major consideration to the human element. When complicated reporting and follow-up procedures are required, more may be lost through poor morale and the cost of personnel services than the savings warrant. The real challenge to school business management is to create in all personnel an appreciation of the proper use of supplies and equipment.

For Further Thought

1. Make a survey of the equipment and supplies used by a teacher in one grade in a local school system. Determine whether or not he or she would use more if more were furnished by the school, and how a change in supplies might change the academic performance of the students.

2. List some situations where furnishing adequate supplies and equipment could save the school money.

3. Develop a supply system for a small school district which has 2,000 pupils, 98 teachers, and 4 buildings. Include principles of supply management and a flow chart, which shows the supply process from the time supplies are planned to the time they are expended.

4. Under what circumstances might it make economic sense to spend more than current losses to control losses?

5. What steps might be taken to offset perceived increases in losses as a result of participatory management?

6. Describe a control procedure whereby losses from a large central warehouse operation are curtailed by the warehouse employees.

7. Survey several school systems to determine the perceived strengths/weaknesses of the computer software they use to control inventory.

Chapter 9

Risk Management

The judge's gavel had sounded and the judgment went against the school. The district was liable for $500,000 damages plus actual medical expenses. The school superintendent and the business manager knew that even if the district's insurance program covered most of the costs, the school district was liable for court costs, attorneys' fees, and probably increased insurance costs in the future. The judge's decision meant dollar expenditures that could not be used for the educational program. But were there other decisions prior to the sound of the gavel that were now translated into reduced educational options and opportunities?

The principal had noticed that the old hickory tree in the southwest corner of the school was showing signs of stress the last two years. This August she noted several limbs were dead and others deteriorating. Since last year, the maintenance of the building and grounds was a site responsibility. Foreseeing problems, she contacted a company that did tree removal and trimming, asked their advice, and then agreed on removal of the old tree before school opened. Early into the project, a worker slipped and fell, and the accident left him with a permanently injured hand, a broken leg, and a seriously damaged hip. Did the principal have a copy of a certificate of insurance from the company which showed liability and workman's compensation insurance? Or was the school on its own?

A tornado struck. The second-grade children took the positions they had learned in tornado drills. The teacher pulled the curtains and shades to reduce glass injuries. The tornado hit the temporary structure they were in a glancing blow but many injuries occurred when the building tipped over on its side. Should the children have gone to the "permanent" structure nearby? What losses will be incurred in dollars, in the educational program, in fear? Walt Whitman wrote:[1]

> There was a child went forth
> And the first object he look'd upon, that object he became.
> And that object became part of him for the day or a certain part of the day.
> Or for many years or stretching cycles of years.

Certainly school districts cannot protect each child from every negative occurrence that may cause pain or fear or disability through the "stretching cycles of years," but it is important to reduce the risk of any harm that could come to the children and the school district.

Several sets of decisions preceded each of the three scenarios. Doing nothing is a decision although perhaps a careless or irresponsible one. If judgments went against the school in each case, the decisions were by default negative for the educational program. Indeed, as the hypothetical situations are written, it might be agreed that decisions were not made thereby resulting in the problems. If the school district wishes to have a risk management program, it should provide for it and begin to *manage* risk.

Risk Management: A Board of Education Responsibility

The school risk management program recognizes that there are many potential hazards in carrying out the activities of the schools. Equipment or facilities may break down and disrupt the educational program. Accidents may happen to employees, contractors, students, or school patrons which may put the schools at financial risk. A risk management program which includes safety programs, training, loss control, and insurance protects public funds so that unfortunate events will not further erode the educational dollar.

The mandated and implied powers of a school board require the school board to manage and control school property and school activities. In the case of buildings and equipment, it is clear that schools may furnish protection through insurance. The protection of loss as related to personal liability still provides problems for schools as discussed farther in the chapter.

A Risk Management Policy Is Essential

Like any other major responsibility of the board of education, the risk management plan should be set forth in a clearly stated school board policy. The business manager should carefully examine board policies to see that they are complete in scope. In the event areas are not covered, such as training or security measures, a recommendation should be made to the school superintendent regarding appropriate policy statements. The policy statements should be in line with state law, codes, and regulations. References to specific regulations or codes should be made in the risk-management policy statement whenever applicable.

The following should be included in a policy statement on risk management: type of protection deemed necessary; who is specifically responsible for the administration of the risk management program within the organization of the school; and what or how much outside consultant help is required. In addition, to place the whole plan on a more positive and corrective note, the risk-management policy statement should outline the service measures that will be taken to guard against potential hazards in the school plant and the educational measures that will be developed to encourage safety and security consciousness among those utilizing school facilities.

Identifying Risks

Identifying risks is the beginning point of an effective risk management program. Certain areas of concern are obvious: catastrophic occurrences, theft, liability for personal injury, vehicular accidents, and employee/student protection. At this point, the school business manager who is ordinarily directly involved with the risk management program makes a set of educational decisions which may be somewhat less obvious. The decisions cannot always be "absolutes" in the educational or business sense. As noted in earlier chapters, the decisions must at the same time enhance and protect the educational effectiveness of the school. An example might be the identification of potential risk in field trips for elementary school children to a metropolitan zoo or museum an hour's drive from their rural school. The authors have known of schools reducing the risk by 100 percent by simply not allowing field trips. Such an educational decision is detrimental to learning. Yet, with proper precautions the field trip may be less risk than the school's football program, and may be more defensible educationally.

Madsen and Walker provided a flow chart of activities and decision points depicting the risk management process (Figure 9-1).[2]

There are several sources available to assist the person charged with risk management to identify risks. Among the sources are records of past performance and examples of excellent communications with unit administrators/supervisors, and use of outside expertise when needed.

Records of Past Performance

Certain records are required such as those mandated by the Occupational Safety and Health Administration. Other records often are mandated by the state for certain reporting purposes. In addition, the risk manager will find an information base regarding activities in all the risk areas an essential identification tool. Such an information base would include, along with many others, cost and claims associated with specific activities such as sports, transportation, maintenance, contracts, money handling, vandalism, and natural disasters. What kinds of injuries are associated with what kinds of activities? Do patterns emerge regarding property losses? Over the last five years, what kinds of accidents have occurred? What kinds of losses have been suffered by the school district? Obviously, a computer-based set of data can be very helpful in manipulating data so they can be analyzed from several viewpoints.

The information base should be expanded and adjusted as activities change so that at any point in time a risk audit can be taken. A risk audit will help the risk manager focus on the often overlooked high-frequency, low-severity accidents as well as the low-frequency, high-severity accidents. A number of checklists or questionnaires are available from insurance companies, independent consultants, and organizations associated with the insurance sector. Using combinations of the aforementioned information along with outside experts may provide a number of ideas regarding what history and kinds of records to include in a risk-management information base.

Changes in activities will require changes in the information base. Among the key sources for learning about the changes are unit administrators.

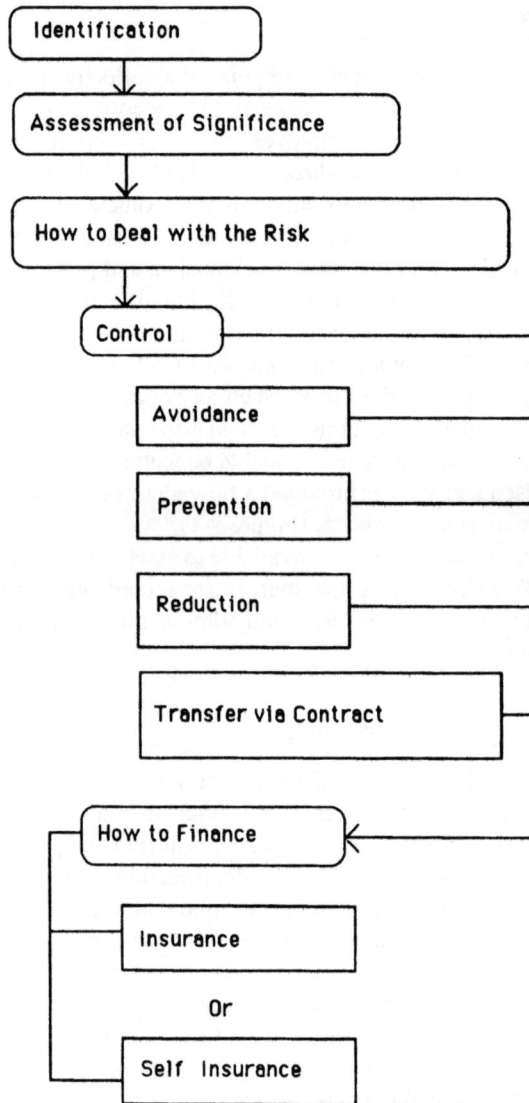

FIGURE 9-1   A Flow Chart of Risk Management Decision Points. (Adapted from Madsen and Walker.)

Communications with Unit Administrators

As noted in preceding chapters, two-way communications are important. The risk manager needs to receive information about new or expanded activities from each unit administrator. Communications include changes in activities, materials, or equipment that may change the risk of conducting the activities. Because of renovations, a summer swimming program may need to be moved to another facility. Are all the safety features the same? Should some provisions be made to reduce added risks? Additional field trips have been planned for a special group of students considered to be academically at-risk. During the field trip the students will be in businesses, theatres, and community buildings for both day and evening events. Is the risk factor increased for the schools? A new school-business partnership has resulted in "internships" for selected students whereby part of their day is spent in performing work for the businesses involved in the partnership. Are the details communicated to the risk manager clearly so that proper steps can be taken to protect all concerned?

Principals, buildings and grounds director, transportation supervisor, special education director, and all other unit administrators should each provide information to the risk manager. Another point concerning risk communications should be noted. Unit administrators cannot communicate to the risk manager the information he or she needs unless they are informed regarding its importance and the type of information that is needed. The risk manager has to assume the responsibility to communicate, in fact educate, other unit administrators regarding risk factors, needed information, and appropriate timing. A close working relationship can be established and maintained so that the risk manager can serve in an advisory capacity, often in the planning stages of changes. Again, the educator role of the school business manager comes into play to assure that wise decisions are made which enhance the mission of the school as well as keeping risk at a minimum.

Outside Expertise

New activities, complicated facilities planning, or a disturbing set of data in the information base may suggest that a person from outside the school district may be helpful. Outside experts may include fellow school business officials, insurance company consultants, the state department of education, state and national professional associations (the Association of School Business Officials, American Association of School Administrators, etc.), or other personnel specializing in risk management. Often the assistance is free or minimal in cost.

Transferring or Retaining Risks

The school district may wish to share the risk of losses with other agencies and schools by purchasing insurance. Candoli et al. note the following conditions that make a risk insurable:[3]

1. The peril insured against must produce a definite, fortuitous loss not under the control of the insured.
2. There must be a large number of homogeneous exposures subject to the same peril.
3. The loss must be calculable and the cost of insuring it must be economically feasible.

4. The peril must be unlikely to affect all the insured simultaneously.

5. The loss, when it occurs, must be financially serious.

Laws and regulations change continuously and vary from state to state, therefore, it is important to review the codes and regulations regarding school insurance before evaluating the insurance program. For example, the Illinois Local Government and Governmental Employees Tort Immunity Act (Ill. Rev. Stat. Ch. 85), 1-101 *et seg*)[4] allows school districts to levy a tax to pay for the cost of risk management. Whether the school should pay for certain types of insurance is still open to question in some states particularly in the area of personal liability. After carefully checking out the state law and board policy, the manager is at a decision point. How best to obtain dollars for instructional purposes versus expenditures for insurance becomes part of the question. Would fewer dollars be spent by sharing the risk with others through an insurance policy, or should the school retain the risk alone or through some cooperative effort with other school districts by self-insurance or self-funding?

Retaining the Risk

A current and complete data base is essential to making a good decision to self-insure. A history of incidents by type, frequency, location, and similar factors to aid analysis will focus on those risks of high-frequency, low-severity that may be good candidates for self-insurance. Jordan et al. noted that glass breakage may be an area where the cost of coverage through an insurance policy may cost more than having glass replaced by the school's maintenance crew.[4]

School districts may not have to self insure alone. Some states permit cooperatives which share risk because they have pooled resources. In Missouri, for example, member school districts constitute the Missouri United School Insurance Council which provides the usual property and casualty coverages. Holley noted that there "are over 200 public entity pooling arrangements in the country."[6] For example a very large percentage of school districts in California are self-insured by some type of pooled arrangement. Florida also has several cooperatives of this type. He cautions that when making a decision to join a pooling arrangement to be sure to compare the costs, coverages, services, ease of local administration, and the school district's control over its own program.

A variation on the theme of self-insuring by means of operating funds, is self-funding. Self-funding is simply setting aside funds designated for covering certain losses. The pooling arrangement noted is one form of self-funding. While economy of scale is a consideration, each district must determine its relative chances for loss and the least costly means of covering the loss.

The following points may be helpful to the school business manager facing the decision regarding self-insurance.

1. Reserve funds must be large enough to cover any reasonable emergency, at least larger than the risk represented by the largest anticipated loss.

2. Extremely hazardous risks should be insured by an insurance company.

3. Investment of reserve insurance funds should be regulated by state law or at least by a firm board of education policy.

4. Regular appropriations should be made yearly to maintain the insurance fund, and any excesses should be rebated at the end of the year.

5. Policy covering the management of the reserve insurance fund should be clearly established and put in writing.

6. Self-insurance should be established gradually unless a fund can be immediately created large enough to absorb anticipated losses.

7. Property within a school district contemplating self-insurance should be geographically dispersed so that a loss affecting all or most units would not be possible.

Many small school districts provide for self-insurance in a variety of areas by setting up maintenance appropriations in their yearly budget. For example, self-maintenance on glass breakage is more reasonable in most cases than glass insurance. In addition, educational prevention programs can cut down this breakage considerably. Collision insurance for a bus fleet is a questionable expense and it will usually be less expensive for school districts to cover their own damages. All-risk policies may be unnecessary if proper management procedures are used. Portions of the robbery, burglary, and theft insurance can be useless, depending on the night-watch situation, banking hours, security measures, and type of neighborhood.

Questions that should be asked before dropping or adding insurance include the following:

1. Would a loss or damage in the area under question seriously hamper the educational program?

2. Can money be budgeted yearly to cover the possible loss?

3. Can the loss or damage be easily corrected by the regular maintenance staff?

4. Can the establishment of reasonable security measures prevent loss or damage?

5. Will the establishment of good management procedures prevent loss or damage?

6. Does the expense for loss or damage appreciably exceed the cost of insurance premiums? Are there enough cases involved to permit the calculation of valid averages? That is, are the losses predictable?

7. Does the insurance company service provide valuable safety measures for the school district which would otherwise be difficult to provide, such as periodic boiler inspections?

Grabill reported the savings realized by one school district in the area of long-term disability.[7] The district was paying premiums up to $78,960. The legislature then made it possible to self-fund long-term disability risk. Given the opportunity, the schools carefully reviewed five years of data, and moved to a partially self-funded program which has provided savings of nearly $29,000 actual dollars to cover a payroll that has increased almost 75 percent.

Transferring the Risk

The most common means of transferring risks is to purchase insurance. There are two categories, property and liability. The following types are the most common and they may be purchased separately or ordinarily in some comprehensive or extended plans which combine them.

Common *property* insurances include:

Fire: Insures buildings and contents against damage by fire. It may also be extended to include smoke damage and other related losses.

Wind: Insures buildings and contents against damage by windstorms and tornadoes.

Boiler and machinery: Insures against losses incurred as a result of boiler or pressure tank explosions. In addition, pumps, fans, compressors, generators, and many other types of machinery may be part of this type of insurance.

Glass: Insures against losses incurred from window or door glass breakage.

Floater or all-risk: A variety of losses may be covered under this type of insurance. Examples include property loss during messenger deliveries, personal property of employees, and a variety of other property losses.

Vehicle: This insurance, divided into two types, protects the school district against (1) loss due to damage or destruction of the vehicle itself, and/or (2) liability for damage and injury caused by the vehicle to persons or property.

Liability insurances commonly purchased by school districts include the vehicle liability noted above plus the following:

Liability: This policy pays for bodily injury damage which may be caused by accidents arising from negligence of employees or from property owned, used, or maintained by the school district.

Workman's Compensation: This protects the school from loss by reason of liability imposed by law for damages because of injury, disease, or death of employees resulting from employment.

Surety bonds: This insurance is of three general types. Fidelity bonds protect the school district against loss or damage through dishonesty of employees. Public officials bonds provide against loss not only for dishonesty but from misfeasance and malfeasance of office. Contract bonds insure against loss due to failure of a contractor to provide services, supplies, equipment, and facilities as agreed on with the school district.

Accident insurance for pupils: This insurance provides coverage for pupils in the school who may be injured while participating in school activities.

Employee Benefits Insurance: Ordinarily this type of insurance includes medical, hospitalization, and major medical coverage. Premium costs are usually shared, with the employee paying a percentage. Life insurance often is part of an employee benefits package.

Although insurance itself has a long historical background, only in the last few decades has responsibility for the school insurance program become a major administrative duty. Even today there is no common pattern of insurance coverage. Some schools may purchase many different types of insurance, whereas others may carry little or no insurance whatsoever. Some states have established state-operated school insurance programs while others have opted to be uninvolved except in areas such as workman's compensation.

Selecting an Agent or Broker

The method of selecting an insurance agent or broker may be one of the most politically difficult problems facing the school district. It involves some of the same political considerations that other purchasing acts involve in that there are many agents writing insurance for different companies in any community. Invariably the attitude prevails that if any insurance is written, local agents as taxpayers should participate.

A distinction should be made between agent and broker. An agent represents a company and, as noted by Vaughn, has a legal relationship whereby the agent can bind a company to a risk. A broker represents the client and cannot bind a company to a risk.[8]

There are four general methods of selecting an insurance provider for the school district:

1. Competitive bidding.

2. Finding the best match between the school district's predetermined objective criteria established by the board of education and the insurance provider. The following criteria are frequently included: financial security of the company; type of service(s) provided; *Best's Insurance Guide* rating; management services and costs.

3. Placing insurance service with an agent's or broker's association which represents the majority of the insurance opportunities in the community.

4. Other means include personal knowledge of the agent. This practice is always open to question and can deteriorate into a patronage practice on the part of the school administration or board.

Jordan et al. cite the following as useful criteria in making comparisons:[9]

- References, particularly from other school districts
- Professional reputation
- Years of experience, especially in writing school coverage
- Amount of insurance in force
- Location and staffing office
- Loss prevention and control services
- Ability to provide personalized service
- Assistance in time loss

- Professional knowledge and training, as evidenced by attaining such standings as chartered property casualty underwriter (CPCU) or charter life underwriter (CPU)
- Access to insurance suppliers

Although one insurance method may be excellent public relations, it should not be used if it results in greater cost. Some cities have insurance associations that will handle school insurance purchases on a nonprofit basis. Even so, an annual review of costs and alternative costs should be made to assure that the most dollars are available to the school's primary mission on a short- and long-term basis.

Bid or Negotiate?

Competitive bidding has proved to be successful in bringing down prices. Some states require competitive bidding either across the board or for specific coverages. As noted earlier, pooling and reciprocal *insurance* arrangements[10] may also influence the price structure in the insurance market. Traditionally, schools may have been paying more than their share of the shared risk. Public schools are buying so much insurance of all types today that they should be considered a risk class by themselves; they would thereby gain advantage in a favorable-risk situation. Public schools should be considered preferred risks because of the following:

1. They are under continuous public scrutiny and subject to heavy criticism if a child's safety is endangered in any way.

2. Public schools through popularly elected boards of education, parent-teacher associations, advisory committees, alumni groups, and taxpayers are subject to closer observation and must be more observant of the will of the people than any other institution, public or private.

3. More provisions are made for inspection and for the regulation of safety features in school than in any other institution.

4. Public school building plans and specifications are rigidly controlled and in most cases must be approved by the state.

5. Personnel working for the public schools are predominantly professional people who are extremely sensitive to the safety of children.

6. State rules and regulations in regard to school bus drivers and bus transportation are extensive in scope and rigidly enforced.

7. Because of the emphasis on safety for children there is a carryover emphasis on safety for all personnel working in the school.

8. Officials responsible for school affairs are not inclined toward dishonesty, misfeasance, and malfeasance of office because of the large number of people to whom they are responsible and the extent of public scrutiny.

The above points should provide a strong argument for the schools to demand competitive pricing.

If the school district wishes to use bidding, it is important to write the specifications very carefully. If the school business official/risk manager is just beginning the process, he or she may wish to seek some outside help from colleagues, associations, or experts in the field of insurance as practitioners or university personnel. State and school board requirements regarding bidding procedures should be followed. Some of the features unique to the school insurance bidding process may be the inclusion of the following:

1. Specific data regarding the property and/or activities under consideration.

2. Data showing claim experiences in the area to be insured.

3. A listing and explanation of associated loss control programs.

4. Forms which are completed by the bidders showing financial status; history of having written similar coverages, claim management services, current rating in *Best's Insurance Guide,* detailed rates per coverage, and payment expectations. Many other areas could be included to ensure that the selection is being made on comparable data.

Some school districts have been able to obtain lower rates through negotiations since the process allows for the companies to offer alternatives. Even if the rates remain the same, maximum allowances may be increased. The caution is that comparable data should be examined.

Liability

Liability of school districts has become a subject of controversy and extremes. As a result, we see a wide variation in liability insurance practices throughout the United States. For years there was some question whether it was legal for schools to carry liability insurance. This question arose from the old doctrine that "the King can do no wrong." In accepting this British common law idea, the state was considered sovereign and therefore could not be sued without its consent. As an agent of the state, the schools were not held to be liable while performing government functions unless liability is created by statute. Those ideas appear to have gone by the wayside and litigation has become commonplace relative to the school's liability.

Transportation as an Example

In the relatively safe confines of the school where factors of safety are controlled by the school administration, accidents which may create liability are rare. The school bus takes pupil and employee away from this sequestered environment and subjects him or her to the many perils of the public highway over which the school administration has no control. There then arises a moral obligation to protect pupil and employee through adequate insurance so that if injury or death results on the highway the entire burden of the damage will not be imposed on the person who suffered the injury. States have recognized this responsibility and passed legislation whereby school districts are either allowed or required to purchase liability insurance for buses.

The well-known Molitor case in Illinois can be considered a landmark in the controversy over the liability of school districts for torts of its agents in regard to transportation and perhaps in regard to all school activities.[11] It was the first case in this country in which, in the absence of statute, the doctrine of governmental immunity was stricken down by a court of last resort.

The case arose as a result of a suit against a school district for injuries sustained by a student when the school bus in which he was riding went out of control owing to the alleged negligence of the driver. In the words of the court: "We are squarely faced with the highly important question . . . should a school district be immune from liability for tortiously inflicted personal injury to a pupil thereof arising out of the operation of a school bus owned and operated by said school district?" The court answered this question in the negative, stating that it found the doctrine of school district immunity to be "unsound and unjust" in the light of modern-day conditions.

> *We are of the opinion that school district immunity cannot be justified on this theory. As was stated by one court, "the whole doctrine of governmental immunity from liability for torts rests upon a rotten foundation. it is almost incredible that in this modern age of comparative sociological enlightenment, and in a republic, the medieval absolutism supposed to be implicit in the maxim, 'The King can do no wrong,' should exempt the various branches of the government from liability for their torts, and that the entire burden of damage resulting from the wrongful acts of a government should be imposed upon the single individual who suffers the injury, rather than distributed among the entire community constituting the government, where it could be borne without hardship upon any individual, and where it justly belongs"!*

The Concept of Liability

Liability has been referred to as the law of torts. There are intentional, absolute, and negligence torts. The school may be held liable for the on-the-job actions of an employee which resulted in injury or loss to another. The school may be liable also for the lack of action by an employee who did not act in the way a reasonable and prudent person would act. Negligence has been the point of many lawsuits.

Maintaining a safe environment and conducting the activities of the school in a safe manner is expected. Not to do so makes the school vulnerable to negative judgments.

Common Types of Liability Insurance

Personal liability insurance protects the school district from injuries and personal property losses incurred by individuals as a result of action by school employees as part of their work.

Professional insurance, or as it is sometimes called *malpractice insurance,* protects the school district against claims of improper or inadequate delivery of educational services.

Worker's compensation insurance is required. It provides workers a route to reasonable and prompt payments for costs connected with on-the-job injuries. A school district should require a certificate of insurance proving worker's compensation for contractors doing work for the school.

The liability insurance market has continued to be volatile. Again, schools appear to be paying more in premiums than seems appropriate. Legislative reforms setting caps on judgments may help. The relationship to claims paid and premiums is hard to understand. Mayer and LeVan report an example: "In 1986 in New Jersey, $65 million was paid in premiums for excess liability coverage and only $1.2 million was paid out in major claims."[12] The risk manager is obligated to study continuously the liability insurance situation and to seek proactive means to reduce the risks through educational programs, continuous two-way communications, and regular, expert inspections.

Proactive Practice

It is clear that waiting for something to happen is not risk management but rather risk reaction. If the school district is to manage risk, the person assigned the responsibility must initiate positive steps toward reducing or finding ways to avoid risk. Normally, this could be considered a business management function. Martini suggested that a wellness program may serve as a way to reduce health care costs.[13] While costs of premiums may be reduced, other losses of time and quality also may be reduced when employees have better energy levels and are absent less frequently. A program aimed at increasing employee wellness may be a good, proactive investment to reduce risk.

One way to avoid risk is to not allow certain activities. This kind of avoidance of risk, however, is occasionally detrimental to educational purposes, as noted earlier in the field trip example. An understanding of the educational process and outcomes is essential to making appropriate decisions. If the risk manager must report to the school business manager, it is possible that the instructional dimension will enter at this point. To rely totally on the school superintendent to strike the balance may be asking more than should be asked. The argument that the school business manager should be grounded in educational practice is again reinforced.

The school district wishing to manage risk will do the following:

1. Appoint an administrator as the district risk manager. This position should be high enough in the hierarchy to stress the importance of the activity.

2. Provide sufficient budget to the activity so that related educational and training activities are conducted regularly; materials and information can be disseminated; and planning time is provided. In addition, sufficient funds should be available to acquire outside expertise on an ad hoc basis if needed. The risk manager, or someone reporting to him or her, should be able to stay abreast of current issues in the field by means of subscriptions, seminars, and professional associations.

3. Encourage team interaction among all unit administrators with a focus on safety and reduced risk practices. Sending memos or holding an annual meeting will not result in the kind of team effort required. Operating each activity in a proactive, safe manner should become part of the routine of practice in each unit whether it is the transportation department, the chemistry class, or play production.

A risk-free environment may not be realistic, but a team effort toward managing risk as a value of proper practice at all levels is realistic. A strong and educationally sound approach to risk management can have a positive effect beyond reduced losses or smaller premiums.

For Further Thought

1. What insurance coverage is mandated in your state?

2. Is there any type of insurance prohibited by your state for purchase by schools?

3. Design a year-long communication process regarding risk management among all units in your school district.

4. Justify the expenditure of any tax dollars for insurance.

5. Compare board of education policy statements from several districts regarding risk management.

6. List the local court cases within the last three years that have risk management implications.

7. List the proactive loss control practices in your school. Compare with other school districts' practices.

8. What is the frequency of school districts being self-insured in your state? In what risk areas are they self-insured?

Endnotes

1. Walt Whitman, "There Was a Child Went Forth," in *The Literature of the United States,* Walter Blair, Theodore Hornberger and Randall Stewart, eds., Chicago: Scott Foresman and Company, 1949.

2. Claudina Madsen and John H. Walker, *Risk Management and Insurance: A Handbook of Fundamentals* (Washington, D.C.: National Association of College and University Business Officers, 1983), p. 35. Also provided in this handbook is an excellent glossary of terms on pp. 64–76.

3. Carl I. Candoli et al., *School Business Administration: A Planning Approach* (Boston: Allyn and Bacon, Inc., 1978), pp. 263–264.

4. Karl R. Ottosen, "Funding Risk Management," *School Business Affairs* 55, No. 6 (June 1989): 33–35.

5. K. Forbis Jordan, Mary P. McKeown, Richard G. Salmon, and L. Dean Webb, *School Business Administration* (Beverly Hills, Calif.: Sage Publications, 1985), p. 376.

6. Darrell L. Holley, "Music to Their Ears: The Missouri United School Insurance Council," *School Business Affairs* 56, No. 6 (June 1990): 29.

7. Thomas G. Graybill, "Self-Funded Long Term Disability," *IASBO Intercom* 26, No. 5 (June 1990): 6; 8.

8. Emmett J. Vaughn, *Fundamentals of Risk and Insurance,* 5th ed. (New York: John Wiley and Sons, 1989).

9. Jordan et al., *School Business Administration,* p. 368.

10. See Allison J. Lapetina, "The New York Schools Insurance Reciprocal," *School Business Af-* *fairs* 56, No. 6 (June 1990): 32–34, for a discussion of reciprocal insuring.

11. *Molitor et al. v. Kaneland Community Unit School District No. 302,* 163 N.E. 2d 89 (1959).

12. David H. Mayer and Donald D. LeVan, "District Liability Insurance Coverage Revisited," *School Business Affairs* 53, No. 6 (June 1987): 11.

13. Gilbert R. Martini, Jr., "Wellness Programs: Preventive Medicine to Reduce Health Care Costs," *School Business Affairs* 57, No. 6 (June 1991): 8–11.

Chapter *10*

Transportation Services

Equalization of educational opportunity is vital to democracy. Every American youth must have the opportunity to develop his or her constructive capabilities to the utmost. America can flourish and prosper and be truly democratic only if the talents of all its youth are developed and allowed to contribute to the well-being of the nation. If restrictions are placed on educational opportunities because of geographical location, or physical, social, and economic conditions, then society must work to remove these restrictions. A factor that plays a major role in safeguarding and enhancing equal educational opportunity is the school transportation system.

The history of school transportation shows that it is inseparably woven into the social and economic development of our nation. Transportation services grew up as an integral part of modern education; the added mobility broke the bonds of rural isolation by making a high school education more easily available to all students. As transportation capabilities have expanded, so have possibilities for adding flexibility to the educational program. Today, school transportation is universally used, and has become a means to realize educational and social goals.

Although the expenditure of public funds for pupil transportation was first legalized by Massachusetts in 1869, not until after World War II did its growth foretell that it would be one of the major auxiliary services of the school. Today those yellow buses carry millions of pupils millions of miles each day.

The State's Role

The responsibility assumed by state departments of education relative to transporting students ordinarily falls into three general areas: (1) control and disbursement of state-aid funds earmarked for transportation; (2) control of transportation factors that lend themselves to central regulation, such as safety, school bus standards, inspections, transportation codes, interdistrict relationships, and reporting; and (3) services to provide general improvement in all areas of transportation, such as leadership conferences, training, and consultant help.

Financing transportation varies widely across the United States. Zeitlin[1] analyzed each state's pattern for funding transportation. Four patterns emerged:

	No. of States
Funding the actual cost	13
Flat rate per unit	4
Multivariate calculations and factors	29
No distinct transportation funds	4

Zeitlin found that the states had three goals regarding funding transportation.[2]

1. Ensure that all districts provide a minimum level of transportation.
2. Encourage districts to provide efficient and effective transportation service.
3. Distribute state funds equitably and so as to equalize the educational opportunities in each district.

Transportation Is Different

School bus transportation as a process differs from all other educational services. It is not contained in or confined to school grounds and buildings. The school bus must make its way on state and county highways where the sheltered atmosphere of the school no longer prevails. Most of the rules and regulations which govern its operation are state laws enforced by state, county, or local police—all noneducational agencies. Thus, positive leadership by the state in the transportation area is necessary. The school district also has a vital role to play. It is necessary for school administrators to provide positive leadership. Unless laws, codes, and policies are developed with the cooperation of professional educators, those regulations may be established with little regard for their effect on children.

Throughout the fifty states, noneducational agencies exert varying control over pupil transportation in a number of ways. Of course all the laws of the road, along with the licensing process for both vehicles and drivers, are established and enforced by noneducational agencies. In many states noneducational agencies have some responsibility for developing school bus standards, and inspecting school buses, sometimes periodically and sometimes on request. Other functions carried out in states by noneducational agencies include training bus drivers, administering special examinations to bus drivers, purchasing buses, and approving routes.

The public school pupil transportation program is only one aspect of an extremely broad area of governmental activity. The following generally accepted educational principle is particularly germane here: *The educational function is so complex that it is accomplished through a number of institutions, agencies, and activities of which the formally organized public school is only one. Cooperation with other educational, governmental, and social agencies is essential to the realization of mutually desirable outcomes.*

While no portion of the educative process can be confined to a single institution, the need for cooperative action is nowhere so pointedly illustrated as in pupil transportation. As a school bus leaves the school grounds it inevitably comes under state control and is subject to interferences from nonschool agencies locally, countywide, and statewide. As the school bus rolls onto state and federal highways where vehicles of all types are traveling, it makes sense to have nationwide uniformity of school bus laws so that motorists will not have to know fifty different state laws relating to school buses.

The problem of building or improving a highway, particularly limited access highways, illustrates the complexity of the pupil transportation system. How will attendance areas be affected? Pupil time on the bus? Isolation of parts of the district? Cost factors if routes are lengthened in miles and time? The reader can extend the list of possible changes and problems.

Pupil transportation is a challenge to democratic action because it involves local, county, state, and national agencies of all types on a day-to-day basis. Local school authorities cannot wait for others to take action. It is up to them to take the initiative; otherwise, procedures may become so firmly fixed that they cannot be changed. Policies, laws, regulations, and codes having an influence on education and the pupil transportation program must be developed in relation to their effect on the school district's children. Only educators working cooperatively at all levels of government can be sure this emphasis is considered.

Private Contract System or School Ownership and Control

It should not be assumed that all pupil transportation systems are controlled and operated by the school. The first transportation programs were organized by parents getting together and making private arrangements for someone to transport their children to school. Later as state and local funds became available, boards of education often continued the practice of contracting with some local person to carry children to and from school. There are even many cases of joint ownership in which the school purchased bus bodies and then contracted with a local farmer to put the bodies on the chassis of their trucks in the wintertime for transportation of children.

Miller argues that contracting for transportation services is an advantage to most school districts.[3] He notes that many school districts face a cash flow problem, leasing is generally not a good option, and additional employee responsibilities are shifted to the school district when the school owns its buses. The major advantages attributed to the private contract system are that

1. It relieves school officials of a major management responsibility in maintenance and operation.
2. Capital outlay expenses for buses and equipment are eliminated.
3. A portion of the complaints and criticisms of the public can be directed to the contractor rather than to the school administration.

There are several cautions to be noted for the school district planning to contract transportation services. Obviously, one is to know the service records, accidents, and on-time performances of the prospective contractors. However, transportation services are just that—a service provided. The service aspect of the contract must be spelled out in detail. The specifications regarding equipment, time, supervision, safety, discipline, maintenance, training, and even how changes will be made need to be clearly detailed. Transporting exceptional students takes special attention.

While contracting for services may appear to relieve school districts of potential hassles and even cash needs, another dimension of pupil transportation may complicate the decision. If the pupils were in a state of suspended animation during the time they spent traveling on the school bus and did not receive or give any input, thought about nothing and saw nothing, then the argument could be made that no learning was taking place. As any pupil or bus driver can testify, such is not the case. For better or for worse, learning of all kinds takes place on school busing trips. The school administrators and board of education need to make a decision regarding whether or not the time pupils spend traveling on the school bus is useful, or potentially harmful, learning time. Is the bus ride a continuation of the home learning environment while riding to school and the school learning environment while on the return ride home? Should the school view the bus as an extension of the school?

Viewed from this perspective, contracting with a private enterprise to operate pupil transportation is no more justifiable than contracting with an outsider to operate school buildings or other equipment.

Advantages attributed to the school-owned pupil transportation system are that

1. It may be less expensive than the private contract system.
2. Buses may be used more easily for other aspects of the school program such as field trips and athletic events.
3. Buses can be operated as an integral part of the total school program.
4. Bus drivers can be selected and trained on the basis of their understanding of children as well as their ability to drive.
5. Control measures in regard to discipline and road procedures are easier to enforce.
6. It fits into the general pattern of public ownership of school buildings and other facilities.
7. Flexibility is possible because adaptations to changing conditions are under the direct control of school officials.
8. It may reduce the legal complexities should litigation occur.

Organizing the Transportation System

In the 1930s approximately two-thirds of the buses used for pupil transportation were contracted. The early practice of private contracting for pupil transportation caused some lag in the development of accepted organizational patterns for handling pupil transportation. Even after pupil transportation became accepted as a public responsibility, boards of education, through custom, were in many cases inclined to let the program run itself. A study of school organization today shows that in too many instances the transportation system in many school systems is viewed as some sort of appendage lacking systematic integration into the total school program.

Pupil transportation requires exacting business management and scheduling; it cannot function without efficient organizational direction and control. Operationally, the pupil transportation program gains its authority at the local level through policies and administrative decisions of the board of education. As an auxiliary service requiring business management skills, its most appropriate place is under the administrative direction of the assistant superintendent for school business management, who through his or her abilities and training as both an educator and business manager is able to build it into an integral part of the educational system.

Legal Basis

The management and control of the school transportation system may involve many legal problems. Since school transportation has grown so extensively, we are not surprised that it has been faced with legal problems as well as educational "growing pains." A study of any of the digests of court cases reveals not only that there has been a great deal of litigation over school transportation but that this litigation has covered a wide range of topics. Because litigation results from dispute and controversy, the topics covered indicate those areas in which local policy should be particularly clear-cut. The topics generally under dispute include the following: authority to use school funds for transportation, eligibility for transportation, determination of distance the child has to walk to meet the bus, responsibility to establish bus routes, liability for bus accidents, insurance, legal responsibility for bus operation, responsibility for bus discipline, status and authority of the bus driver, necessity for a bus driver to be carefully screened and selected and to submit to a physical examination, and eligibility of parochial school students to participate in the public school transportation program.

Early court decisions, in the majority, held that a school had no authority to transport children to and from school unless the state legislature granted it power to do so. Now all states have laws authorizing pupil transportation programs. The courts have unanimously upheld the constitutionality of these laws and have been hesitant to step in and invade the perogative of a local school board in its operation of a transportation system or to permit other agencies or officials to do so. It is well settled that as long as a school board's action does not conflict with any specific statutory provision, the local school board may adopt reasonable rules and regulations for the management of its buses. If the school board does not act in an arbitrary or capricious manner the courts will not interfere. On the basis of this authority the school board may establish bus routes within a reasonable distance of a child's home, determine the number and type of vehicles necessary to transport the pupils of the district, and, in general, use sound discretion in establishing operational procedures. The board of education also has authority over the bus driver, the budget, and discipline.

Policy in Regard to School Transportation

Official policies governing pupil transportation should be adopted and recorded by the local board of education and made known throughout the school district. These policies should present the school board's legal relationship to state and local agencies and then enumerate the powers and duties of the local school board as defined by law. Following the presentation of the legal framework, the policies should describe how the school system will operate within the framework.

Typical local policies may be established under the following headings: (1) objectives; (2) responsibility (superintendent, school business manager, transportation supervisor, principal, teacher); (3) eligibility for transportation; (4) provisions for transporting all categories of exceptional disabled students; (5) selection and training of operating personnel; (6) use of buses; (7) management process such as purchasing, maintenance, and operation; (8) safety; (9) recording and reporting; (10) insurance; (11) discipline; (12) transportation of nonpublic school children; (13) evaluation; and (14) continuing review of policy.

Written policies give consistent direction and stability to the operation of pupil transportation in the community. As the overall guiding force for education in the community, these policies assure proper integration of all activities of the school. Most important, they provide a framework within which the activity must function.

Studying the Transportation Program

When studying a transportation system, the school should collect the same type of information that it uses when studying the need for a new building or a new course of study. In fact, a transportation study should be an integral part of the long-range educational master plan. Understanding the potentialities in transportation allows for flexibility in planning buildings and programs for years ahead. At the same time, an effective transportation system cannot be established without an understanding of the area it is to serve, including predictions of community growth, school enrollment, and expansion in communications. Every segment of study involved in the development of the long-range master plan is also involved in laying the foundation for the transportation system. Once the groundwork is laid by the long-range master plan, the specific transportation survey may then bring the master-plan data up-to-date and add to these data where necessary. Obviously as the planning process is updated, the pertinent information that affects the service of the transportation system needs to be used to refine the transportation plan.

The lack of coordination of data can be a problem. The computer can assist in this regard and since the school business manager ordinarily provides much of the data for the planning process, he or she can use or provide access for the transportation planning and updates. Often school districts conduct or are required to conduct an annual census to identify school-age children as well as children requiring special services. The process varies from school district to district but for the first part of the study the following information is usually required: (1) householder's name(s), (2) address, (3) telephone number, (4) name and date of birth of each child, (5) if of school age, name of school and grade level, (6) special needs of children of any age legally qualified to receive special services. Integrated into the needed data should be specialized placements available in choice programs, magnet schools, or special services schools providing for exceptional children, latchkey programs, and preschool or after-school programing including sports activities. When in-migration or out-migration is a significant factor, the planning task becomes very complex.

The second portion of the study should deal with recommendations regarding management and operation, that is, maintenance, equipment and supplies needed, office procedures, records and reports, and supervisory processes.

The third portion of the study should be coordinated closely with instruction, for it deals with student safety, discipline, student helpers and assistants, and methods of obtaining parent cooperation and advice.

Naturally, the data and recommendations obtained in this transportation study will form the basis for revision and improvement of policies previously developed by the board of education.

Transporting the Exceptional Child

Compliance with laws and regulations regarding disabled children will increase the costs and complexity of transportation services. Some states have discovered it costs four to five times as much to transport disabled students as for the regular student; others even higher. Anthony and Inman note the following factors that affect the cost of transporting exceptional students:[4]

1. The number of handicapped students with a particular handicap being served within a school district
2. Severity of the handicap
3. Location of programs
4. Inefficiency in management and operation procedures

The desire to provide the least restrictive environment for exceptional children would suggest transporting nearly all exceptional children by regular buses on regular routes. This does require special attention on the part of the school district, whether contracting for or operating its own transportation service. As noted earlier, the bus ride provides ample opportunities for learning to take place. In this discussion the authors have used the terms "exceptional" or "special" when referring to pupils with disabilities being transported except when quoting from another work. The term "handicapped" may not apply to many exceptional children insofar as they do not accept or believe what others may try to impose on them—that they cannot, or even should not, participate in our society as those without a disability. If the exceptional student does accept the imposed devaluation, then he or she indeed is handicapped. The bus ride, sometimes adding up to several hours per week, can add to the risk of imposing additional handicaps on the exceptional child. It is an issue which the schools should address as part of their philosophy regarding transportation services.

For those students who should not and cannot use regular buses, a number of decisions have to be made on almost a case-by-case basis. Door-to-door transportation can be provided in some cases by parents who are reimbursed at an appropriate rate, sometimes set by the state. The advantages are obvious. There are risk considerations as well as the need for consistent and punctual pickup and dropping off of the children. Private companies or city transportation companies may be contracted for the service. If the numbers warrant, the school may save some money by operating its own specialized vehicles. More recently, the regular size bus is being equipped to handle wheelchairs. Casey cites Noel Biery's forecast that 54 passenger buses will be fitted with wheelchair lifts to accommodate disabled students.[5] The routes will become longer or more buses will be required given the reduced capacities. Biery suggested that "by 1995 the distinct difference between regular and special education transportation will become blurred."[6]

The school district should clarify proper procedures with parents or guardians regarding notification of illness, schedule changes, and/or claiming reimbursements for parent-transported pupils. As noted earlier in the chapter, the board of education should have clearly stated policies regarding transporting exceptional children.

Scheduling

With special programs requiring different times other than school opening and closing; with planning for exceptional children, magnet schools, parent choice, and increasing size of school districts because of consolidation, the scheduling of pupil transportation can be very complex. A small school district with few buses, limited routes, and low density pupil population will not need to computerize the route scheduling. As some of these factors begin to change, the school business manager may wish to explore some of the several computer route-scheduling programs available. Several advantages accompany computer scheduling such as speed of task completion, ability to consider many factors simultaneously, ability to construct answers to "what-if" questions, and (after the data have been put in and the program is running well) a cost saving.

The modeling capabilities can be of assistance in cost projections, planning questions, and can be responsive to changes. Hennessey described the use of computer scheduling in Lowell, Massachusetts which not only has high diversity, complex sheet configurations and natural barriers, but the added problems of immigration and secondary migration and parental controlled choice.[7] He noted that the use of the computer saved time and money for a fifty-three-bus transportation system.

A number of questions should be asked when considering computerized route scheduling:

1. Does the school district or the vendor have accurate data for current addresses, streets, traffic patterns (one-way streets, permanent changes, or detours, etc.)?

2. Does the hardware/software vendor have an established track record of high performance? Conversations with current clients who have similar needs will help establish the company's credibility.

3. How much of a time commitment is involved, and what kinds of data must be generated by the school district?

4. Does the school run the software or does the vendor run it?

5. Does the software utilize the student data base to generate answers to what-if questions. Salmon[8] suggests that a school district "test" the proposed transportation system to determine how well it will handle such what-if questions as: What if students change addresses? What if routes become overloaded? What if a school closes or one becomes a 7-8 instead of 6-8 school?

6. What kind of consulting backup is provided by the software vendor?

7. Does the software provide for multiple destinations and flexibility, and are those capabilities in place or under development?

8. What actual benefits accrue to the school district? Does the investment pay a real return?

Such considerations provide a beginning for the potential user to analyze a proposed computerized scheduling program.

The Transportation Supervisor

If the school district's transportation needs are large enough to warrant a transportation supervisor, he or she should have a thorough knowledge of bus transportation, operation, and maintenance; competence in business management practices including computer use if required; an understanding of the educational objectives of the school; an ability to supervise effectively and elicit cooperation; a liking for children; and high moral character.

The specific duties of the transportation supervisor are the following:

1. To carry out the transportation policies of the board of education as interpreted by administrative directives of the superintendent of schools, the assistant superintendent of schools, and the assistant superintendent for business affairs.

2. To maintain necessary route maps, records, and reports so that the school administration may be kept informed of the status and needs of pupil transportation.

3. To supervise and train bus drivers.

4. To carry on a continuous study of transportation problems so that necessary changes in traffic patterns, routes, bus stops, and other operational matters may be recommended.

5. To recommend the type of equipment and supplies to be purchased.

6. To supervise the maintenance shop and the servicing and maintenance of equipment.

7. To establish a preventive maintenance program.

8. To keep the assistant superintendent for business affairs continually advised on the efficiency of pupil transportation.

9. To work cooperatively with teachers, principals, and other school personnel in making the school transportation program a valuable service to the instructional program.

Supervisory Training

Occasionally the care with which administrators choose a supervisor for the school transportation program lulls those responsible into overlooking the need to continuously update the supervisor in perspective and skill. The following areas may suggest ideas to explore regarding the performance levels in top transportation unit administrators.

1. Ability to articulate the school's mission.

2. Ability to articulate specific linkages between educational programs and transportation services, e.g., special education, the complexities of meeting choice or magnet schools' needs, or discipline procedures.

3. Ability to identify underlying problems as well as pinpoint symptoms of employee dissatisfaction, with the aim of improving job performance.

4. Ability to analyze equipment use difficulties.

5. Ability to motivate drivers toward excellence.

6. Ability to develop and maintain a teaming environment.

7. Ability to develop or contribute to manuals for drivers and to conduct training programs.

Relationship with Teachers, Principals, and Other Executives of the School

When people with different specific duties have to work together there is a possibility that friction will arise unless responsibilities are spelled out and a willingness to cooperate to achieve a common goal is evident. Probably the first step toward smooth working relationships between the transportation administrator and his or her staff and the teaching staff is the understanding by transportation supervisors and drivers that they are performing a service to the instructional program; therefore, the major justification for their existence in the school system is the contribution they make to education. An operating principle established on the basis of this philosophy is: *Teachers, principals, and instructional leaders should participate in the development of any pupil transportation policy that affects the instructional program.* Decisions regarding the following subjects are among those which affect the instructional program: length and location of bus routes and their effect on attendance area and and class size, bus schedules, discipline on the bus, maximum time spent on the bus by students, distance a child must walk to a bus stop, and number of pupils on the bus. Examples of questions which have little effect on instruction and which might be decided independently of the instructional program include specific location of bus stop, type of equipment used, and bus driver reports.

The principal must be considered the chief administrator of the school plant to which he or she is assigned by the board of education, and as such is responsible for the children from the time they step onto school property, which includes the school bus, until the time they leave it. When the bus is on the school grounds the principal is responsible for the proper supervision of arriving, loading, and departing. He or she sets up safety and educational programs for transported pupils, arranges meetings in which pupil behavior and welfare may be discussed, and promotes programs for student assistants, patrols, and student transportation officers. Any major disciplinary problem is, of course, the principal's responsibility.

As complexities increase, the school business manager and superintendent or assistant superintendent for instruction should cooperatively develop and recommend transportation policies and procedures which will enhance the instructional mission of the school.

The Bus Driver

The school official cannot overlook the fact that anyone who works closely with children has a decided influence on them—a good or bad influence. The bus driver is a daily part of the children's lives; he or she performs an important function, and is a person whom some children, particularly the younger ones, may tend to see as a role model. Add to this the fact that the driver has the life and safety of forty or fifty children at stake and we can see why the bus driver is considered the most important single factor in any transportation program. In every area of management, it is people who make a plan succeed or fail, and transportation is no exception.

Because of the extreme importance of the school bus driver to the transportation program it follows that recruiting, selecting, training, retaining, and supervising the driver are some of the most important management activities in the transportation program.

Obtaining competent drivers is difficult because bus driving may be a part-time job and only a small number of people are so situated that they are able to take on this work. Some schools employ part-time factory or business workers, small-farm operators, retired workers, and housewives as bus drivers. Others may use people already employed by or affiliated with the school, such as teachers, custodians, or lunchroom workers. Because of the character of the job the employment problem is different in almost every community and its solution depends on local conditions. There are, however, certain guiding principles that should be adhered to in all situations. The person should have the following qualifications. He or she:

1. Should consider bus driving a very important employment activity.
2. Must have time available to participate fully in the formal training, in-service education programs, and meetings required of all drivers.
3. Must be free from mental and physical defects which would reduce his or her ability to drive safely, and must have a clean record regarding substance abuse.
4. Must be thoroughly reliable and of good moral character.
5. Should provide assurance that he or she expects to hold the job on a reasonably permanent basis.
6. Must be able to pass rigid tests in both driving and driving safety, including holding a commercial drivers license.
7. Must be of proven maturity and sound judgment.

Branson, Missouri schools use a two-stage process consisting of a reference checklist and a weighted rating scale. The rating scale, or Applicant Review as it is called by the school district administration, consists of items judged to be characteristic of a successful school bus driver:[9]

- Attitude
- Self starter
- Cooperation
- Compatibility
- Initiative
- People oriented
- References
- Communication skills

- Patience
- Enthusiasm, energy
- Appearance
- Previous driving experience
- Owns a telephone

- Organizational ability
- First aid knowledge
- Mechanical knowledge
- Educational knowledge

Driver Training

States may provide training sessions for school bus drivers, or require a minimum amount of participation in approved training to qualify for a certificate. Seldom do these workshops deal with the educational function of the transportation service, at least not in operational ways. Too often, discipline is alluded to as expected but little specific help is given to bus drivers. As a starting point, one school system included the following in its *School Bus Driver Handbook:*

25 Tips on Maintaining Discipline

1. Never give an order you do not mean to enforce.
2. The response of the child is in action. Give your command to stimulate action, not to check it. Say, "do this" rather than "don't do that". Suggest an action which can be successfully obeyed.
3. Give a child time for reaction.
4. Have a reason for what you ask a child to do and when possible take time to give the reason—he can see the point if you can.
5. Be honest in what you say and do. A child's faith in you is a great help.
6. Be fair; it isn't punishment, but injustice that makes a child rebel against you.
7. Be friendly. Always show an interest in what they are doing.
8. Commend good qualities and action.
9. Try to be constructive, not repressive, in all dealings with children.
10. Remember that a sense of humor is extremely valuable.
11. Never strike a child. It may seem to be the easiest way, but it only aggravates the problem.
12. Do not judge misconduct on how it annoys you.
13. Do not take your personal feelings and prejudices out on the children.
14. Maintain poise at all times. Do not lose your temper.
15. Remember—"The tongue is the only keen-edged tool with which grows sharper with constant use." Do not nag, bluff or be officious.
16. Look for good qualities—all children have them.
17. Do not "pick" on every little thing a child does. Sometimes it is wiser to overlook some things.
18. Bear in mind that misbehavior is seldom willful. There usually is a cause and it may be in yourself or some other influence outside the child.
19. Listen for suggestions and complaints from the children.
20. Follow-up all cases which have been disciplined. Be certain that you still have the respect and confidence of the child.

21. Be sincere in your work.
22. Set a good example yourself.
23. Intelligence in handling youth consists of thinking faster than they do. If they can out think you, you are not using your maturity, and the advantage of your larger education. You should see possibilities before they become results. This is the secret of leadership.
24. Defiance to established procedure comes from failure in some adult to keep the situation in hand. If there is danger of a direct break, the child should not be forced. An adult's will should never be pitted against that of a child. It is far wiser to give some simple directions that will be mechanically obeyed and pick up the reins of control in a quiet way.
25. Never hold a child up to public ridicule. It is the surest way of creating a discipline problem.

The handbook provides an opportunity for the schools to emphasize linkages of transportation services to the school's educational program.

Pre-Service Training
Excellent pre-service training not only helps the person do the job well, it is a good step toward retaining good workers. A good pre-service training program reduces stress and tension levels, and responses to given situations are more controlled.[10]

Pre-service training should include riding routes, observing excellent vehicle handling, practice runs, safety sessions, equipment familiarity, and handling emergencies.

In-Service Training
Opportunities to set training agendas should be provided to the bus drivers as well as discussion of district-selected topics. Sharing ideas and techniques provides drivers with timely information that can be put to use immediately as well as providing recognition of their own developing expertise. States usually require annual training sessions conducted by the department of education, state police, or other safety agencies. Information workshops conducted by principals or teachers can be helpful to bus drivers' understanding of what is going on in the schools as well as foster a team relationship between transportation service personnel and instructional personnel.

Combining Job Opportunities

A recruitment and retention problem lies in the fact that driving a school bus is not a full-time job and certainly is not an upwardly mobile job. The enterprising school may find that combining jobs so that a person can be a full-time worker for the school may help in recruiting and retaining good people. There is a definite advantage in having the school bus driver a full-time employee of the school and making the rewards and satisfactions rich enough to attract top-quality people. One of the advantages of placing the administration of the transportation system under the assistant superintendent for business affairs is that he or she is aware of the variety of jobs in the school management area that can be combined with bus driving to allow the school to provide full-time employment. Some of these jobs are school plant maintenance, custodial work, cafeteria work, mechanics helper in the bus garage, and clerical and bookkeeping work. There have been many complaints about these combination jobs, but the weaknesses lie in their planning, establishment, and administration, not in the fact that they are combinations.

The following policies may be of help in developing and establishing combination jobs:

1. Supervisors and administrative officers cooperatively plan the combination job prior to employment. (For example, if a person has a combination cafeteria–bus driving job it was planned by the assistant superintendent for business affairs in conjunction with the transportation supervisor and the school lunch supervisor.)

2. Definite hours are established for each job with sufficient portal-to-portal time allowed so that one job does not encroach on the other.

3. Under no circumstances should a combination job holder be allowed to drive a bus on special runs, such as field trips, which interfere with the schedule of his or her other job.

4. A written job description of the combination arrangement is approved and made available to all parties concerned.

5. A means is established for supervising the employee in the combination job.

6. Frequent review and evaluation of combination jobs is made by the assistant superintendent for school business affairs.

In the field of management and administration we become fettered by tradition and the customary ways of doing things. There is need for more imagination in the way people are employed on the job, and in the way their work is scheduled. This need is particularly evident in school management, because if school facilities are to be fully utilized, the factory-like time schedule of schools will have to be changed. Management must be capable of adopting a schedule that runs, say, from 6AM to 11PM. Instead of accepting a work schedule and job description bound by custom and tradition, job planners will have to think in terms of providing conveniences to the instructional program.

A bus-driving team might be composed of people holding a variety of jobs. A number of full-time drivers who drive regular runs might handle field trips and excursions and perform other work in traffic management; some full-time drivers might also work in the bus maintenance shop. Other bus drivers could have combination jobs such as custodian–bus drivers or cafeteria helper–bus drivers. Then, there could be a number of drivers such as housewives, small-farm operators, and part-time workers who would fill out the rest of the team. There is nothing wrong with having these combinations if the principles and policies proposed earlier are adhered to.

The School Bus

Concern about the transportation vehicle carrying schoolchildren has been with schools since the beginning of school transportation. Stories are told about trustee discussions regarding side curtains on the horse-drawn "school hack," use of warming bricks for cold feet, and providing blankets. Safety is always the first concern. Dependability and economy are high on the priorities list, as is the ever-present cost factor in purchasing a bus.

Purchasing a School Bus

As a rule the school bus is constructed by combining an independently manufactured bus body with a chassis manufactured by one of the nation's large truck manufacturers. Sometimes a school will make its own arrangements for having the body mounted; or the complete unit may be purchased from a chassis dealer. Usually the first method is cheaper and requires very little more trouble, because all body companies can arrange to have their bus bodies mounted on any standard chassis shipped to them.

The principles of purchasing outlined in chapter 7 should be followed when purchasing buses, supplies, and equipment, with all purchases being handled through regular channels. The competitive bid principle is particularly important here.

Determining the number, type, and size of buses most suitable and economical for a school district's pupil transportation system is a scientific process. It requires a careful analysis of many factors:

1. Number of children to be transported for the next five to ten years.
2. Density of population, present and future.
3. Road conditions—width, surface, number of curves, steepness of grades, number of stops.
4. Road building or other major changes causing re-routing.
5. School schedules (if schedules are staggered buses sometimes make two or three short runs instead of one long run).
6. Fuel use/availability (gasoline, diesel, propane/natural gas).

These and other factors can be used to classify the school district's transportation situation. An analysis may then be made of school districts with similar transportation problems to determine what type of bus has proved to be the best for the conditions encountered.

A bus should then be selected according to the conditions under which it must serve. For each situation there is, presumably, a type of bus that will serve best, and the good school business manager can make the right match. Points to be considered in bus selection are:

1. Wheel base and overall size
2. Manufacturer's rated seating capacity
3. Safety and comfort
4. Costs, initial and fuel economy
5. Ease and economy of maintenance
6. Availability of parts and service
7. Maneuverability given road/street conditions
8. Suitability for climatic conditions and terrain
9. Speed, pickup, and general ease of driving

Vehicle Maintenance

The goal of school bus maintenance is to keep the bus running efficiently and safely. If this is to be accomplished, maintenance must be considered more than just fixing actual breakdowns. Rather, it should include a carefully conceived method of anticipating weaknesses and possible trouble spots and correcting them before breakdowns occur, in short, "preventive maintenance." The preventive maintenance program is essentially a management process which requires responsible attention by transportation supervisor, bus driver, and bus mechanic. It is administered by a system of reports, records, and inspections. The reports submitted by bus drivers indicate any unusual circumstance of vehicle operation and any driving problem or road incident which might be a symptom of trouble. Records are used to keep track of various vehicle parts that need replacement after normal use, and to schedule cleaning as well as lubrication and oil change. The computer can be of assistance in large operations by maintaining recommended maintenance schedules and keeping reports regarding performance. A maintenance record can be made available on-line to monitor performance and anticipate scheduling of service. Analyses of costs are simplified so that performance of equipment, e.g., certain types or brands of tires, engines, and so on, can be checked frequently. Careful maintenance and operation can reduce costs per mile significantly.

Collings reported a year-long study of fuel savings in New Jersey in which she estimated fuel savings for the 632 school districts to be $1.6 million.[11] Recommendations in the study included converting fleets to diesel power, use of radial tires, reducing kerosene content of blended fuels, developing a driver incentive program related to fuel-efficient operation, expanding the use of fuel and maintenance records in decision making, and other specific recommendations. School business managers may find a welcome ally in the state's department of energy. Proven practices, software, and training programs may be made available from agencies interested in conserving resources.

Transportation and Instruction

Pupil transportation makes its most obvious contribution to instruction by transporting children to school to be educated. There are other contributions just as important that must be recognized by those who operate the school transportation system. School buses may also contribute to learning by transporting children on field trips and class projects at a distance from the school grounds.

The daily bus trip may be a rich educational experience in learning to live with others, or it may be a source of overstimulation, hilarity, or bickering from which the child cannot settle down while in school or at home. In older children it can provide a dangerous situation when behavior gets out of control. No desirable learning takes place. The professional educator working hand in hand with the transportation supervisor and the school bus driver can establish the bus trip as a laboratory session for democratic living where children learn good manners and responsibility. Sometimes wholesome learning occurs without trained adult direction, but unhappily this is generally not the case. In addition, means should be provided for reinforcing and evaluating a balanced environment as times goes on. The transportation supervisor and the bus drivers he or she manages should be a part of this important planning and organizational process. School bus drivers are silent teachers who can encourage student self-government. Viewed from the selfish interests of good management alone, well-behaved students make driving less nerve-racking, safer, faster, and much more pleasant.

When a school bus is used for field trips and class projects, it becomes, in a sense, a traveling classroom; it enables the pupils to gain direct experiences which clarify and supplement classroom teaching. A good school transportation system accepts its role as an extension of the classroom as being one of the purposes of its existence. Management then must incorporate, as an integral part of its planning, the use of school buses and drivers in a variety of activities, and the school budget must provide the necessary funds for the realistic handling of this phase of the educational program.

If this part of the school transportation program is to work smoothly, several management processes will have to be established:

1. Clear-cut lines must be established for getting approval for the field trip.
2. A simple method must be provided for requisitioning buses.
3. Arrangements must be made so that trips do no interrupt regular bus schedules.
4. Means must be provided to ensure cooperation between the teacher-sponsor and the driver.
5. There must be complete understanding of where liability rests in case of an accident.
6. Controls must be provided to ensure adequate preplanning and preparation.

Summary

The development of the pupil transportation system is inseparably woven into the social and economic growth of this nation. Its original purpose was to equalize educational opportunity for rural children, but it now provides transportation for nearly all children and serves as a traveling classroom in which students are taken on field trips and given experiences outside the classroom which clarify and supplement classroom teaching.

It must be understood that pupil transportation differs from other educational services in that it is not contained in or confined to school grounds and buildings. Operating on the open highway or city streets, the school bus is subject to many conditions not under the control of the school. Many of the rules and regulations which govern its operation are established and enforced by noneducational agencies. The need for cooperative action at all levels of government is particularly important in the pupil transportation area.

Transportation has been faced with legal challenges. Litigation over transportation has been heavy and has covered a wide range of topics. This should serve as a warning to local boards of education that pupil transportation requires intelligent administration and exacting management. The basis for establishing the school transportation program should be a thorough survey. From the data gathered, organizational patterns should be set, policies should be clear-cut, and definitive procedures should be established so that teachers, parents, students, and bus drivers can work together for the achievement of a wholesome educational experience as well as an efficient, safe, and economical means of transit.

For Further Thought

1. Discuss pupil transportation as it relates to equalization of educational opportunity.

2. "Pupil transportation, more than any other auxiliary service of the school, should be under the direct control of the state." Argue for and against this statement.

3. What regulations does the state department of education in your state have regarding pupil transportation? What services does it provide to pupil transportation?

4. Make a list of the situations affecting pupil transportation in which it is particularly important that various levels of government cooperate with schools.

5. Argue for and against the following statement: "Public ownership of school buses is but another step by the state to undermine private business."

6. Diagram a line-and-staff organizational chart for a school transportation system using twelve buses. Using one hundred buses.

7. Develop a set of pupil transportation policies for a suburban school system with thirty buses.

8. Do you believe in a special state financial aid program for pupil transportation? List some of the criteria that should be considered in developing a formula for pupil transportation aid.

9. What responsibility should the driver have for disciplining students on his bus? Set up model procedures for school bus discipline.

10. State your views in regard to having a teacher drive a school bus as a regular part of his or her job.

11. Visit several schools with bus maintenance garages and several which contract for all bus maintenance. How do the costs compare? Why?

Endnotes

1. Laurie S. Zeitlin, "State Pupil Transportation Funding: Equity and Efficiency," *School Business Affairs* 56, No. 4 (April 1990): 23.

2. Zeitlin, °State Pupil Transportation Funding," pp. 22–25.

3. Anthony R. Miller, "Contractor Relationships," *School Business Affairs* 55, No. 4 (April 1989): 40–41.

4. Patricia Anthony and Deborah Inman, "Public School Transportation: State Aid and Current Issues," *Principles of School Business Management* (Reston, VA: The Association of School Business Officials International, 1986), p. 428.

5. Thomas J. Casey, "Special Education Transportation Update and Forecast, "*School Business Affairs* 57, No. 4 (April 1991): p. 11.

6. Casey, °Special Education Transportation Update," p. 11.

7. John Hennessey, "Computerized Bus Routing for 'Controlled Choice' School Attendance Policies," *School Business Affairs* 56, No. 4 (April 1990): 36–37.

8. Stephen H. Salmon, "The Potential of Computerized Pupil Transportation," *School Business Affairs* 57, No. 1 (April 1991): 23.

9. Doug Hammond and Gary Blakey, "School Bus Drivers: Recruitment and Training," *School Business Affairs* 57, No. 4 (April 1991): 28.

10. Hammond and Blakey, "School Bus Drivers," p. 27.

11. Amy Collings, "State Bus Fleet Study Documents Fuel-Saving Measures," *School Business Affairs* 56, No. 4 (April 1990): 28.

$C \quad h \quad a \quad p \quad t \quad e \quad r \quad$ *11*

School Food Services Management

Food service is a continuous management challenge for the schools and an important factor in the education, health, and well-being of youth. Concern for the problem arose in diverse places, including the slums of New York City and the rural one-room school. Interest in food service in schools was stimulated by the suburban movement, the consolidation and reorganization of rural schools, and the nutritional deficiencies of youth caused by the Great Depression of the 1930s.

The National School Lunch Act of 1946 and the Child Nutrition Act of 1966 were the major stimulants to the establishment of unified food service programs throughout the United States. This act and the administrative directives of the U.S. Department of Agriculture and the state departments of education have provided a basis around which have developed theory, principles, and methods that are universally accepted but not universally practiced.

Over 90 percent of the public schools in the United States participate in the Child Nutrition and National School Lunch program.[1] With the near disappearance of the family lunch hour at home, the school lunch program becomes even more important. More and more communities are planning school breakfasts as an essential auxiliary school service. School food services are and will continue to be an important business management function.

Federal Government Participation: Depression Deterrent

The federal government stepped into the school lunch picture during the Depression years. In 1935 Public Law 320 was passed, authorizing the Secretary of Agriculture to purchase certain surplus agricultural products and distribute them free of charge to schools which had school lunch programs. This measure improved the market for agricultural goods and provided lunches for children at low costs. It stimulated local schools to establish school lunch programs in order to take advantage of the free food. It also caused state departments of education to take a hard look at this program because distribution made directly from the federal government to local units violated a sacred states-rights principle, which is: "All contacts by the federal government with local units should be through the state department of education. No federal government agency should deal directly with any school, school system, or any political subdivision of a state on any education project or activity except with prior approval of the chief state school officer."[2]

The free lunch program appeared to be a success. Mothers were happy because it gave their children a hot lunch. Farmers were happy because it provided a market for their goods. As a result further legislation was passed which shaped the structure of our school lunch program as we know it today. The first cash reimbursements came in 1939–1940 with the school milk program. In 1943 this was combined with the "indemnity plan" whereby the U.S. Department of Agriculture (USDA) reimbursed schools in cash for the purchase of specified agricultural products. In 1946, the National School Lunch Act was approved (Public Law 396), the preamble of which is as follows:

> *It is hereby declared to be the policy of Congress, as a measure of national security, to safeguard the health and well-being of the nation's children and to encourage the domestic consumption of nutritious agricultural commodities and other food, by assisting the states, through grants-in-aid and other means, in providing an adequate supply of foods and other facilities for the establishment, maintenance, operation, and expansion of non-profit school lunch programs.*

The act recognized a principle of operation important to federal-state relationships in that it specifically stated, "Funds paid to any state during any fiscal year . . . shall be distributed by the state educational agency." All states have accepted responsibility for establishing, maintaining, and operating the school lunch program and have either a director or a supervisor to handle the details. Because each state was required to pass legislation to show how the federal money was to be distributed, there are differences among state laws regarding the school lunch program. It is important for the school business manager to be familiar with state regulations governing school food services.

The Child Nutrition Act of 1966 complements the school lunch act and the two provide the vehicle whereby Congress funds lunch programs annually. Breakfast programs are funded by virtue of Public Law 94-105 (1975). National overseeing is provided by the Food and Nutrition Service of the Department of Agriculture. The programs administered by the Food and Nutrition Service include:

School lunch
School breakfast
USDA commodities
Special milk program
Nutrition education and training
Child care food

Emergency food assistance
Summer food service for children

Legal Basis

The legal bases for the operation of food services within a school are found in federal legislation, state laws, and administrative policies laid down by state departments of education. In addition, court decisions have played an important part in this legal framework. As might be expected, considerable litigation occurred because school cafeterias compete with local restaurants. Courts have consistently held that boards of education have the authority to carry on any reasonable activity necessary for the proper operation of a school and the education of children.[3]

The activities necessary "to manage and control the affairs and interests of the public schools" have been broadly defined. The accusation that selling food and lunches was putting the school in the restaurant business, and that tax money is therefore being used to the detriment of the private restaurant, has not been accepted by the courts provided it is clear that school operations are not abusive.[4] A school board abuses its rights when, without any educational objective, it performs a proprietary function for the express purpose of making a profit or when, by rules and regulations, it prohibits or discourages children from patronizing certain business establishments.[5]

Court decisions emphasize the educational benefits of the school lunch but have warned that any desire to make extra profit from the school lunch program must be suppressed. There has been an increasing tendency for the courts to consider activities from which a profit is derived as proprietary functions.[6] This may deprive a school district of its immunity from liability and may raise all sorts of questions as far as operating a cafeteria is concerned. In fact, if a cafeteria is operated essentially as a money-making proposition the courts probably would not allow it to continue to operate if suit were brought against it.[7]

What Are the Purposes?

The purposes of the food service program need to be clearly stated. Without clear purposes the program may thrive, but it also can deteriorate to merely feeding those who participate. It is difficult for persons with diverse job descriptions—cooks, teachers, custodians, principals, etc.—to work together toward providing simple, nutritious meals in an efficient, cafeteria-style line and doing so at a break-even cost. Yet, a passing nod in deference to the educational purposes will not suffice. Ignoring the educational possibilities in a food service program is not responsible management. Those minutes spent at mealtime are learning minutes. It is a matter of what is learned in a laizzez-faire approach versus what is learned in a proactive, team-designed environment. The possibilities for positive learning abound. It may be much easier for those persons with diverse jobs to focus on some of the positive learning possibilities than just providing a relatively safe and sane place to eat a meal.

What Is the Role of the School Business Manager?

Indeed, why should a text for school business managers discuss the educational purposes of food services? For decades the American School Food Service Association has pointed out the need for *a team effort* in the educational enterprise.[8] Providing dollars, overseeing compliance with state and federal laws, accounting for funds, and maintaining facilities seem to be sufficient to absorb the school business manager's time available for food service. Such a discussion is appropriate because food service is an important part of the educational enterprise. Consider the following possibilities:

- Learning appropriate, courteous social behaviors in groups.
- Learning proper use of flatware and ways to eat different foods.
- Encouraging cleanliness and sanitation.
- Learning proper nutrition and selection from essential food groups.
- Learning vocational options and skills.
- Learning good management practices.
- Discovering the integrated agriculture, agribusiness, retailing connections.
- Providing opportunities for family/interage interactions.
- Providing opportunities for the developmentally disadvantaged.
- Providing opportunities for unlimited science applications.

The above list is not intended to be exhaustive, but rather a beginning to stimulate the reader's thinking about possibilities. It does make the point that all levels of the school enterprise could profit by an enthusiastic effort to focus on the opportunities. Such an approach requires the manager to plan, communicate, and evaluate the food service program differently from a program which does not aim beyond providing nutritious food at minimum cost for all students. Planning includes all personnel, professional and noncertified, who are involved with food services. Continuous feedback and training is essential. Evaluation includes the learning dimension as well as cost analyses. Obviously, a great deal of organization is required.

Organizing for Service

Several decisions face any school district involved in operating a food service program. Among them are:

Operating the food service or contracting for the service

Self-contained, site-based programs or centralized kitchens

Management decisions at each site or centralized management (includes purchasing, menus, storage, and so on)

Supervisory responsibilities at the principal's level or supervision by central food service professionals

Self Operation or Contracting

This very complex decision must take into account the mission of the food service program, history of local school service, size of the operation as related to per-meal costs, persistent problems that precipitated a decision point, and, of course, the availability of viable food service contractors. As noted in an earlier chapter, the culture of the schools cannot be ignored. Consider the food service needs of a small school district. Economy of scale demands a centralized kitchen with satellite service to three schools. The family atmosphere and commitment of persons to a quality program in each school demonstrated an important value held by parents/patrons, teachers, staff, and students. Centralized purchasing, planning, and some storage reduced the costs but enabled the school district to maintain a self-contained operation. A contracted food service would have been "unthinkable."

There may be situations in which the school district is not meeting the goals of the food service program, cannot operate within available funds, or is encountering other problems of personnel, storage, or supply that seem insurmountable. Frey suggests the following as areas on which to focus when contracting a food service management company:[9]

The development of fair and equitable bid specifications with qualitative standards to ensure that management companies clearly understand the type of program a district wants for its students.

The development of a prototype contract form to be used between the school district and the management company which protects the financial and program interests of both the school district and management company, and precisely sets forth the obligations of both parties.

A comprehensive review and audit process which school districts will follow in tracking the revenue and expenditures of the food service program.

These considerations are not exclusive to contracting for food services, but rather are points that should be well thought out for any food service program, whether it is self-managed or contracted. When contracting, the school business manager should review state regulations governing allowable expenses of the contractor, emphasis on Type A meals by means of price structure, and performance bonding. Other state regulations may apply to the provisions of the contract. The school district should carefully watch the district administrative time needed to manage the contract in comparison with the time it would take to have a self-operated program.

Centralized or Decentralized

The next decision for the school district is to centralize the food service operation or decentralize it. Every aspect of food services must be answered in the centralized or decentralized decision (e.g., menus, personnel, purchasing, storage, and so on). Unless there are long distances and a large number of sites, modifications of the centralized approach are found in most school districts. The advantages of centralizing most food service functions include the following:

1. Economy of scale regarding purchasing, storage, and equipment.
2. Higher levels of expertise regarding planning, evaluation, and personnel selection and training.
3. Menus can be more carefully monitored for quality and meeting requirements.
4. Integration of efforts regarding the educational dimensions of the program become easier.
5. Accounting, financial management, and required reporting tend to be more accurate.

Management decisions ordinarily are made best at the school district level. As noted earlier in the chapter, unique situations may dictate otherwise, at least temporarily, but the school business manager will wish to examine possibilities for change continuously.

Here a word of caution is in order. A school district may choose to operate the food service as a business devoid of educational purposes whether self-operated or run by a contracting service. Van Newkirk of the York, Pennsylvania school district made the choice and clearly stated, "With regard to food service, we are talking about a business, not pedagogy."[10] Van Newkirk described fast-food type items, à la carte items, and the regular Type A lunch. The results were 75 percent participation and a fiscally self-sufficient food service program. In the same article, Strong of the Cambria, Pennsylvania school district noted "We're an educational program. You can't teach nutrition in the health classes and serve junk food in the cafeterias." The Cambria school district returned to a self-operated program. While a contracted service may serve the educational dimension as well, business factors appear to dictate otherwise.

If management decisions are made at the school district level, a set of questions are posed regarding the principal's role. This becomes even more important if a district is committed to site-based decision making. For example:

Should the principal be held responsible for planning and evaluating the educational facet of the school food services program in his or her building? If not, who then should be held responsible?

What appropriate input to the hiring of food service personnel should the principal make? In one school district in a 1990 study by Drake, the central office developed a pool of persons from whom the principals could select. Another central office simply "washed their hands" of the situation and said, "That is up to the principal."

How much influence should the principal have regarding menus? There may be widely diverse community backgrounds between schools in the same district. One school recently had a "tasting fair" at which student representatives had the opportunity to try samples of potential menu items. It was well received by the middle grade students and participation in the lunch program was increased.

Central Kitchen

The central kitchen plan provides an alternative. All food is prepared in a single high-production kitchen and then transported to "satellite" school buildings. Special vacuum containers and portable steam tables are wheeled into trucks and attendants in each school location receive and handle the food and assist in the distribution of items such as bread, milk, and ice cream.

The central kitchen puts the school in the realm of high-speed production, for specialized transportation and coordinated scheduling must be worked out with split-second timing. An example of increased efficiency was provided by Bender who noted that the central kitchen operation in the Dayton, Ohio schools produced 90 to 120 meals per labor hour in contrast to 20 meals per labor hour in the on-site kitchens.[11] Naturally management problems multiply, and without provisions for proper management control a school would be wise to stay away from this operation.

The *advantages* of the centralized kitchen may be listed as follows:

1. Provides great flexibility in serving and eating
2. Allows imagination in planning and designing buildings
3. Saves the expense of providing a complete kitchen unit in each building
4. Centralizes all purchasing and accounting for supplies
5. Allows wide use of labor-saving devices because of large production
6. Permits assembly-line production
7. Centralizes supervision of food preparation
8. Allows uniformity of recipes and food
9. Permits greater specialization of help
10. Provides close control of food and portions
11. May serve as a food distribution center during a local or national emergency

Disadvantages may include:

1. Lacks homey atmosphere of small school kitchen
2. Requires strict and controlled management procedures
3. Requires a large initial expenditure for high-efficiency, multiple-use machines, equipment, carts, and trucks
4. Makes kitchen facilities in older schools obsolete
5. Requires specialized management personnel trained in mass production
6. Tends to duplicate some equipment because it is convenient to have at least a small kitchen in each school for community use

Relationships with School Principal

As in many school business management activities, a question, arises of the relationship of the principal to the school food service program, its personnel, and its operation. The answer depends on the degree of administrative centralization desired by the school administration. The authors adhere to the view that the principal should have administrative control over all activities in the building to which he or she is assigned. Looking at Figure 11–1, we see that the principal has direct administrative control over the eating areas and the food services manager, while technical supervision comes from the office of the director of food services. The principal helps the director of food services in the selection, dismissal, and transfer of personnel. He or she establishes lunch-hour schedules, oversees student control in the lunchroom, monitors serving lines, provides upkeep of facilities and equipment, and encourages cooperation among students, teachers, and food services personnel. The principal provides, as in all affairs of the school, overall administrative leadership and direction to the food services program as it relates to the site for which he or she is responsible.

The director of food services acts as a staff officer for the school superintendent when working with personnel in the various buildings. He or she is recognized as the technical expert on food services. Whenever there are suggestions which might involve or affect education or administration, the director of food services discusses them with the principal, and the principal makes the final decision. Differences of opinion can be settled in staff meetings. In any event, it is highly important that relationships be clearly spelled out and job descriptions publicized so that all personnel understand the organization and operation of the system.

There are always people who attempt to take advantage of irregular relationships. The authors have known principals who insisted on being "boss" in every situation, who failed to respect the technical know-how of central office personnel and considered them snoopers. Also there are supervisors and staff personnel from the central office who sweep

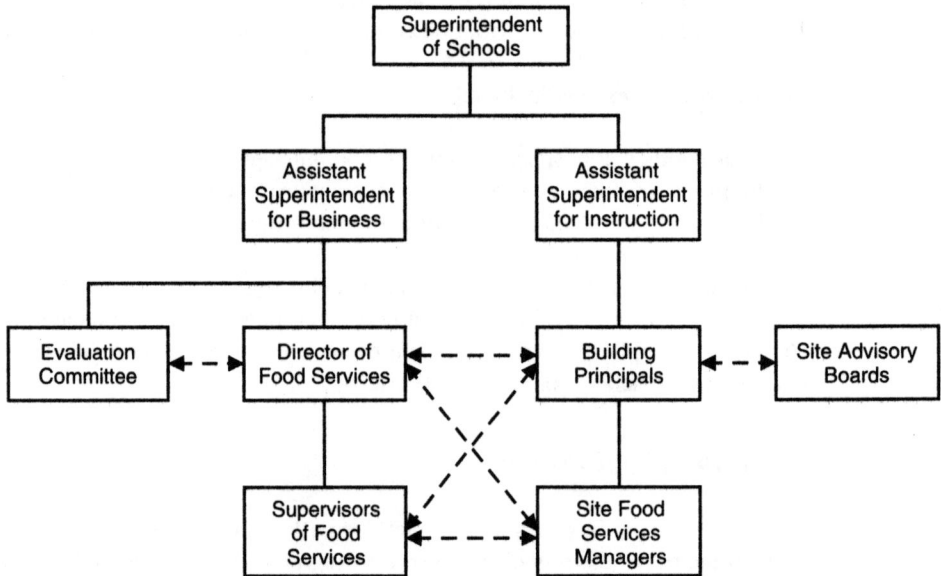

FIGURE 11-1   Administrative Relationships for Food Service Functions.

in to inspect like commanding generals, barking orders for improvement like a first sergeant. Many employees delight in creating confusion by playing one administrator against another, exaggerating one's attitudes and comments, or continually appearing confused themselves for the sake of the dissension and dissatisfaction they may sow. Obviously personnel of this kind are difficult to work with under any circumstances. Their presence should persuade an organization to look carefully at its selection, orientation, and training program rather than at its organizational structure. The presence of a fertile environment for such divisive behavior does require revision of the communication lines and possibly clarification of job roles.

Many buildings have a community/staff advisory group, particularly in the site-based decision-making environment. Such groups provide the food services manager and the principal an excellent opportunity for considering the educational aspects of the food service program.

Staffing

The key to any program is a good and adequate staff. Food services is no exception, and as expected, the food services director is ordinarily the person charged with the school district's overseeing of the program and the one who determines how the program is implemented. In carrying out these functions the Director of food services is responsible for the following:

1. Recruits personnel
2. Hires necessary personnel and inducts them into the system
3. Maintains a pool of personnel for emergencies if necessary
4. Provides for necessary in-service training
5. Appoints personnel to specific schools after they have been interviewed and approved by the principal
6. Plans all menus
7. Standardizes and tests recipes
8. Standardizes procedures and techniques
9. Establishes a central reporting, recording, and accounting system for money received (in cooperation with the accounting department)
10. Works in cooperation with the purchasing department on purchasing
11. Establishes a central recording and accounting system for supplies
12. Inspects and evaluates the programs and serves as chairman of an evaluation committee
13. Recommends to the school superintendent and principal necessary changes in personnel
14. Assumes responsibility for the technical operation of the entire school lunch program
15. Recommends the purchase of necessary equipment
16. Assists in planning food service facilities
17. Works in concert with building principals and parents and other groups to acquaint them with the lunch program and to enlist their support and participation

18. Assists in integrating nutrition education and the school lunch with the school health program and related curricula

19. Prepares state and/or federal reports

20. Sets standards for efficient and sanitary practices in preparing and serving appetizing food

The school business manager will wish to develop a feedback system on each of the tasks of the food service director.

Size of Staff

The size of the food services staff is affected by the number of meals required, efficiency of labor-saving equipment and facilities, and complexity of offerings (e.g., á la carte, number of choices, ease of preparation, and so on). There are several guidelines which can be used to determine the number of staff needed for a particular operation. A commonly used staffing guideline is the one developed by Dorothy Van Egmond-Pannell's, as presented in Table 11-1.

Types of food prepared make a difference in the number and type of staff needed. For example, instead of frozen foods requiring freezers to store, thawing time and space, there are irradiated foods that have a very long shelf life without requiring the special equipment to store or added time to prepare.

Technology is available which will speed preparation, cash management and reporting, and expedite the payment process. A fully computerized system reduces or eliminates

TABLE 11-1   School Food Service Staffing Guidelines

Number Lunches Served	Meals per Labor Hour	Total Hours
Up to 100	$9\frac{1}{2}$	0–11
101–150	10	10–15
151–200	11	15–17
201–250	12	17–20
251–300	13	20–22
301–350	14	22–25
351–400	14	25–29
401–500	14	29–32
501–550	14	32–35
551–600	15	35–36
601–650	15	36–40
651–700	16	40–43
701–800	16	43–50
801+	18	50+

Source: From a mimeographed communiqué from the Indiana Department of Education, October 1986. Guidelines developed by Dorothy Van Egmond-Pannell.

These recommendations do not include hours for breakfast or à la carte. They do allow for some limited menu choices and some labor-saving equipment.

manual record keeping including inventory control. Students using cards instead of cash avoid the perceived stigma of the free or reduced lunch labels. Adamson and Luckman report the results of such a system that began in Salt Lake City, Utah in 1987.[12] Time savings were realized on labor costs and express lines in the cafeteria increased to twenty to thirty students per minute. Preparation for auditing is much more efficient. However, a fully computerized system is expensive, and some schools have successfully used bar code scanner technology coupled with an Apple II to accomplish some of the same savings.

The astute school business manager will seek new technologies that have the potential to pay for themselves while reallocating time and effort to activities that will be more productive and achieve program goals. Providing the food service manager with materials and in-service opportunities may be a wise investment and may change the staffing patterns that have been established over many years.

Menu Planning

State and federal guidelines assist the menu planner to meet nutrition requirements. The USDA commodities program and existing alternatives to it, such as letter-of-credit programs, provide a set of foods which the menu planner may use as a starting point.

Contract management companies find it advantageous to listen seriously to their clients, in this case students, to avoid waste and to increase participation. Regularly monitoring selections and waste is important to careful planning. Some schools have found creative ways to use the available USDA commodities and have combined that creativity with energetic marketing of special meals, special days, and new selections. The marketing idea may integrate nicely with business curricula, closed-circuit television or radio, the art department, and a number of other possibilities.

Since a main purpose of the lunch program is to provide approximately one-third of the recommended dietary allowances (RDAs) for each level in a properly balanced meal, alternative à la carte lines should not create serious dissonance with this nutritional goal.

The Lunchroom Facility

It is difficult to find more than two basic types of school lunch facilities: first, a kitchen opening up into a yawning semibarren room within which students are massed for lunch; or alternately, a kitchen attached to a gymnasium or multipurpose room with some sort of ingenious disappearing tables. In either case the mob design seems to mock the oft-used words that school lunch is basically educational. The lunchroom facilities are educational, because education seldom ceases, but they are not good learning situations. Most criticisms of the school lunch program have their basis in the limitations which the physical plant imposes on the possibilities for good learning at mealtime. True, there have been innovations in food service equipment, in the handling of food, and in its ease of preparation, but little has been done in regard to designing the eating space itself.

The following are some ideas which, used singly or in combination, may help to take the "mass out of the meal," put "learning in the lunch," and at the same time provide freedom in planning.

1. Plan a series of small dining rooms of various sizes clustered around a kitchen. These can be used as classrooms, clubrooms, homerooms, seminar rooms, or meeting rooms. They have possibilities for a great variety of combined uses.

2. Use portable half-partitions throughout large dining rooms to break up the mob atmosphere. Different groupings can be created almost instantly.

3. Use booths throughout portions of the dining area to break up space.

4. Experiment with special bag-and-box lunches for outside eating or away-from-dining area eating (this should not be a regular practice).

5. Stagger schedules for choir, clubs, play practice, and organization meetings so that groups can eat together and meet together on certain days in order to relieve congested dining halls.

6. Establish several combination dining areas in various wings of the building.

7. Mobilize steam tables and food carts so that serving can be flexible and adaptable.

8. Experiment with disposable food containers, preassembled meals, and vending machines. Care should be taken to consider ecological concerns.

9. Place portable, temporary, and even permanent food-counter islands or service units in strategic spots throughout the school building where food may be taken from the kitchen, served at the portable islands, and eaten in nearby rooms.

10. A variety of preportioned servings on recyclable plates/trays, including a choice of menu selection, may provide excellent flexibility and manageability for groups in a variety of activities.

Purchasing

The objective of the buyer for the school lunch program is to buy the most nutritious and appealing foods at the lowest possible price. Two factors distinguish this task from other school purchases: perishables like milk, produce, and eggs must be purchased, and food requirements must be coordinated with available government-supplied surplus commodities before purchases are made.

State and federal guides are available to the food services manager to help determine quantities needed. Over time, the manager will wish to adapt the calculations to local estimates because preparation and cooking methods, servings, and other variables contribute to differences from the guides.

Purchasing ordinarily should be handled through the school district's central purchasing office, which works in close cooperation with the food services department on specifications. The availability of adequate storage will determine how much food can be ordered at one time. Experience has shown that substantial savings can be realized by submitting large orders for bids. Several small schools may find it advantageous to buy nonperishable foods cooperatively. Some state school-lunch departments encourage cooperative buying on a regional and county basis. Schools have realized savings through their large-scale purchases.

Some perishable items are more conveniently ordered daily by the lunchroom manager, with invoices being checked frequently by the director of food services. Perishable items like milk should be subject to competitive bidding procedures. Open-end contracts can be arranged which establish a price per unit if a certain minimum amount is bought over a year's time. The director of food services should make a study of federal, state, and local food and market trends to help the staff select foods that are abundant in supply and reasonable in cost.

Storage is a special problem. Fortunately, the newer shelf-stable foods will have a positive effect on the storage problem since specialized refrigeration needs are reduced. Older buildings, particularly some elementary school buildings several miles from other facilities are hard-pressed occasionally to accommodate some foods that would help menu variety and are thereby limited in options. Maintenance of equipment is a continuing concern and should be part of a maintenance plan along with all other facilities and equipment in the school building.

Supply Accounting and Inventory

Two of the most important management controls in the school lunch program are supply accounting and inventory. These are safeguards against waste, theft, carelessness, spoilage, and oversupply and undersupply of goods. Proper accounting provides for the designation of one person to be responsible for removal or storage of goods in the storage area, a continuing in-and-out inventory, and periodic checking of supplies used with the number of meals prepared and served. Additional accounting may be made by using spoilage charts which record items which have spoiled, and waste charts, which record the amount of food thrown away.

A weekly or biweekly inventory serves as the final accounting step. The actual stock on hand at inventory is then balanced with the various control records to determine the effectiveness of the controls. The frequency of inventory depends upon the size of the operation and the type of stockroom facilities available. A continuous inventory can be set up with computer assistance.

Financing, Accounting, and Controlling

The school lunch program in the United States is an excellent example of federal, state, regional, and local cooperation both financially and programmatically. It is true certain minimum requirements have been established by the federal government and must be followed if a local school district wishes to obtain financial aid. This is appropriate and it should be noted as reasonable. Based on universally accepted health standards, the federal program arouses little controversy. Another redeeming feature is that it is the policy of the federal government to work directly with the state educational agency only. Thus, the local public school district operates through the normal state channels. The state establishes a master plan which covers the operation of all programs in the state. When the plan is approved by the federal government, thereafter all negotiations for federal aid are undertaken by the governing body of the school district in concert with the appropriate state agency. While school district programs are subject to federal audit, irregularities are corrected and settled by the state agency.

The typical school lunch program is supported and financed in the following ways:

1. Federal assistance
   a. School milk program
   b. Partial school lunch reimbursement
   c. Commodities program and possible alternatives
2. State assistance
   a. Supervisory and consultant help
   b. State aid
3. Local assistance
   a. Student fees
   b. School board appropriations
   c. Furnishing of equipment and facilities
   d. Providing of custodial care and maintenance
   e. Local donations
   f. Personnel in-service training
   g. Support services provided through business office accounting, purchasing, personnel, etc.

Budgeting for Food Services

Budgeting for the food services program is based on anticipated participation and projected costs. Forecasts of participation will need to include probable participation in each of regular meals, à la carte, or special lines. In addition, projections need to be made regarding the number of reduced price and free meals that will be provided. Any other anticipated income to the food service program should be included. Panell reminded readers that very tight management control of the food services program is essential because "increasing expenditures, the margins between actual revenue and what a lunch/breakfast should cost have become so small that there is no room for error, waste, over-staffing or over-serving."[13]

Decisions will need to be made regarding what costs will be borne by the food services program. Often certain costs such as custodial care, repair and maintenance of the areas for eating, preparation, storage, and cleanup are not specifically budgeted against food services and may be subsumed by some other budget activity. Simple, inexpensive marketing costs such as newspaper releases, duplicated menu announcements, or incentives should be part of the budget.

An equipment repair and replacement schedule should be built into the budget. The budget does not need to be a limitation to experimentation. The income and cost sides of the budget must be looked at monthly and adjustments made.

Accounting for School Funds

The accounting process need not be rigidly centralized. Cooperation may be achieved by having the accounting department handle payroll, payment of invoices, and bookkeeping, while the food services staff processes state claims and reports, the collection and deposit of money, and the preparation of profit and loss statements.

Records and reports which are a part of good financing and accounting procedures not only assure scrupulous safeguarding of public money and properties but provide necessary background data for improving management.

The required reports for government agencies and filing of claims for partial reimbursement for free and reduced-price lunches and breakfasts demand careful record keeping. As noted earlier, a computer-based charge card or bar code system can make these chores much simpler and more accurate. Because of irregularities noted in claims for reimbursement, the USDA has initiated the Assessment, Improvement and Monitoring System (AIMS). Within this system are review processes now required of the states, as well as a federally operated review. Baeher noted:[14]

What we have now is a three-pronged program review system:

- AIMS, which sets the performance standards and dictates the pattern and interval of State Agency reviews.
- The Federal Review System (FRS) where school districts are chosen by computer in Washington and reviews are done by the federal auditors.
- AccuClaim, which requires school districts operating programs in more than one building to conduct their own on-site review of each school prior to February first.

Each participant in AIMS must check and document monthly the following:

Number of free and reduced-price applications
Free and reduced-priced meals day by day per month
Average daily attendance

Obviously an integrated computer system would be helpful. Reports could be generated with a minimum of effort from a variety of sources. Some records and reports which serve useful purposes are noted below:

1. Daily participation by type and cash report
2. Monthly and yearly summaries of participation and type and cash report
3. Monthly and yearly statement expenses
4. Monthly and yearly operating statement (revenues divided according to source)
5. Summary of hours of work per meal served
6. Record of bids
7. Summary of requisitions
8. Purchase records

9. Cost summary of foods used divided according to source; i.e., USDA commodities, donations, local purchase, etc.
10. Monthly and yearly food supply inventory report
11. Summary of assets and liabilities
12. Small-supply and equipment purchases including repair and maintenance records.

Summary

Operating or contracting food services for a school district is a complex task. It can also be a rewarding task when participation increases, a team effort toward clear goals materializes, and the program goes beyond providing a fast meal in a mass atmosphere. Operating such a program requires vision, communication, and good business practices. A food services program is education. It behooves the school administration to insist that it is a positive educational experience.

For Further Thought

1. Argue pro and con: The schools should not be in the food business.

2. You have been asked to represent the school's food service planning area on a new high school facility planning team. Outline your approach to obtaining appropriate input and indicate the principles on which you wish to base the specifications. List the specifications assuming 1,200 students 9–12, plus a child-care facility for 20 children.

3. Review the forms required by your state to report and make claims for reimbursement.

4. Prepare a teaching unit integrating at least two subjects using the food services facilities as a laboratory.

5. List the types of help available to a school district from the state education department food services division.

6. Find three school districts which operate their own food services and three who contract the food services program. Interview the appropriate persons to see if there are important differences in results and philosophy.

7. Draw a network of communications between district offices to integrate information for proper reporting and management decisions. Assume a centralized decision-making structure.

8. Repeat exercise 7, but assume a site-based structure.

Endnotes

1. *The School Foodservice Handbook* (Reston, Va: Association of School Business Officials, 1987). p. 1.

2. Lee M. Thurston and William H. Roe, *State School Administration* (New York: Harper & Brothers, 1957), p. 343.

3. *Merryman v. School District No. 16 et al.,* Wyo. 376, 5 P.2d. 267 (1931).

4. *Goodman v. School District No. 1, City and County of Denver,* 32 F. 586 (1929).

5. *Hailey v. Brooks,* 191 S.W. 781 (1916).

6. *Richards v. School District of City of Birmingham,* 83 N.E. 2d 643 (1957). *Saway v. Tucson High School District,* 281 P. 2d 105 (Arizona, 1955).

7. *Cook v. Chamberlain,* 199 Wis. 42, 225 N.W. 141 (1929).

8. Leo E. Buehring, "Food Service, Too, Is Education," *The Nation's Schools* 61, No. 1 (January 1958): 63.

9. *Joseph P. Frey,* "The Food Service Factor," *American School and University* (September 1988): 43.

10. Ronald Stainbrook, "Contract vs. District-Operated School Foodservices," *School Business Affairs* (June 1990): 11.

11. Betty Bender, "The Central Commissary," *School Business Affairs* 57, No. 11 (November 1991): 17.

12. Pam Adamson and Michael Luckman, "Computerized Food Service," *American School and University* (March 1989): 107.

13. Dorothy V. Pannell, "Has a Financial Crisis Hit School Food Services?" *School Business Affairs* 56, No. 11 (November 1990): 14.

14. Bonnie Baeher, "AccuClaim and the Federal Review System," *School Business Affairs* (November 1989): 26.

Chapter *12*

======================

Information Services

At the other end of the line is a well-modulated voice, "This is Phil N. Blanque from Channel 99. We have read that nearly half the schools in the U.S.A. are in serious disrepair or are educationally inadequate. Is this true of the buildings in this school district?" In the stack of mail is a letter from a group of parents concerned that their children are in classrooms that are much more crowded than in other schools. Another letter offers help from a group of businesses in the form of desktop computers. This morning's newspaper contained a story of a citizen's tax guard group raising questions (and tempers) about the waste of taxpayers' money spent on debt service for building construction and renovation for facilities used only 185 days a year and only part of those days.

So it goes day after day. Inquiries and requests for information come into the school district's offices continuously. Responses to internal and external public sectors are essential and they need to be based on sound data and information. The school business manager plays one of the key roles in the generation of data and information, the analysis and interpretation of the information, and in providing input to the decisions based on the information gathered. The business offices constitute one of the key nodes in the communications network of the school district. Figure 12-1 depicts some of the sources and directions of communications to and from the business offices.

New regulations regarding handling petrochemicals, a sharp downturn on short-term interest rates, or a major emphasis at a school site on applied technology requires the business manager to have current information and be able to communicate it. The business manager has choices to make regarding the proper role for each communication. Shall he or she serve as a conduit and pass the information along; shall additional information be included; what other information is needed to put the inquiry or input into the proper perspective; shall the information be interpreted and forecasts generated to assist the receiver to make wise decisions? How shall the school business manager decide which route to follow, since it is likely that different answers are appropriate depending on the information received and the receiver targeted?

The Communications Function

Clear Lines of Communication

Who-communicates-with-whom-about-what is important for the school business manager
to know. Past patterns of communication are starting points but may not serve present or
future needs of the school district. The school business manager will need to clarify with
other members of the administrative team what information they need. Beyond that, the
business manager may need to demonstrate what additional information is needed to assist
in sound decision making. Figure 12-1 represents some of the choices but does not answer
the routes to be used in a particular school district. For instance, the school business
manager continuously receives information, perceptions, data, and attitudes from persons
in the community at large because of interactions with them while conducting the business
of the school. The community people will be receiving what they perceive to be informa-

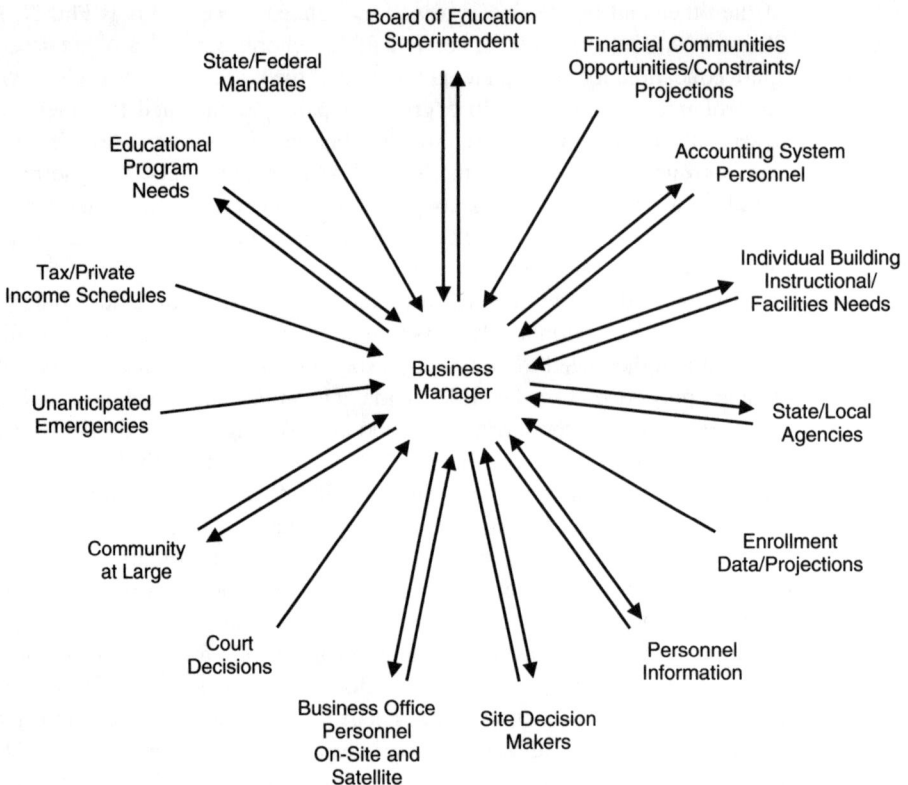

**FIGURE 12-1   An Example of Directions of Communications to/from the
Business Offices.**

tion about the schools from their business office contacts. The exchange of communications is inevitable—how purposeful it is depends on the communications skills of the business manager.

Purposes of Communications

One of the major purposes of communication is to influence. Other purposes include informing as a service or communicating for pleasure. If the primary purpose of communication is to influence, the school business manager is in a position to be one of the important players in meeting the communication needs of the school district. What influences do the school leaders wish to exert? How can the business manager contribute to effecting that influence? The question is, In what is the purpose rooted? The reader can imagine a number of possible answers ranging from personal survival to shining an ego-centered image. The authors suggest that the purposes of the business manager's communications should be that of a member of a leadership team that has a goal of improving the achievement of students. With this attitude toward communication, different answers to some of the questions raised above may emerge. For example, if the purpose of communicating is one of influencing the community to see the real achievements made by students, responses to comments made by officers of financial institutions will be different from responses rooted in the idea of "I'm just doing my job as business manager efficiently." Receivers nearly always try to answer the question, "Where is this person coming from?" Too often the question remains open or if answered, the answer has little relationship to the mission of the school.

Articulating the School Mission

Articulating the mission and/or vision of the schools is the superintendent's responsibility, but it should also be the responsibility of each staff member, including the school business manager, to articulate and clarify that mission to all within his or her sphere of influence. Communications and information services coming out of the various business offices will be designed to enhance the mission of the school. In short, the business manager is part of the instructional effort of the school as a communicator as well as a provider of business services.

Information as a Service

The purpose of information is to assist in making decisions related to the institution's mission, which is student achievement. Decision makers need to be identified and the kinds of information that will help decision makers need to be identified. The school business manager is in a key position to put the emphasis on information *services.*

Users of information available from the school business offices may not be aware of what information is available; they may not know the implications of the information provided; or they may not know what to ask for. As schools move toward more site-based decision making, the number of decision makers increases and the levels of awareness, regarding needed and available information, expands to include building level personnel. Along with other central office personnel, the school business manager becomes a teacher of information awareness and use. To fall short in this role leads to falling short in effectiveness as a member of the leadership team.

Listening and Learning—An Important Factor in Communication

The school business manager acquires another role as a provider of information services, i.e., the role of listener and learner. Users have information to share about how and why they make decisions and factors influencing those decisions. Users' perceptions of how the school business office could help or information that decision makers may have that the business office is not aware of may be useful. Users may be a depository of data useful to others throughout the system. Tapping into the source could enrich the base on which decisions are made. The purpose of the school is better served by a service orientation as opposed to guarding information as a source of power. Occasionally the would-be listener/learner may view the communicator as less well informed and the listener becomes busy forming his or her response rather than keeping an open-minded attitude which leads to learning. Neal[1] suggested the following rules for listening well:

1. Respect others' opinions.
2. Keep emotions under control.
3. Be able to repeat what the speaker has just said.
4. Don't counterattack.
5. Don't deal with too much at once.
6. Examine how questions are phrased.
7. Be careful of assumptions and conclusions.
8. Acknowledge feelings and frustrations.
9. Take time to listen.
10. Listen to how things are said.

A school business manager may find it advantageous to help the transportation director, chief accountant, purchasing officer, and other school administrators become effective listeners and learners so that the total operation becomes more responsive and effective. While all input may not be good input, at least if it is well heard the listener has a better chance to make appropriate responses.

Means of Sharing Information

Just as people have different purposes for communicating so the appropriate ways to communicate may be different. Face-to-face interactions, telephone conversations, written communications, faxed material, "E" mail, data transfers from computer to computer, and the media are part of today's tools to share information. Each tool is suited well for particular audiences and situational constraints. No one tool will do the job for all audiences. The tool should be selected based on the receiver(s) and the type information to be conveyed.

The Potential User

The school business manager wishing to provide information services should be aware that users are not alike in backgrounds, abilities to process information, or attitudes about information. It is wise to assume that a like-job group, such as principals of site-based managed schools, have a wide range of abilities and experiential backgrounds. One method of communicating with them probably will not get the job done. Simply dropping the information on them does not relieve the business manager from responsibility. If the message is not understood, or worse, is misused or ignored, the chance to influence better decisions is lost. Learning how to provide information to the particular audience may be almost as important as developing the information. If there is a range of receptivity within a group of people holding the same job description, it is obvious that many means of communication will be appropriate for a wide range of audiences. Conveying the effectiveness of the supply management program to the school board takes a different tac from reporting the financial condition of the district to the local Rotary Club.

The Type of Information

Massive amounts of data can be moved from computer to computer. Data bases can be used to create hundreds of reports. Memos can be distributed by electronic mail with no time loss, and documents can be faxed across many miles almost instantaneously. If the information to be provided is of a complicated nature involving emotions, feelings, or threat of change, the manager must weigh the value of time lost to use a more personal approach instead of faxing or sending the information by "E" mail. Again, he or she must predict the influential effectiveness of the means chosen.

Management Information Systems

There are many books written, courses offered, and degrees available in management information systems (MIS). It is far beyond the scope of this chapter to prepare the reader in the multifaceted field of MIS. Rather, the following should acquaint the reader with some of the components of an MIS and issues in this field of information services. An information system has the purpose of creating, analyzing, and making available to appropriate users a wide variety of data and information. The creation of data or finding data is the beginning point. Once the data are generated a number of steps follow[2]:

> *Storing*—Proper means of storing data need to be identified based on such criteria as need for analyses, access, and potential users.
>
> *Converting*—Analyses, more usable formats.
>
> *Conveying*—Data ordinarily are not useful only in the original storage area but must be transported to user(s).
>
> *Reproducing*—Multiple copies may be needed in a variety of forms.

Classifying—A decision about the correct headings under which to store the data is most critical.

Synthesizing—Data from many sources may be required to provide adequate decision information.

Manipulating—Meaning of data may be enhanced by statistical manipulation.

Retrieving—Accessibility to appropriate users on demand is important.

Reviewing—What data are needed for how long? Can the system storage and manipulation capabilities deal with massive historical data, or should some data be destroyed?

Destroying—A routine of reviewing data need/use may dictate the elimination of some data.

The above steps, or decision points, are important steps in an MIS. If the school business manager does not lead the decision-making process, he or she should be available for input to the decisions. Some school district organizations have a separate director of MIS, in which case the school business office needs to influence MIS decisions regarding essential data and access. If the MIS is within the business area, it should be open to influence from other areas regarding data and access. On occasion, the "S" (system) is missing and a number of separate information fiefdoms develop. If such an arrangement serves the school district well, then no harm is done; however, the likelihood of optimum utilization is open to question. Duplication of effort, storage, potential conflicting access policies, brokering information for advantages, all are possibilities in the fiefdom arrangement. Decision makers should be encouraged to make the parts work together as a system rather than operating as separate domains.

Making the System Work

People

The primary element in an MIS are the people who operate it and who use it. As noted in other portions of this book, the name of the game is people. The best software running on the fastest, most dependable hardware will be of little use if the people are not in tune with the purpose of the system and the concept of providing an information service to users. Secondly, the system should not be viewed as a static operation, rather it should be a continuously growing one in quality and effectiveness.

We are all familiar with the competent person with a sweet, helpful personality who when a perceived threat to the way he or she has done the job for many years is felt, can become a vicious blocker of progress. The threat comes through many filters such as a perception of the devaluation of the work done up to now, a fear of new technology, a disturbance of comfort, even a feeling of loss! While these human factors are not limited to the advent of MIS, the introduction of an integrated "high-tech" information system can jar such feelings loose. The astute business manager will try to anticipate the potential problems and assure and reassure participants in their roles, how things are going to work, why it is important, and that help will be available. The task is multiplied when there are satellite operations in almost every school.

Hardware and Software

The best first steps are to decide what the system should be able to do with what kinds of data, and what kinds of expertise are available within the school district. Some questions to answer include the following:

- Who needs to use the information?
- Who should not be able to access what kinds of information?
- What technologies are already available for communicating among users?
- How and who are available to input data?
- What kinds of usable formats are needed?
- What subsystems (e.g., payroll and personnel) must be integrated?
- What security checks are needed?
- Is the system to be a total districtwide service?
- How will the instructional decision makers use it?
- How will the effectiveness of the system be evaluated?

The questions above will generate other considerations to address prior to looking for software that will meet the school's needs. Some additional queries might be made regarding:

- Available training support provided by the vendor.
- Available consultant or troubleshooting support free or on a cost basis.
- Continuous updates as new versions are developed and installed free or on a cost basis.
- Will updates require upgrades in hardware?
- Compatibility with a variety of environments, e.g., MS-DOS to/from Apple.
- The track record in similar school districts.
- Compatibility with current mainframe or minicomputers.
- What are the expansion possibilities of the system, both software and hardware?
- What backup systems are available?

Answers to the above queries and others that may arise will help school district personnel to estimate costs beyond the initial software/hardware prices. A wide range of possibilities are on the market. Some companies provide on-line consultant services as part of the software package while others do not. The price usually reflects the services available to the purchaser.

At this point the needed hardware choices begin to emerge. If the instructional decision makers will have access to the system, will additional costs be incurred replacing, upgrading, or adding hardware compatible to the system, or will the present building hardware suffice? Will access be limited to various areas? Will transportation have access to make input and retrieve selected data relative only to vehicle use, maintenance, and efficiency? Will School A have access to School B information?

Control of Access

As implied by the questions above, control considerations should be part of the software/hardware decision process. Guidelines should be developed cooperatively with users or potential users which will create a data input/output request and approval process.

Routine access to certain data should be planned in advance. Safeguards need to be established to protect data as required by law. The areas of personnel and students are particularly sensitive. Hentschke[4] suggested that a committee be established to review policy and practice regarding student information. This committee chaired by the information services administrator would deal with the issues created by ever-expanding data capabilities, perceived needs for information, and changing laws and regulations. The committee would prepare recommendations for the superintendent to recommend school board action to create or modify policies. If feasible, the committee could also deal with the same responsibilities for professional and noncertified personnel data. A large school district may find it necessary to create a second committee for employee data review.

Location of Responsibility and Central Equipment
It does not take long to encounter the question of who is going to control the system and where are the data bases to be housed. Space, existing hardware, and planned utilization will help determine the physical location. The fixing of responsibility may be more complicated. It is often convenient to expand existing responsibilities by placing the additional use where the greatest present use is located. Given the amounts of data already used in business operations, this would locate the expanded information services in the school business offices with the business manager as the administrator responsible for those services. An alternative would be to create a separate service agency dedicated to information services. There are cautions accompanying each alternative. The separate service agency concept creates another step for almost everyone except the school superintendent. The potential for creating a fiefdom is always present, but possibly the most important consideration is that of communication. The individual selected needs to be conversant with all areas. The same concern exists if the system is located in the school business office, but is one additional argument for the idea that the school business manager be a business manager and educator.

Instructional Access
Pressure to develop and maintain a separate MIS may materialize if instructional personnel are not convinced that accessibility and timeliness can be optimized regardless of the location of responsibility. Of course, the same applies to all areas that appear to be outside the central operation. Open communications are necessary to overcome the appearances or the reality of gatekeeping for the sake of gatekeeping. For example, while it is important for accounting control of music instrument inventory, it is also important for the music director in each building to be able to use the information. Data which includes an instrument's age, condition, make, location, person responsible (student), and use with which group can provide the instructional side of the school enterprise as useful information as for the business side. Schools in states requiring an accountability of minutes per week on task for each subject area exclusive of passing periods, certain field trips, etc. can generate appropriate reports for the state in seconds. Using the same data, cost analyses can be generated as easily by the school business office. Test data, attendance/tardy data, substitute teacher data—each may yield interesting information and when combined may provide information helpful in attacking a number of instructional problems.

Integrating instructional systems with other management systems holds a great deal of promise. The Anne Arundel County (California) public schools anticipate increased student achievement as a result of introducing an instructional component to an integrated school information system. Their anticipation is based on reported increases in California Achievement Test scores of Chapter I students.[5] The instructional information possibilities are exciting and will continue to expand. Potential expandability should not replace careful, detailed long-range planning regarding what those future possibilities might be. Kory[5] further encouraged districts to plan with a seven- to ten-year horizon.

Planning a comprehensive, integrated information system may involve potential networking with other community resources ranging from research organizations to governmental agencies.[6] Such an array of possibilities for management is almost dwarfed by the instructional possibilities.

If the information management system is administered by the school business manager, he or she must take care to keep the communication channels open both ways so that user needs are clearly understood. Again, the service orientation is paramount.

Personnel Information

As noted earlier personnel information needs to be safeguarded according to applicable laws and regulations. While safeguards will limit access and distribution of information, they need not limit data entries or careful data analyses. Certification/licensure areas and previous experience may quickly provide the administrator of a school district of 25,000 students with a set of options for transfers or new hires. The possibilities are almost endless. A large school district with a very mobile population resulting from immigrants moving from their initial locations to specific parts of the city is able to predict enrollments in specific schools based on previous patterns of migration within the city. Cost analyses by program and type of population served can help anticipate building budget needs according to population shifts.

Logistical Services

An effective and growing information service can be of great benefit to all the support services. Some of these areas have been noted in chapters dealing with food services, maintenance and operation, transportation, etc. The key is cooperative planning of the use of the service. The administrator of the service shoulders a heavy communication responsibility to open up the potential to what could be a skeptical group of potential users. The transportation director may view collecting and inputting the data as just another thing to do for someone sitting in a windowless office surrounded by keyboards and CRTs and devoid of reality. The transportation director may not be alone in holding some version of that perspective. The task remains one of dealing with people as well as planning data and reports which can reduce costs per mile, per meal, or per square foot of clean terrazzo floor.

Summary

No field in history has changed more rapidly than information services. Given the almost weekly changes in technologies available, the full power of communications and information use is only beginning to be realized. Visual information systems that can tap into other data bases are being developed across the nation in K-12 schools and universities. Access to information is now possible worldwide. An elementary school principal queries a data base in Palo Alto, California; accesses the day's hot lunch program data and generates a report on the number of reduced-price and free lunches; and then returns to a task of graphing financial information for an upcoming presentation to a community study group. Simultaneously, the school business manager is creating a trial-run bus schedule for the next autumn based on enrollment projections and known residents. A report is then generated estimating fuel and maintenance costs based on miles traveled, terrain, distances between pickup points, and numbers of students and their destinations.

One of the key persons in providing and using information services is the school business manager. It is an exciting time to be able to work with information service systems. Their possibilities for instructional use (always the primary focus) and management awareness are limitless.

For Further Thought

1. How would you suggest avoiding the generation and manipulation of data becoming an end rather than a means?

2. What personnel implications may affect the essential education of users to access an information system effectively?

3. What safeguards would you suggest if it were necessary to hire an outside consultant to assist in the development of an information system?

4. In what ways could/should students have access to information systems?

5. How does the concept of participative management fit with an information services concept? Are there synergistic possibilities?

Endnotes

1. Richard G. Neal, "What's That You Say?" *The Executive Educator* 13, No. 11 (November 1991), p. 31.

2. The steps are adapted from Frederick L. Dembowski, "Management Education Systems in Educational Organizations," in *Principles of School Business Management* (Reston, Va.: ASBO, 1986), p. 208.

3. For a discussion of backup possibilities, see James C. Walker, "What to Do Before You've Lost It All," *School Business Affairs* 57, No. 5 (May 1991), pp. 6–10.

4. Guilbert C. Hentschke, *School Business Administration* (Berkeley, Ca.: McCutchan Publishing Corporation, 1986), p. 509.

5. Ross Kory, "School District Information System: Infrastructure of the '90s," *School Business Affairs* (May 1991), p. 21.

6. See Richard J. Lavin and John Phillips, "Improve School-Based Management Through Intelligent Networking," *T.H.E. Journal* 18, No. 4 (November 1990).

Chapter *13*

Personnel Services*

The school business manager is faced with an array of personnel decisions and administrative tasks. Unless there is a personnel department separate from the business office and reporting directly to the central office, the business manager deals with selection through retirement decisions for bus drivers, engineers, groundskeepers, purchasing officers, and many others. Personnel management in public school systems is intended to accomplish the educational mission of the school as stated by school board policy. Accomplishment of the school's mission depends primarily on the effectiveness of the people employed in the various positions within the school district. This includes administrators, instructional staff, and classified or support staff. Personnel management is a set of functions intended to improve the operation of the school system at either end of the personnel process from job hiring to retirement by securing capable people for available positions and retaining their services over time, and by positively influencing the performance of the employees in the various job classifications. This chapter provides an overview of the functions of personnel administration. The functions include nurturing a cooperative working relationship with all employees, human resource planning, recruitment activities, selection processes, induction activities, compensation, staff development activities, effective evaluation procedures, negotiations, and contract management. It is impossible to cover personnel functions in depth in this chapter, but an overview of the various functions is provided. Regardless of the job vacancy the school business manager seeks to fill, the selection and subsequent personnel processes should reflect the overall mission of the schools, which is to provide the best educational experience possible for the students so their earning is maximized.

*The authors wish to acknowledge the primary author of this chapter, Dr. Judy McConnell-Jackson, Associate Dean of the Graduate School at Miami University, Oxford, Ohio.

School Board Mission and Policy Statement

The accomplishment of the goals of a school system will primarily depend on the job effectiveness of the personnel employed. Thus, the philosophy of a school district would incorporate not only the primary statement regarding the mission of the school district to educate students, but would also include policy statements regarding how to facilitate this mission. The school board's mission statement guides the operation of the school district's personnel program.

Mission statements are implemented using a clear understanding of the legal issues involved in personnel management. The school business manager's knowledge of current legislation, regulations, and case law helps him or her to exert the leadership needed to maintain and improve the organization within legal parameters.

School board policies will consider federal legislation regarding employment, particularly addressing the civil rights of current and prospective personnel in mind. Although modifications and changes continue to occur in legislation, with their resulting regulations, promoting a policy of equal opportunity is appropriate. Major milestones on the road to equal opportunity in employment have been[1]:

Executive Order 110925 issued by President Kennedy in 1961; all government contractors are required to have nondiscrimination clauses covering race, color, creed, and national origin.

Executive Order 11246 issued by President Johnson; this created the Office of Federal Contract Compliance and required that every federal contract have a seven-point equal opportunity clause. The clause states agreement not to discriminate against anyone in hiring and during employment on the basis of race, color, creed, or national origin. In addition, contractors have to agree to take affirmative-action measures in hiring.

Executive Order 11375 issued by President Johnson in 1967 amended Executive Order 11246 by adding sex and religion to the list of protected categories. This order is enforced by the Office of Federal Contract Compliance.

The Office of Federal Contract Compliance along with the Equal Employment Opportunity Commission and the Department of Justice provide leadership in the area of nondiscrimination by government contractors.

The Equal Employment Opportunity Commission, established by Title VII of the Civil Rights Act, investigates alleged discrimination based on race, religion, sex, or national origin. Passage in 1972 of the Equal Employment Opportunity Act extended coverage to all employers of 15 persons or more, all public and private employment agencies, all state and local governments, all educational institutions, labor unions with 15 or more members, and joint labor-management committees for apprenticeships and training. The Commission has the power to bring litigation against organizations that engage in practices found to be discriminatory.

Subpart B of Section 504 of the Rehabilitation Act which applies to all state, intermediate, and local educational agencies prohibits recipients of federal financial assistance from discriminating against qualified handicapped persons in recruitment, hiring, compensation, job assignment or classification, and fringe benefits. Employers must provide reasonable work environment accommodations for qualified handicapped applicants or employees unless it can be demonstrated that the provision of such accommodations would cause undue hardship. In addition, agencies which receive assistance under the Education of the Handicapped Act must take positive steps to employ and promote handicapped persons.

An understanding of affirmative action and of the Equal Employment Opportunity Commission is essential for the school personnel manager. Affirmative action practices are meant to correct past discrimination. If, in the past, persons were discriminated against in hiring or promotion, steps should be taken to redress the past inequities. In order to determine if there has been discrimination, the school personnel manager should calculate the percentages and numbers of minorities and females employed in each position within the school district and should compare the presence of minorities and females to their presence in the labor market utilized to recruit. The qualifications of minorities and females currently employed should be noted to determine who among them are qualified to handle more advanced jobs. This information can be used to establish a plan to be sure that there is an appropriate percentage of women and minorities in the school district in the various job classifications. Such a plan can be put in place through the normal processes in the personnel plan through recruitment, selection, placement, and staff development.[2] Equal employment opportunity and affirmative action policy statements can be included in school board policies clearly stating the district's commitment to recruit, hire, and promote personnel without regard to race, creed, national origin, sex, or age (unless sex or age constitute a bona fide occupational requirement). The following examples of school board policy statements regarding affirmative action, and equal opportunity may be helpful in writing or examining existing policy statements:

Equal Employment Opportunity:	The Board of School Trustees hereby directs the Superintendent and all other employees of the school district to take action to prevent discrimination against any employee on the basis of race, creed, religion, sex, age, handicap or national origin.
	The Board of School Trustees directs the Superintendent to take appropriate measures to inform every applicant for employment of the Board's policy against discrimination on the basis of race, creed, religion, age, handicap or national origin, and to inform any applicant who does not wish to work with persons of any race, creed, religion, sex, age, handicap, or national origin, that such applicant should not seek employment in the school district.

The Board of School Trustees directs the Superintendent to make provision to ensure that the place of employment is fair and just, that nondiscrimination policies will be enforced, and that, because of such policies and practices, the school district will attract a diverse pool of qualified applicants.

Affirmative Action: Consistent with the established policy, goals, and objectives of the School Corporation and with the directives provided by the Federal and State Government, affirmative action procedures will be established to ensure equal employment opportunities for all racial minorities and women.

The School Corporation reaffirms its moral and legal commitment to full support of affirmative action toward equal opportunities in employment. The School Corporation further reaffirms its policy not to discriminate against any employee or applicant for employment because of race, color, creed, national origin, sex, age, or physical handicap.

Cooperative Working Relationships

The school business manager normally is assigned the responsibility of working with classified or support personnel in a school district while certificated personnel may be managed through the office of the assistant superintendent for instruction or personnel or by the superintendent. There are many other structures which assign different responsibilities. Some larger school districts have a personnel office separate from all other functions which reports to the superintendent directly. Regardless of the structure, it should be recognized that all employees are working toward the same goal, and all roles are important for the smooth operation of the school system. Care should be taken to nurture a cooperative, respectful relationship between staff persons in all positions. This relationship begins with all personnel being educated and sensitized to the importance of all other positions. The interdependency of positions within the school system needs to be emphasized in order that the mission of the school system to enhance learning is understood by all members of the organization.

People appreciate recognition for the valuable services they render to the organization. Consider the importance of clean buildings; supplies on hand when needed; buses running on time with courteous, careful drivers; safe equipment; nutritious and tastefully prepared meals; and the effective handling of clerical responsibilities. These are only a few examples of important contributions made by classified personnel. Yet, in some instances, the importance of the services of classified personnel goes unrecognized and the personnel processes in place for these employees are not emphasized. In a recent conversation, a building custodian voiced the following concerns: "They (teachers and administrators) treat me as if I am nothing around here. Sometimes they don't speak to me. They don't realize that I live in this neighborhood and my friends know that I'm not happy coming to work here. I could do more around here but it seems like no one appreciates the things I do. I try to be nice to the children to make this a friendly place, but nobody thinks about me." In stark contrast is the situation in 1991 when a senior class selected two custodians to be the commencement speakers.

The challenge to the person assigned administrative responsibilities in the area of classified personnel is to provide leadership in working toward a cooperative relationship among the staff based on an understanding of the value of all positions within the system. The goal is to achieve the objectives of the school district and to help individual staff members maximize their potential. In most situations, respect for employees and their abilities and decent treatment, including concern for the welfare and needs of the individual, helps to bring about commitment from employees in working toward the goals of the organization. Employee needs include acceptance, security, belonging, and a sense of accomplishment. Attention to these needs and to the forging of relationships of cooperation and mutual respect is an important facet of implementing an effective personnel management system.

Human Resource Planning

Human resource planning involves establishing processes to determine staffing needs for the future. Pupil enrollment projections, changes in instructional practices, adjustments in service delivery, and other changes indicated in the school district's long-term plan will impact staffing. Personnel managers can use the projections to forecast staffing needs and provide for training of staff to meet future needs.

The first step in human resource planning is to conduct an *inventory* of human resources. The inventory should profile the current personnel roster. Up-to-date information on every employee should be collected including the name of the employee, date of birth, sex, job title, site of employment, education and training, and any special skills. For certificated personnel, areas of certification should also be included. The employee profiles should be stored in the computer in order to provide easy access to the information. Information can be sorted by age, training, and so forth. This information will be beneficial when planning for in-service activities, when figuring aging patterns of staff to anticipate openings, and to determine those among the current staff who are qualified for promotion.

The next step in planning involves *interpreting the implications for staffing of the school system's long-term (3 to 5 year) plan.* This step involves consideration of what the school district plans to accomplish, what the student population will be in the foreseeable future, and what kind of educational program the school district wishes to operate. The availability of funding and the political climate must also be taken into consideration.

The final step in planning is *establishing discrepancies,* comparing what the schools have available in terms of personnel (from the profiles) with what is needed to adequately staff the programs and services planned for the future. The results have implications for staff development activities if persons need to be re-trained, and for recruitment activities to seek out individuals with the necessary skills for new positions. At the same time, if some employee skills are no longer needed, procedures to reduce the size of the staff (reduction in force) should be formulated in compliance with applicable laws, policies, and contract language.

Recruitment of Personnel

Perhaps the most effective way to make long-range improvements in organizations is to have a sound recruitment program. Recruitment of certificated staff is on the rise due to shortages in some areas, particularly mathematics, science, special education, and minority teachers in all fields. It has happened at "teacher fairs" that there were more recruiters representing the various school districts than there were prospective teacher candidates. It is evident that districts can no longer afford to have a laissez-faire approach to staffing. When specific qualifications are necessary to match the needs of certain positions, school districts are realizing the importance of planned recruitment activities. The teacher marketplace is becoming more competitive causing many districts to fund aggressive recruitment strategies. Some school districts are resorting to offering bonuses, relocation assistance, and rent reductions as incentives for prospective employees. It was recently reported that one inner-city district offered to lease a car as a "sign on" bonus for a potential candidate for a hard-to-fill position! Other school districts are beginning to pattern their recruitment efforts after those used in business and industry, by recruiting continuously, cooperating closely with other educational institutions and employment agencies, and by "stealing" the best personnel from other districts.

Many school districts are now realizing that an active recruitment program is needed to secure quality candidates for classified positions particularly considering retention in the district. Services and facilities which make up school systems are expanding with the resulting increase in the need for capable persons. Classified personnel include persons to staff the transportation services (director, maintenance persons, mechanics, drivers), the food services (director, supply coordinator, cooks, servers), building staff (custodians, maintenance, engineers, plumbers, electricians), office staff (secretaries, clerical persons, computer programmers, receptionists, accountants) and others. Many of these positions require persons trained in specific skills, while in some cases the individuals can be trained on the job.

A recruitment plan can be developed from the information provided in the human resource forecast, budgetary constraints, and other variables that will influence the need for personnel. Recruitment plans for classified personnel can include the following:

Advertising in local newspapers
Working closely with state and local employment agencies
Representation at local and surrounding community senior high career days
Visits to vocational and trade schools
Establishing contacts with high school guidance counselors
Networking with existing personnel whose work habits are of high quality
Consideration of current employees for promotions

Developing a promotion track within the system
Seeking promotable recruits

The assumptions underlying recruitment and promotion practices may begin to be examined by asking, Does the school district have a record of promoting from within, even if the jobs are advertised internally and externally? Does the school district have an in-service program that prepares people to move up, or is it limited to job-specific skills for incumbents? Can the district recruit on the basis of future opportunities for advancement? If not, why not? What kinds of messages are being conveyed to potential recruits as well as to those already within the school system?

An aggressive recruitment program involves incorporating as many of the listed suggestions as possible. Up-to-date records of the successes of recruitment strategies which produce quality applicants may be helpful. Refinements of the strategies can be made continuously as the recruiting picture changes.

The reader may have experienced sending a letter of inquiry about possible openings to a school district or business and then waiting in vain for a reply. The message sent back by the nonreply is "We don't need you," or "We're too busy to be bothered." A prompt reply to candidates who contact the personnel office "out of the blue" or in response to recruitment efforts is important. Pamphlets which describe the school district in general, its goals, mission statement, and general employment information can be helpful. The pamphlet could explain the advantages of employment in the district and could be mailed along with application materials in response to all inquiries. Files should be developed for each application received. If no position is available, the applicant can be informed that although no position is currently available, the application will be kept in the active file for a specified period of time, usually one year. In the event of an opening, files for the position should be pulled and given due consideration along with files of persons applying specifically in response to a vacancy announcement.

The Selection Process

After determining the necessary positions to be filled, and working through the recruitment process to create a diverse pool of qualified candidates, attention turns to the establishment of selection procedures. Selection is critical in order to reduce future problems. The goal of the selection process is to choose competent staff who will both give to the organization and gain from the organization. The following are logical steps in establishing a selection process:

1. Establish accurate, up-to-date job descriptions.
2. Establish the selection criteria.
3. Announce the position.
4. Receive and review the applications.
5. Determine which candidates should be interviewed.
6. Administer appropriate measurement devices or tests.

7. Check credentials and references.
8. Select the best candidate.
9. Make the job offer.

The Job Description

A detailed job description is a starting point for each position within a school district. The job description should be prepared in such a manner that it can be used by both the selection committee and the applicant to evaluate the requirements of the position. The job description is the end product of a "job analysis" which details the skills, education, or training required to do the job, the relationship the job has to other jobs, and what conditions affect the job. This information can be collected in a variety of ways including observation of performance of the job, interviewing the personnel employed to do the job, written surveys of the employees who do the job requiring them to indicate the duties they perform, asking employees to keep a journal of their job activities for a certain period of time, or by hiring an outside agency or consulting firm to prepare the job descriptions.

Job descriptions normally contain (1) job title, (2) job summary outlining the overall responsibilities of the position, (3) qualifications and skills required, (4) job classification, pay scale, and working hours, (5) position of the job in the organizational structure, and (6) the specific tasks to be performed. The cycle is then repeated as changes occur requiring new tasks. An annual review process may be helpful in keeping job descriptions current with job demands.

The Selection Criteria

Selection criteria will include ideal characteristics that would enable a person to be successful on the job. A candidate's actual characteristics should be compared to the ideal characteristics in order to determine suitability of the individual for the position. These criteria can then be used to determine the best persons to interview and to record impressions from the interviews.

Announcing the Position

It is important that a job vacancy announcement be prepared which includes the job title, major responsibilities of the position, site of the position, how to apply for the position, the application due date, and the minimum qualifications necessary for consideration.

The vacancy announcement should be posted in locations which will lead to a high response. For classified positions, advertisements may be placed in local newspapers, neighboring community newspapers, the employment office, local and neighboring high school guidance offices, and should be posted in all school district buildings. It is advisable to allow 2 to 3 weeks following the posting for responses. Persons interested in applying for the position should be given application forms. The application forms are often weighted with qualifications having an specific point value. Weight can be given for experience, certain skill levels, training, and so on. Research on application blanks indicates that weighted applications are the most valid.[3] The deadline for applications to be turned in should be followed by a 2 to 3 week period for the administrator to complete the steps involved in the selection process.

Receiving and Reviewing the Applications

On any given day the school business manager may be seeking persons to fill positions from accounting to window washing. Delegation is the order of the day unless the school district is very small. A well-conceived, consistent process for receiving and screening applications can expedite the process. A specific individual, usually a secretary, should be assigned the responsibility of receiving and coordinating application materials. This staff person would mail applications in response to all inquiries, and upon receipt of applications and other materials, create files for each applicant. The application, reference letters, transcripts, copies of all correspondence from the office to the individual, and all other pertinent information will be placed in the file.

On the day following the advertised deadline for receipt of applications, the files should be given to the individual designated for the initial review of the files. The initial review of the files can be compared with the selection criteria for the position on hand for comparison with the qualifications of the applicants. Files of applicants who do not meet the qualifications specified in the selection criteria and incomplete files should be removed from consideration.

After the first review and elimination, the weighted applications are tallied. In a weighted application, each item on the form related to job performance is given a weighting according to the degree to which it predicts job performance. The total score gives a prediction of job success.[4] Tallying the points from the applications will produce a rank ordering of the applicants. The top three to five candidates should be contacted for interviews and skill tests when appropriate.

Interviewing Prospective Employees

It is good practice for candidates to be interviewed by a central office administrator, the person who will supervise the employee, and if possible, an individual employed in a similar position. Persons serving on the interview team will need to review the files of the candidates before the interviews. The interview team may wish to meet prior to the interview sessions to formulate questions and to review the procedure for scoring the candidates in relation to the criteria previously established for the position. Arrangements may be made for persons serving on the committee to have released time from their job responsibilities. This investment in the selection process is worthwhile for it demonstrates the value placed on the process and the importance of selecting the right people for the available positions.

The team approach to interviewing allows for a comparison of views regarding the candidates and also allows for a good exchange of information regarding the position for the benefit of the candidate. The candidate will be asked questions and will be given the opportunity to question the team members. A standardized set of questions can be developed so that responses from the candidates can be compared. The object of the interview is to gather information from the candidate, and to learn about the candidate as a person.[5]

In certain instances, candidates may be required to take a test to measure skill level. Legal rulings indicate that tests must be clearly job-related to justify their use. Aptitude and ability tests are used most commonly and are justifiable. A person interviewing for a secretarial position can be required to take a typing test to determine skill level, or an applicant for the position of mechanic may be required to demonstrate skill. Some school districts are now requiring teacher candidates to demonstrate teaching ability.

The Reference Check

Personnel specialists often cite the general axiom that "the best predictor of future performance is past performance." It follows that most predictors used to select personnel are measures of past performance. Grade point averages, references from previous employers, information from résumés, and other information from the candidate's past should be closely scrutinized. It is not unheard of for an applicant to falsify information on application forms and résumés. It is in the best interest of the employer to spend the time and energy checking an applicant's references and qualifications before hiring rather than spending time later in termination procedures.

Selecting the Best Candidate

Once all relevant information regarding the candidates is assembled, the candidates can be rank ordered in accordance with scores derived from the weighted application, from the interview, from skill tests where appropriate, and from verified credentials and references.

The school business manager may have different processes of reaching the recommendation decision for hiring depending on the area, job level, and past performances of those charged to screen candidates. The transportation supervisor may make a "final" recommendation to the business manager, but the business manager may wish to be much more involved in the recommendation for a purchasing officer. The person selected should be the person who ranked highest in comparison to the selection criteria in order that employment decisions are fair and defensible.

Making the Job Offer

For classified positions, the school administrator ordinarily recommends to the superintendent the person he or she considers best qualified for the position. The job offer may come from the superintendent, or from his or her designee—the personnel manager, the business manager, or the supervisor. The board of education must approve the issuance of a contract. If the candidate accepts the position, employment may begin at once.

All applicants for the position are notified when the position has been filled (offer extended and accepted). Letters to high ranking candidates who were qualified but not selected can include a paragraph similar to the following: "Thank you for applying for a position within our school district. We sincerely appreciate the interest you have expressed in our district. We regret to inform you that we are unable to offer you a position at the present time. We received applications from many fine candidates making the selection decision a difficult one. We would like to keep your application in our active file for future consideration should other vacancies occur. Thank you again for your interest in our schools." Candidates receiving this information realize that they may still have the opportunity for employment in the future.

Induction Activities

After employees have been hired or transferred to new positions within the school district, induction activities begin. Induction activities are ongoing since staffing often requires transferring of individuals from one site to another. When employees are transferred, induction activities are appropriate to orient the person to the new situation.

Induction activities can contribute to employees assimilation, to their development, sense of security, and to their feeling of belonging. Demonstrating consideration, guidance, and understanding of individuals at this point in the employment cycle can do much to help employees find a reasonable degree of job security and satisfaction. The time and effort spent with employees during induction activities can help circumvent economic loss to the system due to staff turnover. Edmund J. McGarrell, Jr., in his article titled "An Orientation System That Builds Productivity" suggests the following points to remember when planning induction activities:[6]

Early impressions of the organization are lasting; poor impressions lead to staff turnover.

The prearrival period should be considered as part of the induction period and should be used to assist new employees by providing information about the system, the community, etc.

The first day on the job will leave a lasting impression.

New employees are interested in the total organization.

Teach the basic information about the position first.

Time the giving of information to fit the new employee's needs.

Avoid information overload.

Understand the importance of the individuals adjustment to the community.

Focus on the individual rather than groups.

Allow the supervisor to have primary responsibility in orientation.

Emphasize orientation as a must for productivity.

Induction programs for classified and certificated staff should be formulated as follows: (1) determine the objectives of the school district's induction activities; (2) organize the induction process and schedule activities; and (3) follow up on progress of inductees. The induction process should include scheduled sessions to provide information to the new or transferred employee. Information should be provided which may not have been covered during the recruitment and selection process. This information may come from meeting with a central administrator, the immediate supervisor, and with other employees. Planned induction activities should aim to provide information about the community, about tasks to be performed, responsibilities of the position, information about the school system including policies, procedures, mission, the fringe benefit package, and other information having to do with the welfare of employees. The new employee should be given information regarding the interworking relationships of all positions within the system and the specific role that he or she will play within the system. During the orientation process, the employee should be made to feel an important part of the organization.

To aid new employees and to enhance their productivity, many school districts have developed induction programs which incorporate "support groups" for new employees, assigning a "mentor" to the employee and having planned periodic orientation sessions with new employees. The sessions serve as a follow-up activity and can be used to ascertain the employee's progress within the position. New employees can use this time to ask questions and to obtain additional information helpful for job success. Many school districts sponsor intensive training sessions which last several days as an induction program to assist in orienting new employees.

Again, the school business manager has an opportunity to exert leadership in the personnel process for teachers and administrators. He or she can point out the essential support role of the business offices and possibly dispel some myths or misinformation about business processes such as purchasing, payroll, or maintenance. Time taken at this point may lead to some good ideas regarding providing services to the instructional sector.

Compensation

The purpose of the compensation process is to allocate resources for salaries, wages, and benefits in a manner that will attract and retain a high-quality staff with the necessary skills to accomplish the goals of the organization.[7] A salary policy is important for the efficient operation of the school system. A position structure must be established along with a determination of the economic value to be associated with each position. Most school systems use a step-increment salary schedule for both classified and certificated employees. Information can be projected easily from salary schedules and personnel files for budgeting and negotiation purposes.

Fringe benefit packages constitute a continuously growing cost to school systems. Benefits may include vacation and sick leave, medical coverage, life and disability insurance, etc. Fringe benefit packages contribute much to the well-being of school personnel. Classified and certificated personnel should be included in the plan. Information regarding the costs of the fringe benefit package should be shared with personnel, particularly during negotiations. Input should be solicited from employees regarding the trading of certain benefits for certain others.

Staff Development

The terms "staff development" and "in service" are sometimes erroneously used interchangeably. Note the differences articulated by Sergiovanni and Starratt: "In-service works to reduce the teacher's range of alternatives. . . . Staff development and renewal assume a need for teachers to grow.[8] If sound personnel practices are in place, school districts can aspire to operate with employees who are qualified, capable, and committed not only to their job responsibilities, but also to the goals of the school system as a whole. A staff development program is intended to help able staff to become better and to grow on the job. Good staff development programs maximize employee contributions to the goals of the system and promote employee job satisfaction.

The staff development program is also the umbrella for in-service activities. An effective staff development program may require the formulation of a districtwide committee with broad representation of employee groups. The committee would be charged with conducting an assessment of needs, establishing goals and objectives which are reflective of these needs, developing programs to meet the needs, formulating a plan for delivery, and then evaluating the programmatic attempts.[9] The staff development program might include activities such as programs to upgrade skills, train employees in new procedures or the operation of new equipment, educate employees in legal matters, orient staff to new educational programs which are being adopted, etc. Care should be taken to provide activities which will be meaningful and rewarding experiences for the employees. Jordan et al. recommended that the following be included in developmental activities[10]:

- Reinforcement of the pre-service orientation program
- Explanation of changes in the school district's internal organization that will affect employees
- Development of a better understanding of roles, responsibilities, and relationships of different employee groups in the school district
- Improvement in communication patterns among personnel and buildings in the district
- Explanation of changes in work procedures
- Improvement of the skills needed in present positions

Informative, interesting, and motivational sessions will encourage participation. When possible, staff development activities could be scheduled during regular work hours rather than during the evening hours or the weekend. The benefit of such programming should more than compensate for the money spent to fund employee release time.

Evaluation

The evaluation function was discussed in chapter 3; however, there are some areas that need to be emphasized. The focus of evaluation is on the results of the employee's on-the-job behavior as it relates to the required job functions and the purposes of the job for accomplishing the goals of the school. A food service director who provides nutritionally correct food but creates menus that cause drops in participation, or a purchasing officer who is so careful to get the best price that the commodity does not arrive in time so that it can be used, are not meeting the goals of their jobs nor providing service to the overall mission of the school.

An often-neglected aspect of evaluation is the education of those the school business manager must rely on to perform first-line evaluations. Unless the school district is very small, the business manager cannot conduct evaluations of the work of every person in the business area. A series of workshops on evaluation procedures could be conducted utilizing the expertise of the school attorney, the superintendent, the personnel manager, and other individuals knowledgeable in this area. If trained persons are not available from within the district, qualified contract consultants may perform the training.

Evaluation procedures are intended to provide staff members a periodic assessment of their performance, to relate job targets to day-to-day performance, to allow early identification of specific areas in which staff members need assistance, to provide help that is appropriate to the particular needs of the employees, and to provide the employee with specific information regarding strengths and weaknesses. Evaluation procedures are also intended to celebrate and encourage excellent job-related performance. Personnel who are identified through the evaluation process as demonstrating outstanding performance competencies may be later used to help new employees through "buddy" programs. Employees who consistently perform above the standard of expectation should be considered for promotion as openings occur.

Collective Negotiations and Contract Management

The school business manager is usually a key player in collective bargaining because of her/his information and knowledge of costs, probable changes affecting budget, and expertise in projecting the impact of proposals on the dollars available. Certainly collective bargaining is a key process affecting business functions. It is intended to be a bilateral process of give and take between representatives of management and representatives of employee groups for the mutual benefit of both. Lieberman and Moskow defined negotiations as "a process whereby employers make and counter offers in good faith on conditions of their employment relationship for the purpose of reaching a mutually acceptable agreement, and the execution of a written document incorporating any such agreement if requested by either party. Also, "a process whereby a representative of the employees and their employer jointly determine their conditions of employment."[11] Collective negotiations is an ongoing process. It is not a relationship that ends when the agreement is reached. The bargaining process includes all activities involved in contract management; negotiations, compensation, and the resolution of disputes (grievances) which arise during the term of the contract.

The right of public employees to bargain collectively dates back to 1959 when the first compulsory public sector bargaining law in the United States was enacted by the Wisconsin legislature followed in 1962 by President John F. Kennedy's Executive Order 10988 which granted federal employees collective bargaining rights. E.O. 10988 required federal employers to bargain in good faith, defined unfair labor practices, and established a code of conduct for labor organizations. In addition, it prohibited union shops and banned strikes by federal employees. In 1969 President Richard Nixon issued Executive Order 11491 which supersedes E.O. 10988 and served to standardize procedures to bring public labor relations in line with the private sector. The Assistant Secretary of Labor was given the authority to determine bargaining units, to supervise procedures for representation recognition, to rule on unfair labor practices, and to enforce standards of conduct in labor organizations. The Federal Labor Relations Council was formed as a result of E.O. 11491 with the responsibility to supervise the implementation of the order, to handle appeals, and to rule on issues.

The majority of states now have legislation enabling state and local public employees to organize, bargain, or to consult with employers. When permitted by state law, the employer has the duty to bargain with organized employees in "good faith." Good faith bargaining means that the parties agree to provide reasonable proposals which can be backed up with facts and figures used in their preparation. Complete and reliable information and data are needed and must be shared with employee organizations so that they do not negotiate on misinformation. Good faith bargaining also means that the meetings between the parties will be scheduled at convenient hours and that the decisions which are made will not be changed after they are made. The contract is to be in writing and no propaganda is to be used by either side during the bargaining process. The good faith bargaining relationship is defined in the National Labor Relations Board rulings and in court rulings. States which require only "meet and confer" sessions between employer and employees are required to meet at reasonable times to discuss proposals. There is no binding expectation that agreement will be reached.

Initially, bargaining was intended to include wages, hours, and conditions of employment. Certain topics are mandatory to bargain, others are permissive, while still others are unlawful. The line between mandatory topics and permissive topics has become blurred. Most state laws state that negotiations are to be confined to "conditions of employment." Conditions of employment refer to the quality of the employment situation. Conditions of employment have evolved in some states to include teacher bargaining on such items as the following:

Regulation of transfers
Selection of department chairs or team leaders
Determination of the ratio of support staff to teaching staff
Designation of student discipline procedures
Staffing of summer school by seniority
Time limits and frequency of faculty meetings
Released time for union representatives
School calendar
Daily schedules
The composition of instructional committees
Staff development programs
Procedures for evaluation
Assignment of staff
Provision of "just cause" for teacher reprimands
Grievance procedures

Over time, teacher contracts have become increasingly comprehensive and seek to address issues of policy, although it is generally known that policy should not be subject to bargaining. Myron Lieberman, a former advocate of teacher bargaining changed his position, espousing that teacher bargaining rights should be limited. He stated:

What was advocated or opposed in the 1960's on the basis of logic or intuition or speculation or analogy can be tested today against a body of experience. Today there is no excuse for debating whether or how collective bargaining in education differs from collective bargaining in the private sector. The differences are real and important, and they justify this conclusion: Providing public employees collective bargaining rights similar to those provided private sector employees is undesirable public policy.[12]

For better or worse, collective bargaining or something similar to it exists in most states and appears to be here to stay. While it has been stated by some that collective bargaining is getting out of hand, it is a means for personnel to identify and satisfy their needs, and it provides a vehicle to improve the development of personnel.

The Bargaining Process

The collective bargaining process requires preparation and commitment. Ideally it results in management and employee organizations resolving concerns. A key point to remember is that the process does not begin or end at the bargaining table.

The bargaining process includes the following steps:

1. *Preparation.* Current agreements are reviewed for language that may have caused some difficulties during the previous period of the contract. Additional reviews of grievances, contracts in similar school districts, and current changes in laws or regulations that will affect the upcoming contract language will help in the preparation of the district's proposal.

2. *Select the Bargaining Team.* The team should include persons who understand the operation of the school system, who possess the negotiations knowledge, who understand the importance of satisfaction of human needs, who understand the necessity to believe in employees and in employee participation, and who can make decisions for the school system. It is advisable that the team spokesperson be someone other than a school district employee because the spokesperson may be seen by the employees as their adversary. A professional negotiator or the district attorney might serve well in this role. Other members of the team can be free to help during caucus. The superintendent may elect not to serve on the negotiations team although in small districts the school board may expect him or her to do so. The superintendent can make significant impact on negotiations by being available to educate the board about issues relating to the contract, by investigating problems which may result if new language is adopted, and by advising the board and the team on negotiations strategy. The school business manager can be a valuable member of the negotiations team because of his or her knowledge and expertise in budget matters relating to salary, benefits, staffing and enrollment projections, etc. Other possible members on the team might include an experienced building principal, and the director of personnel. If curriculum issues have been allowed into the contract, the director of curriculum could be a member or serve as a consultant when necessary.

3. *Predict Employee's Proposal.* Again, the school business manager can be of great assistance in translating the expected proposals into dollars. Being aware of the positions

of the state-level organization will be helpful in anticipating bargaining positions and language locally.

4. *Formulate the District Proposal.* In formulating the school district's proposal, it is important to identify the district's bargaining goals, both reasonable and hopeful. The goals established should be reflective of a desire for increased effectiveness in management, clarification of language difficulties, and containment of cost. Information about how much money is available should be gathered, priorities should be set, and language formulated. A rationale should be written for items that are high priorities. Items which are not high priorities should be distinguished as being tradeable.

5. *Meeting of Bargaining Teams.* The next step in the negotiation process is for the two teams to meet. An important factor in successful meetings is to listen. Knowledge of what the real issues are is necessary if a settlement is to be reached. An attempt should be made to establish a positive negotiations process characterized by trust and respect. To make the process workable, the negotiation teams must agree on the school district's financial condition, be willing to give and take, and should endeavor to stay calm. Operating guidelines for the meetings should be decided including meeting time and place, role and number of members of the negotiating teams, school district information which needs to be provided, rules for caucuses, procedures for recording agreement and counterproposals, impasse procedures which will be operationalized if necessary, along with other guidelines which the situation in the school district dictates.

When agreement has been reached, the final contract should be signed and distributed to the supervisors. It is important to hold a briefing session with the supervisors to explain all changes in contract language and the anticipated impact of the language changes on management.[13]

When parties with differing interests seek agreement through negotiation, it is inevitable that at times they may be unable to come to a satisfactory settlement. If the school board and the employees' organization cannot reach agreement during good faith negotiations of mandatory subjects, they have reached an impasse. The state of impasse has been reached when during the proceedings neither side will move from its stated position. On the other hand, if one side refuses to meet, an unfair labor practice could result against the party refusing to meet. Many states which have collective bargaining laws have public employee relations boards charged with implementing the law and in most cases with administering procedures to resolve an impasse, which can include mediation, fact-finding, and arbitration. Normally the range of measures used at an impasse begin with mediation first, followed by fact-finding, and where permitted by law, arbitration.

Mediation is usually the first remedy on reaching an impasse. Mediation is an informal process which helps the teams to work out the problem themselves. An individual or panel is chosen by both parties or appointed by the public employee relations board. The mediator serves as an advisor who seeks to reduce the differences through compromise. Mediators sometimes meet with the teams separately to find concessions each are willing to make. The mediator seeks to persuade or influence the parties to reach an agreement but has no authority to make decisions. Normally the mediator is involved in negotiations for new contracts, rather than in mediating grievances under an existing contract.

In the event that disputes are not resolved through the use of mediation, fact-finding can be initiated. In fact-finding, an impartial party or panel conducts hearings to review the evidence, collects facts, and makes recommendations based on the facts in evidence. The process is voluntary and the parties may accept or reject the report.

Arbitration may be the final measure resorted to in impasse resolution. Arbitration involves the use of an impartial individual or panel who collects evidence and facts and makes a decision. Arbitration may be compulsory or voluntary. Compulsory arbitration must be established by statute and may involve compulsory submission to the arbitration process and compulsory acceptance of the decision. Generally, the determination of the arbitrator is enforceable by the courts. In compulsory arbitration, a government appointed agency handles the dispute resolution. In voluntary arbitration, either negotiation team may initiate the action to take the unresolved matter to arbitration. Arbitration is identified in statutes as being binding or nonbinding.

Work Stoppages

When failure at the bargaining table results in an impasse, a possible outcome of the bargaining impasse is a job action. A strike constitutes a withdrawal of services by union members or a lockout by management. In the private sector, a strike is used to impose economic losses on the employer so that it is in the employer's best interest to reach a settlement. In the private sector both employer and employees lose economically. The economic impact on employees may be modified by strike funds or other union benefits.

Strikes in public schools normally do not effect the economic status of the employers or of the employees inasmuch as their major funding is through tax revenues or state government appropriations. Tax monies are not dependent on the operating calendar for the school system and state monies are normally based on enrollment. Schools may continue to receive money during strikes whether the school is open or closed.

Teachers do not normally lose revenue because most states require schools to operate a minimum number of days, normally between 180 to 185 per year. School districts normally make up days lost in a strike to meet the required number of days of operation. Therefore, teachers suffer no real economic loss; however, a strike may or may not have a economic effect on classified personnel.

While the employers and the employees ordinarily do not lose money from a strike in public school systems, loss is suffered by the student body and by the public. Students lose because of the prolonged absence from school. Although the days are technically "made up," they may be made up during normal holiday periods, during and often late in the month of June, and occasionally on weekends. The makeup days may not be well attended. Families may have prearranged vacations, and in some cases parents choose not to send children during holiday periods because they don't feel that their child should be "punished" for the teacher strike. When days are made up in June, students who would have had a chance for summer employment may lose the opportunity. Students planning to graduate and begin summer classes at a college or university also lose.

Parents are also losers during a strike. Many parents, including an increasing number of mothers, work outside of the home. When schools are closed, parents must find alternate arrangements for their children. Older children have been known to congregate in shopping centers, places of business, or on the street. Their presence is not always welcome, sometimes causing community persons to begin to vocalize concern over the strike.

The losses suffered by the community during a strike by school employees causes the political climate in the school district to change. Often, a great deal of pressure will be put on school boards to end the strike and open the schools.

While strikes affecting the operation of public schools tend to be unpopular with the public, it appears that strikes are becoming a part of the negotiations process in public school systems. Although strikes are not the anticipated results of negotiations, plans must be made by the school district in case they occur.

The school district administration should prepare a contingency plan to put in operation in the event a strike should occur. The plan should include procedures to be followed if the school system intends to continue the delivery of services to students, and procedures to be followed if the school system intends to shut down. Included in the plans should be the roles of administrators and supervisors during and after the strike. Although it is wise to have a strike plan ready, it is in the district's best interest to try to work out the problems at the bargaining table.

Grievance Procedures

After reaching agreement on the contract, and having it ratified by both parties, it then becomes the responsibility of the employers and of the employees to make the contract work. Inevitably, problems will arise over the application or interpretation of contract language during the time that the contract is in effect. Grievance procedures are the mechanisms in place to provide for a settlement of such disagreements. Written procedures for the settlement of grievances in many cases are included in the contract. Written grievance procedures are normally characterized by the inclusion of a definition of the items that are grievable, the series of steps to take in filing a grievance, the steps through which a grievance may be appealed for settlement, the time limitations for the presentation of grievances, decision making and appeals, and provision for the final step in unresolved grievances.

The general order of the grievance process is normally from informal discussion of the complaint with the immediate supervisor, putting the grievance in writing and submitting it to the supervisor, appeal to the next level which is normally the department head, and finally appeal to the school board or to an arbitrator. Each step is described in the grievance procedures and includes the time limit for filing an appeal and the time limit for response from the different individuals or boards. Employees have the right to have legal counsel or representation and may seek advice from the union.

Summary

The personnel processes in place in a school system can do much to affect the achievement of the mission of the school district since the goals of the school system are carried out through its employees. A central figure in the personnel picture is the school business manager who oversees many functions essential to the day-to-day operations of the school. The work of the people that he or she selects, supervises, and evaluates can help make the difference between a good school and an excellent school.

The personnel processes include recruitment of a diverse group of qualified candidates, selection of individuals with the capabilities to be successful on the job, adequate compensation of employees through salary and benefits, staff development activities to enhance the employees, evaluation for the improvement of employee performance, and collective negotiations and contract management. Processes should be in place for certificated as well as classified personnel. All personnel processes should reflect the goals of the organization and should adhere to federal, state, and contractual guidelines.

For Further Thought

1. Survey several business managers to determine what personnel functions they are responsible for. Is there consistency?

2. What provisions are made by school corporations to ensure that disabled persons will have opportunities to be hired and to advance?

3. List practical ways to commend excellent work in the purchasing office, transportation, or food services that will be appreciated over time by the persons recognized.

4. Should the business manager be the chief negotiator to reach agreements with non-certified personnel groups? What are the advantages or disadvantages in either case?

5. More often than might be desirable, the orientation of a new employee consists of, "Here is your desk. Let me know if you have any questions." Could the case be made that the investment of time into a thorough orientation program will repay handsome returns to the school district? Under what conditions might that not be the case?

6. What contingency plans do school systems have in the event of a strike of maintenance/operation personnel or food service personnel?

7. What control of access to personnel files is provided, especially when records are available on the computer system?

Endnotes

1. Department of Health, Education, and Welfare, "Nondiscrimination on the Basis of Handicap," Federal Register 41, No. 96 (May 17, 1976).

2. Equal Employment Opportunity Commission: Affirmative Action, Vol. 1. (Washington, D.C.: Government Printing Office, 1974), pp. 18–64.

3. Herbert C. Heneman, II, Donald P. Schwab, John A. Fossum, and Lee D. Dyer, *Personnel/Human Resource Management* 3rd ed. (Homewood, Ill.: Richard D. Irwin, 1986), p. 315.

4. Ibid.

5. Auren Uris, *The Executive Interviewer's Handbook* (Houston, TX: Gulf Publishing Company, 1978), p. 4.

6. Edmund J. McGarrell, Jr., "An Orientation System That Builds Productivity," Personnel 60, No. 6 (November–December 1983): 39–40.

7. William B. Castetter, *The Personnel Function in Educational Administration,* 4th ed. (New York, Macmillan Publishing Co., 1986), pp. 427–428.

8. Thomas J. Sergiovanni and Robert J. Starratt, *Supervision: A Redefinition,* 5th ed., New York: McGraw-Hill, 1993, p. 267.

9. Ronald W. Rebore, *Personnel Administration in Education: A Management Approach,* 3rd ed. (Englewood Cliffs, N.J.: Prentice-Hall, Inc., 1991), p. 166.

10. K. Forbis Jordan, Mary P. McKeown, Richard G. Salmon, and L. Dean Webb, *School Business Administration,* (1985) Newbury Park, CA: Sage Publications, Inc.

11. Myron Lieberman and Michael H. Moskow, *Collective Negotiations for Teachers: An Approach to School Administration* (Chicago: Rand McNally & Company, 1966), p. 418.

12. Myron Lieberman, "Eggs That I Have Laid: Teacher Bargaining Reconsidered," *Phi Delta Kappan* 60 (February 1979): 414.

13. Kathryn Prenn and John Coughlin, "Negotiations: Try a Pragmatic Approach," in the National School Boards Association Up-dating School Board Policies, Jan., 1986.

Chapter *14*

Capital Projects

The process of renovating, additions to, or building new buildings may be divided into four rather distinct phases: (1) long-range planning; (2) short-range planning for the specific structure, (3) construction; and (4) orientation, occupying, and evaluating the facility. Long-range planning was discussed in chapter 4, therefore; in this chapter we re-emphasize some aspects of planning as related specifically to capital projects.

Again, the business manager plays an *educational* role in the building or renovation of an educational facility. The educational purpose of the facility is the primary purpose to be served and the decisions about the process and persons to be involved should be based on that purpose. Both cost-effectiveness and the quality of construction and equipment are important but only as they relate to the effectiveness of the educational activities to be housed. Brick and mortar time is not abdication time from educational responsibilities for the school business manager.

Steps toward a Capital Project

The steps taken in planning the renovation or construction of a school building vary according to state law; the understanding and sophistication of citizens, school board members, and educators in the community; and the extent of building needs. In general, however, the following might be considered universally desirable.

1. Examine the recommendations of a statewide survey of total building needs.
2. Review any regional, county, or area study involving several related school districts.
3. Undertake a long-range study of school district growth in conjunction with municipal growth to predict future building needs.
4. Purchase new sites on the basis of long-range needs.
5. The school administration presents evidence showing the need for a new building based on long-range plans or new developments.
6. The school board authorizes a more thorough survey (a stakeholders' study) of needs.

7. Establish and operate the school study organization.

8. Advise the public and encourage its participation.

9. The school board decides to build on the basis of preliminary reports and findings.

10. Hire an architect.

11. Develop a carefully worded contract with the architect specifically stating his or her duties and responsibilities.

12. Establish the executive building committee and define its organization and responsibilities.

13. The total educational staff studies functional needs of the building and makes recommendations, including how the facility is to be evaluated once in use.

14. The building executive committee makes educational layout and specifications from the recommendations of an advisory committee of teachers and other personnel including staff and classified personnel.

15. The architect makes working drawings and obtains approval from the school board.

16. Develop a long-range plan for financing the building.

17. Obtain approval and advice from the state on the entire building and financing plan.

18. Obtain public approval of the finance plan.

19. Approve final drawings and specifications.

20. Advertise and sell bonds for financing if needed.

21. Develop a construction budget.

22. Supervise the construction (clerk of works, architect, executive building committee).

23. Select furniture and equipment.

24. Make payments to the contractor on the basis of formal progress reports to the architect.

25. Approve all changes on a formally written change order sent by the architect to the school board.

26. Landscape the site.

27. Approve the completed project (architect, executive building committee, board of education).

28. Present the building to the public at a formal open house.

29. Orientation to the use of the facility and beginning the formal evaluation.

It is clear from the above that planning is the key to creating an effective facility. If the new facility or renovated facility is to *facilitate* as its name implies, the linkage to the overall direction and mission of the school must be direct and strong.

Some Decisions Regarding Involvement of People

A glance at the list above alerts the reader that many people and much time will be used in any capital project. The professional lives of the school administrators, particularly in small or medium-sized school districts, will be changed when planning and constructing new or renovated facilities. Time demands will be increased and the interruptions to ordinary time use will mount. At an average cost of $5 million for a new or renovation project (1987 estimates) and more than half the school districts in the country planning a major project, the use of time becomes an important consideration. Large school districts that have full-time professionals in a planning/construction division may not experience the perceived disruptions that smaller school districts may experience. The concern that the ordinary activities of educational leadership are superceded by the capital project is real. On the other hand, if the care needed to create a useful facility is ignored, the potential for spending dollars unwisely has become real.

The problem is acute and may appear unanswerable in the small school where there is no administrative staff to whom responsibilities for the building might be delegated. In many small schools it is not reasonable to recommend the permanent addition of an administrative assistant or business manager to lighten the administrator's load.

Hiring a temporary assistant on a terminal six-month or one-year assignment who would serve as executive secretary and liaison person between the superintendent's office and the building operation may be an answer. Several side benefits also may accrue from this plan. First, it can provide a training ground or internship for outstanding young staff members or graduate students interested in gaining administrative experience, and second, it can provide a transition period for the growing school district and in some cases a permanent position may be established after the building program is completed.

Many school architects complain about a further problem—lack of explicit policies and procedures for their direction and assistance. Operational procedures need to be in written form, which will expedite the planning and construction of the facility. The contact people need to be clearly designated and a clear-cut problem-solving process needs to be spelled out before problems arise.

An Operational Executive Committee

The planning of a school building requires the assistance of many people. There are cases on record where thousands of people have been involved in one way or another on a project—as advisors, consultants, information gatherers, etc. A small working group, however, must actually execute the plans and put them into operation. Execution of the building plan is not a one-person job. It cannot be carried on by the superintendent alone or the architect alone; it requires team effort just as the planning process does. Figures 14-1 (page 238) and 14-2 (page 239) show the possible composition of a building executive committee in both the medium-sized school district and the large school district and its relationship to the board of education and various advisory groups.

It will be noted that in both situations the executive committee includes administrators representing the instruction department and the business department of the school district. The school business manager serves in an official capacity as secretary and chairman in the large-school situation (Figure 14-2). This proposal does not intend to minimize the role of other members of the committee, but rather to capitalize on the managerial skill and the facilities for handling business matters which already exist in the school district under the direction of the business manager. It is important that the committee be chaired by a high-level administrator who has authority to make decisions, arbitrate, organize, and expedite in the name of the executive group and the board of education. In the small and medium-sized school district the superintendent may assume

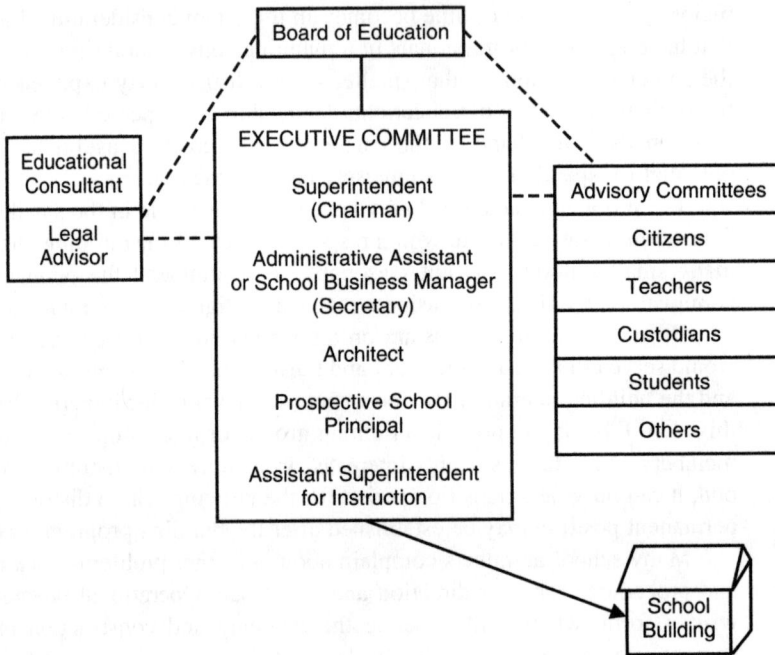

FIGURE 14-1   A Building Executive Committee for a Medium-Sized School District.

this chairmanship, but it should be emphasized that the school business manager who serves as secretary must do most of the work. In the large-school situation the assistant superintendent for business affairs chairs the committee, with the school plant consultant doing most of the work for the committee.

In all cases the prospective school principal is a member of the committee—a point that is often overlooked—for he or she must perform this job in the new building. He or she will be concerned with problems of a more personal and specific nature than the rest of the committee. If an entire staff is to be transferred from an old building, the principal can serve as leader and chairman of this staff group and can be their representative on the executive committee assuming contract language does not prohibit it.

Evaluating Facilities

Facilities should be evaluated on a regular basis regarding their educational effectiveness, safety, cost-effectiveness, and mechanical systems. Evaluating the cost-effectiveness of buildings is closely related to the maintenance and operation processes discussed in chapter 15. Careful records of data gathered in such a way that they can be analyzed over time and by a number of criteria are essential to arrive at a reasonable cost-effectiveness rating of a building.

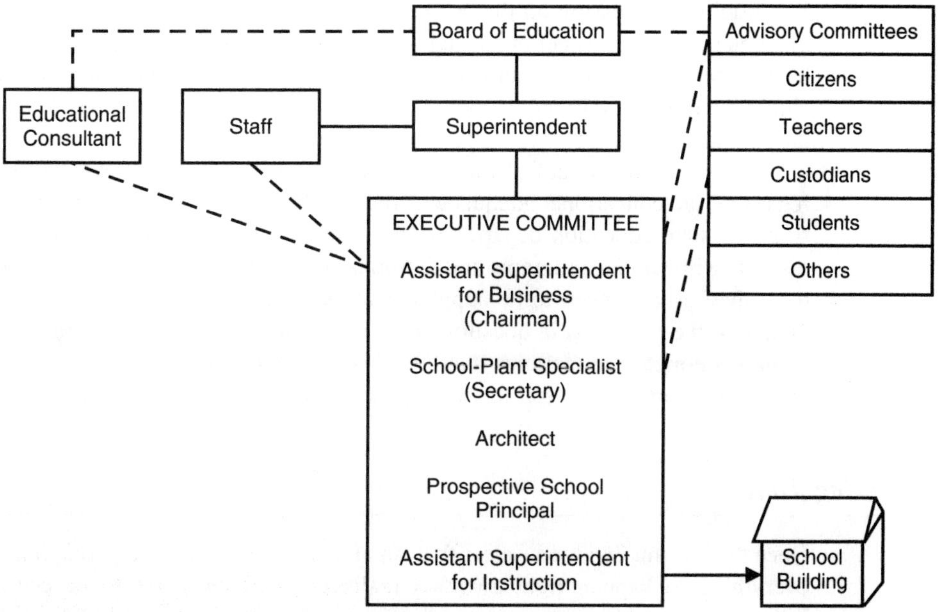

FIGURE 14-2 A Building Executive Committee for a Large School District.

Evaluating educational effectiveness can be a bit elusive and more complicated. As the needs for technology grow, as society imposes mandates or expectations on the school that may or may not be directly related to the school's mission, as problems enter with students who require extensive services, the facilities of yesterday or even today become somewhat of a disability for the educational mission. Schools may not have fiberoptic cables to carry computer-driven visual instruction. Special facilities to accommodate thematic instruction or inquiry-based learning utilizing a number of information sources may be very limited. Support services personnel such as psychometrists, speech pathologists, or special education teachers may find themselves working in and even sharing closetlike spaces suitable for storage but not instruction. Special programs, for instance in reading instruction, require spaces for one-to-one tutorials. Increased interest in preschool programs may result in new programs and space demands. Some schools have incorporated preschool programs in high schools with appropriate space and equipment modifications.

The business manager will need to work closely with his or her counterparts in instruction to determine the educational effectiveness of buildings. As noted in chapter 4, the evaluation process is continuous and the educational evaluation of buildings should be continuous. Instructional or program innovations may change the balance between a building or part of a building from being adequate to being obsolete. A study reported that 43 percent of the nation's schools are obsolete.[1] While age alone does not constitute obsolesence, over 37 percent of the school buildings in Indianapolis, for example, are over 60 years old and 40 percent of those are over 80 years old, one of which is 124 years old.[2]

Additional pressure on the educational adequacy of some buildings comes with the movement toward magnet or specialized schools. A school emphasizing the fine arts will have different educational and facility needs from one concentrating on technology in commercial/industrial applications. If the concept of choice becomes more widespread, the pressure on educational adequacy will increase.

The professional staff of the school is the primary source of evaluative information regarding the educational adequacy of the buildings. Evaluation forms may be available from the state education department, from university personnel, or from nearby school districts with similar programs and facilities. While these forms are helpful in organizing data, they usually need to be supplemented with descriptions of activities that may be unique to the programs in question. Time and money should be set aside for faculty and administrators to see facilities that have been designed for programs similar to those the district has committed itself to via long-range planning.

Planning Time

Once the information seems clear that a major capital project is required, it is easy to want everything to happen right away. A realistic timetable needs to be established. The following timetable was suggested for the construction of a new building of 100,000 to 150,000 square feet with a construction time of eighteen months.

I. Two years and ten (10) months prior to the building occupancy
  A. Send questions to prospective architects and start the selection procedure. (This procedure should take approximately 3 months.)
  B. Send questionnaires to prospective construction managers, if one is used. (The procedure should take approximately 3 months.)
II. Two years and seven (7) months prior to the building occupancy
  A. Hire architect.
  B. Hire construction manager (if this method is used).
  C. Hire financial consultant.
III. Two years and six (6) months prior to the building occupancy
  A. Review scope of the project, budget, and special details with architect and construction manager.
  B. Instruct the architect and construction manager to develop a calendar showing the completion dates for the following:
    1. Concept of the project
    2. Schematic design
      a. Starting date
      b. Completion date
      c. Administrative and staff review
      d. Board approval
    3. 1028 Hearing. (This hearing and form is required by the State of Indiana.)
    4. Design development/Preliminary plans
      a. Starting date
      b. Completion date

c. Administrative and staff review
d. Board approval
5. Construction documents/Final plans
a. Starting date
b. Completion date
c. Administrative and staff review
d. Board approval
6. Bidding
a. Start date
b. Bid date
c. Board approval
IV. Two years and five (5) months prior to the building occupancy, start development of educational specifications.
V. Two years and four (4) months prior to the building occupancy
A. Prepare a budget for the project
B. 1028 Hearing
VI. One year and eleven (11) months prior to the building occupancy
A. Release bid documents to the prospective bidders
B. Ad appears in the local paper that the school is accepting bids.
VII. One year and ten (10) months prior to the building occupancy
A. Accept bids on school project
B. After accepting bids, if a holding corporation is used, meet with bond council and establish a budget
C. If a holding corporation is used it will take approximately four (4) months until the bonds are sold and ground can be broken. (Some states permit special holding corporations to be formed to finance school buildings.)
VIII. Bond issue—between one year and ten (10) months and one year and six (6) months prior to building occupancy
Week 1—Meet with bond council and establish budget.
Week 2—School board approves resolution to advertise proposed lease.
—File petition with state tax board.
—Publish notice of hearing on lease.
Week 3—Conduct formal hearing on lease. The lease must be at least ten (10) days after the advertisement.
—Approve the lease resolution at the same meeting of the formal hearing.
Week 4—Publication of the notice of lease execution.(A thirty (30) day remonstrance period follows from the date of publication of the notice of lease execution. At this point, the public may lodge complaints to stop possible construction. Check state law for such provisions.
Week 8—Waiting period for remonstrance 30 days.
—NOTE: If a remonstrance is filed add 50 to 100 days.
Week 9—After 30 days remonstrance period has expired if no remonstrance is filed, meet with the school property tax board for a hearing on the lease. *Note:* Time needs to be built in according to the tax board's meeting schedule.

Week 10—Approval of state property tax board.
Week 11—Adoption of the bond resolution and approval of the trust indenture.
Week 12—Advertise the sale of bonds two times one (1) week apart.
Week 14—Receive bids on bonds (15 days after the 1st sale notice).
      —Award bids on the same day bids are received.
Week 17—Deliver bonds.
      —Break ground on the day bonds are delivered.

It is clear from the above example that many efforts will be coming together during this time. From the planning process have come data regarding projected enrollments and commitments to existing and possible new programs. A financial plan is in place. The process of gaining community support has begun. Educational specifications have been written. An architect has been selected.

Architect Selection

Every decision in the building process is important, but none is more critical than selecting the architect for the project. Earthman[3] suggested the following steps in selecting an architect on a comparative basis:

1. Identify the pool of interested architects. Obtain names from the American Institute of Architects (AIA) chapter, colleagues in education, and the telephone directory.
2. Send out to the above information about the project and a questionnaire seeking information about the firm.
3. Review materials sent by the architect firm's capability statement and completed questionnaire.
4. Identify five to ten firms that seem capable and interested. Send an additional questionnaire seeking further information including names and addresses of former clients and facilities that can be visited.
5. Review the materials from the above firms and evaluate them so that the list is reduced to three firms.
6. Conduct an intensive background investigation on the three firms by contacting former clients and colleagues and visiting facilities designed by the prospective firms.
7. Hold interviews with the three architects and their staff to gather first-hand impressions and additional data.
8. Visit the offices of each of the firms in order to gain an impression of employees' working atmosphere.
9. Select one firm from the list of three based on the visits, interview of the candidates and interviews of former clientele.
10. Present the candidate firm to the board of education.

Gathering accurate information about an architectural firm's capabilities and performance record is critical. In the process above, questionnaires and interviews provide much of the factual data. Hertz[4] reminded readers that some architects are very good in one aspect, for instance new construction, while not as good in others such as additions or renovations. He suggested seeing facilities the architect has done that would be similar in type to the one being contemplated. Further, the work commitments of the firm needs to be determined so that the school district administration is assured that the amount of attention needed for the project can be given to it.

The American Institute of Architects (AIA) provides a standard form of questionnaire for selecting architects for educational facilities. In addition, the AIA has available a standard form of agreement between the school district or owner and the architect. Topics covered include the services to be rendered, owner's responsibilities, construction costs, architects drawings, arbitration over disputes, termination, payments to the architect, basis of compensation, and other conditions or services to be agreed to by the parties.

Some of the services that the school district could expect from the architect firm include the following:

1. Preliminary plan preparation
   a. Studying and discussing the educational plans with school authorities.
   b. Assisting in making studies of proposed sites in regard to soil structure, topographical relationship, space requirements, harmony of school plant, and relation to utilities.
   c. Preparating preliminary drawings, including floor plans, suggested elevations, location of building on site; developing, in consultation with the educational authorities, any desirable revision of equipment layouts submitted by them; and drafting a brief outline of specifications on which tentative cost estimates can be based.
   d. Securing the written approval of the board of education on final revision of the preliminary drawings; and proceeding with the preparation of the working drawings and specifications.

2. Working drawing preparation
   a. Holding frequent conferences during the preparation of working drawings and specifications with the educational authorities for the development and application of data required for essential planning, choice of materials, anticipated problems in relation to state laws, public utilities, and legal permits and restrictions.
   b. Securing written approval of working drawings and specifications from the board of education and from government agencies as required by law.

3. Assistance during time of bidding
   a. Preparing advertisements for bids after having cleared with the board of education regarding the policy to be used in bidding.
   b. Distributing plans and specifications for purposes of bidding.
   c. Clarifying plans and specifications for purposes of bidding.
   d. Tabulating bids on opening.
   e. Checking performance and financial record of contractor.
   f. Recommendations to client of contractor's reliability.

4. Preparation of contract documents. Contract documents should consist of at least the following, prepared in sufficient copies for the files of the school board, the contractor, and the architect.

    a. Plans, signed by the school board and contractor.

    b. Specifications signed by the school board and contractor.

    c. Copy of proposal signed by contractor.

    d. Contract form properly filled out and signed by the school board and the contractor.

    e. Bond forms executed by contractor and surety.

    f. Certificates of required insurance furnished by contractor.

5. Supervision of construction

    a. No matter how carefully and competently the drawings and specifications for a building have been prepared, unless they are followed the effect is the same as though they had not been prepared or had been done poorly. Consequently, there is a need for adequate supervision of construction. It is regarding this point that misunderstandings frequently arise. It is essential that before construction starts or even before the contract with the architect is signed, complete agreement be reached between the architect and the school authorities regarding the nature and extent of supervision to be furnished by the architect. The AIA has available a booklet *You and Your Architect* which provides a checklist of design services provided by architects as well as other helps particularly useful to persons faced with the prospect of building without a backlog of experience.

    b. On most projects additional supervision should be furnished by a "clerk of the works" who will work under the direction of the architect and will give continuous personal supervision. The decision concerning the employment of a clerk of the works is a matter to be decided by the architect and school officials. There should be complete understanding among the architect, the supervisor, the contractor, the workmen, and the school authorities regarding the payment of the construction supervisor, his or her qualifications and competence, and the lines of authority and responsibility. A great deal of care should be given to the selection of this person.

Educational Specifications

Educational specifications result from the long-range planning process and the facility-specific planning. The executive building committee coordinates and consolidates the specifications that have been generated through a process involving a number of users. The persons involved could include teachers, specialists, directors, principals, community representatives and agency representatives if the facility is to serve the community at large in a variety of ways.

Too often the school district does not assume the assertive role it should in developing educational specifications. The situation may be the result of not knowing exactly how to proceed; not trusting the expertise available within the district staff; confusion regarding whose role it is to develop them, or the press of time, especially in smaller school districts where administrators and teachers often wear more than one hat. Regardless of the reasons, the astute business official would be remiss if the district were allowed to avoid the job. Developing the specifications provides opportunities for clarification of program direction and priorities of activities, special use needs, and a commitment to quality. Well-written educational specifications provide the architect with a description of the activities anticipated, with the number of students involved, with the relationships between and among programs and spaces, and a glimpse of the future use of the facility being planned.

A word of caution is in order. When teachers are asked to assist in the preparation of educational specifications, they are too often left to work unadvised on the requirements for grades or subjects of their own particular interest. They dream great dreams, develop exciting ideas, and then when they submit their report it is tossed out as unrealistic. This is both disheartening and unfair. Prior to the time when teachers become involved in specific planning for their own teaching space they should participate in some type of workshop where the overall building specifications are considered, realistic limitations proposed, and a list of helpful readings developed. The readings will sharpen their thinking and make it more precise. But most important, they can go on to make their plans within a definite frame of reference. Clear lines of communication need to be established so that when questions arise, those developing the educational specifications know where to turn for clarification or information.

Another caution relates to the tendency on the part of educators to try their hands at drawing specifics as if they were the architects. Educators should no more try to enter that turf than the architect should try to enter the instructional matters of the school. The temptation occurs to both. Directing the ideas and information the two groups have to offer each other is a challenge, but well worth the effort if done successfully. On occasion the architect firm will have a well-qualified educator on its staff. While this is a happy situation, the school administrators should not abdicate their responsibility to see that educational specifications are developed which reflect the programs and instructional activities unique to the school district both in the present and the future. The educator on the architect's staff can plan a very helpful role in bringing other ideas and considerations to the district's staff and can serve as a translator back to the architect responsible for developing the working drawings.

Financing Capital Projects

For most school districts, financing school capital projects is a local responsibility. Five states (Alaska, Delaware, Florida, Georgia, and Maine) indicated that they provide more than half the funds needed for school building construction.[5] Three states fund on a "need" basis and four provide thirty percent of the costs.

There are five common ways for the local school district to pay for new school buildings: (1) a pay-as-you-go plan; (2) accumulation from a building and site fund; (3) borrowing on short-term or long-term notes; (4) borrowing through sale of bonds; and (5) any combination of these.

Pay-As-You-Go Plan. Under this plan building expenses are provided out of current revenues. It is indeed a fortunate school district that can construct all the buildings it needs under the pay-as-you-go plan today; the difficulty of putting such a plan into operation in the face of increasing building needs is obvious. If a district is paying off an old debt, the chances are that it cannot simultaneously establish a pay-as-you-go plan.

The chief advantage of the pay-as-you-go plan is that it saves a district from paying interest on borrowed money, which during a twenty-year period may amount to as much as the principal of the debt. Of course, this advantage disappears when low interest rates are in effect. The disadvantages attributed to this plan are (1) there might be a tendency to skimp on needed buildings in order to stay within the pay-as-you-go limits; (2) there is danger that operational funds might be robbed to finance the plan if states did not have distinct barriers between funds; (3) the high taxes needed immediately to pay off a building might be used more profitably by the taxpayer himself; (4) changing economic and social needs increase building needs at one time and decrease them at another, thereby causing inequitable burdens over the years; (5) it is difficult to educate the taxpayer to this type of program.

Building and Site Funds. The building and site fund plan sets aside a certain sum of money annually which is allowed to accumulate. This is then used to finance buildings as they are needed. Thirty-four states make some provision for an accumulating building fund. Like the pay-as-you-go plan, this is an economical way of financing buildings during periods of high interest rates and high prices. However, it has the disadvantages of the previous scheme. An additional objection came some years ago when many would-be financial experts saw these large reservoirs accumulating and accused schools of having idle money in the banks which could better be used by the taxpayer or the teachers' unions for salaries. Instead of setting up some reasonable means of regulating the administration and organization of these reservoirs, some states passed laws banning reserve funds.

Some states have modified the cumulative building funds so that dollars are not accumulated for unspecified, potential future needs, but rather have established an approval process whereby funds can be accumulated for specific, approved capital projects. Such a process encourages good long-range planning.

Some schools have had to bond in the face of huge enrollment increases, but the people, as a rule, have accepted the situation more graciously because they seemed to realize that at least an intelligent attempt at planning had been going on over the years. Bond buyers also look with favor on this evidence of careful long-range planning and are inclined to give more favorable interest rates when purchasing bonds from these school districts.

The pay-as-you-go and building and site fund plans work on much the same principles. Experience has proved that a wise combination of the two is the most desirable type of plan; spreading the burden over a period of time before and after the building is erected provides greater stability in taxation. An emergency building situation is almost impossible for many schools to operate entirely under either plan. Therefore, they must borrow money which will have to be paid back over a period of time after the building is completed. This forces them into the bonding process.

Bonding. Bonding is the most widely used plan for financing school construction. It provides for borrowing money by issuing bonds which the taxpayers of the school district promise to purchase back with interest over a designated period of years. School bonds for the most part are attractive to investors because of certain tax advantages, although they bear interest rates that are lower than those on corporate obligations of equivalent rating. Because school bonding is so widespread it is carefully regulated by state statute. In addition, the courts through the years have ruled on many litigations so that there is a fairly accepted pattern of operation within each state which the investment banker watches carefully. Bond brokers will seldom even consider bonds unless they have what is known as a "marketable legal opinion." That is, an opinion from a recognized specialist in the field of municipal bonds that all necessary legal requirements are met in establishing the bonds.

Bonds are usually classified as follows: *Straight-term bonds* are sold for a stipulated term such as fifteen or twenty years and no part of the principal amount may be paid before the end of the term; *callable bonds* get their name from the stipulation that the seller may repurchase these bonds at any time or at certain specified times; *the serial type of bond* is a regular installment type bond which provides for repayment of principal plus interest at regularly designated intervals.

Straight-term bonds have little to recommend them. They were widely used in financing school buildings years ago, but in many cases they proved to be detrimental to later financing. The major weakness of these bonds is that they must be paid off in one lump sum. This requires a sinking fund because most school districts cannot raise sufficient money in one year to retire all bonds at once. The problem of maintaining such a fund, investing it, and perhaps losing it over a long-term basis has made this kind of financing unpopular at both state and local levels.

Probably the most practical bond issue from the point of view of the borrower is the serial type of bond with callable features. It is the most flexible type of bond and provides for a wide variety of possible conditions. Systematic payments allow for a uniform tax rate and obviate the necessity of maintaining a large sinking fund. Larger payments may be made if financial conditions warrant, and refinancing is possible when emergencies arise.

Borrowing money through the sale of bonds is a highly technical process and most school districts need to secure some expertise to help. Persons employed in banks, universities, state departments of education, or firms specializing in financial consultation may provide assistance. Frohreich[6] pointed out that persons in investment banks or commercial banks are regulated by the Municipal Securities Rulemaking Board while others are not. The state department of education may provide assistance in preparing for a bond issue. Costs associated with the process can be considerable by the time fees for bond counsel, underwriters, fiscal agents, and even the printing of the bonds are totaled.

The school business manager should be prepared to provide information to advisers, underwriters, etc., so that the issue can be properly appraised and marketed. The following may be required:

1. Assessed valuation of property taxable for school purposes showing real and personal property separately.
2. Estimated actual or market value of taxable property.
3. Outstanding bond and note indebtedness stated separately.
4. Amount of dedicated funds applicable to bond principal.

5. Amount and nature of state grants-in-aid which lessen or offset the debt burden at the local level.

6. Record of tax collections for several years showing tax rate, amount of levy, collections during the tax year, and the amount of delinquencies as of the date of the statement.

Bidding

When steps are completed up to selection of contractors to actually construct the facility, the school district must have a process whereby the contractor(s) is determined. The owner or district has to work within the framework of state and local regulations regarding the owner's relationship to the contractors. Clear understandings of who is to pay the contractors on what kinds of arrangements need to be established. The architect needs to have the technical specifications and approved working drawings completed. The school district is then ready to locate potential bidders; provide appropriate documents; receive and analyze bids, and finally award contracts. The following points may be helpful to the school business manager in planning the bidding process.

Safety

Safety is one of the prime requisites of any school building. No one will disagree with the statement that a school building should be a safe place for children. In the controversy that arises in many communities over construction costs, little thought is given to the possibility that the lives of children may be endangered through the false economy of cheap construction or the continued use of old and obsolete buildings.

Safety codes regarding exit requirements, fire safety, and mechanical equipment should be carefully studied and adhered to; however, there may be many situations not covered by state or local safety codes. When it comes to safety of the students and staff, meeting minimums is seldom enough.

Students and staff with special needs are important to consider when safety is concerned. Simple things like grating, swinging doors, and ramp surfaces can be hazardous to the person whose only mobility is a wheelchair. Additional safety concerns arise for the partially sighted or hearing impaired. The Council of Educational Facility Planners International provided the following list of considerations for the safety and welfare of exceptional students[7]:

- At least one primary building entrance, automatic doors (with pressure-sensitive mats and appropriate time-delayed closure) which slide rather than swing open.
- Ramps instead of steps and curbs, both inside and outside buildings.
- Carpeting on floors to reduce slipping and to cushion falls.
- Wide classroom entryways without doors (which permit students free access) but which restrict visual and auditory exposure to the corridors.
- Use of safety glass for doors and accessible windows.
- Avoidance of sharp corners, surfaces, and projections.
- Toilets that are convenient and available, with space and hardware to permit independence.

- Hardware on doors, sinks, and cabinets that can be used by all exceptional students and can be quickly identified by the blind.
- Vertically adjustable chalkboards set approximately 18 to 24 inches away from the wall to permit use by students in wheelchairs.
- Switches, controls and fire alarms within reach of people in wheelchairs.
- Horizontally mounted railings or grab bars.
- Furniture that can be adjusted vertically and horizontally to meet the needs of individuals or groups of students.
- Specially designed storage spaces to accommodate wheelchairs, walkers, standing tables, and other large equipment.
- Raised or recessed signage to identify rooms and spaces.
- Additionally, careful attention must be given to emergency and fire protection systems including easily operated emergency doors, barrier-free corridors, and warning signals that are comprehensible to all exceptional students.
- Fire alarms, for example, must be equipped with audio signals for the blind and visual signals for the deaf.

The site may provide its own hazards because of terrain not conducive to the agile antics of the early adolescent, or because of rocks, stumps, or metal protrusions that could injure anyone. There are other potential hazards. Are the students and staff secured from errant traffic, unauthorized persons, and harrassments from outsiders? Is the parking lot relatively secure from vandals, thieves, and various vendors including drug dealers internal and external to the school?

Violence and vandalism are considerations for school building design. Spaces and material can discourage or encourage both. School officials should point out to the architect the need for safe areas and materials difficult to vandalize and easy to repair or replace.

As a safety factor, an effective two-way communication system must be built into the facility so that all staff are linked. The add-on, two-way radios, or other after-the-fact systems can be helpful in the obsolete building. They should not be the only communication means in a new facility.

Many chemicals are used in a building; they range from cleaning agents, fuel, and insect control to naturally occurring hazards such as radon. The school building may be located near an industry with noxious/toxic gas emissions. The school business manager will utilize a number of experts in dealing with the variety of threats to the welfare of students and staff. There may be few parades on behalf of the effort, but the knowledge of a safe learning environment should be reward enough.

Site Acquisition

In periods of rapid growth over time a school district might find it appropriate to acquire sites for future expansion several years ahead of when the need is projected to occur. Growth tends to drive up prices and early site acquisition is usually a saving of the taxpayers' dollars. In a more stable environment, or especially in areas experiencing declines in enrollment, acquisition of sites is best at the time of identified need.

A number of specialists need to be involved in the decision regarding the school site. The composition of the team might include the school administrator(s) associated with the level of the school being considered (e.g., middle, elementary), a civil engineer, an architect, real estate appraiser, a regional or area planner, and legal counsel. Community representatives may be helpful in providing perspectives from various community constituencies.

Site sizes vary according to density of land use, prices, state requirements, and availability. Ideally the sites should be[7]:

Elementary school: 10 acres plus one acre per 100 students enrolled.

Middle/junior high school: 20 acres plus one acre per 100 students enrolled.

High school: 30 acres plus one acre per 100 students enrolled.

The CEFPI[8] suggests the following questions be addressed for site selection:

Will the site support the educational program?

Is the site's location convenient for the majority of students?

Is the site the right size and shape?

Is the topography conducive to desired site development?

Is the general environment aesthetically pleasing?

Is the site safe?

Is the air quality healthful?

Is the site free of industrial and traffic noise (both air and ground)?

Does the land drain properly and are other soil conditions good?

Does the site have desired trees and other natural vegetation?

Is water available?

Are there easements of any nature affecting the use of the site?

Is the site suitably oriented for energy conservation?

Is the site located on a flood plain?

Is the site near other community services—libraries, parks, museums?

What is the relation of the site to existing educational facilities?

How is surrounding land zoned—will its development enhance the site?

Are utility services available?

Is the site served by public agencies—police, fire department, etc.?

Is the site easily accessible for service vehicles?

Can the land be shared with other community facilities and organizations, especially parks?

Will the site provide desirable open space for the community where it is needed?

Is the site available?

Is the site expandable in the future?

Is the site affordable? Are life-cycle costs reasonable?

Summary

The educational facilities of a community express the values of the community regarding education. Some school buildings may be very simple, straightforward facilitators of forward-looking instructional programs and some may be marble edifices to preserve tradition. Both may show a high regard for the importance of education. So it is with the point of view which the school business manager brings to the planning of a renovation or new school facility. If the point of view is one that emphasizes the educational value; if compromise is necessary, as it always seems to be, and the educational considerations are considered uppermost, then the business manager is functioning as the educational leader he or she should be. The complexities and details of school building planning, financing, construction, occupancy, and maintenance can easily demand top priority, yet it is what happens inside the building that is the most important. The business manager is encouraged to exercise statesmanship in leading the school business office personnel toward establishing the educational priority perspective.

For Further Thought

1. Investigate the ways in which faculty were involved in planning new facilities in your school districts. What directions and information were they provide for their planning input? Did they view their roles the same as those persons leading the planning process?

2. What forms and sequence of financial planning are required in your state regarding approval for building or renovating?

3. In what ways has planning a learning facility changed since the 1970's?

4. Discuss educational specifications with architects? Do their definitions suggest ways to arrive at educational specifications differ widely? What implications does that hold for the facility planner?

5. Can you make a good case for involving custodians and cooks in the planning process?

6. What funding alternatives are available in your state? What is the state share? Local?

7. If architect firms have a checklist of educational specifications already made, why not use them to save the time of many people?

8. What potential undesirable politics may be connected with the bidding process? How would you suggest guarding them?

9. To what agency or specialty would you turn to ensure the freedom from harm due to chemicals used in the building?

10. In what way, if at all, should students be involved in planning an educational facility?

11. If age alone does not constitute obsolescence, what factors do make an educational facility obsolete to the point of being able to convince the public to pay for a new facility?

Endnotes

1. Anne Lewis, *Wolves at the Schoolhouse Door.* Washington, D.C.: The Education Writers Association, 1989.

2. JoEllen Meyers Sharp, "U.S. Schools Falling Down, Report Says." Indianapolis Star, April 29, 1989.

3. Glenn I. Earthman, "Facility Planning and Management," in *Principles of School Business Management* (Reston, Va.: Association of School Business Officials International, 1986), p. 629.

4. Karl V. Hertz, "Reflections on a Building Program, "*School Business Affairs* (January 1990): 22.

5. T. L. Drake, Project funded by Ball State University, 1990.

6. Lloyd E. Frohreich, "Turning Bonds Into Dollars," *Building Education*, National School Board Association (May 1989): A3.

7. Council of Educational Facility Planners International, *Guide for Planning Educational Facilities* (Columbus, Ohio: The Council, 1985), p. F-10.

8. CEFPI, *Guide for Planning Educational Facilities,* pp. F-6 and F-7.

$Chapter$ 15

Facilities Operation and Maintenance

As the visitor drove up to the school building parking area he tried to determine what the broken lines and spots of paint meant. After lining up his car with another nearby, he walked toward the building noting the posts for the ornamental chain barrier around the ample crop of dandelions and crab grass were leaning in almost every direction. The paint on the ceiling of the entrance way was peeling off looking somewhat like the curtains above a theatre stage. The handwritten sign on the right door said, "Use other door."

The impression made by the physical appearance of the school building is often the only basis the ordinary citizen has for evaluating education. Shoddy landscaping, untidy interiors, and poorly maintained facilities suggest that education within the building follows the same pattern. Regardless of the feelings of the professional educator, the school plant is to the noneducator the symbol of state and community education. It sends a message whether the classroom operation within is first-rate, second-rate, or worse.

While buildings, land, and equipment do not make a school, the physical plant can affect in large measure the school's effectiveness. In facilitating the educational process, a building's design, orientation, adaptability, and upkeep may have a decided impact on the aims and methods of modern education. A school building is an instrument of education and the environment created invites children to grow physically, emotionally, and mentally. Thus to the children, the teachers, and the community, school plant operation and maintenance are highly important services.

Definitions

The terms "maintenance" and "operation" often are used interchangeably as if their meanings were the same. However, there is a distinct difference between them, as both in their functions and their place in the budget.

253

The term "maintenance" has been defined as "those services, activities, and procedures which are concerned with preserving, protecting, and keeping the buildings, grounds and equipment in a satisfactory state of repair."[1] In addition to keeping what exists in repair, the concept of keeping the facility effective for its intended purpose can be included in the maintenance definition. The installation of safety or security devices, expanding the number of electrical outlets for computers, or the addition of doors to an open shelving storage area are a part of the maintenance of a building. The manager should be familiar with the state budget codes to determine the budget implications of what should be included under the function of maintenance.

The same source[1] defines "operation" as including "the day-to-day services necessary to maintain the physical plants and grounds in a usable condition for the purposes for which they were intended." Operation includes cleaning, disinfecting, heating and cooling, moving furniture/equipment, adjusting spaces, caring for the grounds and other housekeeping activities that are repeated hourly, daily, weekly, or even seasonally (mowing the lawn, snow removal).

Organizational Patterns

Organizational charts for maintenance and operations functions indicate the variety of ways in which the school district or institution grew. There is little consistency among chart structures even when limited to maintenance and operation functions. In Figure 15-1 the custodial services are separate from grounds maintenance. Energy control and environment control are separate from the maintenance crews. A more common pattern would be to have groundskeeping associated with custodial services.

Figure 15-2 on page 256 shows an organizational chart for the business sector of a school district of approximately 10,000 students. The operations and maintenance people report to the supervisor of buildings and grounds and groundskeeping ordinarily is associated with building operations. It is interesting to note that this structure shows the supervisor of buildings and grounds reporting to the director of facilities and energy management.

If there is a weakness in the organizational structure, regardless of how it developed, it results from the lack of clear-cut communications and understanding of how the organization really works. This is especially true between instructional and support personnel. It becomes easy to let the lines on the chart delimit a free flow of communications. As part of the school district's leadership team, the school business manager must carry his or her share of initiating communications and careful listening.

The organizational structure should be constructed to provide flexibility and adaptability. Change in technologies, state and federal mandates, and societal expectations appear to be coming along at an ever-increasing rate. The ability to provide quick responses to these changes and to new instructional demands as they arise is very important.

Administrative Secretary — Department of Physical Plant — Assistant Director

Energy Conservation Engineer — Energy Control Technician

Central Heating Plant

Central Chilling Plant

Mechanical Project Engineer — Environmental Control

Grounds & Transportation
- Grounds
- Transportation

Custodial Services Moving & Storage
- Plumbing
- Lock & Key Control
- Tool Repair

Building Maintenance & Electrical Projects
- Electrical Technical
- Carpenter
- Electric
- Electronic
- Metal
- Paint

Planning & Construction
- Planning & Safety
- Work Control Technical
- Design Drafter

Office Manager
- Office Assistant
- Work Control Center Secretary

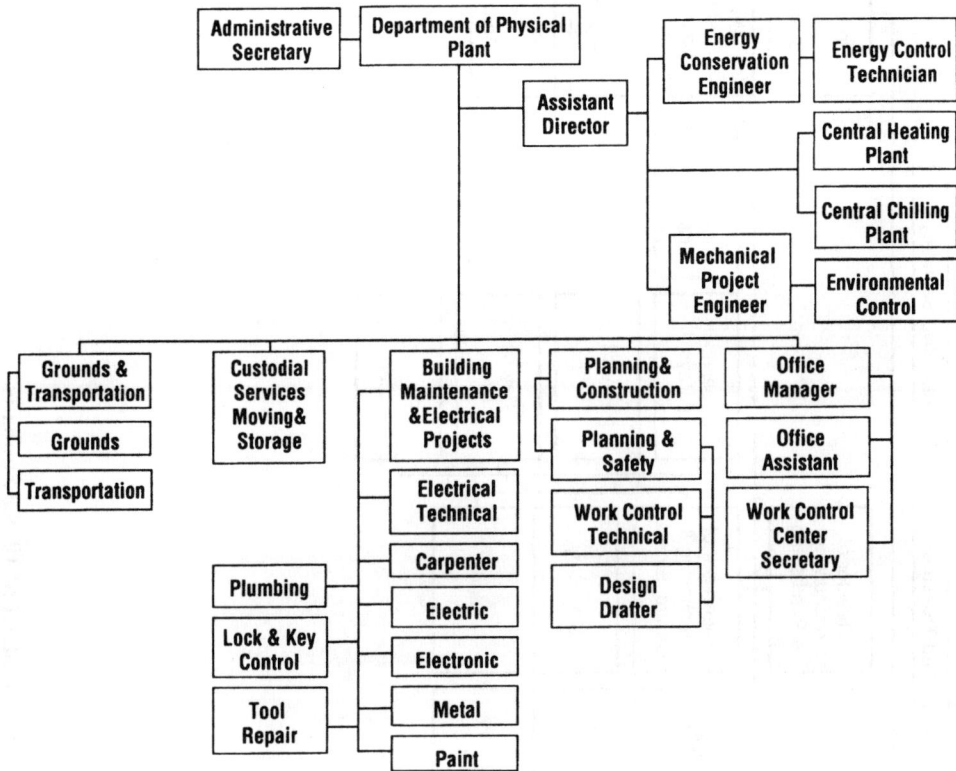

FIGURE 15-1   Example of Physical Plant Organization.

Relationship with the Building Principal

An important consideration in organization is the relationship of the school principal to the maintenance/operations personnel in the building, the director of school facilities, and/or supervisor of custodians. Observations, while serving as consultants for schools reporting maintenance problems, lead the authors to note that invariably one of the contributing factors in any troubled area points to a lack of clear-cut understanding of the administrative relationships of these three positions.

There is no mystery in the area of school operation. The relationships can be easily understood and spelled out, but mutual understanding, respect, and cooperation will still be necessary.

A generally accepted administrative principle is that the building principal is responsible for all activities and functions carried on in the building to which he or she is assigned. Site-based management underscores this principle. This principle, strictly interpreted, gives the principal immediate direction and supervision over all custodial employees in the building. The questions then arise: Why should the principal, who knows little

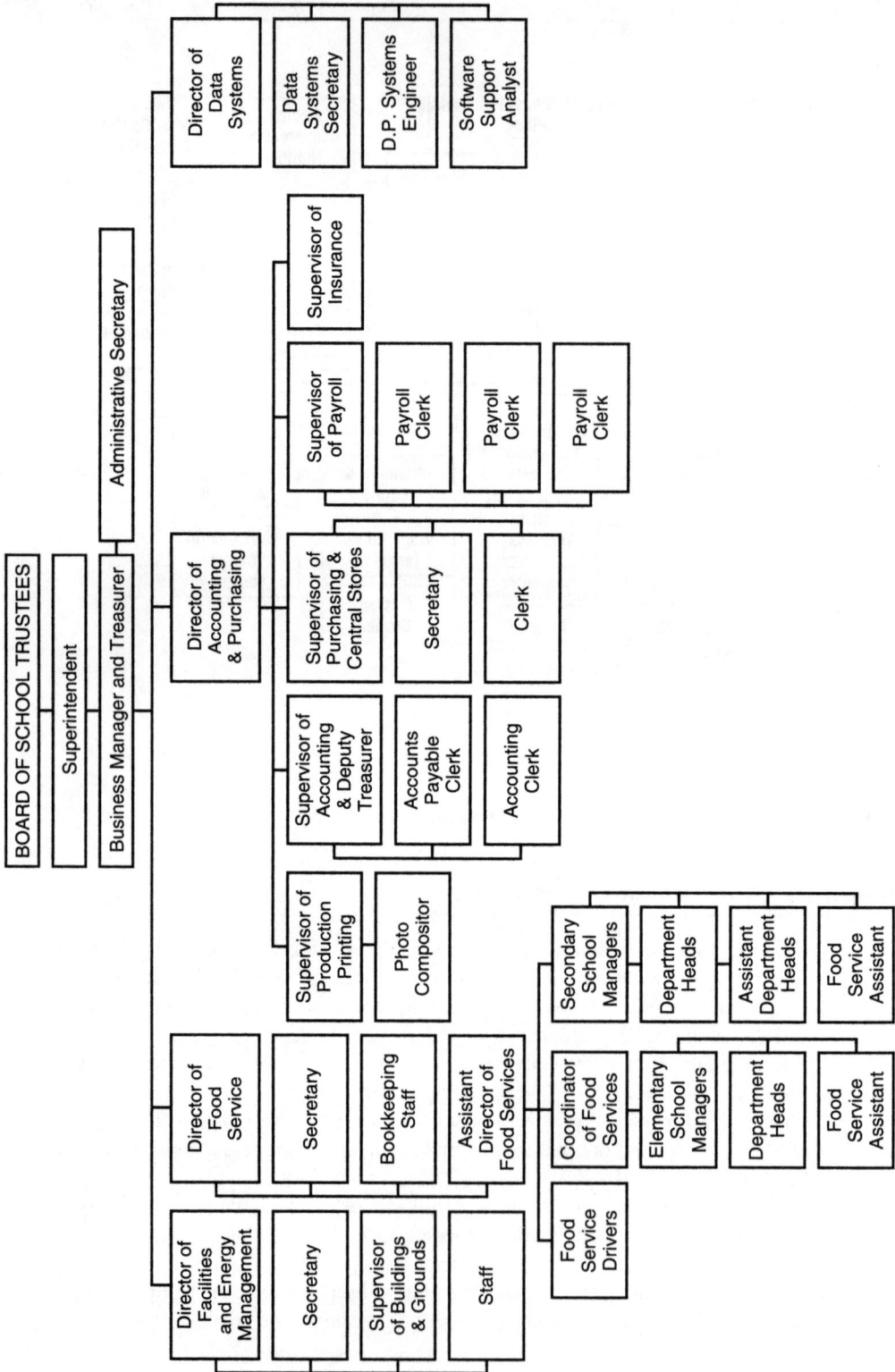

FIGURE 15-2 Organization of the Business Section in a School District of 10,000 Students.

or nothing about custodial work, direct it? What use is a technically trained plant supervisor or director under such a setup?

All personnel working in a school building constitute a unified team established to facilitate the instructional process carried out in the school. Though they are performing many different jobs, they are all working toward one end, that is, student learning. The principal, the established leader of the team, has the responsibility of coordinating activities to accomplish this end. True, many of the people are more expert in their particular fields than he or she is, yet this should not limit his or her administrative responsibility as manager, coordinator, and leader.

The supervisor for custodial services, operating within this framework, ordinarily is given responsibility for and authority over the operational functions throughout the school district—except direct administration of the custodian in a building. By developing schedules, the supervisor can determine what work should be done and he or she can establish standards of how it should be done; by providing supplies and equipment, the means can be furnished to do the work; by inspecting and reporting through appropriate channels, he or she can see that it is done the right way. The principal, however, should still be considered the immediate administrator. Further clarification of relationships may be made by spelling out some of the duties of the supervisor of the school plant operation.

Responsibility of the Supervisor of the School Plant Operation throughout the School District

Relationships between and among roles in the school district are a result of many influences as noted in chapter 2. The structure of the organization under a "pure form" of site-based management will strengthen or weaken some of the responsibilities noted below. The staff consultant role would be expanded greatly if all decisions, including hiring and firing of personnel, were at the building level. On the other hand, if site-based decisions were limited to instructional matters and very limited budget areas, the following responsibilities of the supervisor would require little adjustment.

1. Recruits maintenance/operations personnel.
2. Hires and inducts them into the system.
3. Maintains a pool of custodial personnel for emergencies.
4. Is responsible for in-service training.
5. Is responsible for standardization of housekeeping procedures.
6. Establishes, in cooperation with the principal, work schedules for various buildings.
7. Is responsible for providing necessary equipment and keeping it up-to-date and serviceable.
8. Provides necessary supplies and evaluates them.
9. Assigns personnel to a specific school on approval of the principal.
10. Recommends transfers, additions, and reductions of staff on approval of the principal and the superintendent.
11. Carries out periodic evaluations and appraisals of custodial performance in each school and reports through the central office and the principal.

12. Serves as staff consultant on custodial service to the building principal.
13. Serves as consultant and supervisor to the custodial staff.

Responsibility of the Principal for Operational Activities in the Building

In addition to the often awesome array of activities and responsibilities incumbent on the principal, he or she must carry out these tasks in a context shaped by local history, customs, feelings, and negotiated contracts. The negotiated contract, sometimes hammered out on the anvil of adversity, is a shaper of relationships and cannot be ignored. The responsibilities noted below will need to be interpreted in light of the negotiated contract(s), but should not diminish the intent of keeping the principal as a major player in decisions about the maintenance and operation of the building.

1. Administratively and managerially responsible for the maintenance and operational personnel in the building.
2. Determines in cooperation with the supervisor the personnel needed on both a long-term and an emergency basis.
3. Confers with the custodian on workload and work schedule.
4. Checks and inspects the building, compares schedules with accomplishments, and makes suggestions for improvements.
5. Directs that emergency deviation from schedules be made and out-of-routine chores be accomplished.
6. Interviews and approves maintenance and operations personnel to be assigned to his or her building.
7. Recommends disciplinary action and correction through established channels.
8. Evaluates the custodian's work in line with his or her contributions to the total objectives of the school.

The principal also accepts some responsibility for the welfare of the staff within the building. In so doing, the welfare of the school is maintained or improved. It is responsible practice for the principal to not leave custodial work to chance or to occasional forays to the boiler room. The astute school business manager will see to it that he or she benefits from a coordinated effort between the principals and the buildings section of his or her office regarding maintenance and operations of the building.

Personnel Considerations

Qualifications

The school custodian sometimes is seen as the sage of practical wisdom, the conduit for building gossip, the source of information to the community, and the one who can solve dozens of problems for the teachers and/or students. The good custodian can raise morale and efficiency. He or she not only helps provide a clean and safe environment, but takes care of a seemingly endless array of annoyances from flickering fluorescent bulbs to stopped-up sinks.

He or she is in constant contact with students while working; they observe the quality of the work and the custodian's personal characteristics. If it is a man in an elementary school, he may be one of very few men the students observe at work. The custodian's speech, work habits, and attitudes constitute an important factor in the students' educational environment. As discussed in chapter 1 regarding the school business manager's communication function with the public, building maintenance and operations people are important to the image of the school.

The custodian's relations with the external public are also important. Often he or she is the first person the visitor sees on entering the building, and naturally is the one asked for directions or information. A pleasant, informative answer creates good will. The custodian is often a local citizen of long standing and with more extensive community ties than teachers or administrators. Because he or she is an employee of the school, people ask the custodian's opinions about the school. A slighting remark or a chance word of criticism can often do irreparable damage to the school system. It seems that too many people who are critical of the school hear their criticisms and obtain their opinions from the school custodian. Unfortunately, the situation has not changed over the years for segments of the school patron base.

Neither the selection nor the training of this key person should be left to chance; it should be a carefully planned process designed to bring to the job of custodian the most qualified person possible and to train and educate him or her to a high degree of proficiency. The following may serve as guides for selecting and training maintenance and operations personnel:

1. The selection of maintenance personnel and custodians should be made with a thorough knowledge of their backgrounds, including previous employment, previous legal convictions, physical condition, and education. As noted in chapter 13, follow-up on references is a must. Careful attention to equal opportunity guidelines is essential. A manager does not want to find someone in his employ by virtue of an error in the selection process.

2. Selection of a person should follow the administration and scoring of a test on the knowledge of maintenance and custodial materials, equipment, and methods applicable to the position being filled.

3. Interviews with appropriate persons (e.g., supervisors, principals) should be scheduled.

4. Agreements to hire should be in writing.

5. Provisions should be made for formal and informal programs of in-service training.

6. A work schedule should be posted.

7. Specific instruction should be given concerning the methods and objectives of education in the classroom, particularly in those areas where misunderstanding and disinformation is possible.

8. Custodians should be instructed in the duties they would be expected to perform in a national, state, or local emergency involving their school building.

9. Continuous information and training should be planned and budgeted regarding environmental hazards and/or emergencies.

In-Service Training Is Essential

The important personnel function of continuously improving performance is as important in the area of maintenance and operation of a school building as in any other area. New products, equipment, and challenges face the custodian as well as the electronics technician. Some of the challenges for both include hazardous materials, environmental protection, energy conservation, and protecting oneself and others from diseases and injury. A major concern of the school business manager is his or her responsibility to keep the schools in compliance with federal and state regulations regarding security of property, safety for students and staff, access for the disabled, and so on. The training and education implications for maintenance and operations people are great.

The Learning Team Concept

An often overlooked but critical need for education was noted in item no. 7 above, namely, getting across the concept that everyone is part of a team whose purpose is to improve the learning of students. On occasion the purpose is articulated, or at least is interpreted to be that of providing instruction. Instruction must of course be provided, but the main purpose is not just to instruct but to enhance students' learning. The goal of learning may necessitate new group configurations, different schedules, cooperative activities, extended hours, and a number of other changes that disrupt established routines. Teacher teaming, group learning, and hands-on projects may generate movement and increased noise levels. The departures from tradition may be misinterpreted as loss of control, "horsing around," fun and games, or some other negative interpretation. There is potential for poor communications to those in the custodian's or maintenance person's network, both internal and external. There is also the positive potential for increased understanding and fostering the idea of a community of learners. The astute business manager will anticipate the need, or will have communications established with instructional colleagues who will tell him or her about anticipated changes that could cause disinformation from the facilities crews. If the idea that the instructional and facilities people on the team can help each other accomplish not only their respective roles but to achieve the overall good of improved student learning, then the time, energy and money spent on inservice activities will be worthwhile.

Energy Conservation

The wise use of energy is essential to all segments of society for reasons beyond current and anticipated costs. Depending on foreign energy services causes great concern as demonstrated in the 1970s and early 1990s. Pollution problems abound as a result of burning certain forms of energy sources and serious waste disposal problems are associated with using nuclear energy. Wisdom dictates conservation. This topic is discussed more extensively later in the chapter but it is important to note that conservation is an important area of in-service training for operations people.

Protection against Disease

Many opportunities to contract illnesses come into the building each day. The routines for maintaining clean facilities should be continuously examined and personnel should be given the best possible materials and equipment to do the job. Training in the use of the material is needed, but education regarding *why* certain routines and techniques are employed must be part of in-service training.

The spector of AIDS and of Hepatitis B virus has cast a shadow across the workplace, including schools. Increased potential of children having these infections demand precautions, which means changes in routines and in-service training. Mishler[2] suggests the following as essential if a body fluid spill needs to be taken care of:

1. Wear plastic, disposable gloves with no holes or tears.
2. Contain the spill. It is best to use chlorinated absorbent.
3. Remove the spill and place in a plastic bag.
4. Decontaminate the area with a hospital-grade germicidal detergent.
5. Dispose of the waste in accordance with local regulations.
6. Decontaminate your hands by washing or using an alcohol rinse.

Obviously the above have several in-service, communication implications. In addition, they have budget and purchasing implications to help ensure the safety of all school personnel and clients. These areas are a small piece of the training needs picture but can serve as a beginning point for the school business manager to examine the in-service/pre-service program for building operation personnel.

Operations Manual

Another facet of the training program as well as day-to-day operation is an operations handbook. A methods and procedures manual may be adopted and adapted to a local situation. If none is available within the school district several sources may be helpful such as neighboring school districts; the state department of education; or regional, state, and national organizations.[3] Safety practices, cleaning procedures, schedules, energy guidelines, and references for more information should be part of the manual. Other areas to include may be job descriptions, personnel dress/appearance guidelines, various request forms such as leave, personal days, and transfer. Writing or adapting a manual is time-consuming but a good operations manual may be a time saver in the long run.

Sources for In-Service Help

Large school districts may have training personnel within the district for most in-service needs; however, small school districts may have to rely on outside expertise most of the time. Ordinarily state departments of education provide materials and often workshops, particularly for those areas of required compliance. Again neighboring school districts can provide assistance. Regional groups may hold workshops for operations personnel as common needs are identified. University sponsored study councils which may include up to forty districts sponsor annual events for custodians to gain perspectives and learn new skills and techniques. Commercial companies often are anxious to provide training, but they usually do so only within the boundaries of the products they have sold or hope to sell.

Scheduling Work

Custodial duties consist of many mechanical activities which can be measured. Efficient utilization of tools and equipment can be determined; amount of floor space to be cleaned can be timed and measured, and the way to effectively clean special rooms such as restrooms can be measured. Given the same equipment, area, materials, obstructions, and time of day or evening, the tasks in question should be performed at the same rate from Syracuse to Seattle. It is obvious that not all conditions are the same. Equipment varies greatly. Carpet cleaning can be a time-consuming task, particularly in high traffic areas, yet machines are available with which one person can clean 5,000 square feet per hour. Time-motion type of studies have been conducted in almost all aspects of operations services resulting in "standards" expressed in the number of square feet of floor space that can be swept in one minute. Work expectations have been expressed in units called "room equivalents," which indicate the amount of time expected to perform the tasks associated with cleaning a building divided by the number of rooms in the building. Custodial requirements could then be calculated by using the room equivalent unit. Larger cities and some state departments of education maintain workload guidelines that may be a starting point for a district to examine workloads and scheduling.

The Association of Physical Plant Administrators (APPA) and The Association of Higher Education Facilities Officers have been working on a project to develop guide-lines/expectations for custodial work. The results of the work are classified into levels such as "orderly spotlessness, ordinary tidiness, casual inattention, moderate dinginess, and unkempt neglect." Descriptors appropriate to each area accompany the levels. Schedules ranging from "daily" to longer periods of time are noted for each task pertaining to each area whether locker rooms or stairwells and halls. Data from several institutions were collected on every task regarding the number of minutes required to complete the task. Many discussions were held to account for different conditions (climate, material, etc.).[4]

As school districts develop sets of standards and expectations for particular jobs, a word of caution should be noted: *include the people who do the work in the process.* The process used by the APPA included input from "those who pushed the brooms and swung the mops." One might anticipate resistance to the idea of work expectations in that the expectations may be viewed as the sharp stone at the end of a whip in a manager's hand. Such was not the case in the APPA effort. The standards and expectations were viewed positively as a way to demonstrate that a good job was being done.

A single expectation of square feet to be completed per unit of time can be misused if not adjusted to conditions. The expectations developed by an organization or a commercial company are starting points but should be evaluated locally and according to existing conditions. In other words, an expectation of 4.6 square feet per minute for an entrance-way or 1,932 square feet per day may be quite different if it is a clear, dry day with clean, dry exterior walks, in contrast to a subzero, windy day with heavy snow and virtually uncleaned walks. Table 15-1 lists examples of time required to clean specific areas under ordinary conditions.

These formulas are all calculated on average situations, and the *science* of management is responsible for their development. When applied to people working under a variety of different conditions, they must be used wisely and effectively. This involves the *art* of management. Thus for all intents and purposes a custom-built schedule must be devised for each situation. It may have a scientific base adopted from one of the excellent formulas available, but it should take into consideration the character of the building, the personality of the worker, and the local conditions, equipment and materials.

Specific formulas should be reviewed and revised according to the way the following questions are answered: What is the condition of the building? What equipment is available for use? How convenient are cleaning supplies, equipment, and facilities to the spaces to be cleaned? How often and by how many is the building used? Are there free times available for thorough cleaning? How demanding are the children, teachers, and principals? How friendly and accommodating is the custodian? How much time does the heating system take? How much maintenance work is expected from the custodian? Are there special jobs or errands required of the custodian in a particular school? What special abilities or disabilities does the staff member have that might affect the situation? What are building design obstructions to equipment use?

A custodian can accomplish only so much in one day. The authors have often heard a plant supervisor complain about a particular custodian and then has visited the school where he was working and heard the teachers unanimously agree, "He's wonderful; we love him." On the other hand, many times a supervisor praises a particular custodian for his or her efficiency while the teachers in the school have little or nothing good to say about him or her. Obviously the art of administration is not being skillfully applied in either situation.

The custodian's work schedule should be posted in both the custodian's office and the principal's office. It should be divided into two parts: (1) the daily tasks and (2) the periodic tasks. In a centrally managed school district, the work schedule formulated cooperatively by the worker and the plant supervisor and approved by the principal puts the custodial activities on a sound base for proper management. The truly site-based managed situation will put the plant supervisor in a more consultant role. Properly conceived, the schedule gives the custodian a reasonable workload; it considers the

TABLE 15-1   Examples of Expectations of Work Performed

Area	Square Foot Per Minute	Square Foot Per 7-Hour Day
Locker/changing room	17.3	7,266
Office	42.7	17,934
Public area	14.7	6,174
Stairwell	11.2	4,788

particular abilities of the person and the peculiarities of the building; it serves as a reminder so that necessary tasks will not be overlooked; it avoids overlapping and duplication of work when more than one custodian is involved; it may be an informative device for teachers; it clarifies responsibility; it serves as a plan of work for substitutes when the custodian is ill; it forms the basis for supervision and control by the principal and the operations supervisor.

Table 15-2 shows an example of a custodian's schedule that is sent to all unit heads within the school organization so that information about work expectations can be general knowledge.

Energy Considerations

Discussions of energy and environment considerations seem to be appropriately placed between discussion of operations and maintenance functions since both are involved in managing wise use of energy and maintaining environmentally safe conditions.

The wise use of energy resources has direct short- and long-range effects on student outcomes. An immediate effect is that wise use of energy results in more dollars available for learning purposes. Over the long haul, the benefits of wise energy use range from cumulative added achievement in excellent learning environments to preserving a quality of life on our fragile spaceship Earth. With the above very real outcomes, time and dollars spent to monitor and improve energy could be good investments. Honeyman and Wood noted that according to a Department of Energy report, energy costs will be near $700 per pupil by the year 2000, making the educational energy costs more than $31 billion.[5] Schools using energy sources priced at the whim of external political happenings and crises may find themselves on a roller-coaster-like ride that can cause serious budget

TABLE 15-2   Custodial Services and Schedule

Service Provided	Frequency
1. Prepares building for occupancy	
a. Security (unlocks and locks building entrances)	Daily
b. Clean entrances—inside and out	Daily
c. Replace incandescent bulbs and florescent tubes not functioning	Whenever a light is out
2. Empty waste paper	Daily
3. Restroom maintenance	
a. Remove waste material	Daily
b. Providing supplies	Daily
c. Clean soap and towel dispensers	Daily
d. Clean mirrors	Daily
e. Clean lavatories	Daily
f. Clean urinals	Daily
g. Clean stools	Daily
h. Clean partitions	Daily

TABLE 15-2   *Continued*

Service Provided	Frequency
i. Wash walls	As Needed
j. Sweep floor	Daily
k. Mop floor	Daily
4. Floor maintenance	
a. Sweep or dust mop	Daily
b. Wet mop	As Needed
c. Scrubbing	As Needed
d. Buffing	As Needed
e. String wax	As Needed
f. Apply new wax	As Needed
g. Strip and seal	As Needed
5. Stairwells	
a. Sweep or dust mop	Twice weekly to daily
b. Wet mop	As Needed
c. Strip and seal	As Needed
6. Carpet care	Daily
7. Wall maintenance (spot removal)	Daily
8. General cleaning	
a. Elevator	Daily
b. Blackboards	Daily
c. Windows (inside)	As Needed
d. Doors	As Needed
e. Spot wall clean	Daily
f. Indoor entrances and steps	Daily
g. Cigarette urns	Daily
h. Mats	
(1) Rug	Daily
(2) Link	Daily
i. Drinking fountains	Daily
9. Dust removal	
a. Ash trays	Daily
b. Overhead pipes	Monthly
c. Hall and stairwell walls	Daily
d. Doors and trim	Weekly
e. Furniture	Weekly
f. Sills and ledges	Weekly
g. Venetian blinds	As Needed
h. Grills and louvers	Monthly
10. Care of outside areas	
a. Building dock area	Daily
b. Snow removal	As Needed
c. Snow emergency procedure	As Needed
d. Outside entrance area	Daily

problems. Partial solutions may be found in newer technologies associated with geothermal heating and cooling. Regardless of the energy source "it is estimated that energy consumption and costs can be reduced by 30 percent with the use of simple conservation measures and constant awareness and monitoring of use."[6]

Monitoring

Like any evaluative process, baseline data need to be established. These data are consumption of energy by type, by building, under what kinds of conditions. They can be analyzed by relating them to pupil costs, per square foot costs, and per level of students housed in the building by pupil or square footage. The per pupil and per square foot unit costs are helpful when comparing local costs to regional or state expenditures.

Hentschke suggests that the best unit of comparison is the British thermal unit (BTU) per square foot.[7] The American Association of School Administrators studies on energy use may be helpful to the school business manager for general comparisons. To further refine the comparisons, degree-day data need to be used to make comparisons over time more meaningful. Caution should be exercised to keep additional data since a cold day of 10° F average with calm wind in contrast to a 10° F day with 28 m.p.h. winds can result in very different BTU use in a building.

Gathering and analyzing data are intended to point toward decisions regarding budget, operations and maintenance practices, renovations, building planning, closing and scheduling, and other areas affected by the need to use energy. Good decisions require good data and good analyses. Figure 15-3 illustrates some of the influences on energy use and the implied data/information needs associated with analyses for decisions.

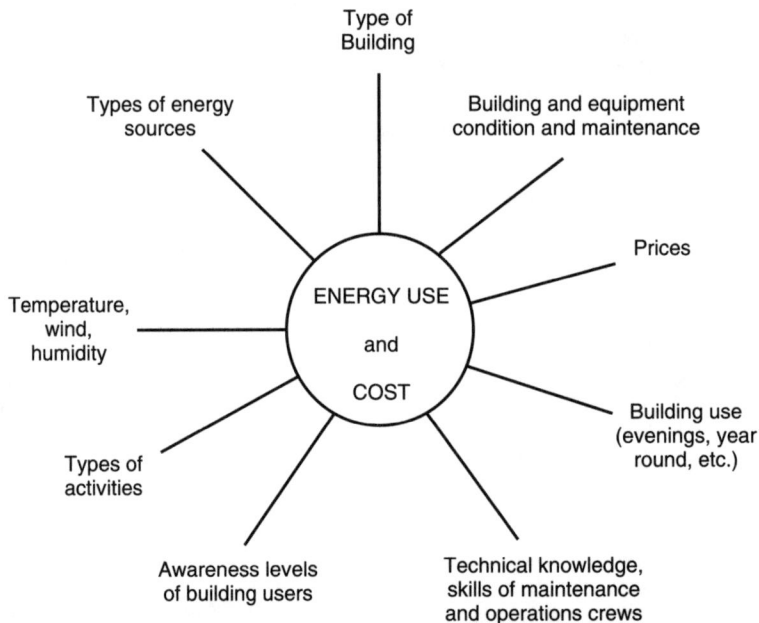

FIGURE 15-3   Influences on Energy Use and Costs.

A Team Approach

The business manager will find an investment in building a team approach to energy use a good expenditure of time. The team includes all building users, even community users. A short session with PTA or community theatre leaders and others may enlist their efforts to conserve. Building administrators, coaches, cooks, and students can join the effort, particularly when they understand the overall impact on dollars as well as the environment.

Principles of Operation

Whole books have been written on the how-to-do-it phase of custodial work; therefore, it is beyond the scope of this chapter to cover completely this phase of school building operation. There are, however, certain general principles which can help one establish a better program.

1. Proper preservation of building and equipment is a long-term savings which ordinarily will more than pay for the salaries or contracts of those who perform care and maintenance services.

2. A single operation standard should be applied throughout the system so that no one school receives preferential treatment.

3. The value of a school plant to the educational process depends on its attractiveness, its cleanliness, its safety, and its availability for use.

4. The way a custodial and maintenance force is organized may in the long run depend on local conditions, but lines of authority should be clearly understood and responsibility specifically delegated.

5. The building custodian is directly responsible to the building principal; it should be understood that the school plant supervisor serves in a consultative capacity only.

6. Building inspections should be made on a periodic basis with the aid of checklists.

7. Custodial workers should participate in planning and in schedule making; they should assist in the development of any policies that affect them. This, ideally, should be outside the formal contract bargaining.

8. The workloads of the custodial force must be constantly evaluated and kept in proper balance.

9. A feeling that they have a common goal will do much to improve the morale of both teachers and custodians and must be constantly encouraged.

10. A school custodian can be one of the most important public relations forces in the school. This must be brought to his or her attention, and in-service educational activities must be developed to improve abilities in this area.

11. Custodial operation is a skilled job requiring technical know-how and certain innate abilities. An outstanding staff may be developed only through careful selection, intensive training, and realistic supervision.

12. A custodian makes a decided impression on the children in his or her building. The custodian must recognize this and gear actions accordingly.

13. A school custodian has neither the right nor the privilege to supervise or discipline children.

14. A school custodian must maintain the same loyalty and professional discretion in discussing the activities of the school as any professional person.

15. Custodians must be able to work cooperatively with others. If they cannot do so, they should not be employed in the school.

16. Scientific methods are as necessary in the school plant operation as in any other administrative activity. Experimentation, time-and-motion studies, cost records, long-range comparative data, objective inspection processes, job and work analyses, and similar processes should be included in the custodial program.

17. Custodians should be employed only on the basis of a written contract duly approved by the board of education.

18. Custodial activities should be so arranged that they will not interfere with normal school operation.

19. Custodians should understand the objectives of education and they should know enough about modern teaching methods to recognize the importance of various activities carried on in the school.

Security

As mentioned in the chapter 9 on risk management, time and money spent preventing problems often pay back handsomely. In the case of building security, not only is the community's investment being protected, savings can be realized in insurance costs, repairs, replacements, and losses of investments in academic projects, books, references, and trauma of possible dislocation.

It is not necessary to detail the magnitude of the potential for problems. Suffice it to say that in a 1988 survey, 74 percent of the schools reported vandalism, 42 percent reported thefts, and 33 percent reported burglaries.[8] Security was noted by 77 percent of the 25,000 schools as a concern. Many factors seem to be coming together to cause widespread concern. As one school business manager observed, "It's not just Halloween anymore." The business manager will want to explore several avenues for improving building security. Some of these are noted below:

1. *Maintaining continuous occupancy by personnel.* To do so requires a round-the-clock schedule for custodians and supervisory personnel. Lindbloom and Summerhays noted a novel approach used by one school district to keep persons on or near school property to discourage would-be vandals or thieves. The school moved families into mobile homes on the school campus. While such a partial solution may be impractical in many situations, it does underline the point of maintaining a continuous presence at the building site as a deterrent to those who would violate security.

2. *Employ or contract for security personnel.* The employment or contracting of security personnel should be weighed against the costs of not so doing. Again, data on losses and possible insurance reductions are needed to compare with liabilities incurred with hiring or contracting security services.

3. *Explore all aspects of security with local law enforcement personnel.* Special needs of or events at the school may create additional security risks. Athletic events, carnivals, concerts, evening adult/community education classes may provide opportunities for would-be vandals or thieves. A thorough discussion of the activities with law enforcement personnel may yield some excellent ideas for improving building security as well as elicit help for the activities.

4. *Examine board policies.* The school business manager should examine board policies regarding the community use of buildings and grounds and holding vandals responsible for restitution; reporting responsibilities if security is violated; and making provisions for training of personnel regarding emergency situations. In the event gaps are noted in the review of the policies, the business manager should recommend to the superintendent changes appropriate for facilities security.

5. *Keep abreast of security technology.* A variety of technologies from burglar alarms tied to a law enforcement office to motion detectors or electronic surveillance devices are available and if one reads advertisements, new applications seem to appear weekly. These tools may be helpful if properly matched to needs. Like buying computer hardware prior to establishing what tasks/output are needed, buying security technology prior to knowing exactly what is needed to supplement other security measures can be a costly exercise in gadgetry.

6. *Establish a disaster plan.* Many natural disasters, vicious acts such as arson, or mechanical or electrical failures can leave school facilities vulnerable to further trauma. The school business manager along with the rest of the leadership team of the school district should develop an action plan for emergencies. If a tornado should destroy a major portion of a building, or an explosion or earthquake rip open a wall and leave other walls weakened, what provisions have been made to immediately secure the property and begin making it safe for persons authorized to be on the property? What provisions can be made to reduce the interruption to the instructional program? What network of calls should be made? What backup systems are available to account for probable losses? What personnel training has been conducted to cope with disasters? Have there been any attempts to coordinate community resources with school resources in the event of a disaster? As the reader can readily see, there are many questions that need to be asked and explored *before* trauma occurs. A disaster should not provide potential looters or "souvenir seekers" opportunities. Nor should a disaster provide an opportunity for a display of unpreparedness for citizens to talk or write about.

Maintenance

There are many ways of organizing a crew of workmen to perform the necessary maintenance of buildings and grounds within a school district. Although it is difficult to categorize these into patterns because of the minute variations possible and labor climates, for the purposes of this text the organization could be arranged based on the size of the school district:

1. A large, highly skilled maintenance staff with central headquarters and fully equipped shops, a supply depot, and a transportation system. The department performs all maintenance in plumbing, heating, ventilation, air conditioning, electrical work, carpentry, painting, cement, and masonry. The only work which is contracted is major remodeling and rehabilitation. Maintenance crews are highly trained technicians organized according to work specialization. This is exclusively a big-city operation.

2. A limited maintenance staff which performs repairs and replacements of a minor, simple, and recurring nature. Members of the staff are as much the handyman variety as conditions will allow. While work is performed singly and in crews, and crews are flexibly staffed according to the work to be performed. Major repairs are contracted out to private concerns.

3. The small centralized operation where several handymen are hired as maintenance people. They may be assigned to specific schools or they may work in all schools, depending on needs and skills. They tackle any job they think they can handle and may get assistance during slack periods from custodians and extra hired help. A typical example is painting. The major painting schedule is set up for the summer slack period. Maintenance personnel, custodians, and extra hired help form a crew to perform this work.

4. The situation where a custodian is a general handyman who has been hired because he or she can do almost anything. The custodian performs minor repairs and replacements in his or her own school and may occasionally go to other schools to help out. When major repairs are necessary, the local plumber, electrician, or skilled tradesman is called in. This pattern is best suited for small schools, and its efficiency depends a great deal on whether or not the school is able to find people with the necessary skills and ambitions.

Contracting for Maintenance or Using the School Maintenance Staff

Probably one of the topics discussed most among people concerned with maintenance is whether maintenance should be contracted. Contract maintenance means negotiating with a painting contractor to do all painting, a plumbing company to repair all plumbing, an electrical contractor to fix all electrical equipment, and so forth. In the noncontract situation, skilled or semiskilled craftsmen are employed by the school to do these jobs.

Of course, as in most controversies, this is not completely an either-or proposition. It is not realistic to assume that all necessary maintenance should be performed by contract. There are many small, necessary activities in maintenance, such as tightening a screw or bolt, adjusting a window shade, or replacing a light bulb or fuse—activities of a simple and recurring nature—which it would be unreasonable to leave until the contract maintenance crew arrived. Local situations such as the following will also affect a decision: negotiated contracts, availability of competent maintenance contractors, ability to get immediate service when required, dependability and competence of contracting personnel, and ability of the school to hire skilled labor. In addition, the small school does not have the variety of choices that the large school has. Taking all these situations into consideration, the following is a list of the pros and cons usually proffered in respect to staff doing maintenance or contracting for maintenance services.

Advantages in Using a Maintenance Staff

There are advantages to having a school maintenance staff:

1. Hourly rates may be lower, there is no profit to be earned, and there is little overhead.
2. School staff may be dispatched quickly and organized functionally. The staff is flexible to changing needs and priorities.
3. The staff is familiar with the school plant and equipment.
4. High standards of workmanship may be demanded of school employees because no one is pushing for a margin or profit.
5. Many communities do not have enough private contractors available to provide a truly competitive situation on contractual work.
6. Repairs may start without wasting time advertising for bids and awarding contracts.
7. School employees will understand and cooperate with the activities of the school.
8. School employees working as a unit have great esprit de corps and concern for doing the job well on a continuous basis.

Advantages of Contracting for Maintenance

There are unique advantages to contracting for school maintenance:

1. It is difficult to purchase and account for all the supplies and equipment necessary for complete maintenance.
2. Contractors have highly skilled and fast-working men who are usually more specialized than a school maintenance staff.
3. Workloads vary during certain seasons of the year so that it is not practical for the school to staff enough maintenance people to handle everything.
4. A centralized maintenance department designed to serve widely dispersed schools involves excessive travel and requires the purchase of expensive transportation facilities and shop equipment.
5. Excessive breakdowns can overtax a balanced maintenance crew.
6. It is easier to get budget money for a contracted operation than for a complete maintenance department.
7. Contracting reduces overhead, the size of the administrative and supervisory staff, and the number of facilities needed.
8. Contracting creates good relations with the private sector and helps support the economy of the community.

Crothall offered the following questions for the school district to ask about prospective maintenance/custodial contractors[9]:

Is there a formalized, cyclical cleaning and maintenance program?
Is there a computerized work order system?
Are routine reports provided to school administrators?
Does the contract allow for customized services?

Are there financial controls on the housekeeping and maintenance programs?
Is there quality management?
How does the contractor supervise employees?
What training is offered by the contractor?
Is there a guarantee of continuity and stability of management?
Are there any added benefits? For example, are bulk discounts given on materials?
Who payrolls maintenance and custodial employees?
What is the financial viability of the contractor?
Does the contractor have a record of delivering what was promised?

Long-Range and Short-Range Maintenance

Maintenance may be divided into four general types: (1) long-range maintenance; (2) annual maintenance; (3) short-range periodic maintenance; and (4) emergency maintenance.

A *long-range maintenance* program considers the expected life of the building and attempts to provide the necessary care, repair, and replacement to keep the building in top condition and educationally adequate for the time expected. Examples of long-range maintenance include replacing worn-out chalkboards and outmoded lighting, replacing a boiler or large electrical motor, pointing outside brick walls, and painting. A top maintenance administrator sees that long-range maintenance is so scheduled that repairs and replacements are anticipated and disposed of before outdatedness and breakdowns take place; at the same time he or she does not waste money by undertaking a task before it is necessary to do so.

Annual maintenance includes those activities which may be scheduled as recurring items each year. They deal with yearly inspections, corrections, improvements, and repairs; they are usually done in the summertime when buildings are empty and machinery shut down. Annual maintenance consists in cleaning, inspecting, and making any necessary repairs on the heating plant, motors, mechanical equipment, and electrical equipment; it includes reconditioning floors, inspecting safety devices, roofs, and plumbing, and completing any painting scheduled for that particular time. Certain phases of the long-range maintenance schedule are a part of the annual schedule; thus long-range maintenance and annual maintenance complement each other. Each is accomplished through proper programming and scheduling. State and local governments often require inspections in public buildings particularly for elevators and food service areas.

Short-range periodic maintenance is a preventive measure. This type of maintenance requires careful record keeping and follow-through so that the many periodic activities are carried out which are required to keep a building and its equipment in good repair. This maintenance usually includes a periodic check of all facilities to replace excessively worn items and identify unreported items that need fixing. In today's mechanized age much time is spent on oiling and greasing and providing periodic tune-ups of motors and mechanized equipment.

Emergency maintenance includes all kinds of items, from a broken windowpane to a collapsed boiler. In a sense it is the most aggravating activity of the maintenance department because a thousand and one things can happen to a building and its equipment especially when there are hundreds of active children around. Maintenance of this type is usually requested on a regular work order made out at the school where the emergency occurs. Standard procedures should be adopted throughout the school system for preparing and carrying out work orders so that proper control can be made of how, when, and where the repairs are accomplished and by whom.

As in all business aspects, there are trade-off decisions facing the business manager. One of the questions is, Do increased planned maintenance activities offset unplanned maintenance? Will heating plant breakdowns be avoided by upscaling the type or frequency of maintenance? These decisions are always made with less than complete information. An approach to costing out the incremental changes and keeping a history of overall cost results may be practical.

Evaluating Maintenance and Operations Functions

Armed with reasonable expectations and data, the school business manager can develop a formative evaluation process which will improve the total operations functions of the school district. As noted in chapter 3 on evaluation, any evaluation should focus on the *result of the work, not the worth of the person doing the work.* The following are considerations regarding the maintenance/operations evaluation process:

1. *Data and information.* Supervisors should have maintenance information on all equipment and facilities. Product specifications should be readily available. Workload expectations should be available for all operations functions. Work histories on buildings and equipment should be accessible.

2. *Job descriptions and individual job goals.* Individualized job goals should be developed at least annually and on an as-needed basis. Records should be generated and kept regarding establishing and progressing toward the goals.

3. *Scheduled observation of work results and work in progress.* Observations should be conducted frequently enough to minimize reacting to complaints. When possible, facets of the observations should be done with a principal or his or her representative regarding instruction-sensitive and public use areas. Carefully designed checklists can be helpful to include all functions as well as to reinforce expectations. The checklists can then serve as documentation of work results.

4. *Provide for input from users.* The principal, the mathematics teacher who uses the window air conditioner for climate control in the computer room, the aide and/or children who deal with the playground equipment and, in fact, all users should have a way to provide input regarding the condition of the facilities they use. A planned process to gather the input could be annual or seasonal. Clear communication channels should be set up for both regular and necessary ad hoc referrals.

5. *Provide for expertise.* Occasionally situations arise where the additional expertise of outside resources may be needed to make good decisions. A network of possible sources could prove valuable especially when time is at a premium.

Summary

Few people stop to consider the importance of operation and maintenance in developing an outstanding school. To the public at large the condition of the building is a symbol of the effectiveness of community education. It may represent a significant, first-class operation or a second-rate one. To the children, the building extends an invitation to grow physically, emotionally, and mentally; to the teacher, good building operation and maintenance make teaching a pleasant activity.

Operation consists in custodial housekeeping activities, whereas maintenance consists in fixing and repairing. The two terms are often incorrectly used interchangeably because the custodian, particularly in the small school, may perform both operations.

One of the major weaknesses in school plant operation is lack of precision in spelling out organizational relationships. The building principal is administratively responsible for all activities and functions carried out in his or her building; therefore, the custodian comes under the principal's jurisdiction. The school plant supervisor serves as a consultant and specialist on plant operation to the entire school system.

It is not a simple matter to develop an operational and maintenance staff that considers itself part of a team dedicated to serving the educational needs of all children and adults in the community. Some do consider operation and maintenance personnel menial laborers; however, they perform work which, when done properly, requires a great deal of technical know-how. It is important to remember, too, that if they are working in a school they are working in close association with children and with the public; therefore, their personal characteristics must pass close scrutiny.

An outstanding operation and maintenance staff can only be developed with (1) proper organization; (2) intensive recruitment and careful selection; (3) in-service training; and (4) adequate administrative supervision and inspection.

For Further Thought

1. Is there a statewide training program available in your state for custodians? Outline what you consider an outstanding training program for school custodians both local and state.

2. In what ways can teachers and custodians cooperate in helping one another?

3. Examine the energy-use data base in your school district. What additional information is needed to make wise decisions regarding use? What kinds of analyses are available? Compare analyses from other school districts.

4. Compare the custodial and maintenance work schedules of at least six school districts. Can you account for the differences other than bargained contract language?

5. Review the security provisions for buildings in your school district. What special events may cause problems?

6. Prepare to explain to a head custodian why a principal who is not experienced in operations should administer the program in her or his building.

7. List several high maintenance items related to the construction of a building.

8. Are periodic inspections contrary to the concept of shared decision making? Discuss.

9. Examine workload formulas in your school district or neighboring districts. Develop improvements in them.

10. Design an ideal structure of organization for building and grounds maintenance/operations functions in a school system of 10,000 enrollment.

Endnotes

1. Association of School Business Officials, *School Facilities Maintenance and Operations Manual* (Reston, Va.: ASBO School Business Officials, 1988), p. 5.

2. Church Mishler, "Reducing the Risk," *Cleaning and Management* 25, No. 10 (October 1988): 20.

3. For example, ASBO published a *Custodial Methods and Procedures Manual,* revised in 1986, which could serve as a starting point for local adaptation.

4. The reader is encouraged to examine a publication from the Association of Physical Plant Administrators (APPA) entitled *Custodial Staffing Guidelines for Educational Institutions.* Jack C. Dudley, ed. Alexandria, VA: APPA: The Association of Higher Education Facilities Officers, 1992 for details regarding time and frequency expectations for a variety of custodial tasks.

5. David S. Honeyman and R. Craig Wood, "Monitoring Energy Consumption: The Energy Use Guide and Energy Use Index Program," *School Business Affairs* (January 1990): 19.

6. Honeyman and Wood, "Monitoring Energy Consumption," p. 19.

7. Guilbert C. Hentschke, *School Business Administration* (Berkeley, Calif.: McCutchen Publishing Corporation, 1986), p. 445.

8. Kenneth Lindbloom and Joel T. Summerhays, "School Security: An AS & U Survey, Part II," *American School and University* 61, No. 1 (September 1988): 51.

9. Graeme A. Crothall, "What to Ask When Contracting for Maintenance and Custodial Services," *School Business Affairs* 55, No. 2 (February 1989): 21–24.

Chapter *16*

The Legal Environment and the School Business Manager

It is not the purpose of this chapter to present a complete treatise on the legal basis of our educational system or to review major instances of litigation relating to the business management of the school. To do so would require many more pages than would be reasonable in a textbook of this type. Rather this chapter will provide a general discussion of school law helpful to the school administrator by (1) reviewing briefly the legal authority of American public schools; (2) explaining the need for the school business administrator to be familiar with and understand educational legislation; (3) exploring the variety of legal sources that interface public schools and create a framework for administrative action; (4) showing the relationships between school officers and the school attorney; and (5) suggesting criteria for selecting the school attorney.

Unfortunately for lawyers and lay citizens alike the general public views legal transactions in public affairs, in business, and even in private civil affairs as a maze to be considered with some distrust and alarm. This attitude, instead of sending people to a lawyer when trouble looms, actually frightens them away. Some people will go to great length to keep from getting themselves involved with a lawyer. As a result a lawyer frequently is hired to get them out of trouble, not to keep them out of trouble.

At the other extreme the authors know a number of school administrators who will not make a legitimate administrative decision without consulting with their attorney, and in many a school system nothing new and exciting ever happens because of the fear of litigation or legal repercussions. A working knowledge of law, and understanding of the purpose of lawyers and how to work with them, will do much to alleviate the situation.

While today, courses on the legal basis of education are generally standard fare in the training of school administrators they are not intended to make an attorney of the school administrator. Rather the purpose should be to acquaint educators, and particularly administrators, with some of the legal fundamentals affecting the decisions they must make. Putting this principle into its simplest dimension, a knowledge of some law is necessary for every citizen. A hunter must know hunting laws, the fisherman fishing laws. The car driver is responsible for knowing traffic laws. We all must know right from wrong, not only morally but also legally. Ignorance may be bliss, but not so far as the law is concerned. As John Selden stated: "Ignorance of the law excuses no man: not that all men know the law, but because 'tis an excuse every man will plead, and no man can tell how to confute him."

It follows that a school administrator, particularly the superintendent and school business manager must know the law concerning his or her professional field—education and the schools. One would not expect a school superintendent or business manager to consult a lawyer every time a professional decision is made, yet to carry a point to the extreme, to be on the safe side he or she would have to do so without some working knowledge of school law. School districts are governmental agencies of the state through which the legislatures carry out their constitutional mandate to provide a system of public education. The courts have ruled that school officers are state and not local officers. The employee (superintendent, business manager) of an agent of the state (school board) acts on behalf of the local board which is a state entity. We have heard many administrators make the statement: "If there is nothing in the law saying we can't do it, we'll go ahead and do it." In the strict sense this is wrong. The legal viewpoint in relation to a school district and employee acting on its behalf is "Unless the law gives you power and authority to do it, you can't do it." Of course the laws cannot specify the what, where, and why of every possible condition: therefore it is recognized that there must be a wide range of "implied powers" in order to permit the exercise of "expressed powers."

Expressed powers are those specifically listed in legislation which authorizes a particular activity. "Implied powers" are not specifically enumerated or mentioned but are activities which one might reasonably expect would be necessary to carry out the spirit and intent of the legislation. Implied powers because of their lack of specificity are a source of much litigation. Fortunately, over the years our judicial system in ruling on this litigation has had a commendable tendency to allow broad leeway to local schools in carrying out these implied powers. As long as an administrator's or board of education's action is "reasonable" the courts generally have accepted the idea that implied powers represent "changes necessary for a dynamic educational system"; therefore, they have understood that narrow, literal interpretations could slow down desirable experimentation. Implied powers then allow progress, growth, and experimentation by providing a frontier where imaginative and dynamic administration can take place. The good administrator searches for the delicate balance between what is necessary for the entire state, as illustrated by expressed powers, and what is best for his local community, as allowed by implied powers.

Implied powers may also serve to establish proving grounds to test administrative practices which may eventually become law. A procedure designed by a school administrator to meet a particular educational problem in a particular school system may spread through an entire state as a logical way for all school districts to operate. The procedure may stand unquestioned for several years and then, because of some question or controversy, the legislature may feel obligated to pass permissive or mandatory legislation to allow it to continue. In this way it becomes part of the school code.

Education Is a State Function

The concept that education is a state function can easily be proved. The roots of the American philosophy of education were firmly embedded in the colonial law that foreshadowed state law; the pattern of our educational system was developed through ordinances governing the territories that were to become states. When the United States became a reality the structural pattern of education as a state function was established by the general reservation of power in the federal Constitution, by positive expression in state constitutions, and by enactment of state school legislation. Today, each state constitution has charged its legislature either directly or indirectly with the responsibility of establishing and maintaining a system of schools. All states delegate certain of these responsibilities to state educational agencies and local boards of education. Thus the springboard for any administrative action was derived broadly from the state constitution and more specifically from state legislation, administrative directives of state educational agencies, and policies of the local boards of education with the courts resolving questions of meaning or intent through judicial review. This made school law a relatively simple matter prior to the mid 1950s with administrators not needing to be knowledgeable about legal matters beyond what was written in the school code.

The Winds of Change

Prior to the 1954 Brown *v.* Board of Education decision the federal government maintained a relative "hands off" policy toward public schools accepting the state function concept more or less "carte blanche." The U.S. Supreme Court had reinforced this attitude through a variety of case decisions through the years. The Brown decision, based on the Fourteenth Amendment to the Federal Constitution, created a noticeable turnabout in attitude. The court in its operative language limited the action of states and its schools by stating: "No state shall deprive any person of life, liberty or property without due process of law," specifically meaning in this instance that racial segregation in public schools is a violation of the equal protection clause of the Fourteenth Amendment and the situation should be corrected "with all deliberate speed." As this case was being reviewed and debated the public and lawmakers became more conscious of the constitutional rights of individuals under the first ten amendments (the Bill of Rights). This precipitated a dramatic explosion in legislation, litigation, and changes in attitude. It now became accepted that U.S. Constitutional standards were definitely applicable in state public school matters. In the late 1950s and 1960s refinements were made in the Brown decision by the U.S. Supreme Court in apparent need to make up for former disregard. In addition the U.S. Congress, urged on by public opinion, jumped on the "bandwagon" by enacting the following landmark legislation:

> *Title VI of the Civil Rights Act of 1964*—bars discrimination because of "race, color, or national origin."

Elementary and Secondary Act of 1965—making federal funds available to local public education for the purpose of serving the educational needs of "educationally deprived children" in both public and nonpublic schools.

Emergency School Aid Act of 1972—provided funds to school districts for eliminating "minority group isolation."

Title IX of Education Amendments of 1972—prohibits discrimination on the basis of sex in educational programs or activities receiving federal assistance.

Education for All Handicapped Children Act of 1975—each state must provide a detailed plan for assuring all handicapped children the right to a "free appropriate public education."

The refinement and expansion of these landmark acts through further implementing legislation, such as the American with Disabilities Act of 1990, did much to limit the discretion of school boards and administrators in the operation of the school. This massive intrusion by the federal government forced the states to develop follow-up legislation. On the whole there was an important tendency for states to become more expansive in their authority when interpreting the reach of the above legislation, particularly as funds were made available to the states by the federal government to assist the local schools in carrying out the details of these acts. Therefore, state departments of education became more aggressive in shaping school policy to enforce state and federal mandates and assure that federal monies were properly expended.

The Source of Authority for Administrative Action

Times have changed radically since 1950 when school administrators worked loosely with the state and a simple school code was an easy reference on matters of school legislation. Today the school administrator must be knowledgeable of a great variety of sources of legitimate legal authority. An understanding of legislation and regulations from these sources provide a base or framework for administrative action giving the superintendent and school business manager a sense of security in the decision-making process.

To review, these sources of authority can be listed in order of precedence: (1) The U.S. Constitution; (2) Federal legislation; (3) decisions of federal courts; (4) implementing rules and regulations of federal agencies, such as the U.S. Department of Education or the Governmental Accounting Standards Board; (5) state constitutions; (6) state legislation; (7) decisions of state courts; (8) implementing regulations of the state departments of education; (9) Attorney General opinions; and (10) local board of education policy.

The above list of sources of administrative authority might tend to overwhelm the pre-service school administrator as he or she contemplates the job ahead. Like any area of necessary knowledge, familiarity increases with use. In addition, it is not necessarily what one knows, but knowing where to find the information when needed is important. Every school should have a central depository for rules and regulations from local, state, and federal sources pertaining to the operation of a school; this depository should be kept up-to-date and properly maintained. Often the school business office is considered the logical place to locate a large part of this depository making the school business administrator the local expert in identifying and defining sources of legislation and any follow-up rules and regulations, especially in the areas of finance, accounting, buildings, risk, and transportation.

Every administrative action, then, fits into a legal framework which guides and directs the school administrator. One naturally expects a professional educator who acts for a school to know this framework as it relates to local school board policy and his or her school. Logically the professional educator might even be more expert in school law than the average lawyer. This means that the school administrator must have a general knowledge of school law in order to make decisions which affect education. In making decisions it should not be necessary to constantly use a school attorney except in exploring new and different areas of action, answering questions of technical interpretation, organizing a legal defense, initiating legal action, or in preparing legal documents.

Right to Employ Legal Counsel

All states have permissive legislation authorizing local boards of education to hire attorneys. The legislation grew from the widespread practice of hiring attorneys, which was allowed by implied powers. An analysis of the several cases contesting the employment of an attorney by boards of education indicates that to deny their employment would render the boards helpless in enforcing the rights of the school district. A Texas court set the precedent for upholding the right to hire an attorney over fifty years ago. The statement of the court in this case exemplifies the conclusions reached in many other similar cases: "The authority on the part of trustees to employ an attorney to institute and prosecute an action in their behalf would exist as a necessary incident of powers to contract, and to sue and to manage and control the affairs and interests of the public schools."[1]

School districts are in a sense state corporations and in some states such as Indiana, the entities are called school corporations. It would be almost impossible to implement the corporate powers of a school district if the employment of legal council was not permitted. Corporate powers conferred on school districts may be found in the respective state laws. A perusal of these laws shows that their implementation requires technical legal advice. The following is a list of the typical corporate powers of a school district although these may vary to some degree in different states and are only granted under the authority of the state: (1) to possess a corporate name; (2) to acquire and hold real and personal property; (3) to convey this property when necessary or appropriate; (4) to contract and be contracted with; (5) to sue and be sued; (6) to receive grants, gifts, and bequests; (7) to make by-laws, rules, and regulations; (8) to exercise the right of eminent domain; and, (9) in general to exercise those corporate powers usually possessed by public corporations of this rank, and to do those things necessary to the attainment of the ends for which the corporation is organized.

The Need for a School Attorney

The growing need of legal assistance results from many factors including increased size/enrollments of school districts; complexity of public laws (e.g., Americans with Disabilities Act); and a society that has been described as litigious. In fact some of the conditions which have created the need for school business managers have also created the need for increased legal assistance. A sample list of the activities requiring legal assistance follows:

1. *School reorganization.* The process of reorganizing school districts into larger, more efficient units often requires school elections, interpretation of state and municipal law, transfer of property, protection of bond holders, and other acts or decisions which might bring about litigation. The annexation movement—in which cities are annexing surrounding suburban areas—is raising many legal questions for both cities and schools.

2. *School sites.* Technicalities arise in consideration of site acquisition, including possible condemnation proceedings, easements, and clearing of title.

3. *Preparing for building.* Other problems precede actual construction, such as petition, elections, sale of bonds, and proper accounting of funds.

4. *New building construction.* The relations of school districts with contractors require legal counsel to protect the public interest.

5. *Personnel relationships.* Contracts, tenure, unions, social security, affirmative action, retirement, and an increase in the amount of progressive enactments in the area of personnel relationships have created the necessity of legal interpretations, hearings, and protection from litigations.

6. *Liability.* With a growth in school facilitating services, such as transportation and school lunch; the activities program, which includes class visits and field trips; the expansion of the curriculum to include hands-on experiences in a variety of settings; and with the intensification of the extracurricular program in athletics and recreation, the possibility of further liability and litigation arises.

7. *School and governmental relationships.* Potential conflicts occur between the board and other governmental agencies over responsibilities for building code, sewage, utilities, sidewalk, and other services.

8. *Disgruntled parent or citizen.* More people are threatening legal action for relief from real or supposed grievances precipitated by actions of boards of education, administrators, or teachers.

9. *Various advocacy groups monitor school action for compliance with public laws such as the Americans with Disabilities Act.* From time to time an advocate will attend school-parent conferences regarding placement of the student. While the advocacy situation does not require the presence of legal counsel for the school, the administrator present needs to know the details of the process and implications of plans made for the student's education. An example would be the implications of an individual's education plan which included full participation in physical education and on the playground. As noted in chapter 15, those facilities need to be accessible to all.

10. *Close a school building.* With the changes in age, character of neighborhoods, shifts in school populations, and advancing age of school buildings a growing number of school buildings are being closed, sold, and even leased. Frequently parents in neighborhood centers will seek injunctions, threaten, or actually bring suit to stop a given school closure.

11. *Civil rights.* The civil rights movement starting in the 1950s stimulated a flurry of legal threats and actual lawsuits to uphold the rights of individuals and groups. A number of organizations and associations accepted as their duty the elimination of racial, religious, and sexual discrimination by legally protecting the civil rights of both individuals and groups.

12. *Student rights.* Student rights are closely akin to civil rights; in fact they are actually a part of them. The truth is students are no longer as malleable as in "the good old days." A growing number of legal controversies fall in the student rights category, i.e., dress codes, free speech in student newspapers and rallies, discipline, personal rights, and even child abuse.

13. *Purchasing.* As a matter of fact, the whole range of school business management activities is a ripe field for litigation. As was noted in chapter 10 the school is one of the top employers of people with one of the largest budgets, owning the most buildings, and particularly in suburban and rural consolidated schools, serves the most meals and has the largest transportation system.

Points to Consider in Employing an Attorney

The question often arises on the matter of selecting a school attorney. A reactionary, overbearing and overcautious attorney can retard school board and/or administrative action. A forward-looking and progressive counsel can do much to promote a dynamic school system.

The most satisfactory basis for selecting legal counsel is a review of the professional qualifications and past services of the lawyer being considered:

1. Is the person in question a highly qualified lawyer in good standing in his or her profession?

2. Is the lawyer a person of unquestioned character and integrity?

3. Are the attorney's methods of procedure in serving clients appropriate for a public institution and particularly for a school district?

4. Does it appear the lawyer in question is the type of person whose personal characteristics will permit a harmonious working relationship with the board and staff of the school district?

5. Has he or she been involved in school law and shown enough interest in it to consider it a specialized part of practice?

6. Does he or she recognize the executive relationships of the school and understand the way to operate as employee and/or consultant?

7. Is the attorney's office, staff, organization, location, and facilities appropriate to the needs of the school district?

8. Would the lawyer being considered be compatible with the administrative team and would they be comfortable with each other?

From a 1992 survey of practice[2] generating responses from 153 school districts, some patterns emerged regarding the use of attorneys by school district personnel. In response to the question "Does the board employ or retain the services of an attorney who advises and/or represents the board of education and the superintendent?" the response was an overwhelming (95 percent) "yes." The 5 percent not employing/retaining an attorney were small school districts of less than 2,000 enrollment. The utilization of attorneys has changed dramatically since the 1960s when only 40 percent of school districts employed legal counsel on a regular basis.

Thirty-two percent of the respondents noted school board members as providing direction to the attorney and 60 percent noted that the superintendent provided direction. Of the 5 percent noting that another administrative person provided direction to the school attorney, only six (4 percent) cited the assistant superintendent for business. It becomes clear that confusion could occur as to who has the prerogative to give direction to the school attorney. A school-board-approved policy can eliminate confusion regarding this matter.

Who has direct access to legal counsel to make inquiries is another matter that should be in policy form. The 1992 study indicated that persons in a wide range of positions had access to make direct inquiries of legal counsel. As expected the superintendent has direct access, but next most frequently noted were school board officers and principals. Over one-half the school districts reported direct access for these people. The assistant superintendent for business was mentioned by only 21 percent of the reporting districts, but as the size of the school district increased, the business manager had greater direct access to make inquiries of legal counsel. The size affected the percentages of school districts providing the school business manager access as noted:

0–1,999	3%
2,000–4,999	23.4%
5,000–9,000	80%
10,000+	71%

Policies should be written so that communication lines do not break down and become tangled as more and more people have direct access to the attorney. The potential for strained relationships may increase unless care is exercised to keep colleagues informed. Additional evidence regarding potential problems was provided in responses to the question "To whom does the board attorney report?" Responses were almost evenly divided between school board and superintendent with many school districts reporting both. In no case was the school business manager cited as the one to whom the attorney reported.

When queried about whether the school attorney's opinions directly affected educational decisions, the respondents were divided evenly with 50 percent saying "yes" and 50 percent saying "no." In practice 40 percent of the respondents reported that the school attorney sat in on all the school board meetings. Butler[3] concluded that the role of the attorney should be more precisely defined. The need for complete understanding of the distinction between educational advice and legal advice cannot be too strongly empha- sized. Often the school attorney is a prominent local person, possessing great influence in the community; he or she places both the superintendent and board of education in an untenable position if in an official capacity he or she takes stands on educational and administrative problems or argues for a particular point of view that must be evaluated on its educational merits rather than its legal implications.

Fees agreed to or charged by attorneys to provide legal counsel to schools vary greatly. Part of this is a function of school district size, problems faced at any point in time, and local pricing for the services rendered. In the 1992 survey of practice, fees ranged from $60,000 to zero. The majority of school districts employed attorneys on a retainer plus fees basis with only four districts (3%) reporting that they employed an attorney on a full-time basis. Interestingly, three of the four school districts doing so had enrollments of fewer than 5,000 students.

For what kinds of legal issues are attorneys hired to give counsel or to represent the schools? The number 1 issue cited by the respondents was teacher dismissal or discipline. Following some distance back was collective bargaining in second place. The size (en- rollment) of the school district appeared to be a factor as to which issues most commonly caused the perceived need to consult with legal counsel. Table 16-1 notes the differences in the top five issues cited by the sizes of districts noted.

TABLE 16-1   Top Five Issues Regarding Legal Counsel by Size of School District

Enrollments	Issues in Order of Weighted Rankings
0–1,999	Teacher dismissal/discipline Collective bargaining Control of student behavior/punishment Suits regarding negligence Special education including 504
2,000–4,999	Teacher dismissal/discipline Collective bargaining Control of student behavior/punishment Suits regarding negligence Suits by outside contractors
5,000–9,999	Teacher dismissal/discipline Special education including 504 Collective bargaining Suits regarding negligence Suits by outside contractors
10,000 or more	Teacher dismissal/discipline Collective bargaining Suits regarding negligence Special education including 504 Suits by outside contractors

The school business manager may be involved in many of the issues ranked as causing the most contact with legal counsel. Inasmuch as bargained contracts with noncertified/licensed staff and collective bargaining was high on all the lists, certainly the school business manager frequently will be dealing with an attorney. In addition, suits by outside contractors appeared on all the lists from school districts of 2,000 or more enrollment. The implication is clear that care regarding the preparation of any contract is essential. Given the number of outside contractors used in the areas of buildings/grounds, food services, transportation, security, etc., the school business manager will want to pay special attention to this aspect of the job. In all enrollment categories, suits regarding negligence were ranked number 3 or 4. Again, given the frequency of opportunity for negligence in the areas noted above, the implications for care in training and quality control are clear.

It was interesting to note that most attorneys serving schools are not perceived to be specialists in school law. Of 153 responses, only 47 (31 percent) indicated the attorney with whom the respondents worked was a specialist in school law. That may be because several school districts hire attorneys for special purposes such as collective bargaining, issuing bonds, special education, and teacher dismissal. The business manager likely would be working closely with the attorney in issuing bonds and possibly collective bargaining.

Administrators will be concerned with selecting the attorney(s) who can do the best job for the clients of the school districts. The following are considerations for establishing and maintaining an appropriate relationship with the attorney.

1. *Attorneys should be selected on the basis of specialization and integrity.* Assuming honesty, there is no other quality so important in an attorney as competence. Local attorneys who are not school law specialists know less about school law than good superintendents—and that's just not enough!

2. *Local legal counsel and special bonding attorneys should be appointed after joint study by the superintendent and board of education.* The board of education and the superintendent must rely on the attorney for sound advice on highly technical legal matters. It is essential that they have confidence in the attorney selected; joint selection helps to assure that confidence.

3. *Special bonding attorneys should be employed for bond issue elections and subsequent steps leading to the acquisition of the bond money.* It is essential to hire a specialist in municipal bond law in school bond elections. It is vital that mistakes that might invalidate an election do not occur in bond proceedings. Unless there is a recognized or "marketable" legal opinion furnished to the bond broker he or she cannot sell school district bonds.

4. *Fees should be based on the time required for services performed by the attorneys involved.* The only equitable solution to the matter of fees seems to be payment for time actually spent in the service of the school district at a predetermined rate. Besides being fair to both the attorney and the school board, this arrangement has the advantage of making it clear to school district patrons what services are being rendered and how much they cost.

5. *Attorneys should receive direction from and report to the superintendent of schools.* The superintendent, as executive officer of the board, should act as intermediary for all items coming before the board of education. In certain complicated legal situations the superintendent may wish to have the attorney report directly to the board. These instances should be the exception to the general rule.

6. *Local legal counsel should attend school board meetings only when specific matters in his or her jurisdiction are to be discussed.* In situations where local counsel intrudes on educational policy, he or she ordinarily is a *regular* attendant at school board meetings. It is desirable to avoid this intrusion by the attorney.

7. *Attorneys should be treated administratively simply as consultants to the superintendent and board of education on technical legal affairs.* It is important that it be made clear to all that the attorney serves in a technical staff capacity to the superintendent. The distinction between line and staff is important to remember.

8. *Board policies and administrative regulations governing the financial and working relationship between the attorney and the school board and superintendent should be written and made a matter of record.* Most problems arise because of inadequate understanding and preplanning. Written policies eliminate these problems.

Two Cases in Point

Case 1.

Dr. Gerald Browne was the newly appointed Superintendent of Schools for Palm Grove, a city of approximately 20,000 people with a suburban environ of 15,000, all of which made up the Palm Grove School District. Superintendent Browne had been hired after an extensive search by the board of education. The former superintendent was released because Palm Grove had experienced several years of conflict and strife over the operation of its schools. Numerous votes on increase of mileage and bond issues had been defeated by the voters and in general there was a noticeable lack of support for the schools. The reasons for the conflict and lack of support was not clear but the criticism eventually focused on the central administration resulting in noticeable antagonism toward the superintendent by the public and eventually the teachers and other school employees.

Dr. Browne was selected as the new superintendent from among over fifty candidates because of his recognized ability as an intelligent communicator, his belief in strong community relations, and his demonstrated skills as a consensus maker in his former administrative position. Hired at the same time was Dr. Charles Foster who would serve as Assistant Superintendent for Business Affairs, a new position in the Palm Grove schools. He came to the school district highly recommended by Superintendent Browne.

One of the planned approaches of Superintendent Browne to bring the school and community together was to arrange events that would encourage the public to attend functions within the several school buildings and to allow use of selected school facilities by the public for nonschool events.

Addressing the board of education at his first official meeting with them Superintendent Browne reviewed some of his plans. He immediately sensed a rather cool and mixed response to his suggestion that there be more public use of school facilities. In addition, there was a negative reaction from the school attorney. Later, quietly digging into the reason for this attitude he noted that some eight years earlier the board had established a policy at the urging of the former superintendent and the present school attorney which stated: "Use of school buildings for nonschool events is an encroachment on staff time, of questionable legality, and fraught with innumerable liability consequences." Dr. Browne decided not to press the issue at the next board meeting but he did inform the board that he was giving Charles Foster, his Assistant Superintendent for Business Affairs, authority to develop a staff study to determine if the use of school facilities by the public was legally possible and if so how much might be feasible and beneficial. The staff study would be presented at a subsequent board meeting.

In developing the staff study Assistant Superintendent Foster contacted the Director of School Plants for the State Department of Education as to the plan's feasibility and legality and was given a definite go-ahead. He then contacted a number of schools in the state of similar size who had an "open-door policy." He wanted to identify the problems they faced in implementing the policy and what rules and restrictions they had to establish to make it work. He then analyzed his own staff situation to determine whether or not the concept could be implemented in Palm Grove without too much disruption of school and without too much additional expense.

The staff study was completed in time for presentation at the next board meeting. Very briefly, it concluded:

1. *While school buildings are legally the property of the state and not the local school district, their management and control, with few exceptions, are left to the discretion of the local boards of education.*
2. *The local board may determine what nonschool use may be made of school buildings within their school district so long as they are used for a nonsubversive activity and so long as the proper maintenance and conduct of the school is not interfered with or any way hampered, and so long as school district property is not defaced or destroyed.*
3. *A fee may be charged for building use to pay for general control, upkeep, and maintenance (most boards did charge fees for building use). However, buildings may not be rented on a profit basis.*
4. *Most boards of education had rules that prohibited the use of school buildings for sectarian, political, partisan, or commercial purposes.*
5. *Boards of education with the most successful plans had formulated very specific terms and conditions governing the nonschool use of buildings. Rules and regulations were clear and unequivocal and drawn in light of local conditions as far as they could be seen or anticipated. Any activity of a highly controversial nature liable to arouse ill feelings, jealousy, and dissension and lead to a misunderstanding was rigidly avoided.*
6. *Most boards had a specific contract developed for building use which had to be signed by a representative of a responsible organization or a committee of ten citizens.*

Assistant Superintendent Foster completed his report by stating: "reasonable public use of school facilities appears to be beneficial to community relations and a plan can be implemented without undue cost to the school district."

Following considerable discussion a motion was unanimously passed which stated: "Our school system was designed to promote public education; any use of school property tending to this end and which does not interfere with the regular school work should be encouraged." The former policy forbidding public nonschool building use was rescinded and Superintendent Browne was asked to work with his staff in developing a new policy and plan for approval by the board at the next regular board meeting. When the policy and plan were approved, the school attorney was asked to draw up a contract for potential building users that incorporated ideas that were in the approved plan. At the same time she was asked to study the potential liability risks which could have possible impact on their new policy.

In reviewing the case one sees a pattern of operation that first looks at the educational implications of community use of school buildings. Using the educational expertise of the superintendent, business manager, and staff the school attempted to develop an ideal "modus operandi" which would benefit both the community and the school. The strong philosophical disposition of the superintendent and business manager was that wide community use of school buildings would improve the community support of the schools themselves. It should be noted that the school attorney was not given an opportunity to discourage what could be desirable community involvement by tying the discussion up in possible legal entanglements. Rather, the administrators did their homework on what was possible educationally and legally and developed a proposed planned pattern of operation based on expressed powers in the school code. They obtained tacit support of the state department of education. At the same time they tapped the experiences of other school districts in the state who had used implied powers to develop successful approaches to community use of school buildings. Only then did they go to the school attorney to obtain the technical legal assistance in implementing the plan.

One may note a similar method of operation when planning and building school facilities (see chapter 14). A study is first made of educational needs, the tentative educational plan is developed by the school administration and staff, and it is brought to the architect who incorporates the educational plan into a technically correct architectural design.

Case 2.

A second situation facing the new Superintendent in Palm Grove affected a small group of teachers and employees but nonetheless caused enough discontent from a few to create a negative morale problem with the entire faculty. The Palm Grove school district extended well beyond the limits of the city including a suburban environs of some 15,000 people of whom approximately 1,800 were school-age children. This situation required an extensive transportation system.

*Many of the teachers lived in the suburban area with school buses driving by
their doors or at the most one to two blocks from them. The former superintendent, however, did not allow teachers and other school employees of the school
to ride the buses to and from their work even in an emergency situation. According to the board of education minutes the former superintendent had recommended this action on the advice of the school attorney because of the liability
problems involved. Assistant superintendent Foster heard of discontent among
the teachers. He could see that, although it seemed to be an insignificant thing,
the negative aspects of this policy caused a morale problem. After conferring
with the superintendent he called a meeting of teachers and employees involved
to discuss the situation. It was agreed that because of work schedules and
requirements it would be unreasonable to allow teachers and employees to ride
buses on a regular basis. However, he could recommend that they be allowed to
ride the bus in an emergency situation on a space available basis. The school
employees agreed this would be a fair approach. From past experience assistant
superintendent Foster knew that permissive legislation recently made part of the
school code allowed a school district to purchase liability insurance which
would protect all riders on the school bus at little cost to the school district. He
suggested to the school superintendent that this insurance be purchased to cover
teachers and other school employees. He believed increased employee morale
would be well worth the investment. The superintendent asked the school attorney to restudy the legal implications in light of the new legislation. On receiving
his report he recommended to the board of education that liability insurance be
purchased to cover school employees riding school buses.*

This case again shows that the alert school administrator may often be more up-to-
date on the school code than the school attorney and certainly he or she should be more
conscious of the educational and organizational implications involved. This is no discredit
to the attorney; rather, it is a natural situation because education associations, administrator's associations, and state departments of education are constantly alerting administrators to educational legislation and its educational implications. While the educational
administrator has a general knowledge of these laws it is up to the school attorney to be
up-to-date on technical aspects of educational legislation and constantly study legal
implications.

Summary

School districts are governmental agencies of the state. Each state has established a
system of public education and provided the necessary legislation for its operation statewide as well as at the local level. Thus, there is a delicate balance between what is
necessary for the entire state as illustrated by expressed powers and what may be best for
the local area as allowed by implied powers. Overarching and completing a massive
framework for public education is the U.S. Constitution and the various regulations
established by governmental agencies. It follows then that in a true sense every adminis-

trative act has a legal basis provided by a broad framework composed of constitutional mandate, and federal, state, and local legislation. Parts of the framework may be rigidly constructed from legislation spelling out step-by-step procedures; other portions may be flexibly constructed from legislation directing "what" should be done, leaving the "how" to local boards of education and their administrators. It is the responsibility of school administrators to know and understand this framework. Only then can they act with purpose and direction.

The position of school attorney has been established to assist the administrator in the technical aspects of school law. The duties of the school attorney are to: (1) assist in technical legal interpretation; (2) prepare legal documents; (3) initiate legal processes; (4) study technical aspects of school law; and (5) discover possible implications that can be drawn from general laws and court decisions.

Regardless of the size of the school district the complexities of educational management require that attention to given to defining the attorney's role. The need to understand the distinction between educational advice and legal advice cannot be too strongly emphasized. Often the school counsel is a prominent and influential person in the community. He or she places both the superintendent and board of education in an untenable situation if in an official capacity the attorney takes stands on educational issues or argues for a particular position that must be assessed on the basis of its educational merits rather than its legal implications. Certainly this is not intended to argue that educational decisions be made in spite of legal considerations, but as an educational leadership team member, the school business manager will want to make and help make the best educational decisions within the legal framework.

For Further Thought

1. Examine the policies of several boards of education regarding the hiring and role of the school attorney.

2. How can a superintendent and board guard against the legal opinions of the attorney becoming in effect educational policy and practice?

3. What implied powers within your state directly affect the role of the school business manager?

Endnotes

1. Arrington *v.* Jones, 191 S.W. 361 (Texas).
2. Thelbert L. Drake and Joseph R. McKinney, Ball State University, 1992.

3. Ted Dean Butler, "The Role of the School District Attorney in Oklahoma," unpublished dissertation, Oklahoma State University, 1989.

C h a p t e r *17*

Summary and Conclusion

Because school business management exists to facilitate and support the learning process it must subordinate itself to that function. The purpose of educational administration is to place the schools' instructional programs into practice through formal structures, personnel and techniques, and then to encourage and enhance this program through continuing support. Administration provides the physical, financial, and educational conditions to optimize learning. In addition it provides a vision of excellence and channels through which all agents and agencies of the school system and the public may work for continuous improvement. The objectives of school business management derive from, and its activities are directed toward, the policies and programs established for the benefit of teaching and learning. The agents who carry out the purposes of educational administration we call the administrative team and the school business manager is an integral part of that team. The school business manager then must be trained and experienced in the field of education with emphasis in business administration and management, for the decisions and recommendations he or she makes affect the educational program and are in final sense educational decisions.

Business management is a powerful and influential activity in educational administration. It essentially deals with all aspects of the school through the management of finance, budgets, purchasing, facilities, transportation, supplies, and a host of other supporting services. One must guard against the possibility that these services become dominant ends in themselves, rather than means to the end of an outstanding instructional program and meaningful learning.

The Administrative Team

Educational administration may be defined as that group of activities that (1) cooperatively establishes and articulates a vision of excellence for the schools; (2) carries on the long-range and technical planning of educational conditions under which educators and agencies can work to provide the best instruction possible to students; (3) provides for implementing the established plan; (4) arranges for the selection, assignment, coordination, and evaluation of all personnel and programs in the plan; (5) provides two-way channels through which information about conditions in the organization may flow; and (6) provides leadership by encouraging conditions through which all agents and agencies of the school may work cooperatively for continuous improvement.

The logical major divisions or units of a school system are instruction, instructional and supporting services, and business and fiscal functions. The prevailing pattern for administering these functions is to have an educational leader appointed as superintendent who acts as chief executive officer with all major unit heads (usually entitled assistant superintendent) reporting to him or her. The unit heads may report to the board of education only through the superintendent. This system is highly recommended because it keeps the business management and supporting services contributory to instruction and learning which is the major purpose of the school.

The potential for conflict and competition between the administrators of the units is high. The school business manager often is in a dilemma as he or she faces the task of operating the unit at a high rate of efficiency and at the same time supporting an instructional program whose definition of effective instruction may be perceived to be at variance with what might be efficient management or fiscal practice. This is why it is so important for the school business manager to have expertise in education as well as business management, and why it is so important for educational statesmanship to prevail in providing a reasonable balance between instructional excellence and fiscal control and efficiency. This is where the administrative team concept is tested and where a superintendent must exert his or her leadership to challenge these unit administrators to work toward an ever-expanding vision of excellence in the achievement of organizational goals and objective. This vision should include both managerial efficiency as well as instructional effectiveness.

Another potential for serious administrative conflict is between the building principal and the school business manager. A generally accepted administrative principle is that the building principal is responsible for all activities and functions carried on in the building to which he or she is assigned. This principle, strictly interpreted gives the principal immediate direction and supervision over all classified and/or supporting employees in the building as well as the teachers themselves. The question which immediately arises is: "Why would the principal who may know little or nothing about such various facilitating services as maintenance, food services, custodial work, etc. direct them? This question becomes especially querulous when one realizes the business management unit has supervisors who are highly trained technicians in these various supporting fields. The answer itself is really simple but requires a great deal of cooperation and coordination to carry out. If the central administration gives the responsibility of instructional leadership of a building to a principal he or she is responsible to see that the supporting facilitating services blend with instructional services and indeed facilitate instruction rather than hamper it. There is no mystery in making this principle work! It does require specifically spelled out operational relationships along with mutual understanding, respect, and cooperation. If a school system is task oriented, turf gives way to task. Supervisors of these specialty services may be given responsibility for supervisory functions throughout the school district except for direct administration control in the building. They may have responsibility for hiring and firing with consultation of the principal. They may develop schedules of work to be done, time and task charts, establish standards for work to be accomplished, and furnish the wherewithal to do the work. By inspecting and reporting through appropriate channels they can also determine that the work is done properly. They then can confer with the principal to help assess the job performance and monitor accomplishment. These relationships properly spelled out make the operation a team effort and help develop the concept that cooperative effort is required if the instructional process is to be properly served.

The Teacher

Management implies efficiency, organization, order, competency, proficiency, effectiveness, direction, control, and other complementary words used to describe a business or organization. Too often, however, management, efficiency, and accountability become ugly words in academic institutions. While teachers and supervisors do rate and grade changes in knowledge, attitude, and skills, there are so many things in education that deal with the abstract and unquantifiable; and further, there is much disagreement as to what changes in knowledge, skills, and attitude are desirable. Therefore, the faculty often views the efforts of administration to promote efficiency and accountability as restrictive, repressive, and even harassing, yet they expect instruction to run smoothly through the use of a great variety of facilitating and supporting services which can be provided only by means of rather elaborate procedures and organization.

Humanizing and harmonizing the management aspects of a school is an important task. However, it cannot be considered the exclusive province of the superintendent or the school business official. It can no more be left to the administration than the famous aphorism, war can be left to the general. It has been shown repeatedly that skilled and active participation of students and faculty as individuals and groups is crucial to the effective conduct of a school. This is as true in school business management as well as in any other area of school activity. We contend that business management becomes a total school responsibility and must pervade the entire system from bottom to top. Without proper input from instruction, school business management cannot properly serve instruction.

How then can the business manager create an atmosphere which gives the teacher a good feeling about management and convince him or her that its services are there for support and to facilitate instruction? Three key words, we believe, will create the right atmosphere. They are "input," "feedback," and "implementation." Any activity carried out by the business management unit should encourage input by teachers, feedback from them as to its value and effectiveness, and finally as much implementation of their suggestions as humanly, financially, and reasonably possible. Equipment is useless if it is not up-to-date, easily used, or if it continuously breaks down. Frustration builds up if supplies are in continuous short supply or if they are not effective. Transportation becomes negative if children come in the first hour or two of school not ready to learn because of lack of control on the bus. Factors which imply lack of understanding and concern for support of instruction are real negatives and build up to bickering and poor morale creating an ineffective school system. Morale improves if the teacher understands that he or she is operating in a professional atmosphere with the tools and supplies necessary to do the job. Teachers are appreciative of the school business manager who is sensitive to the needs of instruction.

Classified Personnel

The school business manager normally is assigned the responsibility of working with classified or support personnel in a school district, while certified personnel may be managed through the office of the assistant superintendent for instruction or personnel or by the superintendent. Regardless of the structure, it should be recognized that all employees are working toward the same mission, and all roles are important for the smooth operation of the school system. Care should be taken to nurture a cooperative, respectful relationship between staff persons in all positions. This relationship begins with all personnel being educated and sensitized to the importance of all other positions. The interdependency of positions within the system must be emphasized in order that the mission of the school systems to enhance learning, is understood by all members of the organization.

People appreciate recognition for the valuable services they render to the organization. Consider the importance of clean buildings, supplies on hand when needed; buses running on time with courteous, careful drivers, and safe equipment; nutritious and tastefully prepared meals; and the effective handling of clerical responsibilities. These are only a few examples of important contributions made by classified personnel, yet in some instances, the importance of the services of classified personnel goes unrecognized and the positive personnel processes in place for these employees are not emphasized.

The challenge to the person assigned administrative responsibilities in the area of classified personnel is to provide leadership in working toward a cooperative relationship among the staff based on an understanding of the value of all positions within the system. The goal is to achieve the objectives of the school district and to help individual staff member maximize their potential. In most situations, respect for employees and their abilities, along with fair treatment including concern for the welfare and needs of the individual, helps to bring about commitment from employees to the goals of the organization. Employee needs include acceptance, security, belonging, and a sense of accomplishment. Attention to these needs and to the generation of relationships of co-operation and mutual respect is an important facet of implementing an effective personnel management system.

In some organizations the people come into their respective jobs, perform the tasks, and leave without ever being part of the "big picture." We have told the story of the two bricklayers who are asked what they were doing. One replied that he was laying brick. The other replied, "I am building a cathedral!" This latter response is startling revelation of a sense of mission and belonging found among some employees who identify with the organization that employs them. This sense of mission ordinarily does not just grow by itself. It must be cultivated and nourished by a leadership that is sensitive to the needs of human beings. Whether or not one has this sense of mission gives the observer insights into the culture of an organization and in some cases its subculture.

The Public and Perception

Educational structure grows out of purpose and practice and is determined and supported by the culture of which it is a part. Thus, all institutionalized education is supported by and under the control of the public—expressed essentially through state organization as far as public education is concerned. Although our schools have become increasingly organized, institutionalized, and bureaucratized they are considered too important by the public to be left alone. In our world, knowledge and skill counts immensely. Education is considered so important nationally that several prominent politicians have proudly proclaimed themselves to be education presidents or governors. In the 1992 presidential campaign the candidates vied with each other as to who would be the more supportive of education.

With increasing support of education accompanied with increase in taxes the public also has determined that education is too important and too costly for them to forget about the accountability factor. Thus, the public's perception and impression of schools is very important in relation to the support they receive. Often the impressions are created by the way schools are managed and by the facilities that the public sees.

The impression made by the physical appearance of a school building is often a key for the way an ordinary citizen evaluates education. Shoddy landscaping, untidy interiors, and poorly maintained facilities suggest that education within the building follows the same pattern. Regardless of the feelings of the professional educator, the school plant is to the noneducator the symbol of state and community education. It sends a message whether the classroom operation within is first-rate, second-rate, or worse. Most people point to their school building with pride. They see it as an important symbol of education and like to believe that it creates an environment which invites children to grow physically, mentally, and emotionally. To the children, the teachers, and the community, the school plant along with its operation and maintenance are highly important.

By the same token, if facilitating and service functions are not performed expertly and with precision the instructional program suffers, and the public's confidence in the total school enterprise is shaken. A breakdown in the business management side of the school's function often becomes apparent to the public more quickly than a breakdown in the instructional side. The layperson feels on familiar ground where problems of management are concerned, but they are inclined to leave instruction to the professional teachers.

If bus service is bad or if school lunches are unappetizing, a mother is fairly sure of what she's talking about when she complains and her criticism is justified. If taxes increase, but necessary supplies and equipment are not available and the school budget cannot be balanced, people will naturally wonder why and ask questions, and when they raise these questions they will have serious doubts about the teaching and learning that goes on in the school.

These negative manifestations especially have impact on the superintendent of schools. A school administrator may have master's and doctor's degrees, be a person with outstanding leadership ability, have state or national recognition as an educational scholar, and yet if the business management details of the school are ineptly administered, the general public will consider him or her a poor administrator and opportunities for showing splendid educational leadership will be diminished.

The Changing Society Reflects on Schools

If the leaders of a school district are going to administer successfully, they must be able to see the district within a larger context. Schools do not exist in splendid isolation regardless of how much some persons within the schools would like to have them be autonomous entities separate from the "evils" of politics and economic realities. Schools are affected by almost every major change in their environments and by many smaller changes. The 15,000 plus school districts in the United States exist in a turbulent ocean of opinion, demands, needs, expectations, and political ups and downs, just to name a few of the currents affecting the sometimes battered school districts. The political changes in the 1990s have shaken an increasingly interdependent world. Along with this, education has been experiencing a fiscal ride somewhat like a roller coaster. In recent years there have been varying periods of rapid growth, decline, population shifts, and economic development and doldrums. Added to these are voter apathy, taxpayer revolts, and state caps on tax increases contrasted with increased pressure to provide more services for more segments of the population and unfunded mandates from the state and federal levels. These volatile situations too often seem to whipsaw the schools into frustration.

The dollar amounts associated with the school business management function and the size of the entire educational enterprise makes it a national target for questions. The K-12 sector spent over $215 billion in 1989–1990 and approximately one in four people in the United States are either students or employees of schools and colleges. At the same time in most small and even large communities the schools employ more people, have larger budgets, own more buildings and facilities, feed more people per day, purchase more supplies, and have larger transportation systems than most business and industries in the community. In spite of this we create the wrong impression when we say schools are *big business*. They have functions that have big business dimensions but they are *not* big business. Drawing parallels with big business does damage to the perceived mission of the schools. Turning out "X" number of graduates at the lowest dollar cost so as to realize "Y" amount of profit is not the mission of the schools. The "bottom line" for schools is how much have the students learned. Perpetuating the big business myth may even give the board of education the idea that its main function is to hold tightly the purse strings rather than to represent the community in establishing a proper balance between the best education possible and what people need and want and what they will support. The same myth may encourage the school business manager to become a watchdog of the treasury and warehouse instead of a servant to the instructional programs of the school.

In the context of change and in the confusion regarding the "bottom line" purposes of the school many new voices and conflicting demands are being heard. Some are inclined to dump certain societal problems in the lap of the schools and say "It's your responsibility to fix them!" Others, often business and political voices, are saying the schools haven't coped with the problems of society but "we can fix the schools so that they can." Traditional faith in the schools has eroded in many places. Thus, the school business manager finds himself or herself as part of a leadership team called to question.

The business manager who is naturally allied to the business/industrial community because of his or her expertise and continuous affiliations can make a significant impact on the direction the support from business and industry will take. However, schools should not be run like businesses. It can be dangerously costly to tinker with teaching excellence by assuming that the "bottom line" for the school is measured in dollars rather than improved instruction which results in enhanced learning. It is the role of all education leaders, and especially the school superintendent and often the school business manager to interpret the real goals of the school to business and industry and at the same time to assure them that although it is not the function of the school to make a profit or to save money for money's sake, it is the function of school administration to operate the school efficiently and effectively and to be properly accountable for getting "one hundred cents" worth of service for every dollar spent. When business and industry realize this and understand the real goals of the school, their special support and helpfulness has done much to enhance education. Many examples of partnership efforts attest to that fact!

Ethics and the School Business Manager

The school business manager deals with that segment of school operation that is susceptible to influential forces which can easily bring ethical and moral questions into play. Being responsible for purchasing thousands of dollars worth of supplies and equipment, planning for expensive buildings and facilities, hiring and supervising scores of skilled and unskilled employees, relating to hundreds and possibly thousands of teachers and other professionals, and dealing continuously with the business and industrial sector, the business manager is in a highly visible position of leadership and faces situations day after day that can test moral character. Many school administrators' careers have been ruined by dealing with these situations in a questionable manner.

In a previous chapter we presented the case study of Fred Fiver, "Local Boy Makes Good." This is a typical example of how a situation can develop where a "good old boy" relationship may cloud issues to the point at which it is difficult to determine right from wrong, or at least make it difficult to extricate oneself from the web of personal loyalties. Dealing with friends and local influential persons in business situations can be uncomfortable, particularly if a hard decision must be made that is not favorable to a friend or local influential person. The only way to avoid such unpleasant possibilities is to have it clearly understood that though friendship is very important, in decisions affecting the management of a school such decisions will be made in a reputable fashion based solely on the concept of what is best for the school. It is important that this same attitude prevails when dealing with employees within the entire school system and particularly within the business management division itself. The obligation to support ethics and integrity is greatest on the chief administrator of a unit because any noted deviation multiplies itself in levels below and can very soon corrupt the entire organization. Arthur B. Moehlman, a distinguished pioneer in educational administration, said many times to his students and in speeches to educational administrators: "Develop for yourself as administrator a meaningful code of conduct and professional ethics, then wear it as a mantle of personal integrity in all of your dealings, both personally and professionally. It will help you avoid temptation and protect you from being tarnished by improper actions and influence."[1]

A professional code of ethics to guide administrators in their activities has been developed over the years by both the American Association of School Administrators and the American Association of School Business Officials (See chapter 1). Both are well thought out and are most worthy of acceptance. A defensible and widely accepted code of ethics is essential for the well-being of a profession; however, no code can be made extensive enough or up-to-date enough to describe what is right and wrong in every aspect of professional behavior. Obeying and following the law itself is also not enough, nor is conforming to the spirit and letter of educational policies and programs of your school, which is also a form of ethical behavior. These are not enough because ethical behavior is much more complicated. Professional and social changes continuously confront the administrator and present new problems involving more comprehensive questions of morality. To give these codes and laws and policies a solid base from which one can operate with some internal security one needs to decide what the basis of his or her own moral standards will be after prolonged examination of one's beliefs. This is not just a simple resolution like deciding "I won't lie, steal, cheat, or break the law" (although these are worthy resolutions). To develop your own set of moral standards requires reading, study, deep thought, prolonged self-examination, and introspection. It also requires serious discussion with fellow students, professors, colleagues, and respected students of philosophy and religion.

It is beyond the scope of this book to discuss all of the examples of unethical behavior that could be considered improper administrative conduct. The following may be illustrative:

1. Lack of concern and respect for the individual

   (a) Racial discrimination
   (b) Sexual discrimination and abuse
   (c) Religious prejudice
   (d) Unjust treatment of students and employees

2. Failure to do what is necessary to further the goals of the organization and to fulfill necessary obligations because of lack of expertise, knowledge, carelessness, and/or laziness. (Many are not inclined to categorize these as ethical. However, as an administrator one is morally responsible for job performance. If proper job performance is not forthcoming this borders on lack of professional integrity.)

3. Favoritism and/or nepotism. This is a practice that will favor relatives or friends in job situations over better qualified individuals either in hiring, promotion, or in duties to be performed.

4. Acceptance of personal favors and/or gifts from those who do business with the school. Because of the position they hold, educational administrators will be shown many personal favors. While these may not be outright bribes they can take on that character without too great a stretch of the imagination.

5. Failure to honor an agreement or contract without just cause.

6. Lack of loyalty to a profession, organization, and/or a colleague whose ideas and ideals can be personally and professionally defended. Often one may experience personal conflict if he or she must choose between one or the other in the course of an experience.

7. Displaced loyalty. This becomes a personal moral problem when one is associated with an employer and/or organization that is involved in questionable practices. Watergate or the Iran-Contra affair are illustrative of the conflict one faces in weighing the loyalty to an organization and office against loyalty to law and morality.

8. Improper administrative procedures. There are many examples of unethical practices in this area, i.e., pitting one employee against another; setting up false situations or "straw men" in order to rally employees to a cause or course of action; and being deceptive in dealing with employees personally for "the good of the organization."

9. Questionable actions which may further your personal or professional career, i.e., manipulation of people, policies, or procedures to reflect more favorably on self and career; self aggrandizement at the expense of others; disparagement of a fellow administrator or rival professional for personal or professional gain.

The role of the school business administrator affects everyone in a school district. The paychecks that everyone looks forward to are part of the business administrator's responsibilities as are the chemicals used to prepare floors in the buildings, the heat in the buildings, and the means available to a fifth grader to study the living canopy in a South American rain forest. True, the school business manager cannot meet the great range of responsibilities mentioned alone. There are many players on the stage, but the business administrator has a major role to play as part of the educational leadership team. As part of that team, the school business administrator must shoulder part of the responsibility for the achievement of students.

The tasks facing the school business administrator seem to be endless as represented by the list of twenty-one functions noted in chapter 1. There is no question that all those tasks must be done right. To do otherwise not only destroys the business administrator's credibility, but undermines the effectiveness of the whole leadership team. To serve as an effective team member, the business administrator not only does things right, but does the right things in regard to the mission of the school. He or she cannot avoid raising questions and taking positions about the effective learning of students without abdicating part of his or her role as an educational leadership team member. No one said it would be easy to be part of a leadership team in an ever-changing context of expectations, obligations, and opportunities. But then, many worthwhile accomplishments are not easy. The rewards of seeing them done well outweigh the headaches by far.

Endnote

1. Arthur B. Moehlman, Professor of Educational Administration, The University of Michigan, 1930–1950.

A p p e n d i x *I*

≡≡≡≡≡≡≡≡≡≡≡≡≡≡≡≡≡≡

Example of a Budget Planning Form for an Individual Building

Form for 1993 Exemplar Elementary School Budget

10-11100-311-7 Instructional Service		$ _____
10-11100-323-7 Repairs		$ _____
Copier	$ _____	
Typewriter	_____	
Piano Tuning	_____	
Other	_____	
10-11100-325-7 Rentals		$ _____
Other	$ _____	
10-11100-332-7 Travel - Conferences		$ _____
Grade Level Conf.	$ _____	
Nat. Conf.	_____	
State Conf.	_____	
Local Staff Develop.	_____	
Other		

10-11100-342-7 Postage $_____

   Stamps $_____

10-11100-360-7 Printing and Binding $_____

   Book Binding $_____

   Handbooks   _____

   Report Card/Covers   _____

   Forms   _____

   Mailing Labels   _____

   Other   _____

10-11100-411-7 Supplies $_____

   Instructional Supplies:

     Kindergarten $_____

     Grade 1   _____

     Grade 2   _____

     Grade 3   _____

     Grade 4   _____

     Grade 5   _____

     Grade 6   _____

   Art   _____

   Music   _____

   P.E.   _____

   Science   _____

   Technology   _____

   Office   _____

   Other   _____

10-11100-411-13 Central Stores $_____

   Instructional Supplies:

     Kindergarten $_____

     Grade 1   _____

     Grade 2   _____

     Grade 3   _____

     Grade 4   _____

     Grade 5   _____

     Grade 6

Art $_____

Music _____

P.E. _____

Science _____

Technology _____

Office _____

Tchr. _____

10-11100-540-7 Equipment (list needed equip) $_____

Art $_____

Lang. Arts _____

Music _____

P.E. _____

Science _____

Soc. St. _____

Technology _____

Furniture _____

10-22220-411-7 Library Supplies $_____

Book Covers $_____

Cards _____

Forms _____

Office Supplies _____

10-22220-430-7 Library Books $_____
(List numbers needed by general category)

10-22220-440-7 Library Periodicals $_____
(List)

10-22230-323-7 AV Repair $_____

10-22230-411-7 AV Supplies $_____

Laminating Supplies $_____

Office Supplies _____

Overhead Proj. Supp. _____

10-22230-460-7 AV Materials $_____

Film $_____

Filmstrips _____

Slides _____

Videotapes _____

10-22230-540-7 AV Equipment $ _____
(List Equipment)

10-24100-332-7 Principal Travel - Conferences $ _____

     Nat. Conferences $ _____

     State Conf.   _____

     Local Travel   _____

     Secretarial   _____

10-24100-540-7 Principal Office Equipment $ _____
(List)

A p p e n d i x **II**

A Sample Budget Planning Document

There are five funds indicated in the budget planning document below: 10 indicates the General Fund which supports the operating expenses of the instructional and instructionally related programs; 20 indicates Debt Service; 35 is for Capital Projects; 40 indicates Transportation; and 60 indicates Preschool Handicapped Programs.

The code may be read from left to right as follows:

11	100	110	3
Elementary	Elementary Instruction	Salaries	School
	200—Middle School	300—Purchased Services	
	300—High School	400—Supplies	
		500—Equipment	

The coding system allows the allocation of dollars by object, by school, by program, and a number of other ways so that the planners can focus more clearly on programmatic needs. The document follows state and GASB guidelines regarding accounting for funds.

1993 General Fund (Fund 010) Budget Worksheet

10,000 INSTRUCTION

  11,000 Regular Instruction

    11,100-110-3 CG Salaries (certified)

      ____ Teacher base $____

      ____ % Increase for
              1/2 of 1992 $____

_____ Additional teachers $_____

_____ Substitutes $_____   (110-3) $_____

11,100-110-4 MG Salaries (certified)

_____ Base $_____

_____ Raise $_____

_____ New $_____

_____ Substitutes $_____   (110-4) $_____

11,100-110-5 NG Salaries (certified)

_____ Base $_____

_____ Raise $_____

_____ New $_____

_____ Substitutes $_____   (110-5) $_____

11,100-110-6 WG Salaries (certified)

_____ Base $_____

_____ Raise $_____

_____ New $_____

_____ Substitutes $_____   (110-6) $_____

11,100-110-7 PG Salaries (certified)

_____ Base $_____

_____ Raise $_____

_____ New $_____

_____ Substitutes $_____   (110-7) $_____

                             Total (110) $_____

11,100-120-0 Prime Time Assistants

_____ Base $_____

_____ Raise $_____

_____ Bonus $_____

_____ Substitutes $_____   (120-0) $_____

11,100-120-3 C.G. Salaries (classified)

_____ Base $_____

_____ Raise $_____

_____ Bonus $_____

_____ Substitutes $_____   (120-3) $_____

11,100-120-4 M.G. Salaries (classified)

____ Base $____

____ Raise $____

____ Bonus $____

____ Substitutes $____ (120-4) $____

11,100-120-5 N.G. Salaries (classified)

____ Base $____

____ Raise $____

____ Bonus $____

____ Substitutes $____ (120-5) $____

11,100-120-6 W.G. Salaries (classified)

____ Base $____

____ Raise $____

____ Bonus $____

____ Substitutes $____ (120-6) $____

11,100-120-7 P.G. Salaries (classified)

____ Base $____

____ Raise $____

____ Bonus $____

____ Substitutes $____ (120-7) $____

             Total (120) $____

             TOTAL [100] ____

11,100-311-3 CG Bradford Woods ____

11,100-311-6 WG Bradford Woods ____

11,100-311-7 PG Bradford Woods ____

          Total (311) $____

11,100-323-3 CG Repairs ____

11,100-323-4 MG Repairs ____

11,100-323-5 NG Repairs ____

11,100-323-6 WG Repairs ____

11,100-323-7 PG Repairs ____

          Total (323) $____

11,100-325-3 CG Rentals   _____

11,100-325-4 MG Rentals   _____

11,100-325-5 NG Rentals   _____

11,100-325-6 WG Rentals   _____

11,100-325-7 PG Rentals   _____

                                          Total (325) $_____

11,100-332-3 CG Travel   _____

11,100-332-4 MG Travel   _____

11,100-332-5 NG Travel   _____

11,100-332-6 WG Travel   _____

11,100-332-7 PG Travel   _____

                                          Total (332) $_____

11,100-342-3 CG Postage   _____

11,100-342-4 MG Postage   _____

11,100-342-5 NG Postage   _____

11,100-342-6 WG Postage   _____

11,100-342-7 PG Postage   _____

                                          Total (342) $_____

11,100-360-3 CG Printing & Binding   _____

11,100-360-4 MG Printing & Binding   _____

11,100-360-5 NG Printing & Binding   _____

11,100-360-6 WG Printing & Binding   _____

11,100-360-7 PG Printing & Binding   _____

                                          Total (360) $_____

                                          TOTAL [300] _____

11,100-411-3 CG Supplies   _____

11,100-411-4 MG Supplies   _____

11,100-411-5 NG Supplies   _____

11,100-411-6 WG Supplies   _____

11,100-411-7 PG Supplies   _____

11,100-411-9 CG Central Stores   _____

11,100-411-10 MG Central Stores _____

11,100-411-11 NG Central Stores _____

11,100-411-12 WG Central Stores   ———

11,100-411-13 PG Central Stores   ———

            Total (411) $———

                TOTAL [400] ———

11,100-540-3 CG Equipment   ———

11,100-540-4 MG Equipment   ———

11,100-540-5 NG Equipment   ———

11,100-540-6 WG Equipment   ———

11,100-540-7 PG Equipment   ———

            Total (540) $———

                TOTAL [500] ———

                TOTAL 11,100 ———

11,200 Middle School Instructional

    11,200-110 Salaries (certified)

       ___ Base $———

       ___ Raise $———

       ___ New $———

       ___ Substitutes $———   (110-2) $———

    11,200-120-2 Salaries (classified)

       ___ Base $———

       ___ Raise $———

       ___ New $———

       ___ Substitutes $———   (120-2) $———

                TOTAL [100] ———

11,200-314-2 NCA   ———

11,200-332-2 Repairs   ———

11,200-325-2 Rental   ———

11,200-332-2 Travel   ———

11,200-342-2 Postage   ———   TOTAL [300] ———

11,200-360-2 Printing   ———

11,200-411-2 Supplies   ———

11,200-411-15 Central Stores   ———   TOTAL [400] ———

11,200-540-2 Equipment   ———   TOTAL [500] ———

                TOTAL 11,200 ———

11,300 High School Instructional

    11,300-110-0 Salaries (certified)

      ____ Base $____

      ____ Raise $____

      ____ New $____

      ____ Substitutes $____   (110-1) $____

    11,300-120-1 Salaries (classified)

      ____ Base $____

      ____ Raise $____

      ____ New $____

      ____ Substitutes $____   (120-1) $____   TOTAL [100] ____

    11,300-314-1 NCA   ____

    11,300-317-1 Stat Serv   ____

    11,300-323-1 Repairs   ____

    11,300-325-1 Rentals   ____

    11,300-332-1 Travel   ____

    11,300-342-1 Postage   ____

    11,300-360-1 Printing   ____   TOTAL [300] ____

    11,300-411-1 Supplies   ____

    11,300-411-14 Central Stores   ____   TOTAL [400] ____

    11,300-540-1 Equipment   ____   TOTAL [500] ____

                                          TOTAL 11,300 ____

    11,450-110-1 H.E. Sal. Cert.

      ____ Base $____

      ____ Raise $____

      ____ Substitutes $____   (110-1) $____   TOTAL [100] ____

    11,450-411-1 Supplies   ____   TOTAL [400] ____

    11,450-540-1 Equipment   ____   TOTAL [500] ____

                                          TOTAL 11,450 ____

    11,510-110-1 ICE Sal.

      ____ Base $____

      ____ Raise $____

      ____ Substitutes $____   (110-1) $____   TOTAL [100] ____

11,510-322-1 Travel   TOTAL [300] _____

                                                       TOTAL 11,510 _____

11,900-110 ISTEP Program   _____   (110) $_____ TOTAL [100] _____

                                                       TOTAL 11,900 _____

                                                       *****TOTAL 11,000 _____

12,000 Special Programs

  12,100 Gifted and Talented

    12,100-110 Salaries, Certified

    ____ Base $_____

    ____ Raise $_____

    ____ Substitutes $_____   (110) $_____ TOTAL [100] _____

    12,100-322 Travel   _____   TOTAL [300] _____

    12,000-411 Supplies   _____   TOTAL [400] _____

                                                       TOTAL 12,100 _____

  12,350 Homebound

    12,350-110 Salary   _____   (110) $_____ TOTAL [100] _____

    12,350-332 Travel   _____   TOTAL [300] _____

                                                       TOTAL 12,350 _____

                                                       *****TOTAL 12,000 _____

14,000 Summer School

  14,100 Elementary Summer School

    14,100-110 Salary, Certified

    ____ Base $_____

    ____ Substitutes $_____   (110) $_____

    14,100-120 Salary, Classified

    ____ Base $_____   (120) $_____

                                                       TOTAL [100] _____

    14,100-360 Printing & Binding $_____

                                                       TOTAL [300] _____

    14,100-411 Supplies $_____

    14,100-411-20 Central Stores $_____   TOTAL [400] _____

                                                       TOTAL 14,100 _____

14,200 Middle School Summer School

    14,200-110 Salaries, Certified

       ____ Base   \$_____

       ____ Substitutes   \$_____   (110) \$_____

    14,200-120 Salaries, Classified

       ____ Base   \$_____   (120) \$_____

                                                TOTAL [100] _____

    14,200-411 Supplies   \$_____   TOTAL [400] _____

                                             TOTAL 14,200 _____

14,300 High School Summer School

    14,300-110 Salaries, Certified

       ____ Base   \$_____

       ____ Substitutes   \$_____   (110) \$_____

    14,300-120 Salaries, Classified

       ____ Base   \$_____

       ____ Substitutes   \$_____   (120) \$_____

                                                TOTAL [100] _____

    14,300-323 Car Repair   \$_____

    14,300-325 Car Lease   \$_____

    14,300-324 Car Insurance   \$_____   TOTAL [300] _____

    14,300-411 Supplies   \$_____   TOTAL [400] _____

                                                TOTAL 14,300 _____

                                           *****TOTAL 14,000 _____

                                              TOTAL 10,000

20,000 Support Services

  21,000 Pupils

    21,200 Guidance Services

      21,200 Counseling

        21,21220-110-0 Salaries, Certified

           ____ Base   \$_____

           ____ Raise   \$_____

           ____ Substitutes   \$_____   (110-0) \$_____

21,220-110-1 Salaries, Certified

    ____ Base $____

    ____ Raise $____

    ____ Substitutes $____   (110-1) $____

21,220-110-2 Salaries, Certified

    ____ Base $____

    ____ Raise $____

    ____ Substitutes $____   (110-2) $____

                                          TOTAL [110] ____

21,200-120-1 Salaries, Classified

    ____ Base $____

    ____ Raise $____

    ____ Bonus $____

    ____ Substitutes $____   (120-1) $____

21,200-120-2 Salaries, Classified

    ____ Base $____

    ____ Raise $____

    ____ Bonus $____

    ____ Substitutes $____   (120-2) $____

                                          TOTAL [120] ____

                                        TOTAL [100] ____

21,220-360-1 Printing   ____   TOTAL [300] ____

21,220-411-1 Supplies   ____

21,220-411-2 Supplies   ____   TOTAL [400] ____

                                      TOTAL 21,220 ____

21,230 Appraisal

    21,230-316 Scoring   ____   TOTAL [300] ____

    21,230-411 Supplies   ____   TOTAL [400] ____

                                      TOTAL 21,230 ____

                                  *****TOTAL 21,200 ____

21,300 Health Services

21,340 Nurse

21,340-120-1 Salaries, Classified

_____ Base $_____

_____ Raise $_____

_____ Bonus $_____

_____ Uniforms $_____

_____ Substitutes $_____   (120-1) $_____

21,340-120-2

_____ Base $_____

_____ Raise $_____

_____ Bonus $_____

_____ Uniforms $_____

_____ Substitutes $_____   (120-2) $_____

21,340-120-3 CG

_____ Base $_____

_____ Raise $_____

_____ Bonus $_____

_____ Uniforms $_____

_____ Substitutes $_____   (120-3) $_____

21,340-120-4 MG

_____ Base $_____

_____ Raise $_____

_____ Bonus $_____

_____ Uniforms $_____

_____ Substitutes $_____   (120-4) $_____

21,340-120-5 NG

_____ Base $_____

_____ Raise $_____

_____ Bonus $_____

_____ Uniforms $_____

_____ Substitutes $_____   (120-5) $_____

21,340-120-6 WG

_____ Base $_____

_____ Raise $_____

_____ Bonus $_____

_____ Uniforms $_____

_____ Substitutes $_____   (120-6) $_____

21,340-120-7 PG

_____ Base $_____

_____ Raise $_____

_____ Bonus $_____

_____ Uniforms $_____

_____ Substitutes $_____   (120-7) $_____

TOTAL (120) _____

TOTAL [100] _____

21,340-332 Travel   _____   TOTAL [300] _____

21,340-411 Supplies   _____   TOTAL [400] _____

21,340-540 Equipment   _____   TOTAL [500] _____

TOTAL 21,300 _____

*****TOTAL 21,000 _____

22,000 Instructional Staff

22,100 Improvement of Instruction & Curriculum

22,110 Curriculum Director

22,110-110 Salaries, Certified

_____ Base $_____

_____ Raise $_____

_____ Substitutes $_____   Total (110) $_____

22,110-120 Salaries, Classified

_____ Base $_____

_____ Raise $_____

_____ Bonus $_____

_____ Substitutes $_____   Total (120) $_____

22,110-130 Staff Development
Workshops   ____   Total (130) $____

                                                   TOTAL [110] ____

22,110-312 Consultants   ____

22,110-332 Travel   ____   TOTAL [300] ____

22,110-411 Supplies   ____

22,110-411-16 Central Stores ____   TOTAL [400] ____

22,110-540 Equipment   ____   TOTAL [500] ____

                                       TOTAL 22,100 ____

22,200 Educational Media Services

22,220 Library

22,220-110-1 Salaries, Certified

____ Base $____

____ Raise $____

____ Substitutes $____   (110-1) $____

22,220-110-2

____ Base $____

____ Raise $____

____ Substitutes $____   (110-2) $____

22,220-110-3 CG

____ Base $____

____ Raise $____

____ Substitutes $____   (110-3) $____

22,220-110-4 MG

____ Base $____

____ Raise $____

____ Substitutes $____   (110-4) $____

22,220-110-5 NG

____ Base $____

____ Raise $____

____ Substitutes $____   (110-5) $____

22,220-110-6 WG

____ Base $____

____ Raise $____

____ Substitutes $____   (110-6) $____

22,220-110-7 PG

____ Base $_____

____ Raise $_____

____ Substitutes $_____   (110-7) $_____   TOTAL (100) _____

22,220-120-1 Salaries, Classified

____ Base $_____

____ Raise $_____

____ Bonus $_____

____ Substitutes $_____   (120-1) $_____

22,220-120-2 MS

____ Base $_____

____ Raise $_____

____ Bonus $_____

____ Substitutes $_____   (120-2) $_____

22,220-120-3 CG

____ Base $_____

____ Raise $_____

____ Bonus $_____

____ Substitutes $_____   (120-3) $_____

22,220-120-4 MG

____ Base $_____

____ Raise $_____

____ Bonus $_____

____ Substitutes $_____   (120-4) $_____

22,220-120-5 NG

____ Base $_____

____ Raise $_____

____ Bonus $_____

____ Substitutes $_____   (120-5) $_____

22,220-120-6 WG

____ Base $_____

____ Raise $_____

____ Bonus $_____

____ Substitutes $_____   (120-6) $_____

22,220-120-7 PG

_____ Base $_____

_____ Raise $_____

_____ Bonus $_____

_____ Substitutes $_____   (120-7) $_____   TOTAL (120) _____

                                                                    TOTAL [100] _____

                                                                    TOTAL [300] _____

22,220-332-0 Travel   _____

22,220-411-1 Supplies   _____

22,220-411-2 Supplies   _____

22,220-411-3 Supplies   _____

22,220-411-4 Supplies   _____

22,220-411-5 Supplies   _____

22,220-411-6 Supplies   _____

22,220-411-7 Supplies   _____   (411) $_____

22,220-430-1 Books   _____

22,220-430-2 Books   _____

22,220-430-3 Books   _____

22,220-430-4 Books   _____

22,220-430-5 Books   _____

22,220-430-6 Books   _____

22,220-440-1 Periodicals   _____

22,220-440-2 Periodicals   _____

22,220-440-3 Periodicals   _____

22,220-440-4 Periodicals   _____

22,220-440-5 Periodicals   _____

22,220-440-6 Periodicals   _____

22,220-440-7 Periodicals   _____   (440) $_____   TOTAL [400] _____

                                                                 TOTAL 22,200 _____

22,230 Audio Visual

22,230-323 Bulbs   _____

22,230-323-1 Repair   _____

22,230-323-2 Repair   _____

22,230-323-3 Repair   _____

22,230-323-4 Repair   _____

22,230-323-5 Repair   _____

22,230-323-6 Repair   _____

22,230-323-7 Repair   _____   (323) $_____

22,230-325-0 Film Rental   _____   (325) $_____   TOTAL [300] _____

22,230-411-1 Supplies   _____

22,230-411-2 Supplies   _____

22,230-411-3 Supplies   _____

22,230-411-4 Supplies   _____

22,230-411-5 Supplies   _____

22,230-411-6 Supplies   _____

22,230-411-7 Supplies   _____   (411) $_____

22,230-460-1 Filmstrips   _____

22,230-460-2 Filmstrips   _____

22,230-460-3 Filmstrips   _____

22,230-460-4 Filmstrips   _____

22,230-460-5 Filmstrips   _____

22,230-460-6 Filmstrips   _____

22,230-460-7 Filmstrips   _____   (460) $_____

22,230-470-0 Corp. Software   _____   (470) $_____   TOTAL [400] _____

22,230-540-1 Equipment   _____

22,230-540-2 Equipment   _____

22,230-540-3 Equipment   _____

22,230-540-4 Equipment   _____

22,230-540-5 Equipment   _____

22,230-540-6 Equipment   _____

22,230-540-7 Equipment   _____   (540) $_____   TOTAL [500] _____

                                                             TOTAL [22,230] _____

22,250 Instruction

22,250-110 Salaries, Certified

____ Base $_____

____ Raise $_____   (110) $_____

22,250-120 Salaries, Classified

____ Base $_____

____ Raise $_____

____ Bonus $_____

____ Substitutes $_____   (120) $_____ TOTAL [100] _____

22,250-323 Repairs $_____

22,250-332 Travel $_____

22,250-343 Maint for Software $_____   TOTAL [300] _____

22,250-411 Supplies $_____

22,250-411-17 Central Stores $_____   TOTAL [400] _____

     TOTAL [22,250] _____

     TOTAL 22,200 _____

     *****TOTAL 22,000 _____

23,000 General Administration

  23,100 Governing Board

    23,110-120 Board Stipend   _____

    23,220-120 Secretary   _____   (120) $_____ TOTAL [100] _____

    23,110-332 Travel   _____   TOTAL [300] _____

    23,110-411 Supplies   _____   TOTAL [400] _____

    23,110-640 Fees   _____   TOTAL [600] _____

      School Board Association   _____

      East Central   _____

      IU Partnership   _____

       TOTAL [23,110] _____

    23,150-310 Professional &
    Technical Services   _____   TOTAL [300]

       TOTAL [23,150] _____

    23,160-670 Pro/scho   _____   TOTAL [600] _____

       TOTAL [23,160] _____

       TOTAL 23,100 _____

23,200 Ex. Adm. Services (Supt).

  23,210 Office of Superintendent

    23,210-110 Salaries, Certified

    ____ Base $_____

    ____ Raise $_____   (110) $_____

23,210-120 Salaries, Classified

____ Base $_____

____ Raise $_____

____ Bonus $_____

____ Substitutes $_____

____ Extra $_____   (120) $_____   TOTAL [100] _____

23,210-323 Repairs   _____

23,210-342 Postage   _____   TOTAL [300] _____

23,210-411-18 Central Stores   _____   TOTAL [400] _____

23,210-540 Equipment   _____   TOTAL [500] _____

                                                        TOTAL [23,210] _____

23,220 Community Relations   _____

23,220-342 Postage   _____

23,220-360 Newsletter   _____   TOTAL [300] _____

23,220-411 Supplies   _____   TOTAL [400] _____

                                                        TOTAL [23,220] _____

23,290 Other Services   _____

23,290-332 Travel   _____

23,290-360 Printing   _____   TOTAL [300] _____

23,290-440 Periodicals   _____   TOTAL [400] _____

                                                        TOTAL [23,290] _____

                                                        TOTAL 23,200 _____

                                                        *****TOTAL 23,000 _____

24,000 School Administration

24,100 Office of Principal

24,100-110-1 Salaries, Certified

____ Base $_____

____ Raise $_____   (110-1) $_____

24,100-110-2

____ Base $_____

____ Raise $_____   (110-2) $_____

24,100-110-3 CG

____ Base $_____

____ Raise $_____   (110-3) $_____

24,100-110-4 MG

____ Base $_____

____ Raise $_____   (110-4) $_____

24,100-110-5 NG

____ Base $_____

____ Raise $_____   (110-5) $_____

24,100-110-6 WG

____ Base $_____

____ Raise $_____   (110-6) $_____

24,100-110-7 PG

____ Base $_____

____ Raise $_____   (110-7) $_____   Total (110) $_____

24,100-120-1 Salaries, Classified HS

____ Base $_____

____ Raise $_____

____ Bonus $_____

____ Substitutes $_____

____ Extra $_____   (120-1) $_____

24,100-120-2 MS

____ Base $_____

____ Raise $_____

____ Bonus $_____

____ Substitutes $_____   (120-2) $_____

24,100-120-3 CG

____ Base $_____

____ Raise $_____

____ Bonus $_____

____ Cafeteria Aides $_____

____ Substitutes $_____   (120-3) $_____

24,100-120-4 MG

____ Base　　　　　　　　$____

____ Raise　　　　　　　　$____

____ Bonus　　　　　　　　$____

____ Cafeteria Aides　　　　$____

____ Substitutes　　　　　　$____　　(120-4) $____

24,100-120-5 NG

____ Base　　　　　　　　$____

____ Raise　　　　　　　　$____

____ Bonus　　　　　　　　$____

____ Cafeteria Aides　　　　$____

____ Substitutes　　　　　　$____　　(120-5) $____

24,100-120-6 WG

____ Base　　　　　　　　$____

____ Raise　　　　　　　　$____

____ Bonus　　　　　　　　$____

____ Cafeteria Aides　　　　$____

____ Substitutes　　　　　　$____　　(120-6) $____

24,100-120-7 PG

____ Base　　　　　　　　$____

____ Raise　　　　　　　　$____

____ Bonus　　　　　　　　$____

____ Cafeteria Aides　　　　$____

____ Substitutes　　　　　　$____　　(120-7) $____　TOTAL (120) ____

　　　　　　　　　　　　　　　　　　　　　　　　TOTAL [100] ____

24,100-332-1 HS Travel　　　____

24,100-332-2 MS Travel　　　____

24,100-332-3 CG Travel　　　____

24,100-332-4 MG Travel　　　____

24,100-332-5 NG Travel　　　____

24,100-332-6 WG Travel　　　____

24,100-332-7 PG Travel　　　____　　　　　　　TOTAL [300] ____

24,100-540-1 HS Equipment _____

24,100-540-2 MS Equipment _____

24,100-540-3 CG Equipment _____

24,100-540-4 MG Equipment _____

24,100-540-5 NG Equipment _____

24,100-540-6 WG Equipment _____

24,100-540-7 PG Equipment _____   TOTAL [500] _____

TOTAL 24,100 _____

*****TOTAL 24,000 _____

25,000 Business

25,100 Business Support Services

25,110 Office of Business Manager

25,110 Salaries, Certified

____ Base $_____

____ Raise $_____   (110) $_____

22,110-120 Salaries, Classified

____ Base $_____

____ Raise $_____

____ Bonus $_____

____ Substitutes $_____   (120) $_____ TOTAL [100] _____

25,110-310 Professional &
   Technical Services $_____

25,110-325 Rentals $_____

25,110-332 Travel $_____

25,110-342 Postage $_____

25,110-359 Legal Ads $_____   TOTAL [300] _____

TOTAL [25,110] _____

TOTAL 25,100 _____

25,400 Operation & Maintenace

25,410 Administration

25,410-120 Salaries, Classified

____ Base $_____

____ Raise $_____

____ Bonus $_____

____ Substitutes $_____   (120) $_____ TOTAL [100] _____

25,410-323 Repairs $_____

25,410-332 Travel $_____   TOTAL [300] _____

25,410-411 Supplies $_____

25,410-411-19 Central Stores $_____   TOTAL [400] _____

25,410-540 Equipment $_____   TOTAL [500] _____

TOTAL [25,410] _____

25,420 Building Maintenance

25,420-120 Salaries, Classified (Maintenance)

_____ Base $_____

_____ Raise $_____

_____ Bonus $_____

_____ Substitutes $_____

_____ Building Rentals $_____

_____ Extra $_____

_____ Painters $_____ (120 Maint) $_____

25,420-120 Salaries, Classified (Custodial)

_____ Base $_____

_____ Raise $_____

_____ Bonus $_____

_____ Substitutes $_____

_____ Building Rentals $_____

_____ Extra $_____ (120 Cust) $_____   (120) _____

TOTAL [100] _____

25,420-323 Repairs   _____

25,420-325 Rentals   _____

25,420-332 Travel/Training   _____

25,420-341 Telephone   _____

25,420-342 UPS/Postage   _____

25,420-381 Electric Heat   _____

25,420-382 Gas Heat   _____

25,420-383 Oil Heat   _____

25,420-385 Water   _____

25,420-386 Lights   _____

25,420-387 Gas, Other _____

25,420-388 Refuse _____

25,420-389 Other Utilities _____

25,420-390 Other _____   TOTAL [300] _____

25,420-411 Supplies _____   TOTAL [400] _____

25,420-540 Equipment _____   TOTAL [500] _____

TOTAL 25,420 _____

25,430 Grounds

25,430-120 Salaries, Classified

____ Base $_____

____ Raise $_____

____ Bonus $_____

____ Substitutes $_____

____ Snow Removal $_____

____ Summer Extra $_____   (120) $_____ TOTAL [100] _____

25,430-323 Repair _____

25,430-325 Rental _____   TOTAL [300] _____

25,430-411 Supplies _____   TOTAL [400] _____

25,430-530 Improvements _____

25,430-540 Equipment _____   TOTAL [500] _____

TOTAL [25,430] _____

25,440 Maintenance of Equipment

25,440-120 Salaries, Classified

____ Base $_____

____ Raise $_____

____ Bonus $_____

____ Substitutes $_____   (120) $_____ TOTAL [100] _____

25,440-323 Repair _____

25,440-325 Rentals _____   TOTAL [300] _____

25,440-411 Supplies _____   TOTAL [400] _____

25,440-540 Equipment _____   TOTAL [500] _____

TOTAL [25,440] _____

25,450 Maintenance of Vehicles

    25,450-412 Tires

    25,450-413 Gas & Oil   TOTAL [400] _____

                                                 TOTAL [25,450] _____

25,460 Security

    25,460-120 Salaries, Classified

        ____ Base $_____

        ____ Raise $_____

        ____ Bonus $_____

        ____ Substitutes $_____

        ____ Extra $_____   (120) $_____ TOTAL [100] _____

                                                   TOTAL [25,460] _____

25,470 Insurance (not buses)

    25,470-324 Property Insurance   _____   TOTAL [300] _____

                                                   TOTAL [25,470] _____

                                                   TOTAL 25,400 _____

                                               *****TOTAL 25,000 _____

26,000 Central

    26,400 Staff Services

        26,491-210 PERF $_____

        26,492-210 SS $_____

        26,493-220 W.C. Insurance $_____

        26,494-220 Group Insurance $_____

        26,495-652 Bonds $_____   TOTAL [600] _____

        26,496-230 U.C. $_____   TOTAL [200] _____

        26,497-210 Teacher Retirement $_____

                                               TOTAL 26,400 _____

    26,600 Data Processing

        26,600-323 Repairs $_____   TOTAL [300] _____

        26,600-411 Supplies $_____   TOTAL [400] _____

        26,600-540 Equipment $_____   TOTAL [500] _____

                                               TOTAL 26,600 _____

                                               *****TOTAL 26,000 _____

                                                 TOTAL 20,000

30,000 Community Services

   32,000 Community Recreation

   32,200-120 Salaries, Classified (Summer Recreational Program)

      32,000-120.00 Basketball $_____

      32,000-120.01 Swimming $_____

      32,000-120.02 Tennis $_____

      32,000-120.03 Volleyball $_____

      32,000-120.04 Other $_____   (120) $_____ TOTAL [100] _____

                                                    TOTAL 32,200 _____

                                                *****TOTAL 32,200 _____

   34,000 Athletic Coaches

      34,000-110 Salaries, Certified   (110) $_____

      34,000-120 Salaries, Classified   (120) $_____ TOTAL [100] _____

                                                  *****TOTAL 34,000 _____

   39,000 Other Community Services

   39,300 Summer Enrichment

      39,300-120 Salaries, Classified   (120) $_____ TOTAL [100] _____

                                                  TOTAL 39,300 _____

                                                *****TOTAL 39,000 _____

                                                TOTAL 30,000 _____

40,000 Non-Programmed Charges

   41,000 Payment to Other Government Units

      41,100 Transfer Tuition

         41,100-370 Transfer Tuition   _____   (370) $_____

      41,300 Area Vocational School

         41,300-370 Central 9   _____   (370) $_____

      41,400 Joint Services

         41,400-370 Special Services   _____   (370) $_____ TOTAL [300] _____

                                                *****TOTAL 41,000 _____

                                                TOTAL 40,000 _____

   GENERAL FUND GRAND TOTAL

A p p e n d i x **III**

Sample Worksheet Indicating Previous Year's Appropriations Compared with Requests and Current Proposals

Exemplar School District #1 Budget Worksheet

6/26/91
8 : 08 : 00

FUND 10 GENERAL

PROGRAM .00 000 BANKMASTER FILE

PROGRAM .00 TOTALS.........

PROGRAM 11100.00

OBJECT CC	ACCOUNT NAME	LAST YEAR APPROPRIATION	APPROPRIATION REQUESTED 1993	PROPOSED 1993	AMOUNT OF CHANGE	PERCENT CHANGE	
110.01 000	ELEM SALARIES (CERTIFED)	4,875,565.00	4,875,565.00	5,220,585.00	345,020.00	7.0765	INCREASE
110.02 000	ELEM SALARIES (CERTIFIED) SUB	83,700.00	83,700.00	81,900.00	1,800.00	2.1505	DECREASE
120.00 000	ELEM SAL - PRIME TIME ASSIST	202,180.00	202,180.00	202,262.00	82.00	.0405	INCREASE
120.01 000	ELEM SALARIES TEACH ASSIST N/	151,327.00	151,327.00	199,740.00	48,413.00	31.9923	INCREASE
311.00 003	ELEM INSTRUCTION SERVICES CG	2,392.00	2,392.00	2,392.00			
311.00 006	ELEM INSTRUCTION SERVICES WG	2,559.00	2,534.00	2,534.00	25.00	.9769	DECREASE
311.00 007	ELEM INSTRUCTION SERVICES - P	2,600.00	2,500.00	2,500.00	100.00	3.8461	DECREASE
323.00 003	ELEM REPAIRS & MAINT	11,171.00	11,171.00	9,000.00	2,171.00	19.4342	DECREASE
323.00 004	ELEM REPAIRS & MAINT	3,120.00	3,120.00	13,130.00	10,010.00	320.8333	INCREASE
323.00 005	ELEM REPAIRS & MAINT	2,841.00	2,732.00	2,732.00	109.00	3.8366	DECREASE
323.00 006	ELEM REPAIRS & MAINT	6,676.00	8,612.00	6,700.00	24.00	.3594	INCREASE
323.00 007	ELEM REPAIRS & MAINT	17,660.00	6,500.00	17,000.00	660.00	3.7372	DECREASE
325.00 003	ELEMENTARY RENTALS	11,232.00	11,232.00	11,232.00			
325.00 004	ELEMENTARY RENTALS	10,400.00	10,400.00	10,400.00			
325.00 005	ELEMENTARY RENTALS	10,345.00	9,948.00	9,948.00	397.00	3.8376	DECREASE
325.00 006	ELEMENTARY RENTALS	6,510.00	6,447.00	6,447.00	63.00	.9677	DECREASE
325.00 007	ELEMENTARY RENTALS						
332.00 003	ELEM TRAVEL CG	613.00	613.00	613.00			
332.00 004	ELEM TRAVEL MG	728.00	728.00	728.00			
332.00 005	ELEM TRAVEL NG	624.00	600.00	600.00	24.00	3.8461	DECREASE

332

FUND 10 GENERAL

OBJECT	CC	ACCOUNT NAME	LAST YEAR APPROPRIATION	APPROPRIATION REQUESTED	PROPOSED	AMOUNT OF CHANGE	PERCENT CHANGE	
332.00	006	ELEM TRAVEL WG	800.00	795.00	795.00	5.00	.6250	DECREASE
332.00	007	ELEM TRAVEL PG	572.00	550.00	550.00	22.00	3.8461	DECREASE
342.00	003	ELEM POSTAGE CG	700.00	700.00	700.00			
342.00	004	ELEM POSTAGE MG	728.00	728.00	728.00			
342.00	005	ELEM POSTAGE NG	728.00	700.00	700.00	28.00	3.8461	DECREASE
342.00	006	ELEM POSTAGE WG	676.00	670.00	670.00	6.00	.8875	DECREASE
342.00	007	ELEM POSTAGE PG	832.00	800.00	800.00	32.00	3.8461	DECREASE
360.00	003	ELEM PRINTING & BINDING	416.00	416.00	416.00			
360.00	004	ELEM PRINTING & BINDING	624.00	624.00	624.00			
360.00	005	ELEM PRINTING & BINDING	1,040.00	1,000.00	1,000.00	40.00	3.8461	DECREASE
360.00	006	ELEM PRINTING & BINDING	364.00	360.00	360.00	4.00	1.0989	DECREASE
360.00	007	ELEM PRINTING & BINDING	624.00	600.00	600.00	24.00	3.8461	DECREASE
411.00	003	ELEM SUPPLIES CG	6,240.00	6,240.00	6,240.00			
411.00	004	ELEM SUPPLIES MG	7,592.00	7,600.00	7,600.00	8.00	.1053	INCREASE
411.00	005	ELEM SUPPLIES NG	7,114.00	6,841.00	6,841.00	273.00	3.8375	DECREASE
411.00	006	ELEM SUPPLIES WG	7,635.00	7,560.00	7,560.00	75.00	.9823	DECREASE
411.00	007	ELEM SUPPLIES PG	8,968.00	8,624.00	8,624.00	344.00	3.8358	DECREASE
411.00	009	CENTRAL STORES SUPPLIES	6,928.00	6,928.00	6,928.00			
411.00	010	CENTRAL STORES SUPPLIES	6,520.00	4,390.00	6,520.00			
411.00	011	CENTRAL STORES	7,176.00	6,900.00	6,900.00	276.00	3.8461	DECREASE
411.00	012	CENTRAL STORES	7,111.00	7,040.00	7,040.00	71.00	.9984	DECREASE
411.00	013	CENTRAL STORES	6,314.00	6,072.00	6,072.00	242.00	3.8327	DECREASE
540.00	003	ELEM CAP OUTLAY EQUIP	3,120.00	3,120.00	3,120.00			
540.00	004	ELEM CAP OUTLAY EQUIP	4,563.00	4,500.00	4,500.00	63.00	1.3806	DECREASE
540.00	005	ELEM CAP OUTLAY EQUIP	4,563.00	4,388.00	4,388.00	175.00	3.8351	DECREASE

333

Glossary

Account   A division of a fund under which are recorded similar transactions.

Accounting   The process of recording events regarding the acquisition, disbursement, or analyses of money, objects, or property.

Accounts receivable   An accounting of monies, goods, or services owed to a particular account.

Accrual basis   A means of accounting whereby expenditures are recorded immediately as liabilities and income is recorded when earned.

Activity fund   Monies derived from class fees, athletics, concessions, concerts, etc., not within the tax revenues provided locally and from the state.

Affirmative action   Processes designed to address past inequities.

Appraisal   The process of estimating the value of property, work, or a program.

Appropriation   An act of assigning an amount to a school, or to a fund or account for the purpose of authorizing expenditures and obligations.

Arbitration   A required settlement between groups by a predetermined agent.

Assets   Items owned by or owed to an entity (e.g., school district) that have value.

Audit   The process of determining the proper recording of transactions, the accuracy of the recording, and for the making of recommendations to correct deficiencies.

Bond   A written obligation to pay a specified amount at a specified time, usually with interest due at specified periods over the life of the bond.

Bond rating   An estimate of a borrower's ability and history to meet the terms specified by the bonds.

Budget   The translation of educational needs into a financial plan which expresses the educational program the community is willing to support for the budget period, usually one year.

Budget Document   The written form of the educational program translated into costs and revenues for the upcoming year.

Budgeting   The process of developing a budget including planning, evaluation, document, approvals, and control.

Capital projects Fund   A fund limited to acquisition, renovation, planning, building, and equipping real property.

Cash basis   An accounting of revenues only when received and expenditures only when cash is disbursed. See *accrual basis*.

Categorical aid   Funds provided usually by the state or federal levels limited to a specified purpose, e.g., special education.

Central Kitchen   One kitchen prepares food for and distributes food to a number of satellite sites for serving.

Centralized budget   A budget developed by, allocated by, and controlled by a single district office.

Compensation   The salary, wages, and benefits provided an employee in return for services.

Continuous budget   A planning process in which the budget is refined continuously via evaluation and daily operation.

Contracted services   Services by companies or persons not on the regular payroll of the district.

Cooperative purchasing   An arrangement among districts whereby they jointly purchase agreed-upon items to take advantage of buying power.

Cost center   A small unit of the district/program as designated by a separate account or set of records, e.g., secondary language arts, or the middle schools.

Credit   A decrease in the assets and an increase in liabilities recorded in a fund.

Debt Service   A separate fund, usually required by law, which accounts for revenues and expenditures relative to loans and interest.

Decentralized budget   A budgeting process resulting in individual schools (or programs) being responsible for the development and control of their own budgets.

Educational plan   A written expression of the means whereby the school district expects to achieve its educational goals.

Educational specifications (facility)   The description of goals, activities, persons involved, and relationships with other program activities and spaces.

Electronic purchasing   A system based on computer-generated purchase orders at either the central office or local sites.

Employee benefits (fringe benefits)   Compensation beyond salary to include such things as health insurance, leave, retirement, and disability coverages.

Encumbrances   Contracts, salaries, fringe benefits, purchases, etc., chargeable to a fund prior to being paid.

Equipment   Nonexpendable apparatus to be used over time without being expendable.

Expressed powers   Legislatively specified powers of a governmental unit.

Fidelity bond   A written guarantee against loss resulting from actions of the employee bonded.

Fixed assets   Real property, machinery, furnishings, and equipment.

Fixed charges   Cost recurring such as employee fringe benefits; interest on loans; insurance, and in some states utilities, which are a separate allocation from the state.

Food Services   The planning, preparation, serving, and accounting of meals and snacks in connection with the schools' program.

Foundation   A private entity separate from the school district which receives private gifts and disburses funds for the benefit of the mission of the school district.

Functional budget   A budget built from the starting point of educational needs, a plan, and the involvement of the community.

Fund   An accounting entity with its own assets and liabilities, e.g., transportation.

General fund   A fund which ordinarily accounts for all transactions such as instruction and instructional support other than those funds required to be separate, e.g., debt service, transportation, etc.

Human resources planning   Processes used to forecast needs and to select, assign, and/or train personnel to meet those needs.

Implied powers   Unspecified activities necessary to carry out mission specified.

Incremental budgeting   The increase or decrease of the current budget on a line-item basis, resulting in the next year's budget and usually resulting in little programmatic changes.

Induction   The process of acclimating a new or transferred employee to the job expectations and content of his or her assignment.

Insurance Agent   One who can bind an insurance company to a risk.

Insurance Broker   One who represents the client (school district) and cannot bind a company to a risk.

Internal audit   A process designed to determine the adequacy of internal controls; safeguarding of assets; and reliability of accounting and reporting systems. Ordinarily reports to the superintendent.

Inventory   A record of a class of item on hand at a given time showing amounts, descriptions, values and in some instances dates of acquisition, costs, and specific locations.

Investments   Income producing products (notes, real estate, etc.) for long- or short-term income.

Invoice   A document describing the goods or services, prices, quantities, etc., received from a vendor.

Levy   An amount of taxes imposed by a governmental unit such as a school district.

Liability   An obligation to pay as a result of purchases or contracts fulfilled.

Liability insurance   Coverage against possible losses due to judgments rendered against the school district or its employees.

Maintenance   Activities to repair, replace, or prevent malfunctions of equipment or facilities.

Management information system   A process of gathering, organizing, and providing and controlling access to data for analyses and decision making.

Mechanical budget   A simple revenue-expenditure accounting process largely ignoring needs or programmatic changes.

Mediation   A means of settling differences between groups by arriving at consensus or agreeable compromise.

Negotiations   A formal process of exchanging proposals until agreement is reached on the issues.

Operation, facilities   The day-to-day processes of cleaning, arranging furniture/equipment, groundskeeping, etc., to keep the programs operating effectively and safely.

Organizational culture   The shared beliefs, values, "ways of doing things" in an organization.

Organizational structure   The human and material relationships established to reach the organization's goals.

Property insurance   Coverage of losses or damage of property due to fire, natural causes, theft, etc.

Purchasing agent   The individual designated by the school district to procure goods and services for the district's programs.

Scanning, active   A process of searching for issues or occurrences in the environment that may have an impact on the school district in the near future.

Scanning, directed   A process of narrowed focus of scanning the environment for potential to impact the district.

Scanning, passive   A process of noting environmental occurrences by chance or by a particular interest of an individual.

Securities   Negotiable or non-negotiable instruments such as bonds, notes, mortgages, etc.

Self insurance   The school district retains the risk of loss by covering them from its own resources rather than purchasing insurance.

Self-pay purchase order   A purchase order usually initiated at the building level that has a check attached to pay for the goods or service.

Site-based budgeting   Budget decision making usually at the building level within centrally prescribed parameters.

Site, facilities   Land and all improvements, excluding buildings.

Standardization (purchasing)   An agreement by users on size, weight, general ingredients or components, and performance under specific circumstances of a particular item to be procured.

Student management system   A system of generating information about student status, schedule, health, obligations, address, contact numbers, and a variety of other locally needed data needed to provide services to and decisions about students. Reporting functions are often outcomes of the student management system.

Supply management   The purchasing, receiving, storage, distribution, and accounting of supplies used in the operation and maintenance of schools.

Surety bond   Covers damages or losses caused by the actions of persons named on the bond.

Transfer of risk   Ordinarily the purchase of insurance against loss.

Trust funds   Funds held by the school district as a trustee, often for specific, designated purposes.

Zero-base budgeting   A process which assumes that each program area rejustifies its needs for each budget period with only the highest priorities receiving funding.

Selected Readings

Association of School Business Officials. *The School Food Service Handbook.* Reston, Va.: ASBO, 1987.

Association of School Business Officials. *School Facilities and Operations Manual.* Reston, Va.: ASBO, 1988.

Cali, James F. *TQM for Purchasing Management.* New York: McGraw-Hill, 1993.

Council of Educational Facility Planners. *Guide for Planning Educational Facilities.* Columbus, Ohio: The Council, 1985.

Dembowski, Frederick L. "Management Information Systems in Educational Organizations." In R. Craig Wood, ed. *Principles of School Business Management.* Reston, Va.: Association of School Business Officials, 1986.

Drake, Thelbert L., and William H. Roe. *The Principalship.* 3rd ed. New York: Macmillan Publishing Company, 1986.

Electronic Learning: Special Supplement. Scholastic Inc., September 1989.

Frohman, Alan L., *The Middle Management Challenge: Moving from Crisis to Empowerment.* New York: McGraw-Hill, 1993.

Hall, Richard H. *Organizations: Structures, Processes, Outcomes.* 5th ed. Englewood Cliffs, N.J.: Prentice-Hall, 1991.

Harman, Kay. "Culture and Conflict in Academic Organizations: Symbolic Aspects of University Worlds." *Journal of Educational Administration* 27, No. 3 (1989). pp. 30–54.

Harris, Ben M., Kenneth E. McIntyre, Vance C. Littleton, Jr., and Daniel F. Long. *Personnel Administration in Education: Leadership for Instructional Improvement.* Boston: Allyn and Bacon, 1985.

Hartman, William T. *School District Budgeting.* Englewood Cliffs, N.J.: Prentice-Hall, 1988.

Hentschke, Guilbert C. *School Business Administration.* Berkeley, Calif.: McCutchen Publishing Corporation, 1986.

Hersey, Paul, and Kenneth Blanchard. *Management of Organizational Behavior.* 5th ed. Englewood Cliffs, N.J.: Prentice-Hall, 1988.

Hill, Frederick W., et al. *The School Business Administrator.* Reston, Va.: Association of School Business Officials International, 1982.

Johnson, H. Thomas, and Robert S. Kaplan. *Relevance Lost: The Rise and Fall of Management Accounting.* Boston: Harvard Business School Press, 1987.

Jones, Thomas H. *Introduction to School Finance Techniques and Social Policy.* New York: Macmillan Publishing Company, 1985.

Jordan, K. Forbis, Mary P. McKeown, Richard E. Salmon, and L. Dean Webb. *School Business Administration*. Beverly Hills, Calif.: Sage Publications, 1985.

Madsen, Claudina, and John H. Walker. *Risk Management and Insurance: A Handbook of Fundamentals*. Washington, D.C.: National Association of College and University Business Officers, 1983.

McGuffey, Carroll W. *A Handbook on Professional Certification of School Business Officials*. Reston, Va.: Association of School Business Officials, 1980.

McLaughlin, Milbrey W., and D.C. Phillips, eds. *Evaluation and Education: At Quarter Century*. Chicago: National Society for the Study of Education, 1991.

Miller, Harold. *An Administrator's Manual for the Use of Microcomputers in the Schools*. Englewood Cliffs, N.J.: Prentice-Hall, 1988.

Owens, Robert G. *Organizational Behavior in Education*. 4th ed. Englewood Cliffs, N.J.: Prentice-Hall, 1991.

Posavic, Emil J., and Raymond G. Carey. *Program Evaluation: Methods and Case Studies*. 4th ed. Englewood Cliffs, N.J.: Prentice-Hall, 1992.

Rebore, Ronald W. *Personnel Administration in Education: A Management Approach*. 3rd ed. Englewood Cliffs, N.J.: Prentice-Hall, 1991.

Schmitt, Neal (ed.) *Personnel Selection in Organizations*. San Fransisco: Jossey-Bass, 1993.

Sergiovanni, Thomas J., and John E. Corbally, eds. *Leadership and Organizational Culture*. Urbana: University of Illinois Press, 1984.

Stronge, James H., and Virginia M. Helm. *Evaluating Professional Support in Education*. Berkeley, Calif.: Sage Publications, 1991.

Terplan, Kornel. *Communications Network Management*. Englewood Cliffs, NJ: Prentice-Hall, 1992.

Tidwell, Sam B. *Financial and Managerial Accounting for Elementary and Secondary Schools*. Reston, Va.: Research Corporation, Association of School Business Officials, 1985.

Vaughn, Emmett J. *Fundamentals of Risk and Insurance*. 5th ed. New York: John Wiley and Sons, 1989.

Ward, James G. "School Business Administration in an Information-Based Learning Society." *The Journal of School Business Management* 3, No. 4 (January 1992): 21.

Webb, L. Dean, John T. Greer, Paul A. Montello, and M. Scott Norton. *Personnel Administration in Education: New Issues and New Needs in Human Resource Management*. Columbus, Ohio: Merrill Publishing Company, 1988.

Wood, R. Craig. *Principles of School Business Management*. Reston, Va.: Association of School Business Officials International, 1986.

Index